Godard and the
Essay Film

Godard and the Essay Film

A Form That Thinks

✦

Rick Warner

NORTHWESTERN UNIVERSITY PRESS
EVANSTON, ILLINOIS

Northwestern University Press
www.nupress.northwestern.edu

Copyright © 2018 by Northwestern University Press.
Published 2018. All rights reserved.

Printed in the United States of America

10 9 8 7 6 5 4 3 2 1

Library of Congress Cataloging-in-Publication Data

Names: Warner, Rick, 1977– author.
Title: Godard and the essay film : a form that thinks / Rick Warner.
Description: Evanston, Illinois : Northwestern University Press, 2018. | Includes
   bibliographical references and index.
Identifiers: LCCN 2018002309| ISBN 9780810137370 (pbk. : alk. paper) | ISBN
   9780810137387 (cloth : alk. paper) | ISBN 9780810137394 (ebook)
Subjects: LCSH: Godard, Jean-Luc, 1930– —Criticism and
   interpretation. | Experimental films—History and criticism. | Subjectivity in
   motion pictures.
Classification: LCC PN1998.3.G63 W37 2018 | DDC 791.4302/33092—dc23
LC record available at https://lccn.loc.gov/2018002309

For Gigi

CONTENTS

Acknowledgments	*ix*
A Note on the Text	*xi*
Introduction	*3*
Chapter 1 Research in the Form of a Spectacle	*19*
Chapter 2 A Critical Poetics of Citation	*65*
Chapter 3 Refiguring the Couple: Love, Dialogue, and Gesture	*111*
Chapter 4 To Show and Show Oneself Showing: Essayistic Self-Portrayal	*153*
Coda Stereoscopic Essays for the New Century	*195*
Notes	*223*
Index	*255*

ACKNOWLEDGMENTS

My research on the cinematic essay began when I was a doctoral student at the University of Pittsburgh, where I benefited greatly from the instruction and support of Adam Lowenstein, Colin MacCabe, Marcia Landy, Lucy Fischer, Daniel Morgan, Randall Halle, Neepa Majumdar, and Mark Lynn Anderson. Adam and Dan deserve special mention for their careful guidance when this book was in its earliest stages. I am also very grateful to Colin for enabling a rare visit with Chris Marker in Paris in the summer of 2006.

Some of this book's ideas grew out of conversations with Karla Oeler (who formatively introduced me to *Histoire(s) du cinéma*), Matthew Bernstein, Nina K. Martin, David A. Cook, Evan Lieberman, Alex Greenhough, David Fresko, Anne-Gaëlle Saliot, Michael Moses, Isaac Julien, Sam di Iorio, Andrew Utterson, Pavle Levi, Timothy Barnard, Kevin J. Hayes, Ken and Flo Jacobs, Scott Durham, Jennifer Cazenave, Mike Levine, Hassan Melehy, Sam Amago, Julia Haslett, Yaron Shemer, Gabriel Trop, Richard Langston, Christopher Pavsek, Karen Redrobe, Toni D'Angela, Steve Carter, Kyle Stevens, Murray Pomerance, and Clint Bergeson.

I wish to thank Warren Breckman and James English, the conveners of the 2011–12 Penn Humanities Forum at the University of Pennsylvania, for the opportunity to present an early draft of material contained here. Timothy Corrigan was a warm host during my time at Penn and was generously supportive when we discussed my project. My thanks to him and to Nora M. Alter for inviting me back to Philadelphia to participate in a symposium in memory of Chris Marker at the Slought Foundation in 2013. I owe my gratitude to Jason Kuo and the other organizers of an essay film symposium at the University of Maryland in 2014. I was touched by their invitation to speak, and received valuable feedback there from Caroline Eades, Liz Papazian, Luka Arsenjuk, Jonathan Auerbach, and David Johnson.

Special thanks to Trevor Perri, Maggie Grossman, Anne Gendler, and the full production team at Northwestern University Press, who have been a genuine pleasure to work with. Thanks as well to the manuscript's anonymous readers, and to Alexander O. Trotter, who compiled the index.

Alternate versions of some material included in this book appeared previously in *Critical Quarterly*; *The Essay Film: Dialogue, Politics, Utopia*, edited by Elizabeth A. Papazian and Caroline Eades (Wallflower Press, 2016); and *The Global Auteur: The Politics of Authorship in the 21st Century*, edited by

ix

x
Acknowledgments

Seung-hoon Jeong and Jeremi Szaniawski (Bloomsbury Academic, 2016). My thanks to the publishers for permission to rework that material here.

At the University of North Carolina-Chapel Hill, key support came from the Institute for the Arts and Humanities. I thank the other fall 2015 faculty fellows for their insights regarding my project, and Nelson Schwab III, whose donation made my fellowship possible. Several of my colleagues in the Department of English and Comparative Literature offered advice and support: Mary Floyd-Wilson, Beverly Taylor, Bland Simpson, Jessica Wolfe, John McGowan, Eric Downing, Shayne Legassie, Jane Thrailkill, Tyler Curtain, Danielle Christmas, and Taylor Cowdery. Most of all, I am indebted to my teammates in the Film and Media Studies program, Gregg Flaxman and Inga Pollmann, for their inspiration and feedback.

My parents, Arlene and Richard Warner, and my sister, Jennifer Burgess, have been so greatly supportive and encouraging that I cannot begin to thank them enough here.

Most profoundly, I thank my wife, Gigi, to whom this book is dedicated. I could not have finished this study, or formulated its most important claims, without the energizing effect of her intelligence, compassion, joviality, and charm.

A NOTE ON THE TEXT

In English-language film criticism, some of Jean-Luc Godard's films and videos (e.g., *Histoire(s) du cinéma*) are known exclusively by their French titles, and some are known primarily by their English translations or substitutes (e.g., *Contempt* for *Le Mépris*). Throughout this book, I use whichever title is the more common in North American film scholarship written in English (some Godard films have different titles in the UK, such as *Slow Motion* instead of *Every Man for Himself*). Where necessary, I offer parenthetical translations. I apply this same principle to other artists' works that are known mainly by non-English titles in English-language discussions. For the sake of readability, when referencing dialogue, onscreen text, and vocal narration in projects by Godard and other directors working in languages other than English, I use English translations and cite the original when it is relevant to my analysis. This choice makes for a more economical reading experience, but it should be remembered that some of Godard's multilingual wordplay—a key part of his essayistic process, as it is for Michel de Montaigne's—is lost in translation.

Godard and the
Essay Film

INTRODUCTION

> I play
> You play
> We play
> At cinema
>
> —Jean-Luc Godard

From Orson Welles to Raúl Ruiz, a number of the most innovative artists in the history of cinema have made "essays" with images and sounds as their principal instruments. As a wave of recent scholarly and curatorial efforts has shown, the essay film became a genre of sorts in the aftermath of World War II and its catastrophes. Since then, directors situated in various national and transnational contexts have made essayistic works by renegotiating the boundaries between fiction and documentary, rethinking the critical utility of montage, and expressing the intelligence and personality of the filmmaker in new ways. From the breakthroughs of the Left Bank group in France (Chris Marker, Agnès Varda, Alain Resnais, and Georges Franju) right up to the present, there extends a tradition of essayistic commentary on historical and current events that embodies one of the most important legacies of modern cinema.[1] This book explores the distinctive goals, procedures, and challenges of this cinematic tradition through a study of the contributions of one of its most virtuosic practitioners, Jean-Luc Godard.

For decades, this tradition suffered from critical neglect. If film scholars have only recently begun to give it concerted attention, this is largely because of the major problems of definition it has long posed—its mutable nature, its borrowings from a vast assortment of other genres and idioms both pictorial and linguistic without quite committing to any of them, its diversity of styles and agendas across cases, and thus, its resistance to generic classification. There is still a tendency to use the term "essay" as a vague pigeonhole for quirky, personal documentaries, but recent efforts have engaged the practice with greater clarity and insight. Trailblazing studies by Phillip Lopate, Nora M. Alter, Paul Arthur, Laura Rascaroli, Michael Renov, Christa Blümlinger, and Timothy Corrigan have established a canonical record of the essay film's history.[2] From this scholarship, one can glean a loosely agreed-upon view of the essay film's distinctive attributes: a hybrid combination of fiction and

3

nonfiction; the prominent display of the film essayist's subjectivity through voiceover and/or physical self-portrayal; an open-ended structure and manner of expression that often relies on an eclectic montage of both found and newly shot material; a self-reflexive disposition regarding the techniques used and goals pursued; a leftist political stance that may range in tone from activism to more tentative rumination; and a rhetoric of "direct address" that looks to build a collaborative bond with an especially alert spectator.

One of my tasks in this book will be to expand on, refine, and converse with these extant accounts of the essay film. Yet I will also be concerned to radically reopen the question of what constitutes an essayistic process. My sense is that for all the recent gains that have been made in canonizing the essay film, the methodological pressure to build a cohesive generic category has sometimes led to approaches that quell the unruly energies of the cinematic practices at stake. Laura Rascaroli's *The Personal Camera: Subjective Cinema and the Essay Film* was notably the first English-language monograph to put forward a general theory and generic grouping of the essay film. Although she astutely surveys many of the gestures that film essayists deploy, her framework imposes two restrictions that leave us with a limited appraisal. First of all, her argument suggests that the essay lives wholly in the sphere of subjective documentary, in films structured around the "first-person" perspective and persona of the filmmaker.[3] She attends to hybrids of fiction and nonfiction, such as Godard's *Notre musique* (*Our Music*, 2004), but fiction counts in her analysis only as a pretext for the documentary aspect, where, she maintains, the essay most properly locates itself.[4] Her classificatory scheme in *The Personal Camera* doesn't allow for an essayistic cinema that exists squarely within the dramatic workings of the fiction film. Secondly, her definition of the essay turns on an "I-You" rhetoric of direct address whereby the overtly asserted authorial persona (the "I") of the filmmaker issues a call to the spectator's involvement. *Directness* is paramount in this formulation. Rascaroli's film essayist is an inscribed subject who "wish[es] to communicate with the spectator directly, to establish a contact with the embodied audience." This, she affirms, is the "utopian" mission of the essay that speaks to "the urgency of its project."[5]

Rascaroli wisely makes the relationship between essayist and viewer the crux of her claims in *The Personal Camera*. Without this emphasis, the "essay" term serves as little more than a label. Her book also marks a valuable advance beyond less meticulous taxonomies that frame the essay film more as a monologue than a dialogue.[6] I, too, am going to focus on the special rapport this kind of cinema builds with its spectator, but my examples—which I will draw primarily, though not exclusively, from Godard's corpus—will demand a more nuanced treatment of the ways in which this rapport develops. As will become evident in the chapters ahead, Godard purposefully avoids and undermines the sort of relational directness that Rascaroli theorizes. The "I" of himself as essayist and "you" of the spectator are forcefully

Introduction

in play in his reflections, but this entails levels of ambiguity and tenuousness that conflict with Rascaroli's general model of communication. I am going to pursue a conception of the essayistic that is more in step with Godard's style, where obliqueness and obscurity very often prevail. What is more, I am going to claim that he operates as an essayist in several of his fiction films, without any loss of reflective potency. In scholarship, it is common to separate Godard's "essays" from his more narrative projects, but I will show that this convenience stands at odds with how he has long defined himself as an essayist.[7]

Timothy Corrigan's book *The Essay Film: From Montaigne, After Marker* gives an account that I find more conducive to understanding Godard's exemplary status. Even as Corrigan defines the genre as a performance of a questing, self-critical intelligence, usually that of the director, his study everywhere emphasizes the unstable and changeable character of essayistic subjectivity. Not unlike Rascaroli, he privileges "the dialogic activity of essayistic thinking" as a key definitional trait and values the viewer's contribution therein, but he does this without insisting on a firmly anchored authorial agent who necessarily addresses us directly and whose first-person viewpoint guides the proceedings.[8] "Essayistic thought," for Corrigan, externalizes "personal expression," yet the ideas, queries, and speculations of the essayist are "determined and circumscribed by an always varying kind, quality, and number of material contexts in which to think is to multiply one's selves."[9] The viewer doesn't have a fixed position either but instead becomes an equally volatile subject, "made and remade" in an experiential encounter where "the lack of a single, dominant, or sometimes even coherent discourse disperses that viewing subject through its pastiche of forms, its mix and subversion of generic structures, and its cannibalization of narrative teleologies or lyrical voices." Essayistic investigation "becomes the necessary recasting of subjective experience in the shifting interstices that define worldly experience itself."[10]

If this conception of the audiovisual essay better suits Godard's enterprise, so too does Corrigan's flexible set of case studies. In addition to examining documentary reflections by the usual suspects in discussions of the genre (Marker, Varda, Harun Farocki, Nanni Moretti, Ross McElwee, Werner Herzog, and others), Corrigan adopts the philosophical novelist and critic Robert Musil's notion of "essayism," which Musil elaborates in *The Man Without Qualities*.[11] Narrated by a third-person voice that slides sometimes ambiguously between omniscient and limited perspectives, Musil's massive, unfinished novel entangles a fictional plot with critical reflections concerning its protagonist's aversion to doctrines that pretend to supply incontestable truths. Corrigan's recourse to Musil's novel adroitly allows for the passage of an essayistic disposition into the narrative fiction film. Indeed, when Corrigan examines two films that are partly fictional dramatizations of actual events, *Elephant* (Alan Clarke, 1989) and *Close-Up* (Abbas Kiarostami,

1990), he stretches his criteria well beyond the voiceover-driven essay film on the model of Marker's experiments.[12] In a more recent piece, he goes further in this direction by showing how Terrence Malick's *The Tree of Life* (2011) displays an essayism that inhabits the film's elliptical gaps and unfurls along its branches and streams, linking a cosmic history of the universe to an impressionistic narrative about the struggles and tragedies of a middle-class family in Eisenhower-era Texas.[13]

We will see that on both sides of the fiction/documentary division it confounds, Godard's output demands this widened and more elastic definition of essayistic cinema. Even in his films, videos, and televisual projects that do not quite match the specifications of the "essay film" as it tends to be classified, an essayistic spirit still motivates his methods. This is why it is frequently necessary to invoke the adjective "essayistic" and the Musil-inspired concept "essayism" (which alludes not to a genre but to a cast of mind that thinks openly and provisionally about the chaotic modern world) in the face of Godard's reflections. I will demonstrate that Godard is not unique among cinematic essayists in this respect. As concerns the work of many directors, "essayistic" and "essayism" are essentially cognate terms that index where the practice ventures beyond its assigned boundaries. They name the transgeneric character of the essay, its propensity not to stay put within a single set of attributes, however loose.

Another advantage of Corrigan's account is its careful attention to the essay film's literary heritage. Compulsory references to Michel de Montaigne as the inaugural essayist are routine in overviews of the essay film, but Corrigan traces out this lineage to a more extensive degree than usual. He charts the evolution of a Montaignean manner of inquiry—adaptively recalibrated by literary essayists such as Joseph Addison, Samuel Taylor Coleridge, Virginia Woolf, Jorge Luis Borges, and James Baldwin—as it passes between multiple continents over five centuries and, in time, assumes cinematic guises. What stands out as a welcome adjustment in Corrigan's reference to Montaigne is the care he takes *not* to fetishize the "coherently personalized expression" of the essayist. Corrigan rightly observes that this Montaignean legacy is predicated on a tendency of the reflective writer to "dramatically trouble" and "disperse," rather than merely put forth, his or her authorial subjectivity.[14]

My own approach in this book will maintain that Godard's corpus indeed participates in a Montaignean lineage, but in order to show this, I need to push further in explaining what this literary-philosophical tradition of the essay involves and how it becomes cinematic. I do not wish to fabricate a one-to-one resemblance between Montaigne and Godard. After all, there are many notable discrepancies between them—historical, political, biographical—such that neither essayist is the double of the other. My comparative investments in Montaigne have to do with the precise meanings he confers upon the word "essay," meanings whose full dimensions and implications are sometimes lost in commentaries on his work.

Introduction   7

Montaigne and the Act of Essaying

For Montaigne, the word "essay" is not simply a synonym for "article" or "thesis." Derived from the Latin *exagium* ("weighing"), it denotes the testing of ideas and perspectives—an "attempt," which the French *essai* carries more emphatically than the English variant. At the time of Montaigne's writing in the late sixteenth century, "essay" was a nonliterary term with connotations linking it to apprentice work, the trial-and-error stumbling forth of the artisan in training. Adopting this term for his written reflections, Montaigne embraces its sense of *errant improvisation*, and he mobilizes this aspect in order to throw suspicion on any system of knowing, scientific or philosophical, that does not stem primarily from one's own mental and—no less important for Montaigne—physical impressions made in the erratic flow of daily experience.

This etymological context of the term has been widely mentioned, but what tends to be ignored is that "essay," in Montaigne's inaugural usage, does not mean a self-contained piece of nonfiction writing on a particular topic. When he chose the title *Essais* for his writings, which were first published in 1580 and then, expanded and modified, in 1582 and 1588, this was not quite to indicate a "collection of essays" in the now-familiar sense. According to Montaigne's own terminology, the individually numbered sections of his book (such as "On Conscience" or "To Philosophize is to Learn How to Die") are not "essays" but "chapters" or "stories." His volume's main title refers more precisely to the fundamental impetus of his endeavor: what I would like to call the act of *essaying*. This reflective act is more intensified, more convoluted, and more expansive than the parameter of the chapter allows.[15] Montaigne's volume is less a collection of discrete articles than an overlapping, seemingly infinite series of trials, tangents, exercises, and meditations—a network of essaying that develops within and across separate chapters that generally consider their declared titles as jumping-off points, and that are bound more strongly by manner and mood than by theme or content. (In annotated editions published after his death, this accretion and overlay is made literal when strata of his original and revised writing coexist on the page.)

Montaigne's essaying is thus a diachronic affair that spins a web of reflection across the essayist's *expanding oeuvre over time*. This method is one of "repeated tentatives" and "resumed ponderings," yet at each moment, this process of continual revision and addition remains "inchoative," since the work "implies the abundance of joyous energy that never exhausts itself in this game."[16] It thus makes only partial sense to compare any single "essay film" and a chapter in the *Essais*, because each chapter is a field where multiple paths of essaying interweave. Further, we need to recognize that a genuine Montaignean essayistic cinema is evinced less by directors (such as Wim Wenders) who occasionally make "essay films" in the narrowly categorical sense than by the rarer breed of *prolific essayists* who reopen and rethink their earlier output while devising new experiments (such as Godard, Varda, Farocki, Alexander Kluge, and Peter Greenaway). A Montaignean definition of the practice must train its sights not just on single works but also on *recursive and accretive forms* that refigure still-evolving pursuits across an essayist's body of work.

I want to highlight four aspects of Montaigne's approach with regard to how they prefigure essayistic cinema as I will define it in this book. These correlated features—principles of work—are not comprehensive of Montaigne's example in the *Essais*, but glossing them will throw into relief the predominant aspects of his practice. For Montaigne and for Godard also, these are the key critical gestures around which the diachronic and revisionary development of the essayist's thinking revolves.

1. *Self-portraiture*. The *Essais* are personal but not autobiographical in the sense of imposing a chronological narrative with Montaigne as its central protagonist. Though he does relate much of his private and public life, in his prefatory address, "To the Reader," he enlists the metaphor of painting to distinguish his task: "Here I want to be seen in my simple, natural, everyday fashion, without striving or artifice: for it is my own self that I am painting."[17] But this is no portrait for which he sits still. He tries to capture the *mobility* and *transience* of the self he is testing, the short- and eventually long-term vacillations that reveal anything but a consistent character and outlook. As he famously remarks, "I am not portraying being but becoming" (III.2: 907–8). Registering transience, his self-portrait has a serial structure over time. His studies of himself in various "poses" over several years can be seen as a parallel project to the self-portraits of two of the founders of the genre in the West, Albrecht Dürer and Rembrandt van Rijn. The literary-philosophical essay and painted self-portrait materialized more or less synchronously in sixteenth-century Europe, with both practices heralding a shift toward a new and recognizably modern view of selfhood, invested in rigorous self-scrutiny and self-investigation.[18]

Montaigne asserts that once he captures "in the flimsy medium of words" the chaotic and spontaneous shape of his thinking, what results is not so much a record of his deeds—which he insists would say more about "Fortune" than himself—but an inscribed body: "I am *all* on display, like a mummy on which at a glance you can see the veins, the muscles and tendons, each piece in its place" (II.6: 426). His constant emphasis on the corporeality of his book extends to its content. He does not shy away from writing vividly about his bodily functions, his sexual proclivities, his illnesses, his injuries, and his own impending death. Erich Auerbach points out how these details are "essential ingredient[s]" of Montaigne's self-portrait, "so intimately fused in their concrete sensory effects with the moral-intellectual content of his book that any attempt to separate them would be absurd."[19] Montaigne goes so far as to write that the *Essais* and their author are on a continuum physically, bound by one vital substance: "I have not made my book anymore than it has made

Introduction 9

me—a book of one substance [*consubstantiel*] with its author, proper to me and a limb of my life" (II.18: 755).

Montaigne shows up in the *Essais* in all his self-avowed ignorance, having mastered no field of knowledge or discipline of inquiry. He portrays himself not as an expert but as a thinker whose speculations unmask the presumptuousness of expertise. Furthermore, although he understands that his literary self-portrait necessarily calls for the construction—the fiction—of a textual persona whose "I" *appears* spontaneously identical to himself, he insists that he and his book are one: "Elsewhere you can commend or condemn a work [*ouvrier*] independently of the author [*ouvrage*]; but not here: touch one and you touch the other" (III.2: 909). Through this mental and bodily fusion of author and book, the *Essais* actively complicate, redouble, and disperse the inscribed self of the author. The work doesn't figure the essayist as a coherent, unitary agent (or cogito) toward which the writing everywhere reverts, but rather articulates a fluctuating, fragmentary self as it verges into relations where the essayist shares the labor of reflection with others, be they other authors invoked through his citations, or other readers with whom he tacitly connects. One everywhere recognizes Montaigne's abiding style and wittiness, but he is often at pains to establish his authorial identity as riven and contradictory.

2. *A critical poetics of citation.* Montaigne relies methodically on a style of citation that differs from the way in which anterior sources are invoked in Western literature prior to the Renaissance. Reflecting on the profuse citations in the *Essais*, he refers to them as *emprunts* ("loans"), as though to respect their status as matter borrowed from authorities. But in actual practice, he aggressively transforms what he quarries, sometimes masking or misquoting the original source, sometimes tweaking it for his own needs. He defends these methods as fair game since they follow naturally from his "treacherous memory" (II.10: 469) and his inclination not to read books in their entirety but to "dip into" them: "As for anything I do retain from them, I am no longer aware that it belongs to somebody else: it is quite simply the material from which my judgment has profited and the ideas and arguments in which it has been steeped. I straightway forget the author, the source, the wording and the other particulars" (II.17: 740). Elsewhere Montaigne notes how he methodically "transplants" existing statements into his "own soil." He admits that his appropriations result in "some of the richer flowers" in his garden, thoughts and "reasonings" that he himself could not have mustered. Still, he instructs: "Do not linger over the matter" cited, "but over my *fashioning* of it" (II.10: 458, my italics). He contends that ultimately his citations belong to him as much as honey belongs to the bees that have "ransacked flowers" to produce it (I.26: 171).

Of course, Montaigne's memory is not as defective as he claims. His "forgetting" works in the service of a playful, albeit ambivalent refunctioning of citational procedure in the context of the humanist education he received. He at once mimes the reverential gesture, endemic to the Renaissance, of looking

10   Introduction

to the ancients when they have wisdom to offer, *and* reimagines this gesture by making citation an activity of free thinking that inventively challenges and rewrites authority.[20] Montaigne is usually remembered as a conservative thinker, but Hassan Melehy has pointed out that the early modern writer's strategies of citation conflict with this overgeneralized view by propounding an antiauthoritarian perspective that spills over from textual-intellectual to institutional concerns.[21]

3. *An impulse toward dialogue.* Montaigne borrows from a host of preexisting idioms, such as the aphorism, moral lesson, letter, and, most importantly, dialogue. He repeatedly turns to Plato's dialogues as a way to describe by comparison the expressive style he wants to achieve, a marriage of poetry, open-ended conversation, and the rhetorical impression of an improvised search. He admires how Plato's written discourse "sparkles throughout with poetic power and daring, and presents the characteristics of its frenzy" (III.9: 1125).

In the *Essais*, dialogue with others is not merely hinted at but dramatized in the flow of the text. Montaigne sometimes uses citations as though they are interjections demanding his response; for example, a quote from Virgil, "Where are you heading, so far off course?" prompts his self-conscious discussion of the unpredictable "jumps and tumblings" of poetic prose (III.9: 1124–25). He also raises questions about himself with quotation marks, temporarily donning the voice of an interlocutor: "Since I cannot hold my reader's attention by my weight, *manco male* if I manage to do so by my muddle. 'Yes, but afterwards he will be sorry he spent time over it.' I suppose so: but still he would have done it!" (III.9: 1126). Conjuring up an atmosphere of conversation, Montaigne's text inscribes the skeptical thrust of the dialogue form: its ability, as a drama of contrast, to test assumed truths and stave off consensus while staying in the register of a provisional exchange of ideas.

Although Montaigne couches the *Essais* as a solitary project he carries out while isolated in the library tower of his family estate, a stress on interpersonal interaction fuels his thoughts on many topics, not least friendship, and inflects the manner by which he insinuates a conversation with the reader. In their very conception, the *Essais* were directly inspired by the premature death of Montaigne's close friend and correspondent, Étienne de La Boétie, and Montaigne frames his reflective task as an effort to somehow continue their intellectual exchanges. "If I had somebody to write to, I would readily have chosen [the letter] as the means of publishing my witty chatter," he states. "But I would need some definite correspondent, as I used to have, who would draw me out, sustain me, and lift me up. For to correspond with thin air, as others do, is something I could only manage in my dreams" (I.40: 283).

However, not just any reader suffices to join in the tacit collaboration he hopes the *Essais* will provoke. In the midst of extolling the "poetic gait" of Plato's dialogues, Montaigne declares, "It is the undiligent reader who loses my subject, not I" (III.9: 1125). This is less an abrogation of responsibility, or

Introduction

an admission that he revels in misdirecting readers, than a playful acknowledgment of the major challenges his readers must face. *The Essais*, after all, are riddled with incompletion, from skipped steps of reasoning to thoughts he puts aside before exploring them to satisfaction, through to sentence structures that lack syntactical order and closure. The "diligent" reader, then, must not only keep pace with the essayist's wayward perambulations, but assume a constructive role where arguments are left unfinished.[22]

There is more to Montaigne's underlying interest in dialogue than his fondness for Plato's Socrates and his personal grief over his friend's death. The religious wars that raged in France for the better part of his adult life magnified his skeptical mindset and called for a rethinking of self-other relationships. His essaying must be understood, in part, as an imagined antidote to the dogmatic non-thought that lay at the source of the bloodshed.[23] He responds through an inquisitive style that takes into its own procedure the inconstancy and ambiguity of the modern world he ponders. This style implies that dialogue is only achievable to the extent that we make ourselves "at home in existence without fixed points of support."[24]

4. *The essayist as narrator*. Montaigne enlivens the *Essais* through narrative digressions. He claims, with false modesty, to be a bad storyteller ("the best tale in the world withers in my hand" [II.17: 725]), but at various turns, the essayist relates his thoughtful commentary in the form of stories, whether borrowed from literary, philosophical, religious, or historical sources, or taken anecdotally from his own experiences. In fact, telling stories seems to be Montaigne's preferred means of studying human behavior (and although he confesses to taking poetic license with his yarns, he insists that this only improves their impact as illustrations).[25] His essaying rejects not narrative itself but rather the restrictions and assurances of *conventional narrative order*.[26] As he words it, his "rough," disjointed style necessarily flouts rulebound narrative structure and fluency, its promise of conclusiveness (II.17: 724–26).

Godard as Cinematic Essayist

In each of these respects, Montaigne is a distant but profound forerunner of a tradition of essaying that Godard—another resourcefully "bad" storyteller—adapts into cinema. The affinities of method and purpose between these essayists are more than superficial, their different media of "writing" notwithstanding. According to Jean-Pierre Gorin, Godard's onetime close collaborator, Godard confessed on multiple occasions his "dream to be Montaigne."[27] Of all the film essayists I examine in this book, Godard is among the most Montaignean—that is, if we consider his essaying over the duration of his career, and not just a handful of works that meet the taxonomic criteria of the single, self-contained "essay."[28]

Godard is the protagonist in my study in part because his output over six decades—in film, television, video, and multimedia installation—bears out in extraordinary ways this prolific sense of working as an essayist. *Godard and the Essay Film* offers the first rigorous analysis of Godard's essayistic tendencies across the early, middle, and late stages of his corpus, with a view to showing how these different stages interrelate.[29] Through chapters focused on reflective processes I have just ascribed to Montaigne's *Essais*, I sketch out a conception of essayistic activity that casts light on some of the most intricate features of Godard's work: how he tests out ideas in a convoluted fashion without presenting a forthright thesis; how he willfully obscures his authorial subjectivity through ample appropriations of already extant sounds, images, and critical discourses; how he deftly combines film and video with the media of painting, literature, and music; how he inhabits his experiments in body and voice; and how his critical reflections on the powers and limits of cinema intertwine aesthetics with matters of political resistance, ethical responsiveness, and historical reckoning with the wars and atrocities of the twentieth century.

Despite, or rather because of, this focus on Godard, the stakes and resonances of my claims will encompass many other directors who work either firmly within or on the outer margins of the essay film. This book delves into Godard's reflective tactics in order to reevaluate the larger history of essayistic cinema as a whole, opening up new inroads into apprehending this elusive practice. Chapter 1 retraces, modifies, and enlarges on what has become the canonical history of the essay film's post-World War II genesis. I do this by accounting for both the "essay film" as a quasi-genre *and* for the presence of essayistic gestures in narrative films that do not quite fit the parameters of that category. I then illustrate how Godard's own expressed conception of working as an essayist productively calls for this definitional suppleness on our part, oscillating as it does between both narrative films and more documentary productions. My analysis corroborates the director's claim that his role as an essayist stems from the fact that when he made the transition from film criticism to filmmaking, he never stopped being a critic but began to use the medium of cinema to write his critical reflections. I explain how this critical essayism works both in a narrative venture, *Contempt* (*Le Mépris*, 1963), and a film more readily classifiable as an essay, *2 or 3 Things I Know About Her* (*2 ou 3 choses je sais que d'elle*, 1967). The chapter broadens the scope of what qualifies as essayistic, and discusses Godard's early exploits in relation to those of Marker, Resnais, Varda, and other central players in modern cinema who are less frequently described as essayists, such as Roberto Rossellini.

Chapter 2 turns to Godard's corpus in order to do justice to a Montaignean attribute of essayistic cinema that has not been sufficiently dealt with by other scholars, namely, the prevalent reliance on citation: the creative and critical reuse of preexisting sights, sounds, and texts drawn from

Introduction 13

all manner of sources. I show how, and why, citation serves the agendas of a variety of film essayists, and how their citational acts conduct a dialogue in two overlapping respects at once: with other authors whether living or dead, and with the viewer, who is challenged to catch and make sense of these intertextual threads. I follow a trajectory in Godard's oeuvre from the end of the 1960s through to the late 1980s, inspecting how his citational methods think through an abiding set of tensions between a politically militant mode of essayistic expression on the one hand (best exemplified by the films of Guy Debord) and a more openly tentative mode on the other. I detail how Godard's use of borrowed material persistently cooperates with his gestures of address to the spectator, and I explore the ways in which newly emergent technologies, such as the video mixer, alter the tone and texture of his reflections as he increasingly fashions himself into a historian of cinema and the twentieth century. After working through *Le Gai Savoir* (*The Joy of Learning*, 1969) and *Ici et ailleurs* (*Here and Elsewhere*, co-directed with Anne-Marie Miéville, 1976), this chapter culminates with a reading of the citation-driven montage in his video series *Histoire(s) du cinéma* (1988–98). This chapter, in short, interprets Godard's citational habits within the larger context of what I call a "post-militant" turn of the essay film—a move into more tentative forms that do not abandon leftist engagement so much as they address ethical and political matters by other means. I show *Histoire(s)* to be a high-water mark in this context, on the strength of its contingent attempt to bring together at least two spectators who may share in its montage-based discoveries.

Chapter 3 returns to the claim that narrative fiction films can be powerfully imbued with an essayistic spirit. At the same time, I further consider how essayistic thought, for Godard and also for other practitioners, does not settle into singular, first-person subjectivity but rather gravitates toward critical intimacy with others, toward what I define as dialogical "twoness." I take up this aspect particularly as it materializes around a thematic concern with coupling. I illustrate how this steadfast concern connects Godard's narrative films and more documentary-like essays, opening up feedback loops between them. Now focusing on the late stage of his career, I bring to bear an original understanding of how his long-term partnership with fellow filmmaker Anne-Marie Miéville serves as a self-reflexive and partly autobiographical basis around which he stresses the dialogical workings of essayistic reflection. Through readings of their joint ventures such as the televisual *Soft and Hard* (1985) and the MoMA-commissioned video *The Old Place* (1999), and through comparisons with the filmmaking dyad of Jean-Marie Straub and Danièle Huillet, I show how Godard-Miéville personify a condition of seeing and thinking together that is vitally at stake in Godard's late stage. I also trace a fascination with the study of physical gesture in their projects together, connecting it both to their depictions of male-female relationships and to their mindful, essayistic regard for their own creative gestures of montage. I ultimately account for how their couplehood incarnates a sort of "twoness" in which doctrinaire politics gives way to a more speculative manner of inquiry, and in which the binding force is one of love—not *eros*, but what registers instead as *philia*, a rapport of friendship.

Chapter 4 continues in this vein by probing the interpersonal dimensions of Godard's essaying as they arise in his self-portraiture. I save this feature for last because by that point in our journey, we will be in prime position to grasp how such acts—far from being self-absorbed—open onto the relational interstices between self and other. I weigh the ramifications of four of his self-inscriptive tendencies that gain force across a series of late works: *Scénario du film "Passion"* (1982), *JLG/JLG: Self-Portrait in December* (1995), *Histoire(s) du cinéma*, and *Notre musique* (*Our Music*, 2004). The first tendency is Godard's push into greater retrospection regarding his own significance in the history of cinema, with the director reexamining and also materially reworking his earlier output. The second impulse I examine is Godard's vacillation between Romantic displays of his technical virtuosity and more self-deprecating performances that chip away at his legendary status as an auteur. Third, I closely investigate how Godard depicts himself not as a filmmaker so much as a *viewer* within his own work, a figure whose performance methodically attunes us to a montage-based form of vision and thought that he wants to share. I stress how he resorts to *indirect* address and refuses the pose of an "I-You" structure of communication with the audience. Finally, the fourth inclination I highlight in this chapter is Godard's staging of a sort of dissolution of the authorial self by which he enters into the fabric of his work, becoming "consubstantial" with it, dissolving into the weave of citations out of which it is composed. The self-portraiture of Welles, Farocki, Varda, and other essayists comes in for pointed comparison.

Godard and the Essay Film concludes with a coda in which I consider how filmmakers and media artists with essayistic temperaments have daringly experimented with 3D cinematography since the turn of the twenty-first century and in response to the mainstream film industry's reinvigoration of the stereo format. I survey these essayistic projects and then focus on two of Godard's late projects on this score, both of which he shot using varied grades of digital video: *The Three Disasters* (*Les trois désastres*, 2013), a *Histoire(s)*-like video essay; and *Goodbye to Language* (*Adieu au langage*, 2014), an essayistic narrative film. My goal in the coda is to show how the stereoscopic stylings of these endeavors both amplify and complicate the striven-for bond between essayist and viewer. I discuss the ways in which these works negotiate the boundary of the screen, reconfiguring it as a threshold as they reflect on the affordances and constraints of 3D imagery. I show how Godard's aggressively disconcerting use of the 3D format appeals to our involvement through intricate parallax effects (both recessive indications of depth and protrusive pop-outs) that place our habits of perceiving and thinking under strain. I make clear how Godard's use of 3D, far from being a gimmick, indispensably informs *and interrelates* multiple strands of

Introduction

work in *Goodbye*'s chaotic mix of dramatic narrative and intellectual essay. I spell out how the film's stereo effects go hand in hand with its dreamlike, bifurcated plot concerning two couples; its indictment of totalitarian state-craft in liberal democracies; its lament for failed leftist revolutions; its use of a dog as an intercessor; its inscription of Godard as narrator and actor; its citations of French phenomenological accounts of self-other interaction; and its meditation on Godard's earlier work with Miéville. My readings of these 3D projects bring the book's claims full circle and speak to essayistic cinema's continued relevance—aesthetic, political, philosophical, and techno-logical—in the new century.

On Essayistic Spectatorship

In addition to broadening the criteria for what qualifies as an essayistic pro-cess, and calling attention to diachronic, *multi-work* gestures of reflection, *Godard and the Essay Film* aims to furnish a more thorough account of the viewing experience this kind of filmmaking offers. Though existing stud-ies spotlight the interaction between the essayist and an equally inquisitive viewer, this dynamic tends to be handled too abstractly, through reference to the films' rhetorical devices alone, without the critic delving deeply enough into the sensory, affective, and mental processes that particularize this medi-ated interaction when the viewer plays along.

If essayistic cinema unfolds as a personal, reflective encounter for and with an especially diligent spectator, then why does it tend to be written about at arm's length in film scholarship? That is, why do relatively few readings of the audiovisual works in question keep faith with the peculiarities of the viewing situation into which we are thrown? I am thinking of the snares, the contradictions, the refusals of resolution, the witty peregrinations that charm us yet also run off and leave us on a first pass, the superabundance of materi-als, the discoveries we share in along the way, and, of course, the humbling, never-fading impression that there remains more, much more, to be noticed, unknotted, and looked into. *Godard and the Essay Film* grows out of a desire to provide, through the example of my own critical approach, a more finely detailed record of the viewer's role. I want to explore the contours and path-ways of the "mutual galvanism" (to invoke Friedrich Schlegel's apt phrase)[30] between essayist and spectator. I intend to do this both at the level of the moment-to-moment unfolding of single works *and* at the level of the film-maker's essaying over a long series of experiments. My tenor of engagement is such that I am going to write less *about* the essayistic undertakings I deal with in these pages than from a critical vantage located within their rhythmic hold. I am going to take into account the many frustrations and obstacles that come with encountering these frequently esoteric films and videos, which demand *multiple, obsessive viewings* (more so than most other cinematic traditions),

16   Introduction

and which often seem to do as much to foil our participation as they do to foster it. Essayistic cinema galvanizes a *repeat* viewer, someone who not only answers the invitation to study convoluted arrangements of images, sounds, texts, and ideas on a recurring basis, but also has the cineliterate ability to think in comparative terms about the essayist's larger oeuvre.[31]

To consider just one illustrative case for the moment, Chris Marker's essayistic notion of the "Zone," a memory-charged realm of refashioned electronic imagery in his film *Sans soleil* (*Sunless*, 1983), can hardly be made sense of in its thematic density unless one understands (1) how it materializes as a response to Marker's disillusionment with certain strategies of militant protest in the fallout of the defeat of the New Left in the late 1960s and 1970s, which Marker gravely documents in his prior film *Grin without a Cat* (1977); (2) how it is derived from Andrei Tarkovsky's philosophical science fiction film *Stalker* (1979); (3) how Marker, in his later video portrait of Tarkovsky, *One Day in the Life of Andrei Arsenevich* (1999), interprets the Zone in *Stalker* as a desperate, utopian effort to restore human belief following a strange, large-scale catastrophe; and (4) how, within the crystalline structure of *Sans soleil* itself, Marker's electronic Zone recycles images that have already been displayed onscreen, enacting before us a repetitive process of scrutiny. Such are the intertextual and comparative paths we are encouraged to scour if we join the reflection.

The critical approach I am describing may sound like a reversion to traditional auteurism and its search for perduring themes. I focus mainly on the work of one director, and there is no denying that the serial and recursive style of inquiry I have extracted from Montaigne's project bears similarities to the notion of the auteur as an artist whose preoccupations find continual expression, with his or her "signature" decipherable to a knowing audience. For auteurism as well as essayism, the relationship between filmmaker and spectator is distinctly *long-term*. Godard stands out not only as one of the most esteemed auteurs in cinema history, but also as one of the French critics who ushered in the auteurist outlook at the dawn of the New Wave. And yet, through our examination of his shifting concerns and approaches over time, we will see that his cinematic essayism has as one of its core principles a drastic modification of the traditional concept of the auteur and an effort on his part to vacate its excessive individualism. By following Godard's own revisions on this score, we will arrive at a working definition of our cooperative role that focuses not on the director as a genius creator who alone is responsible for everything of value in the work, but instead on a potentially shared activity of thought that benefits from cinema's special power to unearth and display mysterious links between events, materials, and persons. To borrow Adam Lowenstein's useful reformulation of auteurist reception, we will see that Godard's essayistic style configures "cinema's coming-into-being *between* director and viewer" as a "living negotiation rather than a predetermined certainty."[32]

Introduction 17

Godard most reminiscently describes the general spirit of his essayistic enterprise in his 1962 interview with *Cahiers du cinéma* when he states: "Cinema, Truffaut said, is spectacle—Méliès—and research—Lumière. If I analyse myself, I see that I have always wanted, basically, to do research in the form of a spectacle."[33] There is more to this assertion than an unorthodox crossing of fiction and documentary. Godard's compression of "spectacle" and "research" defines an experimental effort to challenge and enlarge the perceptual and psychic aptitudes of the viewer. My object in this book is to show eventually how Godard and other audiovisual essayists seek to *retrain* the viewer through their open-ended screen pedagogies—how they endeavor to pass along not simply knowledge, but the nimble ways of making connections that they themselves display through montage. My hope is that approaching essayistic filmmaking in this way will uncover a deeper understanding of its past, present, and future importance as a collaborative and heuristic practice. As more than just a genre, more than an influx of first-person subjectivity into documentary, essayistic cinema presents itself as a necessarily speculative guide for living, reflecting, and feeling with images and sounds amid the dizzying complexities of their circulation in the multimedia landscape. If this cinematic tradition is finally commanding vibrant interest in global film culture, this is surely because it stands in timely need of attention, now as ever.

The subtitle of my book, "A Form That Thinks," a phrase I have adopted from Godard's vocabulary, warrants a refined explanation at this point. Godard asserts this phrase in titles and voiceover narration in *Histoire(s) du cinéma*, particularly episode 3A. Critics have used this evocative expression to sum up the essay film as a whole, but for Godard in his late period, it describes less an already constituted genre than an *aspirant* notion of his craft to actualize, or at least make newly possible, what he deems to be cinema's originary (and frequently forgotten) calling as an instrument of reflective thought. Godard's use of the phrase goes beyond generic purview, includes popular cinema, and is embedded in a deep history, at once aesthetic and philosophical, in which the cinema struggles to make good on its visionary promise as a tool of and for critical reflection. Godard at times writes and speaks about the film medium as though it were a sentient, thinking entity in its own right, and to be sure, the phrase "a form that thinks" affirms that films (and works of art in other media) can think via aesthetic gestures and processes that enact, not simply evoke, noetic functions. But Godard, as I will show in chapter 4, uses this phrase to reflect on a *potential* circumstance of shared thought to which the spectator's thought becomes added, tethered.

I want to make one final point, for now, about the relationship that essayistic filmmaking cultivates with its audience. Critics have tended to define this mediated interaction in idealistic terms as a contract predicated on a mutually enlightening exercise of critical thought, one that heroically annihilates the viewer's passivity and espouses progressive ideas. While numerous essay films fit this perspective, there are also many essayistic filmmakers who maneuver in less serviceable, less entirely trustworthy ways. Most of the works I am going to study are *seductive* turnings of thought that don't always abide by rational argumentation. What T. S. Eliot wrote of Montaigne's infectiously evasive manner also applies to Godard's: "He does not reason, he *insinuates, charms, and influences*; or if he reasons, you must be prepared for his having some other design upon you than to convince you by his argument."[34]

This point needs emphasis precisely because certain essay films stress it themselves, urging caution even as they invite us into their unruly inquiries. The first episode of *Histoire(s) du cinéma* presents several implicit warnings for the viewer, through titles and clips from other films. When Godard cites Welles performing a magic trick in the droll preamble of *F for Fake* (1975), I take it that this asks us to be on guard about the essayistic interaction for which we are being recruited. *F for Fake* both relies on *and satirizes* the "trick" of authorial direct address, exposing it as duplicitous (fig. I.1). Welles's film, like Godard's video series, still desires and needs our complicity, but simultaneously warns against the credulous acceptance of its own rhetorical schemes. Together, these two major instances of essaying effectively remind us that the dialogical interaction in which we are called to take part is not reducible to the rhetoric of address that transmits this call. They acknowledge that the collaborative thinking of essayism begins in response to such gestures of address, that these gestures are themselves under self-critical watch, that in playing along we risk being seduced by an unreliable authorial discourse, and that our work as spectators—to paraphrase the intertitles from the beginning of *Histoire(s) du cinéma*—comes with unusually steep demands.

Figure I.1. The film essayist as magician: *F for Fake* (Welles, 1975).

Chapter 1

✦

Research in the Form of a Spectacle

> Godard quite frequently is an essayist . . . That the actual ideas expressed in his films are often specious is a fact of less importance than the way in which they are paraded before us; it is this element of intellectual spectacle that is irreplaceable, not the ideas themselves. This might appropriately be called a "cinema of ideas," but his approach is also and principally an aesthetic attitude, in the same sense that Sartre's essay on Baudelaire is a work of art, no matter what one's opinion of the ideas expressed and despite Sartre's own distinction between art and literature.
>
> —Noël Burch

> I am an essayist with a camera . . . A self-critical one. But in self-criticism there is criticism. The modern novel is always at the same time a novel and a search for an answer to questions such as: "Why write?" "What is writing?" And painting too conveys an anxiety about the empty canvas and about the meaning of the act of painting. It is the same in the cinema. "Why does this shot stop here rather than there?" "Why show this rather than that?" You want a complete object but you never get anything but silhouettes.
>
> —Jean-Luc Godard

Godard is famously by his own judgment an "essayist" who writes his critical reflections in and through the medium of cinema, and he has framed his work in such terms since the outset of his career. But what precisely does this self-characterization mean? What does it imply about his methods and ambitions? Does it pertain more fittingly to some stages in his prodigious body of work than to others? What, for us, is the interpretive utility of the term "essayist"? How does it offer insight into Godard's seminal importance in the history of cinema? What legacies of the practice—whether literary or audiovisual—does the French-Swiss director take part in, prolong, and

19

actively reshape? And to what extent does his work support comparisons with other, perhaps kindred "essayists with a camera"?

These questions have not met with anything like a consensus in debates around the topic. Arguments have differed widely as to what, in the first place, constitutes an "essay" composed of sounds and images. Just as the essay in literature has long been difficult to pin down as a genre,[1] its cinematic status remains far from settled, even as the label "essay film" has gained currency in recent years among reviewers, programmers, and film and media scholars alike. In critical overviews of the practice, Godard is often named as a major innovator alongside Chris Marker, Harun Farocki, Agnès Varda, Alexander Kluge, and others who breach the separation between fiction and nonfiction in order to set loose an especially agile and resourceful style of inquiry. But the definitions and taxonomies that claim these roughly compatible figures reveal significant variations once they extend beyond the initial guideposts of "personal," "subjective," "self-reflexive," "protean," and "unorthodox." Depending on the commentator, Godard is said to contribute to an essayistic cinema that primarily follows from a literary tradition tracing back to the *Essais* of Montaigne,[2] to one that more specifically incorporates *cinéma vérité* into dramatic situations,[3] or to one that, as a more general direction within documentary, explores first-person enunciation in a postmodern age in which the "aura of objectiveness" surrounding the recorded image has all but vanished.[4]

Inspired by Godard's own statements, critics have used the "essay" label in reference to his work quite liberally. Yet only a handful have offered sustained discussions of the essayistic aspects of his productions, and across those accounts are glaring discrepancies as to what the term "essay" means and which films and videos (and which stages in his oeuvre) are to be counted. Such differences are to be expected, given the mutability of the essay form itself. But where the other essayists he might be compared to are more amenable to a basic, encompassing definition, Godard seems to trouble the essay category as much as he encourages it. For many trying to delineate the practice, his example is both essential and unyielding. Phillip Lopate, in his pathbreaking survey, deems Godard's place and influence in the larger field of the cinematic essay a "mixed blessing," on the grounds that although his films are self-referential, pensive, and dedicated to complex ideas, they refrain from communicating what he himself truly thinks and wishes to allege. "Just when you think you've got him, he wriggles away. When he whispers observations in *Two or Three Things I Know About Her* [1967], how can we be sure those are really his opinions?"[5] For Lopate, Godard is both too evasive and too willing to entangle his own arguments within a chaotic patchwork of other discourses he borrows. "He is too much the modernist, fracturing, dissociating, collaging, to be caught dead expressing his views straightforwardly." Only in rare cases does a "synthesizing, personal voice" take command and grant itself the final word. For these reasons, Lopate argues

Research in the Form of a Spectacle

that with the two possible exceptions of *Letter to Jane: Investigation about a Still* (co-directed with Jean-Pierre Gorin, 1972) and *Ici et ailleurs* (co-directed with Anne-Marie Miéville, 1976), the term "essay" does not accurately apply to Godard's work.[6]

Uncertainty as to how Godard figures as an essayist has moved others to dismiss the notion almost entirely. David Bordwell, in an analysis of Godard's films up to *Week-end* (1967), writes that the designation is "relevant to Godard's work only as a filmmaker's historically conditioned alibi for unusual narrational strategies."[7] Finding the term "comforting but empty," he argues that it poorly explains "the orneriness" of Godard's style. An essay, for Bordwell, "organizes reflections around a body of evidence or examples and proceeds in logical or emotional order to a conclusion," and so to describe a Godard film as an essay is to misjudge its structure, reduce it to banal points such as "modern life commodifies human relations," and neglect the actual "conditions within which the difficulties emerge and have consequences."[8] He concedes that Godard's work after *Week-end* sees "the emergence of truly essayistic forms," but offers a vague sense of what this means; "essayistic" seems to suggest a politicized "mixing of modes" drawn from documentary, European art cinema, and "historical-materialist narration."[9]

In spite of these categorical disagreements, I intend to show that the "essay" term indeed has a strong bearing on Godard's sound and image practice at multiple stages in his career, and that his self-description as an essayist, "a self-critical one," is entirely relevant, even crucial, to our apprehension of his work. My argument in what follows and in the chapters to come is that the essay distinction, if pressed rigorously enough, can illuminate some of the most demanding and complicated facets of his enterprise, above all its "element of intellectual spectacle," the ways in which ideas "are paraded before us," as Noël Burch puts it in the above epigraph. It is also my contention that while Godard is an idiosyncratic essayist, he is not an anomalous one. Paying attention to his evolving tactics will sharpen our sensitivity to the essayistic traits of numerous other directors working in a variety of cultural situations—including both documentarians and figures who mainly make fiction films. Though Godard's work doesn't neatly submit to categorical definitions, it remains instructive for an understanding of how an essayistic reflection operates on the move, how it conducts its thinking in an open-ended register while seeking our contribution. In order to grasp the director's exemplary nature, we will have to entertain a versatile conception of what an "essay" entails. Godard is a key practitioner of the form precisely because he so often forces a reappraisal of its defining features—its generic alignments, aesthetic and political motives, and inscriptions of authorial and spectatorial subjectivity. As will become clear as we move along, Godard's essaying reduces neither to Lopate's paradigm of forthright and personal confession nor to Bordwell's emphasis on tautly coherent point-making. It emanates, rather, from a more deeply ingrained impulse to convert the cinema into an all-out laboratory of critical reflection, with its stylistic resources, from framing and camera movement to editing and *mise en scène*, working as essentially inquisitive instruments. And the stakes of this aspiration turn on the audiovisual essayist being able to draw an especially diligent spectator into the fold of a difficult and never quite finished experiment.

In this chapter, I am going to tease out the ways in which an essayistic attitude asserts itself during Godard's formative stage. For a number of scholars, *2 or 3 Things I Know About Her* (1967) signals his initial foray into the "essay film." This is because that undertaking is the first in his corpus to display, all at once and in a systematic manner, the traits that recent definitions of the practice have gravitated toward: it has an "exaggeratedly subjectivized" voiceover commentary; it blends documentary and fiction; it reflexively interrogates its own principles; its address to the viewer is both intimate and challenging; and its montage, instead of advancing a plot, wagers a discursive argument.[10] However, this perspective ignores the important fact that Godard described himself as an "essayist" much earlier in his career, with a less formulaic definition in mind. In his frequently quoted interview that appeared in *Cahiers du cinéma* not long after the release of his film *My Life to Live* (*Vivre sa vie*, 1962), he maintains, in a passage that still goes some way to encapsulate his body of work, that he makes "essays in novel form or novels in essay form: only instead of writing, I film them."[11] He stops short of mentioning a particular example; the thrust of the remark is more to suggest a sensibility that infuses his very approach to working with sounds and images. As I will explore in greater detail below, this combination of "novel" and "essay" is not so much a generic construct as a critical disposition toward cinema and its possibilities that, in some measure, carries over from his formative experience as a film critic.

Godard's early estimation of himself as an "essayist" seems unpromising at first glance. He wavers between two pairings of "novel" and "essay," slipping a noncommittal "or" between them and leaving us to wonder how a "novel in essay form" is perhaps distinct from an "essay in novel form." Are these separate options for his cinema, or two ways of construing the same process? How do his films of the *early* 1960s confirm this declaration? If Godard is resolute in calling himself an essayist but is reluctant to spell out what comprises such an activity, this is not because his view is unfounded. Rather, his view revolves around a broader, less uniform range of variables and expedients than those that more recent studies of the "essay film" have privileged. For one, his use of the term "novel" indicates that a fiction film, no less than a documentary, can be an apt occasion for an "essay" to materialize. Secondly, his statement productively cautions against treating the essay in too prescribed a fashion. His mercurial conjunction of "novel" and "essay" suggests that the value of the one term relative to the other must be refigured anew by each work that tries out their synthesis. His self-definition conveys not a lack of clarity so much as a refusal to endorse generic norms established in advance.[12] Despite our own need to classify, then, we have to be careful not to obscure this undecidability, this provisionality, that inherently marks the essay as an experimental pursuit.

My approach in this chapter will address these unavoidable problems of circumscription by examining Godard's early work in relation to both the "essay film" and a more elastic sense of the "essayistic." I take the former term to name a relatively cohesive, quasi-generic tradition that arose after World War II. As studies by Laura Rascaroli, Timothy Corrigan, and others have shown, the essay film, while having forerunners such as Dziga Vertov's *Man with a Movie Camera* (1929) and Luis Buñuel's *Land without Bread* (1933), came into being in the 1950s and 1960s, with France as its most fertile site of production. In the short films made by the Left Bank directors Alain Resnais, Marker, Varda, and Georges Franju (films that Godard knew well and wrote about for *Cahiers du cinéma*), French cinema witnessed an outpouring of new styles that substantially rethought the dividing lines between the real and fictive, between reporting on actual events and drifting into more daringly subjective reflection. I will start by reconsidering this history of emergence, because this will acquaint us with the type of filmmaking to which Godard more or less adheres for the first time with *2 or 3 Things I Know About Her*. But at some point, I will widen the scope, with reference not only to Godard but also to other cinematic arch-modernists of the postwar era, by observing traces of the "essayistic" in productions that fall outside the "essay film" category, in films that are less outwardly recognizable as essays from a generic standpoint but which bring to bear the requisite spirit of investigation.

By "essayistic," then, I refer to a less constricted *mode*. In my usage, this adjectival term both specifies the animate workings of the essay *and* allows for their extension into the domains of other expressive genres and idioms, including fictional narrative.[13] Literary scholars have long accounted for the modal migration of the essay's ruminative energies and processes into the fictions of such authors as Fyodor Dostoevsky, Joseph Conrad, Marcel Proust, Virginia Woolf, Robert Musil, Hermann Broch, and Jorge Luis Borges.[14] Godard's provisional crossings of the novelistic and the essayistic beckon toward a similar phenomenon in the history of cinema, one whose lineaments and effects have not yet been adequately explored.

This way of dealing with the films may seem to complicate an already fraught field instead of fine-tuning the inductive logic that accords the essay its own branch in intellectual cinema. But this balanced and more supple perspective will allow us to integrate Godard's unruly work into a larger reflective form that includes other filmmakers as well. Welcoming his exemplarity in this way will have two key consequences as we move forward. First, it will guard against a superficially schematic criticism by directing our attention primarily to the elemental details and gestures of a speculative process that must be studied in the midst of its unfolding. And second, it will grant us ample opportunity to align our approach as closely as we can with the sort of viewing experience on which the essayistic depends. By giving Godard his due as an essayist, we will arrive at a more scrupulous account of how the practice works, while taking part in the very interaction we are describing.

The Primary Material Is Intelligence

Over the past two decades, film scholars writing in French, German, English, and Spanish have established a canonical history of the essay film as it emerged after World War II—a history replete with major figures, critical sources, and an inventory of enabling factors and conditions.[15] These studies have converged around two primary texts considered as manifestoes or forecasts of a new film practice on the horizon: Hans Richter's "The Film Essay: A New Form of Documentary Film" (1940) and Alexandre Astruc's more broadly referenced "The Birth of a New Avant-Garde: La Caméra-stylo" (1948).

Richter, himself a filmmaker and activist with ties to the interwar avant-garde, addresses his argument to young talent he wishes to lure away from the commercial feature. Conceiving of ways to move beyond the traditional documentary, he theorizes an approach dedicated to the expression of abstract ideas and processes:

> In its effort to make visible the invisible world of imaginations, thoughts, and ideas, the essayistic film can tap into an incomparably larger reservoir of expressive means than the pure documentary film. One isn't restricted in the film essay to the representation of external appearances or to a chronological sequence. On the contrary, one must bring together material from everywhere, and for this reason, one can jump throughout space and time: for example, from objective representation to fantastic allegory and from there to an acted-out scene. One can represent dead or living, artificial or natural things. Using everything that exists and that allows itself to be invented— just as long as it can serve as an argument for the visualization of a basic idea. With this abundance of means even "dry" thoughts and "difficult" ideas assume a color and entertaining quality that an audience requires in order to enjoy the content.[16]

Richter's formulation of the "film essay" anticipates emergent practices in two basic senses. First, it entails the freeing-up of imaginative thought from the dual constraints of chronological order and matter-of-fact representation by which images dutifully record surface appearances. The thought that animates the materials and arguments is able to determine its own logic of composition and proceed by its own ideational volition: it may, if it sees fit,

Research in the Form of a Spectacle

"jump throughout space and time" and between contrasting styles, "fantastic" or "objective." It is further able to draw on a much "larger reservoir of expressive means" than is typical in documentary, its charge being to give shape to processes that do not have a concrete structure afforded in advance. As a case in point (and not altogether a hypothetical one since he refers to his own films *Inflation* [1928] and *The Stock Market* [1939]), Richter broaches a problem that has beguiled many modern artists (Sergei Eisenstein and Bertolt Brecht among them): how best to represent the stock exchange? For Richter, no "A to Z" reportage, confined to protocols of objectivity, would suffice; it would take a constructive play of forms and the goal would be not just to visualize "the economy, the needs of the public, the laws of the market, supply and demand, etc.," but to make these ideas intelligible. "Even that which is not visible must be made visible." For Richter, the "essay" distinction is relevant in that it "refers to the treatment of difficult topics in a generally *accessible* form."[17]

A second anticipation of the cinematic essay has to do with Richter's call to "bring together material from everywhere," a notion Godard will later second with his claim that "one should put everything into a film" (*GG*, 238). Richter here touches on the form's frequent use of preexisting images, sounds, and texts—a reliance that at once strengthens its ties to the Montaignean essay in literature (where, as we saw in the introduction, inventive citation is crucial) and connects it to the variegated history of the compilation film. Richter's argument encourages a definition of the essay film that considers the likes of Godard, Farocki, Marker, Kluge, Guy Debord, Hartmut Bitomsky, and Edgardo Cozarinsky in the shadows cast by previous innovators of found footage (e.g., Esfir Shub, Joseph Cornell, and Nicole Védrès), as well as alongside more contemporary recyclers who tend to be slotted into the "experimental" category (e.g., Daniel Eisenberg, Abigail Child, Gustav Deutsch, and Klaus Wyborny).[18] Of course, the use of archival footage is a common element of most expository documentaries, but the essay—which neither casts its materials as self-evident bearers of information nor fully subordinates them to a vocal authority—submits what it gathers to critical gestures that unearth fresh meanings and associations. While Richter welcomes this work on intellectual grounds, he advises that it remain enjoyable for its audience. His view of the essay, poised as it is between the documentary and the experimental avant-garde, is flexible as to the means and matter that can be employed, but he insists that the reflective argument should be "entertaining," a spectacle that allows difficult and even prosaic concepts to "assume a color." An essayistic venture must be exciting enough to coax the viewer "to come along, think along, and feel with it."[19]

Richter's call for a cinema of ideas found an echo, eight years later, in Astruc's more famous article on the "caméra-stylo" (camera pen), which was first printed in the socialist-leaning journal *L'Ecran français*. Sensing the arrival of an "avant-garde" within the mainstream, Astruc discerns a cinema on the rise in which the filmmaker at last becomes the equal of the novelist, painter, and philosopher.[20] More than a rallying cry for the primacy of the auteur, the piece, through its scriptural metaphor, puts forth a demand for an audiovisual "means of writing just as flexible and subtle as written language."[21] What Astruc means by "writing," a term he deploys with a subdued Sartrean emphasis, is a manner of articulating complex thought, "writing" as an adaptable pursuit that, as Sartre had recently urged in "Situation of the Writer in 1947," should move beyond the book and journal article into newer, more public media forms.[22] Astruc makes the case that the film medium is advantageously equipped to

> tackle any subject, any genre. The most philosophical meditations on human production, psychology, metaphysics, ideas, and passions lie well within its province. I will even go so far as to say that contemporary ideas and philosophies of life are such that only the cinema can do justice to them. Maurice Nadeau wrote in an article in the newspaper *Combat*: "If Descartes lived today, he would write novels." With all due respect to Nadeau, a Descartes of today would already have shut himself up in his bedroom with a 16mm camera and some film, and would be writing his philosophy on film: for his *Discours de la Méthode* would today be of such a kind that only the cinema could express it satisfactorily.[23]

Without suggesting a template, Astruc is adamant about what this expanded field of possibilities should *not* put into practice: neither the ploddingly conventional shot structures of the popular narrative film, nor the "heavy associations" of the avant-garde of the 1920s, whose use of montage he dismisses as "old hat."[24] He maintains, in tones reminiscent of André Bazin's "evolution" of film style, that the medium has progressed to a point where it no longer requires the juxtaposition of images to convey ideas, that relationships *within* shots—brought to bear "in every gesture of the characters, in every line of dialogue, in those camera movements which relate objects to objects and characters to objects"—make for greater expressive dexterity where thought is concerned. "It is by clarifying these relationships, by making a tangible allusion, that the cinema can really make itself the vehicle of thought."[25] Here Astruc is notably at variance with Richter's embrace of associative montage, and where Richter welcomes the copious use of already extant material, Astruc discourages too firm a reliance on other texts.[26] Filmmakers, he believes, should carry out specifically cinematic reflections in their own right, albeit with the ambition of creating "works which are equivalent, in their profundity and meaning, to the novels of Faulkner and Malraux, to the essays of Sartre and Camus."[27]

The polemical thrust of the *caméra-stylo* concept is to increase available options for—and raze industrial barriers to—directors wishing to bring

Research in the Form of a Spectacle

popular cinema into closer contact with the intellectual currents of the moment. Astruc's text is further significant for the well-nigh utopian revolution in film culture it imagines, on the side of reception. The same technology that allows the modern-day Descartes to put his ideas on film also makes possible a public exchange of ideas unbound by the movie theater:

> It must be understood that up to now the cinema has been nothing more than a show. This is due to the basic fact that all films are projected in an auditorium. But with the development of 16mm and television, the day is not far off when everyone will possess a projector, will go to the local bookstore and hire films written on any subject, of any form, from literary criticism and novels to mathematics, history, and general science. From that moment on, it will no longer be possible to speak of *the* cinema. There will be *several* cinemas just as today there are several literatures, for the cinema, like literature, is not so much a particular art as a language which can express any sphere of thought.[28]

Though the "essay" is just one possibility Astruc names, he gestures toward what becomes one of its fundamental traits, beyond its aspiration to match literary and philosophic discourse with filmic writing: its public vocation and role in the cultivation of what Corrigan has called a "dynamics of interactive reception."[29] A judicious reading of both Richter's and Astruc's positions alongside their other writings and activities of the period indeed suggests that the essay form, as much as it heralds a cinema of personal and philosophical expression, bears with it a progressive impetus and concern for the share of the audience.

To be sure, the essay films that appeared in France following the war did so firmly within the context of altered conditions of exhibition and reception, from a resurgent ciné-club scene to the setting up of networked *art et essai* theaters that specialized in innovative features and short subjects that otherwise would not have found distribution.[30] As Corrigan argues more cogently than other recent theorists, the will to experiment out of which the essay film developed was in many respects nourished by a matrix of cultural, institutional, and economic factors through the 1950s and then on into the next decade. Conceptually, for Corrigan, an essayistic cinema arose during this period as a performance—through borrowed and refigured forms—of an "unsettled subjectivity" putting its views to the test and raising concerns meant to inspire debate. Charged from the outset with "dialogic potential," it addressed, challenged, and tried to galvanize viewers in a decidedly public "forum for thinking ideas."[31]

In this formative period, the significance of the short film cannot be overstressed.[32] Neither can the role played by the filmmakers who would soon make up the Left Bank contingent of the New Wave. With Varda, Resnais, and Marker, as well as with the slightly more autonomous Franju, the short film, far from being a mere training ground for the direction of features, proved a uniquely resourceful format. It served as a veritable laboratory for aesthetic invention and often cunning social polemic, launching a host of new styles that mixed fiction and nonfiction and put a roving, inquisitive voice on unprecedented display.[33] Some of these productions were financed and distributed independently, and some were state-commissioned to promote a certain viewpoint, but even in the latter cases, there surfaces, within the resultant film, a questioning, poetic attitude that renders the work anything but a clear-cut message. For instance, Varda's short films sponsored by the French Tourism Office contend with, more than cater to, a touristic gaze. *Ô Saisons, ô châteaux* (1957) offers itself as an illustrated guide to the Loire Valley castles, but in the voiceover narration, the recounting of facts (a female voice) intermittently gives way to lyrical readings (a male voice) of poems by Ronsard, Marot, and Villon, and these recitations coincide with graceful tracking shots and cutaways that—likewise departing from the main itinerary—cast an analytic and appropriative gaze onto details of edifices, or abandon the chateaux entirely to take in natural landscapes. *Du côté de la côte* (1958) similarly intersperses its lively portrait of the French Riviera with "somersaults" of irony, as Godard puts it in his sympathetic review of Varda's short films, which for him inaugurate the improvised "sketch" in cinema, much as it functions in painting or a journal entry that records passing impressions (*GG*, 112–13).

A far more scathing example of subversion is Franju's *Hôtel des Invalides* (1952), which Noël Burch interprets as ushering in the essay film according to a meditative interplay of "antithesis and thesis" that insinuates itself "through the very texture of the film."[34] Commissioned by the French Ministry of the Army, the film assumes the shape of a guided tour through the imperial armory museum in Paris only to mount a thinly disguised attack on the institution and its values from within. Structurally, the film follows a young, naive couple and their elderly guides through the collection, but this journey through the past military achievements of France is disturbed at each step by intimations of the horrific and fantastic. An antagonistic spirit makes itself felt when the guides' remarks about the artifacts are countered by dissenting formal gestures: a dance of shadows across the gallery, elliptical cuts that animate a mannequin in arms, a sudden modulation of music on the soundtrack, a flurry of machine-gun fire that interrupts ceremonial horns. When we are led to inspect a bronze statue of General Mangin, the camera semicircles its head to show the damage by a cannonball to its cheek and neck; and this upsetting image is later echoed by a close-up of a veteran sitting through a commemorative service inside the building's chapel, his face disfigured from combat. Franju at times veers from subtle into unsubtle commentary, as when—by means of a wipe that erupts from the center of the screen—the film jarringly cuts from a shot of the couple snickering to newsreel footage of an atomic cloud. Yet *Hôtel des Invalides* does not, in

Research in the Form of a Spectacle

the end, offer a straightforward condemnation. As the two lovers leave the museum unfazed, while children perform a military march outside, and birds coil upward into a late-autumn sky, the film retains stubborn ambiguities, unresolved problems regarding the epistemic status of its own images and the logic by which we are to parse them.[35]

The centrality of the Left Bank directors to the essay film's expansion had to do not only with their articulations of "unsettled subjectivity" but with their attendant obsessions with time, memory, and historical trauma. This nexus of themes received its most virtuosic treatment in the shorts made by Resnais and Marker. Over three of their joint projects—*Statues Also Die* (1953), *Night and Fog* (1955), and *Toute la mémoire du monde* (1956)— these filmmakers, in rough accord with Franju's methods, confronted the lingering effects of the wars in Europe and denounced, through barely disguised references and allegories, French colonialism in Africa. But they did so through even more sophisticated arrangements of documents and voices. *Night and Fog* works as a seminal instance of the essay film because of its probing confrontation with the Nazi death camps through a commentated montage that redresses collective forgetting. Its essayistic tenor is manifest in the formal alliance of the slow-tracking camera and the "self-interrogatory" voiceover written by the poet, essayist, and camp survivor Jean Cayrol, with Marker's assistance.[36] The essay film has an urgent message (one of its allegorical motives is to inveigh against atrocities committed by French forces in Algeria and expose the complicity of the French public),[37] but it doesn't pretend to deliver a complete, authoritative record of events. From the first shots, as the camera glides across a rural landscape and negotiates the barbed fence that still, in 1955, encloses Auschwitz and separates it from the outside world, the film admits an impossibility of direct documentation. It then carries out an anxious, increasingly brutal series of oscillations: between present and past; between vivid color and coarse, black-and-white stock; between newly captured and archival material; between static and moving images; between scenes of plenitude and equally disturbing scenes of absence; between vocal fluency and stunned silence. The elliptical digressions provoke the question as to who, *in addition to the Third Reich*, was and remains accountable.

The film is composed with an exacting rhythm, yet functions less as a thesis that has been worked out in advance than as a search for a means to mount a reflection with the resources at its disposal. As William Rothman argues, *Night and Fog* must "discover a way to discover,"[38] and we might add that it must also discover a way to bring the audience into this process. Working in combination with the voiceover (as well as with the erratic score by Hanns Eisler), the mobile framing and disjunctive montage have a strange kind of entrancing effect, even while rousing critical attention. As the horrors escalate, we find ourselves caught between revulsion and wide-eyed engagement, not so much "distanced" from the unfolding images as drawn into a receptive mood where ethically minded thought can confront, instead of "deny," the traces of incalculably more gruesome events. The film further conditions our reception through gestures of apostrophe, moments that invoke or internally configure our participation, implying, in some cases, a mutual understanding with the filmmakers.[39] The narrator at one point breaks off from detailing scratch marks on the wall of a gas chamber to slip into second-person address: "The only sign—but you have to know—is this ceiling scored by fingernails."[40] There is also a running play on the point-of-view structures of narrative cinema and their suturing of the viewer into the space of a scene: both the camera that investigates at eye level and inserted photographs of witnessing inmates stitch us into a circuit of gazes, without letting us settle into uncomplicated identifications.[41] *Night and Fog*, because of its struggle to reckon with the past as it still colors the present, has been foundational not only for scholars attempting to categorize the essay film, but also for essayistic filmmakers who have taken up the violent catastrophes of the twentieth century and the Holocaust in particular—a varied lineage that reaches from Godard's *Histoire(s) du cinéma* (1988–98) and Harun Farocki's *Images of the World and the Inscription of War* (1988) back to Alexander Kluge and Peter Schamoni's *Brutality in Stone* (1961).[42]

For most accounts—and justifiably so—Marker emerged as the supreme cinematic essayist over the next several decades. Now directing films on his own but still engaged in numerous other collaborative endeavors, he did more than his contemporaries to extend the essay from the short film into feature-length examples.[43] *Letter from Siberia* (1957), his eccentric travelogue/epistle, has become a locus classicus in debates about the audiovisual essay, due in large part to André Bazin's prescient take on it as an "essay documented by film. The important word is 'essay,' understood in the same sense that it has in literature—an essay at once historical and political, written by a poet as well."[44] For Bazin, who comes to Marker's project after having closely followed the shifting tides of postwar documentary (through pieces written on films by Jean Vigo, Jean Painlevé, Jean Rouch, Védrès, Varda, Franju, and Resnais),[45] *Letter from Siberia* merits the "essay" distinction because of its new technique of voiceover commentary. Bazin writes that in a more traditional documentary with a narrator, points are asserted through images whose indications are made to seem as if they are self-sufficient and beyond suspicion by a voiced authority that nevertheless remains in a secondary position. "With Marker it works quite differently," he continues. "I would say that the primary material is intelligence, that its immediate means of expression is language, and that the image only intervenes in the third position, in reference to this verbal intelligence." Bazin terms this innovation "lateral montage," arguing that the essay-filmmaker's ideas gain force not through successive images so much as through tension-bearing, "lateral" relays between what is shown and what is said.[46]

The example he cites of this method in action—the moment in which Marker replays the same series of shots filmed in the city of Yakutsk, each

Research in the Form of a Spectacle

time substituting a different commentary and different music—is indeed emblematic of the essay film as an acutely self-questioning form. Three events make up the sequence: a public bus passing a luxury car on the street, the vehicles headed in opposite directions; workers down on their hands and knees mending the road; and a local man with "a somewhat strange face, or at least, little blessed by nature," as Bazin phrases it, walking past and shooting a glance at the camera. On the first pass through the series (there are four passes in all), the voiceover (which, it should be pointed out, is *guardedly* personal in that it filters and approximates Marker's authorial perspective as a traveler-observer instead of putting it forth directly)[47] contemplates the footage and raises the question as to how one might "objectively" document and convey the feeling of hope in the air ("undeniable energy, enthusiasm, and the will to work") without the sequence ultimately being received as grist for opposing ideologies, that is, as either "the worker's paradise" or "hell on earth." This question motivates three subsequent passes with commentaries that change in tone from pro-Soviet to anti-Soviet to ostensibly more neutral, although neutrality itself turns out to be an equally unsatisfying pretense. Marker's gesture here goes beyond negating the other three commentaries with his own, less flawed one. The essayistic impact of the varied repetition isn't just to satirize the Cold War dogmatism but to question the power of the spoken word (and of the soundtrack more broadly) to lay claim to and organize the visual matter it accompanies. Marker, of course, goes on to speak fluently for images that do not speak for themselves, but he does this having conferred onto the visual fragments he handles a certain non-fixity of signification, having acknowledged the "lateral" interaction between the said and the shown as beset with qualms.

There is another way in which this segment evinces an essayistic spirit. The conflict Marker dramatizes is not just between voice and image, or between personal reflection and the chimera of objectivity, but between shooting and editing stages—between the moment of capture and a later moment of inspection and assembly. The repetition of the Yakutsk footage follows from a critical exigency that reasserts itself in stronger tones throughout Marker's body of work (and underwrites the refrain in *Grin without a Cat* [1977, 1993], "You never know what you are filming"). Marker's essaying often stresses the need to study, question, and perhaps revise the same images repeatedly, whether he has filmed them himself or culled them from an archive. Much of what he does as an essayist involves a reprocessing of the already made and viewed, from his electronic alterations by way of the "Zone" in *Sans soleil* (1983) that try to release new, untapped potentialities from scenes of the political upheavals of the 1960s, to the analyses of archival footage in *The Last Bolshevik* (1993) that detect signs and warnings suggestive of an entire historical epoch (e.g., the gesturing Russian dignitary who, "before Lenin, before Stalin," orders the poor attending a parade to remove their hats). In essence, Marker—and this can be argued of Farocki,

Godard, Kluge, and to some degree of Varda—translates to the screen the ecstasies and agonies of the editing suite, the sensations of working with an overabundance of collected material that demands intensive scrutiny but puts up resistance. This lends the finished work the feel of ideas and relations still being tried, the sense of a form being sought.

Because of his intelligent commentaries that put across a distinctive authorial voice despite their use of multiple personae, and because of his forms of montage that evoke the vicissitudes of thought and memory, Marker is frequently said to be *the* most important essayist of audiovisual media, and thus the director who most brilliantly answers the prophecies of Richter and Astruc. Indeed, the key place of Marker in the emergence narrative I have just outlined—what we might summarize as the *caméra-stylo* account—is so widely accepted that the term "essay film" has become synonymous with "Markeresque."

The strength of this record of the essay film's postwar genesis is that it can be extended to a variety of other essayistic styles in international cinema, well beyond France. The hybridization of fiction and documentary, the blatantly subjective self-inscription on the part of the director, the reflexive concern for the formal and epistemological capacities of the medium, the use of disjunctive montage with a contrapuntal voiceover commentary, the dialogical address to the viewer as a co-producer of the work—these combined attributes are traceable across a broad plurality of idioms including but not limited to the missive, the diary, the self-portrait, the portrait more generally, the sketch or rough draft, the pseudo-documentary, the archival compilation, and the travelogue. This *caméra-stylo* definition can encompass inveterate essayists who rarely stray from its principles (Kluge, Farocki, Gorin, Marker, Varda, Johan van der Keuken, Trinh T. Minh-ha, Patrick Keiller, David Perlov, Ross McElwee), as well as directors of narrative films who turn to it more occasionally, such as the Orson Welles[48] of *Filming Othello* (1978) and *F for Fake* (1975); the Wim Wenders of *Notebook on Cities and Clothes* (1989), *Tokyo-Ga* (1985), and *Lightning over Water* (1980); the Raúl Ruiz of *The Hypothesis of a Stolen Painting* (1979) and *Of Great Events and Ordinary People* (1979); and the Pier Paolo Pasolini of *Notes Toward an African Orestes* (1970) and *La Rabbia* (1963). This account can shed light on the approaches of somewhat more traditionally positioned documentarians (Humphrey Jennings, Joris Ivens, Werner Herzog). And, with minimal strain, it can be stretched to include more fiercely political avant-garde examples from Debord's film-pamphlets, through Godard and Gorin's 16-mm projects with the Dziga Vertov Group, to some of Jean-Marie Straub and Danièle Huillet's lessons and dialogues, which, in their obstinate singularity, perhaps border on the essay film without typifying it.

Various other directors hover around the essay film without being paradigmatic examples, including Peter Greenaway, Jonas Mekas, Robert Kramer, Dušan Makavejev, Marguerite Duras, the Aleksander Sokurov of his "elegies," and the Roberto Rossellini of *India: Matri Bhumi* (1959). While the essay film flourishes in western Europe and North America, this *caméra-stylo* formulation—as Rascaroli has shown—allows one to trace, in other parts of the globe, overlaps between "second" and "third cinema" cultures as defined by Octavio Getino and Fernando Solanas.[49] Granted, in the more militant "political film-essay"[50] of Latin America, with *Hour of the Furnaces* (Solanas and Getino, 1968) as its most epic incarnation, the stress on personal, auteurial expression that spans most European and North American variants of the essay film is in scarcer supply, as reflects its critique of bourgeois individualism. But the self-inscriptive director has returned with a vengeance in later approaches that reconceive third cinema aesthetics. For instance, Hamid Naficy's relevant category of "accented cinema" is constituted by many essayistic (although Naficy doesn't adopt the term) strategies that self-portraying filmmakers use to mine structures of feeling particular to exilic and diasporic experience. Reflexivity, direct address, stylistic and generic hybridity, epistolarity, incompletion: these traits suggest resonant commonalities with the essay film, and thus, it is no surprise that Ruiz, Trinh, Marker, Godard, Varda, Mekas, the Ivens of *A Story of Wind* (1988), and Chantal Akerman figure for Naficy as key references or case studies.[51]

All the Expedients: Essaying beyond the Essay Film

This *caméra-stylo* definition goes some way to map and systematize the essay film along these intersecting routes, provided that we handle the shared traits as loose family resemblances rather than as hard-and-fast rules of a genre. To its credit, such an account gives the "essay" term a weightier distinction than more casual journalistic uses; it has brought attention to many gifted filmmakers around the globe who were previously overlooked; and it paves the way for further research into the history of a form that is still evolving and capable of impressive achievements (such as Patricio Guzmán's *Nostalgia for the Light* [2011], Kirsten Johnson's *Cameraperson* [2016], Raoul Peck's *I Am Not Your Negro* [2017], and Varda and JR's *Faces Places* [2017]). But given the sheer variability of the films at issue, this perspective runs the risk of becoming overly schematic, and still leaves us with a partial, somewhat distorted outlook. After all, if the essay, as its etymology and Montaignean inheritance suggests, is indeed a provisional exercise, if it embodies a process of exploratory thought, then why should it necessarily consign its cinematic presence to a set of generic structures and attributes all branching out from documentary? Why should it concentrate *all* its resources around a paradigm situated mainly on one side of the very boundary between fiction and nonfiction it means to challenge?

Taking these questions on board, I want to suggest that the essay film, as plotted out above, is not the whole story, the whole history, of the essayistic in modern cinema. Instructive here is a definition that Edgar Morin once submitted: "Talking of the essay film, I would rather refer to the attitude of he who attempts to debate a problem by using all the means that the cinema affords, all the registers and all the expedients."[52] While theorists have used this quote to support resolutely documentary-centered views of the practice, Morin offers a more fluid conception and suggests a more extensive horizon of variables by which an essayistic approach can manifest itself. All the means, all the registers, all the expedients: such an allowance in no way prohibits the filmmaker from taking on a greater quotient of fiction, of drama, so long as an attitude of debate remains intact. And to do so would actually be in closer keeping with the *caméra-stylo* as Astruc originally intended it. We should keep in mind that even as Astruc proposes new options for documentary, the *caméra-stylo* takes inspirational cues from fiction filmmakers (namely, Welles, Jean Renoir, and Robert Bresson). Acknowledging an essayistic bent within narrative fiction would, in fact, comply with Astruc's prescriptive point that a cinema of thought can be achieved through dramatic staging as well, including not simply montage but *intra*-image forms of expression that range from dialogue and performance gesture to mobile camerawork.[53]

Once we entertain a broader set of expedients for the essay form, Godard's partnering of "essay" and "novel" appears less like a whimsical, half-accurate framing of his own oeuvre than a statement that compels us to consider an alternative notion of cinematic essaying for which he, rather than Marker, is perhaps the most prolific director. I will soon take up Godard's early work to show how it forges a separate, if not a wholly unrelated, path of reflection. But first I want to speak to the extent to which an essayistic spirit, well before and beyond Godard, overflows the essay film and arises in projects more within the bounds of fiction that inaugurate and continue the modern cinema of postwar Europe.

Jacques Rivette's "Letter on Rossellini" (1955) intuits a definition of essayistic filmmaking that is just as prescient as Astruc's and Richter's manifestoes. Published in *Cahiers du cinéma* as a defense of Rossellini's progression across a series of films following *Rome Open City* (1945), the article revolves around two connected arguments: first, that Rossellini, especially with *Voyage in Italy* (1954), ushers in a genuine modern cinema; and second, that in doing so, he awakens the medium, "hitherto condemned to narrative, to the possibility of the essay."[54] Rivette's notion of the "essay" is an unusual one. For him, it names "the very language of modern art" (*Cahiers du Cinéma*, 199) and as such he locates the practice across a variety of linguistic and pictorial media, including painting. Granted, his take on *Voyage in Italy* resonates in a certain sense with more recent conversations around the essay film. He writes that Rossellini, very much in the tradition of Montaigne, offers a highly personal meditation—a "home movie" (196) that purports to be a melodrama but works more fundamentally as a "metaphysical essay, confession, log-book,

Research in the Form of a Spectacle

intimate journal" (199). Yet Rivette's use of the "essay" designation is not, in the last analysis, typological. It has more to do with a *regard*—a look, an attitude—that infuses the film. He stresses throughout that Rossellini's cinema is animated by a "faculty of seeing" that "may not be the most subtle, which is Renoir, or the most acute, which is Hitchcock, but it is the most active," performing as it does an "incessant movement of seizure and pursuit" (197).

For Rivette, this regard that distinguishes Rosselini's cinema as essayistic gains its special dynamism, its "unremitting freedom," from a radical departure from the linking mechanisms of classical *découpage*, that is, from a system determined a priori as to how the shots succeed each other, how they organize action in the service of a story. With each shot, *Voyage* seeks another manner of "ordering," composed to a rhythm of "gamble, tension, chance and providence" (*Cahiers du Cinéma*, 198). This opens the fiction at each instant to accident and improvisation, while retaining the precision of a rough sketch that penetrates its subject more effectively, more movingly, than a deliberate style could manage. Moreover, Rossellini's look at the world uses the camera as an instrument not of recording so much as one of detection: rousing our anticipation, riveting our eyes to the screen, the film holds out a constant promise of our possibly witnessing a "miracle," no less, in the midst of the everyday (198). It pulls us "ineluctably towards the as yet unknown," and where it succeeds in netting something unplanned—an event, an emotion, an undulation of what Rossellini would consider the real itself—the film not only surprises us but "burden[s] us" by refusing to resolve its questions internally. "It is then up to us in silence," Rivette writes, "to prolong this movement that has returned to secrecy, this hidden arc that has buried itself beneath the earth again; we have not finished with it yet" (194). For Rivette, Rossellini's essayism comes down not just to the personal characteristics of his film—his collaboration with his then-wife, Ingrid Bergman, and so on—but instead to an attempt to confront the modern world through a style appropriate to its perceptual challenges. "These films contain the only real portrait of our times; and these times are a draft too. How could one fail suddenly to recognize, quintessentially sketched, ill-composed, incomplete, the semblance of our daily existence?" (195).

Some recent discussions of the essay film have handled Rivette's article as an intriguing but off-the-mark episode in the coinage of the term. But his notion of "essay" shows a rare sensitivity that draws us toward a deeper, genetic relationship between the practice and the modern cinema itself. The most interesting question his piece still raises is not whether to bracket off *Voyage* as an "essay" that is structurally analogous to *F for Fake* and *Sans soleil*, but whether the postwar modern cinema is inherently given to essayistic procedures.

In Rossellini's *Voyage in Italy*, essayistic elements are indeed afoot. The occasion for their incursion is a marital crisis that an English couple, Alex (George Sanders) and Katherine (Bergman) Joyce, undergo on a trip to

Naples, where, removed from their ordinary habits and surroundings, they come to realize their contempt for one another. The film increasingly assumes the feel of a travelogue, and the Neapolitan atmosphere becomes primary, exceeding its role as a backdrop for the drama. We are given to observe the city's aesthetic objects, mysterious landscapes and natural phenomena, sites that captivate and bewilder as they reveal the ancient past to be a continuing force within the present. Through the sightseeing of Katherine, as she studies the bronze statues at the Museo Archeologico, then examines the echoing cave of the Cumaean Sibyl, then photographs and interacts with fuming sulfur vents at the Phlegraean Fields, and then attends the Fontanelle ossuary, Rossellini dramatizes and reflects on the role of spectatorship. Across these events, the mobile camera, cutting, and swells of non-diegetic music highlight a series of near-epiphanies for Katherine,[55] but the regard of the camera also affirms its autonomy in these moments, as an inquiring consciousness equally fascinated by the objects and events on view, in spite of the tour guides' comically deficient remarks (fig.1.1). Loosely comparable to what occurs in the films by Franju and Varda cited above, an essayistic attitude surfaces in critical tension with an official itinerary structuring an examination of the past through its relics. And for Rossellini this voyage, while it is topographical, affective, and mental for the characters, is most profoundly a cinematic

Figure 1.1. Katherine on the cusp of an epiphany: *Voyage in Italy* (Rossellini, 1954).

Research in the Form of a Spectacle

one—it tries out a form in which fiction and documentary intermingle, a priori design gives way to fortuitous pursuit, and teleological action yields to a contemplative vision that elicits a new, more thoughtful and venturesome kind of spectatorship.[56]

Rivette's account of Rossellini's film valuably urges a rethinking from the ground up and particulars outward of what constitutes essayistic expression. It stands as a still-needed reminder that dramatic fiction is just as rightful a province for essayistic form as documentary. But what other cases make this amended outlook necessary? Where else, besides *Voyage*, in the incipient postwar modern cinema do we find experiments that abide by essayistic principles despite not quite counting as "essay films" holistically speaking? And which other commentaries in the vast critical literature on the subject of cinema's innovative upheavals after the war lend themselves to defining such a widened ambit of essayism?

Useful here is Corrigan's claim that Gilles Deleuze's cinema books furnish a theoretical framework that is remarkably "sympathetic" to the workings of "essayistic cinema in general," even though Deleuze himself says nothing about the essay film and ignores some of its leading practitioners, most surprisingly Marker.[57] Indeed, Deleuze's account of the "time-image" that ushered in a radically transformed modern cinema after the war at mid-century has been a touchstone for debates about the essay film. No doubt there are insights that come with positioning the essay film as an offshoot of what Deleuze outlines in *Cinema 2*, but it is important to preserve the fact that he leaves aside the essay as a distinct grouping. If strong sympathies exist between his modern cinema of thought and the fragmentary, unclosed, uncertain, and aleatoric operations of essayistic form, this is because *Cinema 2* speaks—wittingly or not—to a broader distribution of the essay's modal presence than is typically conceded. Put another way, it is the very cogency of Deleuze's *not needing* the essay as a category that gives us cause to adjust our critical antennae. Instead of applying his definition of modern cinema to a particular genre he ignores, perhaps we should move past the genre so as to acknowledge how much of modern cinema is functionally essayistic.

There is something of a paraphrase of Astruc in Deleuze's view that "great directors" are "thinkers" whose creative deeds in effect couple the question "What is cinema?" with "What is philosophy?"[58] Rivette's take on *Voyage* as an essay looks ahead to and comports with Deleuze's account of the time-image's arrival at the start of *Cinema 2*, which likewise treats Rossellini's film as a maiden case. Stressing how Katherine figures as a spectator within the film, unable to react to events that confound her sensory habits, Deleuze writes: "This is a cinema of the seer and no longer of the agent" (*Cinema 2: The Time-Image*, 2). Over and above affinities of form, Deleuze's study verges conceptually on the essayistic where he describes a cinema that renders a thinking process forced to confront its own limits, blockages, and insecurities, its "impower" in the face of chaotic or dull situations that define an

38   Chapter 1

intolerable, cliché-filled postwar milieu (*The Time-Image*, 164–73). Deleuze's filmmaker-as-thinker is tasked with inventing and exploring new forms of perception, with discovering newly credible and habitable links between humans and the world (170–73).

One of the dawning examples of modern cinema that carries out this initiative in a boldly essayistic fashion, while not quite counting as an "essay film," is Alain Resnais's collaboration with Marguerite Duras, *Hiroshima mon amour* (1959). Take how the film generates a love story from out of its disjointed prelude, which alternatingly stages a tender, apparently post-coital dialogue and orchestrates a documentary mapping of contemporary Hiroshima, surveying its forms of collective memory (including film and photography) and remaining scars from the atomic blast. As the film intercuts between the love scene and images from around the city, two trancelike voices, one male and one female, engage in a conversation—but these voices are as yet unfastened to the lovers on the screen, their bodies truncated by the frame, their faces suppressed. As these free-to-float voices combine with elliptical montage and the fluidly traveling camera (returned from *Night and Fog*), the prelude expresses a "cogitative agility"[59] that fluctuates between the past and present, the real and imaginary, the traumatic and erotic, the psychic and somatic. The film performs a style of thought that does not emerge from within a personalized, neatly coherent subjectivity but courses through disparate beings and histories, along multiple lines of fracture, all the while raising suspicion as to the sufficiency of its own endeavoring.

Other examples of essayism in modern cinema that make use of fictional narrative include Straub and Huillet's *Not Reconciled* (1965), Alexander Kluge's *Yesterday Girl* (1966) and *Artists Under the Big Top: Perplexed* (1968), Tomás Gutiérrez Alea's *Memories of Underdevelopment* (1968), Nagisa Oshima's *The Man Who Left His Will on Film* (1970), and Krzysztof Zanussi's *Illumination* (1972). Just as the fragmentary opening of *Hiroshima mon amour* functions as an embedded essay film of sorts, the non-ending of Michelangelo Antonioni's *Eclipse* (1962), as Denis Lévy has suggested through a comparison to the films of Jean-Daniel Pollet,[60] can be viewed as the intrusion of an essayistic rumination. The scene empties out the already tenuous tale of a love affair, leaving it behind and undecided as the camera returns to a suburban street corner at dusk—no longer to watch a dalliance between the main characters but, instead, to continue in a more investigative mode its study of "natural" and "built" elements as they intersect in public space, to conduct a reflexive play of light and darkness as the evening sets in, and to evoke, through headlines from the newspaper of a passerby and a parting close-up of an eerily bright streetlamp that soon shares the screen with a FIN title, an atmosphere of looming thermonuclear disaster.

Essayism infiltrates these works in different ways, but its presence as a thinking, searching manner of expression produces a disjointed stratification of narrative in each case. Plot, character, diegetic world, continuity syntax, point of view—these elements recognizably persist to varying degrees, but are made to contend with each other and assume unconventional functions that renegotiate our orientation. This essayism supplants not narrative altogether but the rules and road maps of traditional narrative order, calling for less deterministic arrangements and logics. Moreover, it recuperates a meaning of "fiction" (from the Latin root *fingere*, "to shape, form, devise, feign") that gets lost in the restriction of the term to either dramatic narrative on the one hand or falsehood on the other. Dorrit Cohn reminds us that "fiction" harbors a philosophical valence that concerns the "translation of mental experiences" and processes into textual forms.[61] The films at issue, then, are fictionalized both in their "feigned" story aspects and in their formal rendering of essayistic thought.[62]

Narrative essayism in modern cinema endured over the decades, well into the twenty-first century. Corrigan reads both Terrence Malick's *The Tree of Life* (2011) and Lech Majewski's *The Mill and the Cross* (2011) as films that digressively "detour into an essayism" so as to critique the "teleologies and agencies" of narrative as an organizational system.[63] For Corrigan, the essayistic strategies in these films wield a *"dissipative"* energy that disturbs and spaces out the narrative, making room for thought in the narrative's crevices and beyond its limits.[64] Essayistic operations work in contrapuntal ways in two other recent narrative films, Todd Haynes's *I'm Not There* (2007) and Jem Cohen's *Museum Hours* (2012). An experimental biopic, *I'm Not There* fractures its narrative into a freewheeling collage in order to both examine Bob Dylan's changeable identity through six divergent personae and to question the foundations of individual subjectivity itself. (For our purposes, it is notable that Haynes's film accomplishes this effect partly through a citational engagement with Godard's films of the 1960s, with a view to rethinking their sexual politics.)[65] For its part, the essayism of *Museum Hours* supplements its narrative dialogue, between a male museum guard in Vienna and a visiting American woman, with a digressive lesson in attention—a lesson that begins with close inspections of canvases by Rembrandt and Brueghel and then moves to the streets and architecture surrounding the museum to offer a modest, gently pedagogical study of quotidian life in the city.

Deleuze's *Cinema 2* further approaches the essayistic and identifies one of its abiding purposes when he articulates a "pedagogical" impulse that becomes more starkly evident at a later moment in the time-image's maturation. In the midst of detailing how modern cinema develops new expressive forms from the ruptured agreement between visible and audible components—that is, from the insistent non-correspondence of sights, sounds, and acts of speech that each take on a puzzling autonomy—Deleuze contends that such fissured arrangements attain to a new "readability" of the visual-acoustic field. The shots must now be "read" in addition to being seen or heard, and this effort of reading must confront and even compensate for severe opacities in the film's disjunctively layered composition. As Deleuze explains it, while citing

Noël Burch's analysis of Yasujiro Ozu's violations of classical syntax, "it is as if the shots are themselves turning, or 'turning round,' and grasping them 'requires considerable effort of memory and imagination, in other words, *a reading*'" (*The Time-Image*, 244–45). A call for careful and vigorous perceptual labor is contained in this formulation whereby the spectator of the film has to "relink" visual, auditory, and linguistic layers that both maintain their separation and press toward their expressive limits, resulting in lacunary silences and gaps that demand a constructive response on our part. "In short, what we call reading of the visual image is the stratigraphic condition, the turning-round [*retournement*] of the image, the corresponding act of perception which constantly converts the empty into full, recto into verso" (trans. modified). For Deleuze, this re-linkage on the viewer's part, this mental supplement to material form, constitutes "a new Analytic of the image" (245).

Deleuze argues that with this new regime of the image a "whole pedagogy is required." For we are not simply plunged into a chaos of unlinked elements and left to our own devices but, as it were, guided and trained: newly attuned through the exploits of certain directors who assist our readings by dint of their model interrogations of the time-image itself. Deleuze pulls close to the essayistic when he singles out Rossellini, Straub-Huillet, and especially Godard as such visionary pedagogues. Partially seeing this practice of reflective lessons, which shouldn't be conflated with documentary, as an interventionist response to televisual and electronic imaging, Deleuze credits Rossellini's telefilms such as *The Taking of Power by Louis XIV* (1966), *Blaise Pascal* (1972), and *The Messiah* (1975) with spawning this direction of work, through "reinvent[ing] a primary, absolutely fundamental, school, with its lesson in things and its lesson in words, its grammar of discourse and its handling of objects" (*The Time-Image*, 247).

Whether one inducts Deleuze's auteur-pedagogues into a genre of the "essay film," there is no denying that this *"pedagogy of perception,"*[66] which returns the filmmaker and spectator alike to "primary school" so as to unlearn old habits and start again,[67] speaks in vital ways to the history and continued mission of audiovisual essayism more broadly. Of all the key players whose efforts call for a revised, extended account of the essayistic along these lines, it is Godard, I want to argue, who does so with the most far-reaching consequences. His shape-shifting body of work satisfies the forecasts of Astruc, Richter, and Rivette in complex ways that are not as readily available to other film essayists from Marker to van der Keuken who are more tightly bound to the documentary format.[68] When the customary separation of fiction and nonfiction ceases to hold in Godard's films and videos, when "spectacle" and "research" go hand in hand, the upshot isn't merely or most significantly to install a personal, self-conscious agency that renders the production more subjective. The form of essaying he demonstrates goes beyond these general factors and stages its questioning along finer gradations concerning the elemental codes and conventions of the film medium. No less

Research in the Form of a Spectacle

than authorial commentary in the filmmaker's own voice, the treatment of a dramatic, fictionalized scene may stir up an exercise in speculative thought. Between his middle and late career stages, Godard in a sense inherits the pedagogical vocation of Rossellini, albeit in a notably different manner of composition and address to the viewer. The trajectory of that work, which is less a straight evolution than a series of trials between cinema and television and back again, gives rise to a profound exploration of the aesthetic, historical, and ethical capacities of the image—a veritable schooling in perception that will be more our concern in the chapters ahead. For now, I want to focus on how Godard's essayism begins.

Course and Discourse: A Critical Apprenticeship

In his writings for *Cahiers du cinéma* in the 1950s, Godard took note of the innovations in the short film more attentively than the other eventual New Wavists associated with the journal. While he was reluctant to ascribe a distinctive "ontology" to the short film versus the feature, he saw in the shorts by Franju, Varda, and Resnais a new practice geared to the reinvention of filmic expression, within conditions of experiment harking back to the beginnings of the medium. Their short subjects, he observes admiringly, "attempt the impossible" in that they try to recapture the "instinctive spontaneity" of early cinema through an exercise of "purposeful intelligence" (*GG*, 107–16). It is possible to trace an apprenticeship toward essayistic work over the five shorts that Godard himself directed prior to *Breathless* (*À bout de souffle*, 1960), from the close documentary observation of a labor process in *Opération "béton"* (1955) to the more capricious *Une Histoire d'eau* (1958), which reweaves existing footage from an abandoned project for François Truffaut and enlists a densely allusive narration spoken by a young woman (Anne Colette) with sporadic intrusions by Godard. But according to the French-Swiss filmmaker's self-definition as an essayist, which we have yet to consider in sufficient detail, it is rather his experience as a film critic that lays the groundwork for his use of the practice.

If we circle back to Godard's oft-quoted summation of his own practice from his lengthy *Cahiers* interview in 1962, and if we pay closer attention to what he implies by "essayist," we can appreciate just how important the concept of "criticism" is to his junction of "novel" and "essay":

> As a critic, I thought of myself as a film-maker. Today I still think of myself as a critic, and in a sense I am more than ever before. Instead of writing criticism, I make a film, but the critical dimension is subsumed. I think of myself as an essayist, producing essays in novel form or novels in essay form: only instead of writing I film them. Were the cinema to disappear, I would simply accept the inevitable

and turn to television; were television to disappear, I would revert to pencil and paper. For there is a clear continuity between all forms of expression. (*GG*, 171)

By the terms set forth in this passage, Godard's consideration of himself as an essayist (even as he makes feature-length fiction films) follows from two intimately related premises: first, that he has remained a film critic despite having transitioned from a linguistic to an audiovisual medium, this being a claim he has rehearsed several times over with unflagging conviction; and second, that this continuation of criticism supposes a fundamental sense of fluidity between media. The second point may sound strange coming from a director who (unlike Marker, with whom he is often contrasted on this score) is sometimes said to be a staunch proponent of filmic specificity in the face of newer media threatening its survival. What "essay" defines here is a spirit of inquiry that continues from his criticism into his filmmaking, effacing the division of labor between them; it names a reflective means that shifts with ease between the linguistic and the pictorial, between potentially "all forms of expression," thereby permitting Godard to carry on with his tireless experiments even pending the cinema's disappearance.

The fate of cinema, to be sure, becomes a pressing question in and for Godard's late work, and I will explore the intermedial dimension of this comment when we turn to that phase of his output. At the moment, I am more concerned to ask how this notion of the essayistic informs his early period, how it grows out of his written criticism. Where, precisely, should we look and listen for the "subsumed" critical aspect of his filmmaking? And how is it that the essay form makes such an adaptive transition possible?

"Writing was already a way of making films," Godard says during the same stretch of the 1962 interview, "for the difference between writing and directing is quantitative not qualitative" (*GG*, 171). That Godard did consider writing articles and making films to be on a critical continuum finds support in the fact that his most active span of contributions to *Cahiers* occurred in the six months leading up to the filming of *Breathless*. Between February and July of 1959, he authored thirty-one articles, and this followed from a steady stream of pieces he wrote over the preceding three years, after having published very little between 1952 and 1956. As Brian Henderson points out, these writings show Godard continuing to think through some of the issues that preoccupied his earlier criticism (e.g., his ambivalent reception of the theories of Bazin, in particular the latter's privileging of the long take), but they also display a mindset that is increasingly drawn to the potential of a full-blown modern cinema.[69] Whether his concern is for the relationship between documentary and fiction, or the marriage of "freedom" (the sensation of chance and spontaneity in Rossellini) and "rigor" (methodical design in Lang and Hitchcock) in a single project (*GG*, 79, 180), Godard is frequently disposed in these pieces to interpret the films he addresses as setting

Research in the Form of a Spectacle 43

a precedent for the reflective kind of filmmaking that he intends to undertake himself. Among the tendencies he imagines, more than he legitimately identifies in other films, is one of intensive, self-critical involution, what Henderson refers to as "Godard's nascent concept of the meta-film, the film made out of knowledge of film history and/or the film about film."[70]

Godard puts forward rather surprising examples of this tendency, and what counts by his lights is neither exactly the Brechtian reflexivity one tends to align with his own work nor simply the plot-based inclusion of a film's production, as in *Sunset Boulevard* (Wilder, 1950) or *The Bad and the Beautiful* (Minnelli, 1952). Citing directors as different as Rouch, Franju, and Nicholas Ray, Godard finds a propensity for metacritical reflection that declares itself at the level of style, through shot-to-shot operations relative to convention. In a striking, if somewhat forced, analysis of Anthony Mann's *Man of the West* (1958), he claims to have witnessed "an admirable lesson in cinema—in modern cinema" (*GG*, 117). For Godard, the film is inspiring because it manifestly entwines critical and creative faculties, and because it gives a Griffith-like impression of cinematic reinvention, of renewing the genre to which it contributes and the very syntax it self-consciously enlists. Mann's western, he writes, "both shows and demonstrates, innovates and copies, criticizes and creates." It therefore unfolds as "both course and discourse, both beautiful landscapes and the explanation of this beauty . . . both art and the theory of art" (*GG*, 117). Godard, eager to project into the film the elements of modern cinema he most admires, goes still another step in claiming that this process of "course and discourse" entails some measure of trial and improvisation. Studying a shot that was surely prepared ahead of time, he seizes on a short-lived delay between the movement of Gary Cooper and the response of the tracking camera as evidence that Mann's practice is caught between "the instinctive and the premeditated" (*GG*, 120).

Godard perhaps strongly misreads *Man of the West*, but what should interest us here is the desire his article sounds for a self-critical mode in which the "finished" film offers itself to the viewer not as the necessary result of preconceived ideas, but rather as the extension of a thinking process that to some degree remains open and contingent. It is this longing that provides the initial grounds for Godard's vocation as a film essayist. The fusion of "essay" and "novel" he soon claims for his own visual-acoustic work continues to explore the combinatory possibilities of "course" *and* "discourse," "research" *and* "spectacle," "rigor" *and* "freedom." Together, these nontraditional pairings sketch the ambitions of his early directorial efforts and, more to the point, indicate where his essayism comes from and where in the texture of a given work we might look for evidence of its reflective energy in action. Some readers will likely protest that what this alleged sense of the essayistic still lacks is an overtly asserted authorial personality, of the kind that critics have tended to tack onto Astruc's *caméra-stylo*, but in Godard's case, *before* such an inscribed enunciator shows up, the critical exploration is, as it were, unvoiced and articulated through stylistic means as the role of the essayist is left more implicit.

To corroborate this claim for the essayistic springing conceptually in Godard's oeuvre from a continuance of criticism, let us look at a telling scene in *Contempt* (1963), a film that has seldom if ever been labeled as an "essay." On the surface, there are certainly more likely candidates among Godard's New Wave productions. One thinks straightaway of the *cinéma vérité*-style questionnaires in *Masculine Feminine* (1966), which, for Italo Calvino and Noël Burch, invite the "essay" term.[71] One might also consider *A Married Woman* (1964) for its intriguingly suggestive citation of *Night and Fog*, sociological use of collage, and offbeat dialogues that make permeable the diegesis while exploring, among many other topics, the fraught links between romantic love and theatricality. Godard's treatment of Weimar-era German cinema through the lenses of film noir and science fiction in *Alphaville* (1965)—which, as Jonathan Rosenbaum argues, "brings social and aesthetic insight equally into focus" and merits consideration alongside the canonical studies of German Expressionism by Siegfried Kracauer and Lotte Eisner[72]— could also lend support to the carry-over of criticism I wish to mark.

If *Contempt* is a less predictable example, it is no less relevant. Although not an "essay film" in the taxonomic sense, it turns on moments of essaying that correspond to the logic of "course" and "discourse" that Godard wrote about as a critic. The film, which draws its Italian setting and most of its plot from Alberto Moravia's 1954 novel *Il disprezzo*, concerns a young French couple on the brink of their marriage dissolving as the husband takes a job as a script rewriter on an international co-production of an adaptation of Homer's *The Odyssey*. The drama of miscommunication, which spans the couple's relationship and the film-within-the-film's contentious making, becomes a thematic springboard for Godard's reflexive mulling-over of a number of pressing concerns for his work in 1963, from the decline of classical Hollywood, to the shifting production climate in western Europe, to the already threatened sustainability of the New Wave in France.[73] As Jacques Aumont among other commentators has pointed out, *Contempt* ruminates on the bleak state of things through an "embittered discourse on the film industry," lampooning the "big-budget epic" while itself being a version of it.[74] And while the film is immersed in the traits of modern cinema, it playfully adopts certain technical characteristics of the classical cinema whose passing it laments: it complies with a three-act structure and uses, for melodramatic effect, a lush score, vivid Eastmancolor stock, and the anamorphic widescreen format.[75]

The reflexive and allegorical components of *Contempt* have been dealt with extensively by others. What I would like to examine in finer detail here is the way in which Godard critically probes these matters on a shot-to-shot basis, through a speculative process that effectively writes itself into the film's fabric, so as to essay a reflection into—not just offer a commentary on—the aesthetic issues that are centrally at stake.

Research in the Form of a Spectacle

At the time of its release, Godard described *Contempt* as "an Antonioni film shot by Hawks or Hitchcock,"[76] implying a modernist enterprise with residual investments in the classical. Such a mingling of styles is nowhere more evident and fascinating than in the long apartment scene that runs through the middle third of the film as the young couple, Paul (Michel Piccoli) and Camille (Brigitte Bardot), argue and circulate throughout the unfinished rooms, trying out different poses and postures as if searching for some form of mutual abidance in the maze-like interior. The scene channels, without discordance, the innovations of Antonioni (the relentless play of frames-within-frames, the "autonomous mediating gaze" of the camera)[77] as well as the *mise en scène* of Minnelli (a delicate, anxious choreography of motion and gesture in domestic space, the cuts relatively sparse and unimposing, the camera mid-range and itinerant, the color pitched to emotional shifts in the CinemaScope frame). What deviates from classical convention is that the scene meanders on for over thirty minutes, without much serving to advance or complicate the plot. And yet it does build toward a forceful if somewhat mysterious climax in its final minutes.

The scene begins to edge toward a dramatic conclusion as Paul and Camille sit down on either side of a table with a white designer lamp at its center. We see them in a profile two-shot, framed almost symmetrically against a large window. Just as Paul switches on the light, an axial cut takes us to the middle of the lampshade, which now dominates the widescreen image (fig. 1.2). Cropped and "flattened out" against a shallow background in softer focus, the object is suddenly less a lampshade than a blank field that lights up at random while the camera shuttles back and forth between the two characters, and while Paul tries, and fails, to pinpoint the exact moment his wife stopped loving him. "Since we were at Prokosch's?" he asks. "When you saw me pat Francesca Vanini's behind?" Camille shakes her head, then replies, "Let's say it was that. Now it's over. Let's not talk about it."

Figure 1.2. The lampshade between Paul and Camille: *Contempt* (Godard, 1963).

With this unorthodox maneuver, Godard puts motivations of technique and *mise en scène* intensely into question. Initially, there is some suggestion that the tracking camera follows from Paul's desire to learn the cause of Camille's scorn, but as their conversation goes on it becomes apparent that the camera's mobility and concentration have, by the standards of classicism, only an arbitrary relation to his intentions. In the conspicuous absence of shot/countershot cutting, the camera's course and tempo are not determined by speech. Instead of conducting a tennis match of queries and reactions, Godard here stresses, in a single, unbroken take, the intervening space that dialogue scenes often reduce or omit. As for the lampshade, one might be tempted to see it as an obstacle that divides the characters and accentuates their emotional rift—their inability to connect in the scene. It seems to me, rather, that Godard is affectionately mocking such use of objects in Hollywood melodramas from the 1950s.[78] Rendered abstract, the lampshade resides where shots and countershots would customarily pivot in the exchange (or in the space the cuts would skip across, depending on camera position). Visually, conceptually, it is not so much an object as a zone that the camera studies with each alternating pass. The tenor of the shot isn't to underscore, in unambiguous terms, "alienation" (this already being a cliché of the European art cinema that Godard stylistically references), but to trace and examine the spatial interval that both unites and separates this volatile couple.[79]

The moments that follow continue to explore this idea—oddly enough by resorting to the very device Godard has just avoided. Paul and Camille both rise and revolve around the lamp in opposite directions; after a semi-violent scuffle, the musical score resurfaces and Camille makes to leave. We cut to a medium shot of Paul now calmly pursuing her as the camera recedes at the same rate. Then we cut to a legitimate countershot from his implied viewpoint, this shot pushing through the doorway as she turns and says she despises him: "J'te méprise!" Here, too, the mobile camera is crucial: the shot and countershot combine with a striking ebb and flow, a pull-and-push effect expressed frontally (figs. 1.3–1.4).

Though it is emotionally resonant, this scene-ending alternation is puzzling. Why, at this decisive juncture—literally a threshold moment for both the couple's relationship and the film's metacritical reflections—does Godard use shot/countershot, *the* classical technique for interlinking two shots and figures in a continuous scenography, just seconds after eschewing it? And why does he stray here from the tendency elsewhere in his work to reject this device at all cost? *Masculine Feminine* and especially *My Life to Live* derive their shot structures principally from a gymnastic evasion of the procedure, whether they handle dialogue in stretched-out takes, switch back and forth between head-on framings instead of between over-the-shoulder setups, or tinker with all manner of inventive pans and tracks in place of editing. What, then, motivates this use of shot/countershot in *Contempt*?

Research in the Form of a Spectacle

Figures 1.3–1.4. Paul approaches Camille (backward track); in the countershot, Camille voices her contempt (forward track): *Contempt*.

It helps to recognize, first of all, that this shot/countershot between Paul and Camille is a citation, less an intertextual allusion than a borrowing from the repertoire of another filmmaker whose formal thoughtfulness Godard values. To put it in Godard's own parlance, the moment is "shot by Hitchcock." Godard had earlier ascribed this visually striking device of shot (backward track) and countershot (forward track) to Hitchcock in a 1957 review of *The Wrong Man* (1956). There he notes the example where the "wrong man" crosses the threshold into the city jail, and he points to another key use at the close of *I Confess* (Hitchcock, 1953) where the priest suspected of murder approaches the "right man" whose guilt he has learned in confidence (*GG*, 52). Hitchcock, as Godard very likely noticed,[80] would use the procedure again in *Vertigo* (1958), first when Scottie (James Stewart) tails "Madeleine" (Kim Novak) around San Francisco, and then, once more, when Scottie walks into an open grave in his nightmare.

48   Chapter 1

If *Contempt* calls some of these references into play (Godard after all wanted to cast Kim Novak as Camille), it is no simple matter of *hommage* when the mobile shot/countershot occurs. Godard critically revises the maneuver for his own purposes. For Hitchcock, it is chiefly about point of view, a character's subjective gaze as it crosses a distance and fastens onto an object or person, procuring the spectator's involvement on the basis of a "psychological mimesis," as P. Adams Sitney puts it, whereby the sharing of a character's field of vision lets us "come to know them and identify with their curiosity."[81] In *Vertigo*, the binding force is one of desirous pursuit (shot) and magnetic allure (countershot). But for Godard, the character's look is of less importance than the rhythmic, almost musical interaction of bodies in the scene—indeed, the countershot steadily draws away from Paul's sightline as it pushes through the doorway. The lens distortion (a bowing of the door frames in both shots) imparts an air of estrangement and the camera sustains its own observational intensity, performing here as it does elsewhere in *Contempt* a detached curiosity, more inquiring than knowing.

This scene becomes less enigmatic if we consider how it puts to work some of the defining functions of the essayistic that we have already touched on in this chapter. The care Godard takes to separate the roving eye of the camera from the limited viewpoints of his characters allows for the assertion of a more independently observant gaze, one that can be understood as a variant of the pursuant regard that Rivette attributes to Rossellini's approach in *Voyage in Italy* (another key reference for *Contempt*).[82] This look is authorial, but to equate it with the "I" of Godard alone would be to miss how its to-ing and fro-ing compels a joint exploration through which the viewer might come to assume a shared inquisitiveness. In *Contempt*, this pull to engagement has a certain aim, or rather a guiding prospect that inspires each of the film's formal maneuvers as we are made to concentrate on the gestural subtleties of human interaction—namely, the prospect of somehow detecting the play of feelings and forces that circulate in *the space between* these two characters. As Alain Bergala explains this almost scientific task:

> Godard utilizes the resources of cinema—as others would an electronic microscope or laser scalpel—to see something that would otherwise escape our ordinary perception, how one passes, in a fraction of a second, between two shots, from misunderstanding [*méprise*] to contempt [*mépris*] . . . Experimenter, [Godard] expands a tenth of a second and the small space between a man and woman to the level of Cinemascope and an hour and a half long film, as Homer had done before him on the scale of a decade and the Mediterranean.[83]

In the apartment scene, Godard flirts with multiple and seemingly incongruous aesthetic systems (Antonioni, Minnelli, Hitchcock . . .) not simply for the sake of intertextuality but with a view to studying the charged space between his

Research in the Form of a Spectacle

49

central couple, his objective being to capture the elusive passage from *méprise* to *mépris*. It is this notion that informs his recasting of shot/countershot. In his hands, the device becomes—like the extended lampshade shot it follows and whose principle it continues rather than contradicts—yet another means of measuring intervallic tension, the vacillating currents of mood, thought, and sentiment between Paul and Camille as their bitter separation draws near.

The scene's layering of narrative "course" and critical "discourse" thus demonstrates an essayistic temperament through its openness and ingenuity at the level of technique. Godard's unexpected use of shot/countershot, the linchpin of popular cinema's continuity syntax, displays what I would like to call—adapting a term from Robert Musil's *The Man Without Qualities*—a "possibilist" conception of the film medium: that is, an inclination to rethink and revitalize the basic tools of cinematic expression, without subscribing to a credo against certain techniques.[84] Critics tend to saddle essayistic filmmaking with an allergic aversion to popular cinema, when in fact many film essayists draw nourishment from popular forms and devices for which they find fresh applications. Instead of rejecting shot/countershot, Godard saves it for a moment when its fuller potential can shine through. It is this reflective stocktaking of possibilities, this refusal to discard as unfit even the humblest, most orthodox of expedients, that in large part distinguishes *Contempt* as a work consisting of essayistic moments.

Hence, in this scene that tests out different traditions of staging and rethinks the grammar of narrative cinema, the essayist's commentary surfaces through a critically allusive disposition of form. Although there is nothing like direct authorial address in *Contempt* (unless we count the gaze of Raoul Coutard's camera back at the audience in the film's opening shot), the apartment scene tacitly invites the viewer to take part in the speculative thinking Godard brings to bear on shot/countershot. Ordinarily, the device ensures continuity and narrative intelligibility for an audience primed to absorb and follow content. Godard, on the contrary, figures the interstitial gap between the main couple as a site of sustained puzzlement, not just for Paul and Camille but for the viewer as well. After all, we don't come away from the scene with a feeling of Godard's optics having *satisfyingly* revealed something. The scene engages a problem of filmic expression that calls for further thought and experimentation.

An Attempt at Cinema, Presented as Such

Now that we have seen how an essayistic spirit initially takes shape as a critical activity in Godard's work, we are in a better position to grasp both the change his practice undergoes in the second part of the decade with *2 or 3 Things I Know About Her* and the implications this shift raises within the larger history of the essay film.

50   Chapter 1

Shot in tandem with his other film *Made in USA* (1966), which supplies a coda of sorts to his New Wave period, *2 or 3 Things* is, for most commentators, the start of something new, something different in Godard's career. For essentially the same reasons, it is also the first of his projects that theorists and historians of the essay film now tend to accept as a canonical instance, more often than not by a logic of assimilation to the model established by the Left Bank figures. Without disputing these views wholesale, I want to suggest that we refine them so that Godard's shift figures as a matter of degree more than kind, and so that we can be sure that our sense of *2 or 3 Things* as an "essay" locates this term's meaning less in an amalgam of structural traits than in the sinews and flows of an itinerant critical process.

That Godard quite consciously approached *2 or 3 Things* as a filmic essay is suggested by a cryptic fragment in a prose piece he wrote around the time of the production: "Those of Lacan, Althusser and Barthes were made obsolete by those of Montaigne."[85] One can surmise that the "those" to which he refers are *essays*, his provocation being that Montaigne's essayistic style of writing far surpasses, in its modern relevance and potential, that of the leading intellectuals in 1960s France. This strong veneration of the early modern essayist lends credence to the view that Godard had Montaignean methods in mind for his own project.

The features of *2 or 3 Things* that together summon the essay film category—its crossing of fiction and documentary, its reflexive concentration on the film medium, its voiceover spoken by the director himself, its ironic renewal of the "city symphony" genre,[86] and its periodic use of intertitles and citations from a variety of fields—all find precedent in Godard's prior endeavors. Considering just his verbal commentary, it evolves from a practice of vocal self-inscription that begins as early as his short films and grows ever more sophisticated in his feature films across the decade, ranging from his Wellesian vocal substitutions in post-synchronization for the voices of other actors to his impulsive narrating persona of *Band of Outsiders* (1964) whose wavering between omniscient and poetic, more brazenly subjective modes already hints at an aptitude for more overt essayistic reflection.[87] *2 or 3 Things* may be the first "essay film" that Godard makes resembling those of Marker and Resnais (Debord's films are perhaps a more likely influence),[88] but it comes, in part, as an outgrowth and intensification of his earlier work.

What is different about *2 or 3 Things*—what makes it a change in direction between early and middle stages for Godard—is the *extent* to which it enacts an interrogation that, of necessity, requires the spectator's rapt involvement, as a co-investigator thinking and perceiving alongside the essayist. If his earlier films, through their essayistic interplay of "course" and "discourse," already alert us to an expansion of the medium's stylistic and conceptual resources by using the rudiments of cinematic expression as critical instruments, now Godard appears more markedly intent on eliciting our participation—as if he has taken more to heart Richter's insistence that an

Research in the Form of a Spectacle

audiovisual essay must, without oversimplifying its subject, excite us into sharing and sustaining its reflective task.

The film lifts its topic from a controversial article by Catherine Vimenet on the existence of prostitution among the inhabitants of the *grands ensembles*, the high-rise apartment housing on the Paris outskirts, built in the mid-1960s under a national replanning initiative. Godard's film, which is shot mostly on location in the Sarcelles region as the complex is being built, sets out to observe, and to document by way of a drawn-from-life fiction, a particular woman, Juliette (Marina Vlady), in her routine as a part-time prostitute over the span of twenty-four hours. In its portrait of a female character and a city in transition simultaneously, *2 or 3 Things* forms a loose trilogy with *My Life to Live* and *A Married Woman*. But Godard, in two texts he wrote for *L'Avant-scène du cinéma* shortly after the film's release, insists that he is trying a new approach. He admits that his previous films have a "newsreel" component in their attention to current events, but he maintains that in *2 or 3 Things* there is an amplified degree of "pure research" that lets his process weigh more heavily on the audience:

> What I am doing is making the spectator share the arbitrary nature of my choices, and the quest for general rules which might justify a particular choice. . . . I am constantly asking questions. I watch myself filming and you hear me thinking aloud. In other words, it isn't a film, it's an attempt at film and is presented as such. (*GG*, 238–39)

Godard had already taken to calling his films "attempts," most adamantly *Pierrot le fou* (1965) (*GG*, 215, 223). With *2 or 3 Things*, however, this notion underlies a goal that is more deeply sociological in nature as he embarks on a thorough study of the structures that govern the day-to-day events and interactions of modern life. Atypically forthcoming in his explanation for readers, he outlines his approach in four separate but coinciding "movements," which I will quote and paraphrase in brief:

1. "Objective Description": of both objects and subjects
2. "Subjective Description": of both subjects and objects
3. "Search for Structures": the sum of 1 and 2 "should lead to the discovery of certain more general forms; should enable one to pick out, not a generalized overall truth, but a certain 'complex feeling' [*sentiment d'ensemble*]"
4. "Life": the sum of 1, 2, and 3 and their discoveries will potentially "bring us closer to life than at the outset," which might be grasped in the film, "if not all the time, then at least in certain images and certain sounds"

This approach might seem too deliberate to qualify as essayistic, not to mention absurdly ambitious in its scheme to arrive at "life" itself, but each

52   Chapter 1

movement is shot through with doubt. Godard, in parentheses, qualifies each descriptive procedure as "at least [an] attempt at description." Consistent with an essayistic manner, there obtains a core tension between methodic design and uncertainty over how to proceed. Not knowing what to call this effort, he states: "a film like this is a little as if I wanted to write a sociological essay in the form of a novel, and in order to do so had only musical notes at my disposition." And then, with greater urgency: "Is this cinema? Am I right to go on trying?" (*GG*, 241–42).

This uncertainty forms an integral part of the film itself. What comes across in Godard's voiceover narration, which he performs in a faint whisper, is an anxious hesitation as to how to progress from one moment to the next—where to place the camera? what to concentrate on? when to start a shot and when to end it?—since each choice on his part will inevitably come at the cost of other key factors that impinge on what he isolates. In his particular use of "lateral montage" (Bazin) there is, besides a counterpoint between voice and image, a sense of thought reaching its outer limits, confronting its "powerlessness" (Deleuze). Godard's anxiety, along with the crisis of knowing that subtends it, inhabits the very title of the film, which equivocates between "two *or* three things," harbors multiple referents for the pronoun "her," and puts pressure on the "I" as well as the "know."[89] A compressed articulation of (and primer for) the film's concerns can be found in the trailer that Godard himself created. Through a series of intertitles, the word "her" (*elle*) points, beyond Juliette, to "the cruelty of neocapitalism," "prostitution," "the Paris region," "the bathroom that 70% of the French don't have," "the awful legislation on *les grands ensembles*," "the physics of love," "the way we live today," "the war in Vietnam," "the modern callgirl," "the death of human beauty," "the flow of ideas," and "the Gestapo of structures." The trailer, no less than the articles Godard wrote, prepares us to watch the film in a particular way: in its slippages and openings out around the singular feminine pronoun, it enacts a certain *complex perceptiveness*—a modality of spectatorship that might permit us, in step with Godard's quest, to negotiate between Juliette's activities and her entire social milieu.

"Complex," *ensemble*, is a weighted term, referring as it does to the highrise housing, the set of structures dictating Parisian life, and a form of vision and thought that is capable, through the medium of cinema, of dealing with a multiplicity of these factors at once. Looking into two pivotal scenes, I want to argue that the film's functioning as an essay consists, most crucially, in Godard's attempt both to exercise this manner on his own and to extend it to the viewer, in the hope of attaining at least temporarily, for himself and for us, the "complex feeling" he stresses in his article.

Three-quarters into *2 or 3 Things*, Godard's voice (once again) disturbs the onscreen action: "How do you describe an event? How do you say or depict that at 4:10 P.M. this afternoon, Juliette and Marianne came to the garage at the Porte des Ternes where Juliette's husband works?" This event is already

Research in the Form of a Spectacle

underway onscreen. The women, in a bright red Mini steered by Juliette, turn rapidly into the car wash of a Mobil filling station with a distinctive red, blue, and white color scheme. There are actually two pieces of action that Godard interjects questions around; the second is a verbal exchange between Juliette and her husband at a gas pump as he comes to her window, kneels, chats with her (dialogue we don't catch due to the muting of other sounds that the entry of Godard's voice occasions), eyes his wristwatch, and then leans in for a kiss. The chronology of these happenings is left unclear, and Godard complicates matters further by showing them twice, not exactly the same shots but slight variations on them: he repeats some of the same camera *setups* but the characters inhabit the frame differently, their gesturing is different, and there are different sync points between sound and image tracks. (For example, the first time that Juliette and her husband kiss, it sparks, just this once, both a cut to a nearby sign that reads "friction proofing" and a piercingly loud car horn.)

Following—or joining—Godard as he thinks through the material takes no small amount of exertion. The constant wordplay as the camera isolates letters of the signage in and around the station, finding words within words, asks us to view each passing shot as strangely legible. The odd links between text and image (soon in his narration, Godard will call himself both a "writer" and a "painter") tie in with a strategy of composition whereby *mise en scène* commands our attention on a chromatic basis, the tricolor patterns marking resonances between things and people, subjects and objects. The scene, lacking a dramatic center, radically turns our focus onto quotidian details and surfaces, onto what Georges Perec (a kindred figure whom Godard cites elsewhere, in *Masculine Feminine*) calls the "infra-ordinary" elements of social life.[90] There is no built-in hierarchy that distinguishes readily between the significant and insignificant. And Godard's voice is not only more tentative than edifying; it is also (if we listen to his French rather than read its subtitled translation) so faintly audible as to put us on the very edge of our aural sensitivity.

Godard's voice cuts in again: "How to say what happened? To be sure, there's Juliette, her husband, the garage. But are these the words and images to use? Are they the only ones? Are there any others? Am I talking too loud? Am I watching from too far or too close?" He considers whether to take note of the leaves in the trees adjacent to the gas station, or the cloudy sky, or words painted on the walls. He has, of course, already made his decisions in the shooting and assembly of the film, but this coupling of the "result" with his indecisive voiceover suggests that each shot, each fragment, on offer stems from a virtual range of alternative views. In his prior films, as we saw with *Contempt*, he had already sought to have us think of the work as a series of formal choices, but *2 or 3 Things* makes us more sharply conscious of what we *aren't* seeing and hearing at a given moment, of what each well-composed shot lacks.

"In images," Godard now says, with an air of defeatism, over a shot of Juliette's car being washed, "anything goes, the best and the worst." At

54   Chapter 1

this point in the scene it may look as though Godard, hampered by self-consciousness, submits to the fact that the subjects and objects under his observation outstrip his abilities to rein them in. Yet seconds later, as we watch the gas pump incident play out for a second time, with minor changes, he enthusiastically relates his ambition:

> I am doing nothing other than searching for reasons to live happily. And now, if I push the analysis further, I find there is simply a reason for living. Because, first of all, there are memories and, secondly, the present and the facility for stopping to enjoy it, in other words, for having caught in passing a reason to be alive and for having kept it for a few seconds, after it has just been discovered amid the unique circumstances surrounding it. The birth into the human world of the simplest things, their appropriation by the mind of man, a new world where men and things will at one and the same time know harmonious relations—such is my aim. It is, in the end, as much political as poetic. And it explains, in any case, this longing for expression. Whose? Mine: writer and painter.

This divulgence, with its accent on "living," follows from his statement just moments earlier—as he shows close-ups of Juliette and Marianne positioned against and dimly reflected within an interior window of the car wash—that things, objects, can be suffused with vitality, while "living persons are often already dead." Godard here offers us more than just a riff on then-fashionable concepts of phenomenology that influence his thinking; read in the overall context of the film and its assault on consumer capitalism for its forcing of the French populace into essentially one or more forms of prostitution, his comment makes evident that he is trying not only to describe the constraining structures of modern life—the deadening routines they impose and so forth—but to awaken us to a liberating condition that is still within reach.

He goes on to pursue this reenergizing "birth into the human world of the simplest things" in the sounds and images that follow. The last few lines of his narration fall on a shot of swaying tree limbs reflected on the hood of the just-washed vehicle, as sunlight glints through the foliage. In this way, the film uses a surface to capture and integrate, in a single image, an object that resides beyond the frame. This gorgeous, almost abstract image of the reflected trees is trailed by an insert of a fuel meter with its large digits revolving, counting out francs (figs. 1.5 and 1.6). For all the elliptical breaks and divagations in Godard's montage, this is a moment where two successive shots in fact work contiguously—they compare two different orders of time that correspond to different modes of being in the world.

The shot of the meter represents time as a measured quantity (as a category of space), a notion that is further stressed with the repetition of Juliette's husband checking his watch as he crouches near the pump. In other words,

Figures 1.5–1.6. Reflections of trees and sunlight on the car hood, contrasted with the rotating gas meter: *2 or 3 Things I Know About Her* (Godard, 1967).

it represents clock time—the time of habit, custom, schedule. The shot of the meter also lends this quantification of time a monetary value and thus connects the scene to the film's larger arguments regarding the temporal logic of consumerism. As Douglas Morrey explains, *2 or 3 Things* propounds the view that in the market economy the consumer is "occupied" by an unrelenting flow of products, and the moment of purchasing longed-for things, rather than offering satisfaction, redirects desire toward things not yet obtained. Intrinsic to this form of captivation is "a linear, irreversible sense of time that always appears several steps ahead of those trying to *live* in it."[91]

Godard works around this insert of the gas meter and offsets its connotations. The shot of the tree limbs reflected on the Mini figures in the scene as a kind of lyrical release from the time of habit and routine. For the instant, it transforms the hood of the car into a canvas and suggests, in concert with Godard's voiceover, a "new world" latent in the surfaces, colors, and contours of the landscape under inspection.[92] Over the shot of the meter, Godard whispers, "It's 4:45 P.M." We cut abruptly to a shot that zooms in on a cluster of trees around the Mobil sign (a movement that reverses a zoom-out from the same tree limbs a few shots earlier). He continues: "Should I have talked about Juliette or the foliage, since in any case it's impossible really to do the two together? Let's say both trembled gently at this beginning of the end of an October afternoon." Godard thus says more than he can quite show us, and implies a "trembling" that includes both Juliette and the leaves. The zoom pushes in until the Mobil sign vanishes and the foliage, buffeted by a light wind, fills the frame. This camera gesture cordons off the garage scene and its faintly epiphanic stirrings. A transitional phrase from Beethoven's sixteenth string quartet leads into a shot of a young woman stepping out of a taxi on the Champs-Élysées with a man we know to be a pimp: back, thus, to the cycles of prostitution and consumerism.

As the garage scene indicates, Godard essays the overarching aims of his project through a putting of perception on trial (his and ours), one shot after the next. In an exercise structured on imperfect repetitions, he fosters an interplay of memory and alertness to what materializes in a contingent present, in the midst of everyday occurrences. As "writer and painter," he espouses a facility not only to "stop" and "enjoy" but also to "discover," this being essential to what he calls "living happily." Bearing these key concerns in mind, I want to examine, en route to concluding this chapter, an earlier scene in *2 or 3 Things* where Godard's essaying has a still more profound expression and where the sense of discovery is more palpable, although still somewhat fugitive in its ultimate effects. Let me say that by traditional standards, my analysis is going to be excessively detailed, but I take this to be a necessary measure in accordance with the work itself and the micro-analytic attention it demands.

The scene in question, the best-known of the film, takes place inside a bustling café in inner Paris. Godard prefaces the scene by saying over shots of construction workers and of Juliette traversing a busy street: "I examine the life of the city and its inhabitants and the bonds between them with as much intensity as the biologist analyzes the relationship between the individual and race in evolution. It is only thus that I can attack problems of social pathology, forming the hope of a truly new city." The scene starts to unfold as Juliette enters the café, walks past a young man to her left playing pinball, and greets the bartender, shaking his hand after it juts awkwardly into the frame. She turns and reports—as though delivering an aside and without returning the gaze of the camera—"To define myself in a word? Indifferent." She then makes her way over to a booth where a young woman has just called her, and Godard, using traditional continuity editing in a strange key, matches on action as they shake hands. That is, he cuts smoothly and without delay according to their gesture, which begins in the first shot and is completed in the next.

The complexity of this scene, and the manner in which Godard studies the inter-corporeal bonds between people while treating this fictional event as

Research in the Form of a Spectacle 57

indicative of actual forces at work in Parisian society, requires a more complete analysis than I can offer here. For our purposes, it will suffice to inspect what the scene gradually declares as its primary (though not its only) focus: the interaction between Juliette and the young man we first see at the pinball machine near the door. The clatter of pinball dominates the soundtrack in the scene's first half, keeping his importance in play even from offscreen. In a further anticipation of what the scene is working toward, there is an arresting shot of these two characters sharing the frame as Juliette returns to the bar and buys a pack of cigarettes. We see them together in silhouette, against natural light pouring in from the street where cars are speeding past, crossing and accenting the already charged space between the figures of these characters. Juliette at this point seems not to pay him any notice, but he shoots her a furtive look.

Their potential link soon becomes a greater focal point. In a three-shot, the man from the pinball machine is shown seated and reading a newspaper while flanked on either side by Juliette and another female character we haven't been shown yet who is smoking and flipping through a magazine. The film sizes up this ensemble of figures from different vantages, as a subtle game of glances and gestures develops among them; and Godard vocally joins in as a fourth participant by asking questions and referring to this emergent woman as a double for Juliette, her "likeness" and "fellow creature" (*semblable*).

In a close-up, Juliette stares intently at the other woman (whom we can detect out of focus in the wall mirror behind Juliette, along with the man as well) and furrows her brow in a mix of curiosity and confusion. That some feeling or thought is starting to impress itself on her (and on us) is underlined further by incipient notes of Beethoven's sixteenth string quartet, the same piece used in the garage scene, which briefly overtake the ambient noise.

Just as Godard's voiceover speculates that "perhaps an object is a link allowing us to pass between subjects, therefore to live in society, to be together," the film cuts to a close-up, angled downward, of a spoon stirring a cup of espresso. This close-up begins one of the most intensely essayistic passages in Godard's entire corpus. The film cuts between progressively closer views of the coffee and a repeated two-shot setup of Juliette and the young man, his figure in profile and her face tucked into the frame just over his shoulders, imbalancing the composition whose right half is now conspicuously vacant. While the two of them make occasional, more than casual eye contact, Godard's voiceover assumes an even more restless tone as his reflection on the linking potential of an object compels him to face up to the gravest limitations of his endeavor. "Since social relationships are always ambiguous, since my thoughts divide as much as they unite, since my speech brings nearer by that which it expresses, and isolates by that about which it is silent, since a wide gulf separates my subjective certainty of myself"—the film cuts back to the espresso, pictured from a steeper angle, its foam swirling clockwise—"from the objective truth others have of me, since I always find myself guilty, even though I feel innocent, since each event changes my daily life, since I fail to communicate, to understand, to love and to be loved"—a spoon enters the frame somewhat jarringly and stirs the dark liquid—"and each failure makes me experience my solitude more deeply . . ."

The coupling of Godard's confession with the espresso, which soon fills the entire screen, turning it into a kind of night sky, effectuates the film's essayistic mood at its peak expression. It is tempting to say the film becomes essayistic in its foregrounding of Godard's individual cogitations, the notion being that he steals the scene from the characters and takes possession of the espresso to which no one else can lay claim, given the geometry of relations established by the cutting. But such a view is reductive and, from a technical standpoint, wrong. The espresso may be indistinctly situated, and it may be apparent that Juliette and the other woman are drinking a coke and a beer respectively, but if we engage the scene as closely as Godard hopes, it becomes evident enough that it is placed in front of the young man.

In the aforesaid close-up of Juliette furrowing her brow while Godard hypothesizes about the connective potential of an object, the young man can be spied in the wall mirror: he is in soft focus but still reasonably distinct, and with his right hand he is most definitely stirring a cup (we can also hear the corresponding clinking sound). In fact, the very next shot, which is the first to show the espresso up close, executes a classical match on action that recaptures and continues his stirring motion. His possession of the coffee is then further confirmed by the spoon that slips into the frame from the right and is laid down on the saucer.

This is a hard-to-catch detail, but it is just the sort of inter-shot relation that is vital to the essayistic work of the scene. The three successive shots, from Juliette to the espresso and then to the young man smoking, coordinate with Godard's concurrently stated proposition that an "object" may allow us to "pass between subjects" (figs. 1.7–1.9). The scene's syntax assigns the coffee cup to the young man and implies that the gradually closer views are conceivably from *his* visual perspective. The vocal commentary, crossing with and complicating these shots, isn't a personal appropriation on Godard's part; it defines his locus of self-inscription as a relational field between characters. Hence the espresso is neither his nor the young man's exclusively. Through a kind of free-indirect discourse, the object belongs to them both at once, and the ambiguity (or sleight of hand) of its cinematic placement is pressed into the service of an effort whose significance is in fact transpersonal.

The last moments of the café scene build to a crescendo, the delicate force of which bears on both Godard and Juliette. Over the coffee and its spiraling foam, now shown in extreme close-up from directly above (fig. 1.10), Godard persists with his anxiety-filled reflection: "Since I can't escape the objectivity that crushes me, nor the subjectivity that expels me, since I can neither rise to a state of being, nor fall into nothingness, I must listen, I must look around more than ever, at the world . . . my fellow creature [*semblable*], my brother."

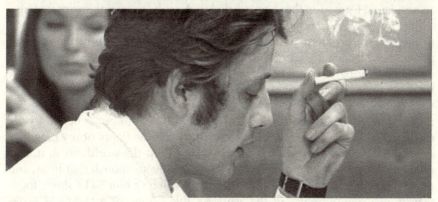

Figures 1.7–1.9. "Perhaps an object is a link allowing us to pass between subjects": *2 or 3 Things I Know About Her.*

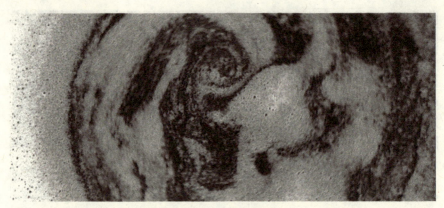

Figure 1.10. Espresso with eddying foam: *2 or 3 Things I Know About Her*.

We cut briefly to the two-shot of the young man turning to glimpse at Juliette, who stares back and then looks away again, as he does the same. We then return to the espresso. The foam has dissolved and left a pack of bubbles in the center of the frame. "The world alone," Godard's voice continues. "Today, when revolutions are impossible, when bloody wars threaten me, when capitalism is no longer sure of its rights and the working class is in retreat, when the progress, the lightning progress of science makes future centuries hauntingly present, when the future is more present than the present, when distant galaxies are at my door . . . my fellow creature, my brother." Bubbles pop and others slide to the center, congregating until they too rupture into an accidental formation that I can't help but describe as resembling parted lips.

Just as the cluster breaks, there is an upsurge of traffic noise and a cut back to the two-shot, Juliette and the man again trading looks. When he glances down, we cut back (again according to his point of view) to the espresso as a sugar cube, barely noticeable, sinks into the now pitch-dark liquid. The sound falls silent with the cut, until Godard asks: "Where does it begin? But where does what begin? God created the heavens and the earth, sure. But that is a bit cowardly and facile. One should be able to put it better, to say the limits of language are those of the world, that the limits of my language are those of the world and that in speaking, I limit the world, finish it, and one inevitable and mysterious day, death will come to abolish that limit, and there will be neither question nor response; it will be a blur." The shot's focus wavers over new bubbles in the espresso, this being not a technical problem for the camera operator (or, if it was, Godard has made clever use of this problem) but a visual counterpart to the vocalized concern about vagueness. "But if by chance things again become sharp"—exactly with the word "sharp" (*nette*), the shot's focus returns to maximum clarity—"this can only be with the appearance of consciousness [*conscience*]. After that everything will connect."

Research in the Form of a Spectacle

The focus pull and gradual, returned swell of Beethoven's string quartet together lend the scene the feel of an epiphany, as though Godard has managed at least a temporary escape from the hindrances about which he frets, namely his solitude, his incapacity to "communicate," and more generally the entrapping interiority that the close-up view of the espresso at one level suggests. But Godard also transfigures this ordinary object (no less than he does the hood of the Mini, or the lampshade in *Contempt*). The framing strategically obscures the cup so that the lively substance it contains becomes a cosmic field of elements, swirling, collecting, dispersing. The shot appears as an emblem of self-absorration, only to soon give way to the very sensation of a social *ensemble* that is ultimately at issue in the film. And however we translate the precise meaning of the word *conscience* in French, it is clear that Godard's use of it revives an emphasis on the usually downplayed prefix *con-* ("together with").

That this epiphany also extends to Juliette is underscored in the scene that follows the last shot of the espresso and conveys an exhilarating release from it. As the Beethoven continues, the film presents three brief shots of Juliette walking briskly through the same stretch of the city, each image a variant on the same event, captured from an alternate angle and with varied commotion. Speaking in voiceover for the first time, she remarks: "I don't know where or when, only that it happened. It's a feeling I have searched for the whole day. There was the smell of trees. I was the world, and the world was me." If Godard-as-narrator has managed to free himself from withering constraints, Juliette has (at the same time) overcome the "indifference" she voiced at the start of the scene as her most singular trait. As viewers, we are just as perplexed as she is about the event in question, and yet we share her conviction that something indeed happened to *almost* shake her out of her daily mechanical routine: this impression she can't quite recall would seem to have sprung from her nonverbal interactions with the young man at the café, the ambiguity of which suggests both amorous attraction (she is perhaps there to pick up clients) and something grander and more encompassing, in line with Godard's research.

Although Juliet is no direct stand-in for the director,[93] she does provide a filter within the film's fictional world through which the essayistic reflection passes and registers an impact. The repeated apostrophe "my fellow creature, my brother" crucially indicates, through an intertextual reference, that the film's viewer has a stake in this epiphany as well. Godard recycles these words from Baudelaire's *The Flowers of Evil* (1857), its prefatory poem "To the Reader," where they serve as an extraordinary instance of reader address. For Baudelaire (whose undertaking can be read as a rough forerunner to Godard's in that its "Parisian Scenes" respond with a mix of curiosity and barbed critique to the renovation of Paris engineered by Baron Haussmann), these invocatory words, as uttered by the lyric poet, assume an identification with the reader, a likeness couched as a shared malady of "Ennui" and its attendant traits of "folly, error, sin, avarice." Baudelaire's apostrophe insists that his readers, like it or not, will see themselves mirrored and implicated in his inventory of the charms, vices, disharmonies, and debasements of life in the city. Yet this avowed kinship, if considered within the scope of *The Flowers of Evil* as a whole, is also marked by the possibility of *reversing* one's alienation and numbed receptivity, through a poeticizing consciousness that comes to terms with the prevailing conditions of modern experience. Godard, too, is both repelled and fascinated by the mutating landscape he surveys in the hope of finding a "new world" obtainable within it. As the essayist comes to understand that his most viable move is to "listen" and "look around" even more acutely, he reuses Baudelaire's phrase (changing it from a shrill reproach to a whispered appeal) to affirm this mission as turning on a sustained, intimate relation with the viewer he is addressing, an *accomplice* who stands to become attuned to the kind of perceptiveness Godard himself tests out.

In light of our analysis, I would like to set down some refined conclusions as to how *2 or 3 Things* operates as an essayistic reflection. First, as was the case with *Contempt*, what matters here is not reflexivity per se but the more specific ambitions of a self-critical intelligence whose intensive deployment is open-ended, searching, and at least tacitly dialogical in its attraction of the viewer. Earlier, I referred to Godard's reflexivity as "possibilist" on account of his readiness to repurpose even the most familiar and abused forms of mainstream cinema. We can see this disposition still at work in *2 or 3 Things*, in Godard's selective and inquiring use of continuity principles. In the café scene, the grammar of popular cinema assists his research and is itself an object of that research. Godard compounds this possibilist mentality with a sense of constructive uncertainty. Due to its technical nature, cinema requires the director's finalized choice. This of course provokes the anxiety that tempers each shot of the film. Through the framing and cutting, and through tensions between what is said in voiceover and what is shown, Godard makes exacting decisions that nevertheless point up alternative options; he lends a strongly felt lack of completeness to even the most studied composition, and thereby opens up his aesthetic system to prolonged essayistic questioning.[94]

Second, *2 or 3 Things* demonstrates that essaying is less a matter of the film possessing certain technical or structural traits in keeping with a generic template than it is of establishing a kind of regard and relation for which many expedients may suffice, whether they are borrowed from the documentary or from the fiction film. This regard and relation is something that comes about, potentially, between the filmmaker and a viewer who is lured into the thinking process on visual and acoustic display—a process that enacts an investigation without the surety of desired results. That we *can* join in the exertion is without guarantee. The apostrophic invocations in *2 or 3 Things* do not automatically produce the sort of viewer—the "fellow creature"—they implicitly address. I will have more to say about the nature of this rapport in the chapters to come. For now, I will just stress that this longed-for bond is itself a matter of repeated negotiation carried out from both sides of the screen.

Finally, Godard's example exposes a problem at the heart of the received argument that the cinematic essay is a personal venture that flows from and accentuates the first-person subjectivity of a markedly visible or audible author. To apply such a simplistic view to Godard is to misinterpret how he uses his own body and voice within his work, even during his early and middle stages. As we saw in our inspection of the café scene in *2 or 3 Things*, if Godard features as a participant in the "ensemble" of Juliette, the other woman, and the young man, if *his* musings over the espresso dominate the soundtrack, this is not simply for the purpose of airing his own viewpoint and thus stabilizing a directorial subject as a privileged voice. The scene offers a nimble expression of the essayistic precisely because it performs an invigorating *escape* from the strictures of selfhood and subjectivity that some definitions of the practice (Lopate's, for instance) hold to be essential. Not only does the work of the scene challenge and render suspect the distinction between "subjects" and "objects"; it also conjures up a stirring epiphanic force that spans both Godard and Juliette and, at least for the moment, enables them to overcome their separateness and connect with the ruined modern world they haunt, because it is made newly sensible.

Godard's essayistic research comes with the promise of seeing anew, within a hitherto neglected range of potentialities. But we have to work toward this intensified vision before we can quite grasp and wield it—the film we accompany is a training exercise for this purpose. This effort demands, from Godard and I believe from us as well, a sacrificial relinquishment of unified and centered subjectivity. As I will eventually argue, seeing and thinking in close concert with the film's attempts requires that we enter into a relationship whereby we, too, become other than ourselves.

Chapter 2

✦

A Critical Poetics of Citation

> Godard leaves the impression of an earlier film, rejected, contested, defaced, torn to shreds: destroyed as such, but still "subjacent." The film only functions in relation to simultaneous referents, more or less tacit but proliferating, encroaching on each other so that they themselves ravel up and weave the entire filmic texture, since ultimately one can feel that there is nothing, no phrase, shot or movement, that is not a more or less "pure" citation or referent: the important thing being, during the course of the film, not to try to identify all these referents, which would be both impossible and pointless, but to realize (to see within the perspective of the idea) that *everything* is referential; though the referents are set with traps and dissembled, deconsecrated.
>
> —Jacques Rivette

> Do not linger over the matter but over my fashioning of it. Where my borrowings are concerned, see whether I have been able to select something which improves my theme: I get others to say what I cannot put so well myself, sometimes because of the weakness of my language and sometimes because of the weakness of my intellect. I do not count my borrowings; I weigh them.
>
> —Michel de Montaigne

To provide a more thorough account of Godard's resourcefulness as an essayist, we will need to consider at length his intricate use of citations. Allusions, salutes, parodies, borrowings, and outright appropriations: such forms of drawing on anterior sources have made up an ample part of his cinema since the 1960s (and this proclivity traces back to his written articles, which bristle with references not just to films but to literature, painting, and classical music). As we saw in the previous chapter, in our discussions of both *Contempt* and *2 or 3 Things I Know About Her*, Godard's allusive tendencies add depth and

65

richness to his essayistic reflections in crucial ways: without the combined aesthetic evocations of practices by Hitchcock, Minnelli, and Antonioni, the apartment scene in the earlier film would be unduly protracted; and without the Baudelaire-supplied apostrophe ("mon semblable, mon frère") that Godard repeats during the espresso cup rumination in *2 or 3 Things*, his bid for the viewer's complicity would be less pronounced and substantial. Very little of what Godard says in the climactic café scene could be said to be "his" thoughts, given that the ideas he puts forward are a mélange—albeit a crafty one—of passages lifted from Ludwig Wittgenstein, Martin Heidegger, and Jean-Paul Sartre, though the scene makes no acknowledgment of this.

Whether Godard conceals his borrowings or renders them explicit, his methods in this respect have long shown a mischievousness that—far from compromising his legitimacy as an essayist—cements his place within an enduring Montaignean lineage. The Montaignean essay constitutes itself through a style of citation that invests the cited matter with new values and meanings, without necessarily retaining the source's intent. To be an essayist is to reshape and sometimes to subvert the very "authorities" to which one turns. Further, this citational process involves a thorough contamination of the essayist's own registers of subjectivity, a blurring of the line between self and other. Echoing Montaigne's pretense of a bad memory (II.10: 469–70), Godard has often claimed not to know the particular origins of his citations and not to be able to distinguish what he has invented from what he has taken from elsewhere.[1]

Characters in Godard's films at times recognize their sources, as in *Contempt* when Fritz Lang quotes Bertolt Brecht ("Hollywood") and Friedrich Hölderlin ("The Poet's Vocation"). But Godard, here again like Montaigne, tends to cite without naming the original and marking the citation as such. A more recent tendency of his films and videos is to defer attribution until the end credits, where surnames and first initials of other authors appear in a partial, transient list, without the mention of specific texts or the indication of where references have occurred.[2] If these habits refrain from communicating a direct, secure connection between the cited matter and its source, they follow from a conception of authorial labor that dispenses with the Western myth of original creation. Across his career, Godard has flouted both legal and artistic observances that shore up Romantic ideas of individual authorship, his early, polemical attachment to the *politique des auteurs* notwithstanding. Jacques Rivette fittingly calls Godard an "intertextual terrorist,"[3] and Jean-Pierre Gorin summarizes Godard's work as an extended "assault on the notion of intellectual property."[4] Indeed, French courts have more than once found Godard in violation of copyright, leading him to argue for a legal distinction between a "citation" and a mere "excerpt." In a 1997 interview with Alain Bergala, he explains that while an "excerpt" makes unaltered use of preexisting material, a "citation" is a creative act in its own right and should require no permission fees. On occasion in his late films and videos, intertitles defend his own unlicensed practice of citation, framing it as his advocacy for

A Critical Poetics of Citation 67

open culture. *Vrai faux passeport* (2006), which consists of twenty-nine shots sampled from other films, ends with defiant titles onscreen: "This was 29 subpoenas [*citations*] to stand trial. Copyright for all."

A reliance on citational procedures goes well beyond Godard in the field of the audiovisual essay. Several exemplary figures make extensive use of all manner of citable documents: film and television footage, literary texts, photographs, newspaper stories, reproductions of artworks, audio recordings, advertisements, and so forth. One thinks of Guy Debord's filmic use of Situationist *détournement*, of Alexander Kluge's utopic bid to wrest from the items he collects the promises of an unfulfilled past, and of Harun Farocki's equally eclectic but more forensic reworkings. For these and other directors from Chris Marker to Jean-Marie Straub, citation is a vital instrument of essayistic reflection that reanimates the products of history as a living archive—one in which the fiction/nonfiction division is on principle refused. It engineers comparisons between different genres and media, allowing the director to draw from a variety of disciplines while questioning the limits of specialized knowledge. The gesture of citation opens the audiovisual work onto lines of interconnection that test our competence. It also puts the essayist in close contact with the voices and views of multiple others, often to the point of destabilizing the "first-person" subjectivity that some accounts of the essay form insist on leaving intact.

Granted, for each of these filmmakers, citing other works tends to be a rather calculated process that yields an incisive commentary, but at the same time, their gleanings can establish a convoluted play of references and personae into which their own, authorial subjectivity at least partially dissolves. Consider how Marker invokes Plato's allegory of the cave in *The Owl's Legacy* (1989), his television series exploring the foundations of modern Western civilization in Greek antiquity. Two narrators—one male, the other female—speak the parts of Socrates and Glaucon respectively. What we are shown onscreen corresponds to what Socrates asks his interlocutor to envision: a dark chamber where captive spectators believe the shadowy forms on the wall to be "real things" on which to base their knowledge. In Marker's reenacted version of this legendary passage from book VII of the *Republic*, the prisoners study a television monitor with upturned faces. The male narrator, changing roles from Plato's Socrates to Marker's surrogate, refers to a 1940 essay by the philosopher Simone Weil that likens Plato's cave to a "movie house" and the illusory events it puts on display. But Marker's point is not to rehash what, since Weil, has become a familiar theoretical take on Plato's allegory that reads it as prefiguring how the technological apparatus of film deceives its audience. Instead, Marker works against that iconophobic stance by underscoring a possibility it ignores.

A key to sensing this purpose on Marker's part lies in the episode's preceding sequence in which the historian Jean-Pierre Vernant deciphers another Greek myth, also set in a dark cave, that allegorizes the *utility* of images.

According to Vernant, the canny way in which the mortal Perseus approaches and defeats Medusa in her lair, using a reflective shield not only to foil her deadly countenance but to capture and redirect the power she emanates, thus turning it to his advantage, is rich with meaning: it implies a human will to confront and overturn the horror of death through artificial images that usurp its petrifying force. For Marker, this tale also pertains allegorically to cinema—but in a different, more liberating sense. The logic of construction asks us to consider Vernant's persuasive explanation of this tale *over and against* Weil's reading of Plato's cave. Marker stages this conflict through the use of film clips that sporadically interrupt both segments in the episode and forge a contrast between them. To be exact, he inserts footage from *Hiroshima mon amour* (Resnais, 1959) showing the two nude, caressing bodies—male and female—that interlock and converse in its remarkable first minutes. It is that image that fills our screen, displaces the grim reenactment of Plato's allegory, and coincides with our narrator's rebuttal to Weil: "How could she accept that this inferior art form should find within the cave the power to negate the cave, to disarm the Gorgon, to tie itself to the thread of human creation, and, finally, to create its own myths?"

Imparting a lesson of his own, Marker invokes *Hiroshima* as demonstrating a post–World War II modern cinema that rouses critical thought from within the cave and embroils its viewers in a studious confrontation with the horrific past, at the breached boundary between fiction and documentary. In addition, his own deed of citation, his clever capture and reuse of Resnais's film, itself figures in the episode as a kind of Persean shield—a reflective device targeted against the deadening proto-cinematic scenario that Plato's Socrates and, much later, film theorists imagine. Marker in this way self-consciously confers on his own essayistic approach the capacity to "disarm the Gorgon."[5] And yet the intertextual and multivocal threading of the episode is such that his individual voice loses something of its ground. The ideas surface and develop through a layered interplay of dialogical exchanges, a montaged series of male-female interactions that extends to Marker's implied stand-ins, interlocutors, and collaborators.[6] Offering a metapoetic gloss on his own critical method, the episode casts citation as a means of exploring *polyphonic* lines of thought, at the necessary expense of a unitary authorial subject.

With Godard, such a process comes with several added difficulties. What we are offered in the way of guidance is typically more sparing, more obscure, and less trustworthy (as Rivette tells us in the above epigraph, the references tend to be "set with traps"). The citational component is more profuse, and it frequently reaches beyond individual texts and artworks to involve entire aesthetic traditions, both popular and avant-garde, that exert a shaping influence on his stylistic choices within a given project. Enlarging on this characteristic as it concerns his investigations into the history of cinema by means of cinema itself, Nicole Brenez goes so far as to maintain that *every* expressive act on Godard's part is a citation: "All the texts, sounds,

A Critical Poetics of Citation

shots and cuts in his work are citational and, if they ever appear original, it is simply because we have not yet come across the reference."[7] If Brenez perhaps slightly exaggerates this claim, her perspective remains instructive. She confronts the very real challenge of catching and interpreting what in fact *is* a citation, but instead of calling for a desperate, exhaustive search for purely intertextual meanings that hold the key to Godard's mysteries, she points up the need to take careful notice of *material effects* that bear on his citational work, right down to the details of particular shots and transitions between them. We shall see that Godard's citations, besides being intertextual, are often intensely *textural* in the forms and relations they weave.

These allusive and formal complexities only increase when we consider Godard's output as a whole. As I made clear in the introduction, the specific lineage of essaying for which Montaigne stands as a deep progenitor doesn't simply hold that the author composes more or less discrete "essays." To work as an essayist in the Montaignean tradition is to forge reflective pathways that link together multiple works over time. This form creates loops and folds between sometimes markedly different stages of the essayist's thinking, as prior themes and commitments undergo revision. In Godard's case, citations can have a special diachronic function by enabling not just references to texts by other authors, but also circuits of association internal to his own self-conversant oeuvre. His citations occasionally telescope his past and present projects, as though to gauge his progression while prompting the viewer to compare his deeds accordingly. What, for us, makes this affair rather complicated, over and above the demands I have already mentioned, is the fact that Godard has resorted to many different strategies of citation throughout his career—some more cinephilic, some more politically militant, and some more in the vein of historiography and a philosophical weighing of ideas.

In this chapter, I am going to meet these challenges by concentrating for the most part on a specific kind of citation that has a pivotal function in the French-Swiss director's development as an essayist: his material reuse of other films. I will inspect citational moments in which a cinematic source is not just alluded to—as when the apartment scene in *Contempt* evokes other film styles—but is physically *sampled and reshaped* as it is brought into the fabric of Godard's undertaking. My reasons for this limited focus are threefold. First, it will offer further insight into how Godard's essayistic sensibility began in his early period and thereafter preserved aspects of its initial calling. We saw in chapter 1 that his estimation of himself as an "essayist" subtends his claim to still be a critic whose chief tools are images and sounds. Here, I want to illustrate how his sampling of other films corroborates this claim. I am going to examine the evolving ways in which his body of work responds to a concern he voices early on: the need for an audiovisual means that brings film criticism and film practice into material convergence.

Second, this focus will let us explore continuities between Godard's early, middle, and late stages without ignoring what sets them apart. When dealing with the major transitions in his career, critics have at times used his changing habits of citation as grounds for upholding rigid boundaries between his periods and privileging one over another. One common perspective is that the citations in his New Wave films delight in uncritical, postmodernist surface play and reveal the mindset of a bemused aesthete who hasn't reached intellectual maturity, whereas his late efforts, as though to atone for his reckless youth, reference other texts and thinkers in a more sophisticated and soberly reflective fashion.[8] This fairly reductive contrast both fails to appreciate the critical charge of his early work and leaves aside more nuanced connections between career stages that Godard himself avows, as part of his abiding essayism. To be sure, he makes amends in his late period for his previous missteps, but with those changes come substantial reaffirmations as well. If the later films and videos move his research in novel directions, they also return to and materially recompose his previous work. This is an involution no less than an evolution, and sampling from within his own corpus is a key vehicle of this essayistic doubling-back. My argument in this chapter will move through four stages of his output in the order of their occurrence, building up to his historically minded montage of cited matter in his video series *Histoire(s) du cinéma* (1988–98). We will discover that by the time he makes *Histoire(s)*, his citational method critically includes multiple inscriptive and associational strategies that have accrued from his earlier stages, gestures ranging from friendly *hommage* to biting, politicized critique.

Lastly, by studying Godard's evolving work in this light, we can describe more fully the attempted dialogical bond between filmmaker and viewer that lies at the heart of essayistic cinema. To cite, from the Old French *citer* and the Latin *citare*, is "to call forward"; it is to issue a summons in the context of an inquiry where additional voices, perspectives, and materials are urgently required. While Godard's citational acts orchestrate a dialogue with countless other authors, they also call the observer to enter the critical fold, summoning *us* to take part in the reflection at hand. We will see that Godard's gestures of citation, for the duration of his career, tend to coincide closely and indispensably with viewer address. What stays constant even as his practice goes through radical changes of tack is that his gleanings appeal to more than just our recognition, our already gained knowledge and "cultural capital." More often than not, Godard calls us to join in a bracingly new consideration of the material he reworks. His citations test our sensory and mental capacities each time we engage them.

Film Criticism in Its Own Right

As I showed in our last chapter, the leap Godard makes in his formative period from the written word to the moving sound-image brings to fruition a kind of modern cinema—which he first envisaged in his journal articles—that

A Critical Poetics of Citation

combines "course" and "discourse" in a film's stylistic unfolding, with each shot reimagining expressive resources of the medium. Godard's integration of already produced sounds and images happens initially as an outgrowth of this concerted reflexivity, but his sampling of other films entails more than an impulse to foreground the cinema itself. His metacritical bent (like that of Farocki, another critic-turned-director whose essaying also shows the lasting impact of that conversion) needs to be seen partly in the context of his reaction against how film criticism is ordinarily practiced.

Godard's earliest directorial efforts already embody the view that cinema can and should be criticized by way of cinema, that the medium comes with its own speculative powers waiting to be actualized and tested. By the middle of the 1960s, he begins to argue that such a pursuit isn't just an option but a necessity on which the relevance of film criticism turns. His hybrid role as both a critic and filmmaker, who challenges the customs of both vocations, accords him an aptly double viewpoint. In certain interviews and writings of the period, he suggests that film criticism should draw closer to its object of study by no longer restricting itself to the written word. In the same time frame, his filmmaking continues to rethink and enlarge the domain of criticism by pushing it into the realm of audiovisual expression.[9]

Godard speaks to this two-sided problem in "*Pierrot* my friend," a tortuous prose piece he wrote for a 1965 issue of *Cahiers du cinéma*. He responds with ambivalence to an invitation from the editors to discuss his most recent film, *Pierrot le fou*: "You say, 'Let's talk about *Pierrot*.' I say, 'What is there to talk about?'" His misgivings follow from his conviction that something about film, unlike literature, inherently resists and evades the linguistic critical discourse applied to it. Film criticism, he continues, should be "a matter of understanding the poetic structure of a film, a thought that is, of managing to define that thought as an object, of seeing whether or not that object is living and of eliminating the dead." But film criticism, withdrawn conventionally as it is from the vital, luminous "attributes" of its object, fails in this essential task. "Difficult, you see, to talk about cinema," he contends, alluding to Jean Epstein, "the art is easy but criticism impossible of this subject which is no subject, whose wrong side is not the right, which draws close as it recedes, always physically, let us not forget."[10]

In "Let's Talk about *Pierrot*," an interview in the same *Cahiers* issue, Godard sets forth his ideas in more concrete terms. When his interviewers (Jean-Louis Comolli, Michel Delahaye, Jean-André Fieschi, and Gérard Guégan) gripe about film criticism having become severely "repetitive and impoverished," he agrees, offering that

> the problem of film criticism arises because, like art criticism, it is not a genre which exists in its own right. All the great art critics have been poets. Only literary criticism exists in its own right, because its object blends with its subject. Otherwise, all the interesting books of

72   Chapter 2

criticism on painting or music have been written by great creators
from another art. Film criticism is much the same. (*GG*, 229)

This begs the question as to how film criticism might "exist in its own right,"
how it might pass into cinematic form, with sounds and images used to comment directly on sounds and images. As the discussion takes up this issue from
the vantage of film production, Godard reiterates his signature claim that he
is still a critic despite no longer writing articles, and this leads one of the interviewers to propose in kind: "With films like *Pierrot le fou* and *Le Testament
d'Orphée* [Jean Cocteau, 1960] it is as though there were two columns, one
of images, the other of comments explaining the significance of the images."
Godard subtly alters this claim and expands on hypothetical possibilities:
"The commentary on the image forms part of the image. One then could
imagine criticism similar to Michel Butor's novels, which are more or less critical commentaries on events. The criticism would be the dialogue of the film,
with photographs and comments: the whole thing would comprise a critical
analysis of the film" (*GG*, 230). Now thinking far beyond his earlier formulation of "course" and "discourse," Godard calls for a more collage-like means
of realizing a critical cinema. He suggests, in part by referencing Butor,[11] that
cinema makes way for criticism through its fragmentariness, multiple registers, and ability to incorporate and recombine heterogeneous materials.

Godard has restated these basic arguments many times over, at once reaf-
firming his continued role as a critic *and* objecting to orthodox film criticism's
far remove from the sounds and images it purports to judge. In a public
debate with Pauline Kael in 1981, he not only tells the celebrated American
film critic that her reviews of his films give him no helpful feedback, but he
takes issue with the model of criticism she endorses. "What have we *seen?*"
he asks her. "We should look at it [the film under inspection]. A real critic
would project it now."[12] Although Kael shrugs off this idea as perversely
impractical, he is adamant that a critic should "bring in the evidence," as he
memorably words it, by seizing hold of the film itself and studying it before
an audience. He insists this isn't just an alternative approach, but a measure
without which no valuable film criticism can exist.[13]

By the time he aired this grievance to Kael, Godard had already begun
to experiment with ways of achieving, through video, a critical enterprise
founded upon the material inscription of ready-made images and sounds. He
took to this work in preparation for what would eventually become his magnum opus, *Histoire(s) du cinéma*, an eight-volume video series that "brings
in the evidence" to an extravagant degree. Without a doubt, *Histoire(s)*,
along with his other late video projects that exhibit a similar citational style,
looms especially large in the context of our present inquiry. It brings to a
head Godard's prodigious search for an audiovisual form in which cinema
is redoubled, dissected, and inventively opened out by means of its own
substances and techniques. The series also stands as a consummate feat of

A Critical Poetics of Citation

essayistic expression, as several commentators have agreed (in debates on the essay film, it stands second only to Marker's *Sans soleil* [1983] in terms of its canonical esteem).[14]

But the manner in which *Histoire(s)* cites and critically investigates cinema history is shaped by aspirations that play out much earlier in Godard's work, well before his adoption of video. His comments in the mid-1960s on audiovisual criticism in fact paraphrase ideas that his filmmaking had—with greater fluency—already put to use. Some of his earliest features in effect "bring in the evidence" by integrating other films for the point of a reflective exercise—one that recognizes and rhetorically includes the role of the audience. This becomes an almost ritual act for the director: at each stage in his volatile career, such material citations act in part to renew, reinforce, or radically modify a certain rapport or contract with his spectator. I want to survey a few of these moments with an eye to how they anticipate his late videographic style. Doing so will not only prepare us to understand the importance of *Histoire(s)* as an essay that brilliantly culminates Godard's efforts to merge film criticism with film practice; it will also go some way to highlight the diachronic and dialogical sense in which his gradual progress toward that goal is itself a core aspect of his essayistic temperament.

Viewing Scenes of Viewing

Godard's sampling of other films begins in his New Wave stage, under the loose pretext of his characters visiting a movie theater. In some of these instances, the film they see is of Godard's own making, such as the silent short of the society woman bathing in *Les Carabiniers* (1963) that provokes the rube in the audience to grope the screen, or the Bergman-like art film that shows a glum sexual interlude in *Masculine Feminine* (1966). But there are other cases where the film he implants within his diegesis is, in fact, an anterior production by another director and where its recycling in his hands occasions a flourish of metacritical thought. These moments (at least the first two I am going to examine) have received much scholarly attention, but I want to pull into relief a recurring motif that has not been sufficiently dealt with by others. Each of these scenes, through its portrayal of the viewing situation itself, acts at some level to address and interpolate Godard's own viewers. Though all of Godard's films from the era can be said to acknowledge the audience in one fashion or another (the most conspicuous being the performers' disturbances of the "fourth wall" when they gaze and speak directly into the lens), these reflexive scenes constitute a specialized form of *implicit address* whereby the citational call coincides with an invocatory staging of spectatorship.

Breathless samples sounds from two Hollywood genre films—a thriller and a western—in order to comment on Michel (Jean-Paul Belmondo) and

74   Chapter 2

Patricia's (Jean Seberg) adventurous but ill-fated romance. First, when she darts into a local cinema to evade a police detective, the action coincides with dialogue spilling out from a theater showing Otto Preminger's *Whirlpool* (1949), specifically a scene in which the heroine tries to persuade her doubting lover of her truthfulness. When Patricia rejoins Michel on the street, they plan to see a "cowboy film" together that same night. As they exit the frame, a not-yet-sourced orchestral score grows louder on the audio track, mixing with gunfire and galloping horses. These sounds continue across a fade to black into the next scene, which consists entirely of a single shot held for almost thirty seconds—a close-up of Michel and Patricia kissing, in what appears to be a movie theater, with light, ostensibly from the screen, billowing over their faces in profile.

But the scene is odd in a number of senses. The "cowboy film" they have chosen to see falls beyond Godard's frame, never appearing to us directly. Only the slightest contextual cues locate the couple in time and space. The compactness of the close-up prevents any sign of other moviegoers in the audience, and it is mainly the tinny, reverberant tone of the sampled sounds that imply an auditorium.[15] Sonically, the scene becomes stranger as the climactic shootout intersperses with French-language dialogue that is too lofty for a western: a male voice, speaking in poetic verse, counsels "Jessica" to "flee, flee, flee, broken memories"; and then a woman's voice responds by assuring "Sheriff" that their "story is noble as it's tragic" and no "drama" or "detail" can render their love "pathetic." After a fade to black, we see an exterior, nighttime shot of Michel and Patricia leaving a theater that has a large banner for Budd Boetticher's *Westbound* (1959) above its entrance.

The ease and economy of this scene all but disguise its complexity. While the music and gunshots indeed come from the soundscape of Boetticher's film, the spoken dialogue is drawn—without attribution—from two noted French lyric poems, Louis Aragon's "Elsa, I Love You" (from *Le Crève-coeur*, 1941) and Guillaume Apollinaire's "Hunting Horns" (from *Alcools*, 1913). The male and female voices speak lines from Aragon's and Apollinaire's texts respectively, as if in conversation. Godard alters these original poems by adding genre-appropriate names for the speakers and thus grafting their lines somewhat more smoothly onto *Westbound*, though the friction between high and low forms is still comically felt. He also makes his own role as author more indelible in that *he* speaks the part of Sheriff, inscribing himself vocally in this transatlantic collage of texts, figures, genres, and media.

Although they are semi-covert, the literary citations thematize the tenuous state of Michel and Patricia's romance. Tom Conley has shown that Godard's choice of these poems brings to the scene an ulterior layer of political commentary, along with a motif of love imperiled by an external threat of armed conflict. "Hunting Horns" (which Apollinaire wrote on the eve of the First World War) and "Elsa, I Love You" (which Aragon wrote soon after the fall of France in 1940) together open a traumatic-historical frame within which

A Critical Poetics of Citation

Breathless obliquely documents an escalating Cold War, in particular Eisenhower's 1959 visit to Paris and talks with De Gaulle on the prospect of a nuclear coalition. Michel and Patricia seem oblivious to these associations, but the film, as Conley argues, situates their precarious Franco-American *amour fou* against the backdrop of failed diplomatic "accords" that had previously led to "worldwide disaster" and that might, in the current context, do so once again.[16]

The lovers' obliviousness also factors within Godard's dramatization of the film-viewing experience. The offscreen positioning of the "cowboy film" makes for a frontal study of Michel and Patricia's behavior, and they are visibly *not* watching the film in front of them, absorbed as they are in their kiss (it would be inaccurate to call them "viewers"). This element of staging distinguishes Godard's scene from the more conventional type of *mise en abîme* where the representation of film spectatorship is plot-based, psychological, and indicative of character interiority (as in Ingmar Bergman's *Summer with Monika* [1953] when the young couple watch an escapist romance that elicits stereotypically gendered reactions). But neither does Godard's work here partake of the more Brechtian version of this kind of scene in which the portrayal of film viewing is more joltingly confrontational and self-allegorizing (as in Ferdinand Khittl's essayistic *The Parallel Street* [1961], where an audience *in* the film is tasked with putting unrelated film clips into the right order, the penalty for failing to do so being their death).

The reflexivity of the cinema scene in *Breathless* is such that we do feel ourselves, as viewers, invoked. We sense this even as Michel and Patricia embody spectatorship in a fashion inconsistent with our own, more engaged activity as we weigh the film's citational and visual-aural peculiarities. But there is indeed a link, a correlation, between ourselves and the kissing couple onscreen, a link that emerges at the figural level and has to do with a cinephilic conception of the medium as being capable of near-magical displacement and substitution. Although Patricia and Michel do not watch the "cowboy film," they are still intimately of a piece with its romantic scenario in that the spoken exchange between Jessica and Sheriff strangely correlates with *their* bodies. As Marie-Claire Ropars puts it, Godard's entwined lovers become for the moment a "screen" onto which the visually out-of-field romance is projected and transferred.[17] In this way, the scene leads us to consider what it seems at first to elide—namely, the threshold between audience and spectacle, a zone of intimate contact defined by slippages, exchanges, and doublings. And the frame effectively situates us, not just the characters, within this locus, as the gently shuddering gaze of the camera (the shot is handheld) marks the unstable border between fictional worlds.

Godard's suspension of the establishing shot that tells us the couple's exact whereabouts allows for a more abstract treatment of the cinema. Up until that disclosure, the space in which the lovers take shelter is less a definite setting than a liminal chamber within which events and characters lose anchorage. Each coordinate of the scene is made uncertain, and it would appear that what Godard's cinephilia enshrines is the destabilizing power of cinema, as medium and as mercurial environment (in this respect, the scene compares more readily to Raúl Ruiz's *Life Is a Dream* [1986] or Abbas Kiarostami's *Shirin* [2008]). That said, the scene gives equal stress to the cinema's power to bring about a harmonious union between spectators and to do so amid, not in spite of, such uncertainty. This power is what the couple's kiss internally signifies. If we are implied to be swept up ourselves in this play of transferences, it is not because Michel and Patricia stand in as our clear-cut surrogates. Rather, it is because they are figural constituents of the idea of cinema through which the scene asks us to ponder our own engagement, perhaps our own loss of a fixed, external position before the screen. (In essence, Godard's exercise moves us to reflect on a filmic version of the possibility that Jorge Luis Borges called the "partial magic" of work-within-the-work enfoldments: "If the characters of a fictional work can be readers or spectators, we, its readers or spectators, can be fictitious.")[18]

In the third tableau of *My Life to Live*, when Nana (Anna Karina) goes to a showing of Carl Th. Dreyer's silent masterpiece *The Passion of Joan of Arc* (1928), Godard again reflects on the cinema's transformative impact. He samples the original film and this time we see it vividly, its dimensions filling the entirety of our frame. He intersperses a scene of Dreyer's forlorn Joan (Renée Falconetti) being told of her execution with close-ups of Nana gazing in the direction of screen. The editing (part Godard's, part Dreyer's) folds Nana's distraught reactions into a series of shot/countershot exchanges between Joan and one of her male inquisitors (played by Antonin Artaud). The clips from Dreyer's film register syntactically (for us) as point-of-view shots, keyed to a vantage we share for the moment with Nana.

The most commonly averred readings of this famous scene submit that Nana is shown to identify with Joan's anguish, and that the latter's death foreshadows Nana's own fatal trajectory. But however far that line of interpretation takes us on psychological or intertextual grounds, we should notice that Godard essays a more fine-grained and provocative reflection through stylistic means. He excises a portion from Dreyer's original scene and, midway through, begins to print the intertitles as subtitles, so the shot changes occur more immediately, without disruption.[19] The first reaction of Nana (there are only two) directly succeeds and mirrors a close-up of Joan. Then, also without delay, the same shot of Nana interlocks with a shot of the Artaud character as if the two figures belong to a continuous scenographic space (although Godard's dark theater boldly offsets Dreyer's white backdrop). Here again the embedding of a film within the film unsettles the limit between fictional worlds, between the spectator and the spectacle; and the fact that Godard never shows both Dreyer's film *and* Nana together within the same frame has the effect of obscuring the physical boundary of the diegetic screen in the theater.

A Critical Poetics of Citation

Through this fastidious incorporation of Dreyer's drama, Godard gives us to contemplate the affective power of the close-up and shot/countershot cutting. He uses these very techniques in order to draw a pictorial, cross-diegetic comparison between the two heroines—hence the affinities of scale and camera angle by which Nana/Karina appears relative to Joan/Falconetti. The former's tears, which match those of the latter, might lead us to infer her experience as one of psychological identification, but stylistically, texturally, what Godard in fact presents to our gaze is an uncannier kind of connection: Nana/Karina *becomes* Joan/Falconetti. While the first folded-in reaction shot of Nana achieves a visual parallel, the second effects a *substitution*, as Nana takes Joan's place in the order of shot/countershot interactions with the Artaud character (figs. 2.1–2.3).

Nana, notably, is joined by others in the audience. The first shot inside the theater shows her seated in the presence of two anonymous men, one a few rows behind her, another on her immediate left, his face hidden from our view. Godard's staging triangulates a relationship among these characters. There is a dramatic similarity between Godard's and Dreyer's diegetic situations in that Nana, like Joan, finds herself in the company of two men, one more encroaching than the other. We learn shortly that under the ruse of an amorous date, she has convinced the man beside her to buy her movie ticket—a desperate transaction prefiguring her turn to prostitution. More to the point, her connection to Dreyer's heroine is formed in contrast to the lack of accord she feels with her fellow audience members. The scene's reflexivity elicits consideration of our own empathic and perceptual involvement in the social space of the theater. But far from just distancing us, the scene carves out space for a receptive mode in which critical scrutiny and affective investment run together: Nana/Karina's glycerin tears move and absorb us, even as we regard them as elaborately citational.[20]

Intriguing scenes in which characters visit a movie theater also occur in *A Married Woman* (1964) and *Pierrot le fou*. In the former case a clandestine couple, the titular heroine and her lover, rendezvous at the Orly airport cinema in a theater showing—implausibly and in spite of the fact that the theater's décor advertises Alfred Hitchcock's *Spellbound* (1945) instead—Resnais's *Night and Fog* (1955). Godard cuts between the couple and shots from Resnais's lead-in sequence, all while the narration of *Night and Fog* alleges that even the most seemingly pedestrian events and places can be linked to a concentration camp. "Even a road where cars, farmers, and lovers pass by." The citation suggests Godard's lovers inhabit a postwar landscape in which the camps have persisted in subtler, commercialized guises in French society.

Pierrot le fou features a no less quirky scene in which Ferdinand (Jean-Paul Belmondo) visits a theater and takes in a series of short films, clutching in his hands the same text from which he delivers a lengthy recitation at the beginning of the film, Élie Faure's *History of Art: Modern Art* (1937).

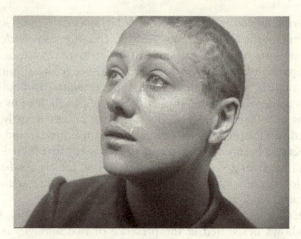

Figures 2.1–2.3. Nana folded into the shot/countershot syntax of Joan's interrogation: *My Life to Live* (Godard, 1962).

A Critical Poetics of Citation

While Ferdinand's eyes move between his book and the screen, Godard at first splices in newsreel footage that documents the escalating war in Vietnam; then, without a transition, he samples a scene from a film in which Jean Seberg points her 16-mm camera at the audience and raises a question about the hazy border between artifice and reality where acting is concerned. This obscure film is in fact Godard's own short *The Great Swindler* (1964). He thus cites both from without and from within his own corpus, in a way that not only investigates the relationship between documentary and fiction, but also in effect reunites Seberg and Belmondo from *Breathless*.

In these early examples of Godard's material citations of already existing films, we can see much more than a cinephile's tribute. These citations are critical, essayistic acts on his part that perform an analysis on the sampled scene, while at the same time fantastically obscuring the difference between alien matter brought in and the fictional worlds of his own making. Godard's citations both incite and excite his audience, addressing us indirectly and imploring us to join in the reflection by deciphering layers of significance. It isn't enough for us to identify the sources of the citations. If our viewing is implicitly stressed in these scenes, it is because the citations are not mere references but sensory *events* to be closely beheld for their values onscreen. We have to examine not only the intertextual ingredients but the dynamic audiovisual mix within which they are transfigured.

Between Collage and *Détournement*

In the mid- to late 1960s, between *Pierrot le fou* and *Le Gai Savoir* (1969), Godard's poetics of citation undergoes an intense period of evolution. After the end of the New Wave, as his practice begins to gravitate toward Marxist-Leninist militancy, he experiments more and more with collage as a structural device, not just in particular scenes but as a means of composing his films in their entirety. Indeed, already by the middle of the decade, many of his commentators—detractors and defenders alike—deem "collage" the best term for his procedure, and with good reason. It defines a set of attributes that have come to distinguish his filmmaking: the discordant linkage of disparate phenomena (whether between or within shots); the palpable impression of the film not as a linear sequence but a paratactic bevy of images, words, noises, and texts; the irreverent blending together of the lofty with the vulgar; the collapsing of "high art" into a shared domain with the objects and accessories of daily middle-class life in consumer society; the flouting of borders between different media; inserts of typographic and handwritten text; acoustic cut-ins that disrupt the shot from all sides; and, as the result of all these aspects taken together, the conversion of the film frame from a "window on the world" into a volatile canvas on which debris of the world affixes and competes, as compositional surface.

Historians of Godard's career, from Peter Wollen to Antoine de Baecque, have illustrated that throughout the decade, his collage methods are informed by an assortment of artistic models and cultural developments: Pop Art, André Malraux's comparative form of studying the history of art through photographic details of works in *The Voices of Silence* (1951), Henri Langois's Surrealist-inspired methods of film programming, and to a lesser degree the innovations of the *nouveau roman* ("new novel") in France.[21] I want to briefly take up the director's relationship with a figure whose presence in this gallery of influences often goes unmentioned, namely Guy Debord, who is perhaps most notorious in Godard scholarship, when invoked at all, for being among Godard's staunchest denigrators.

The assaults that Debord and his fellow cohorts of the Situationist International directed at Godard's films in the 1960s are relevant to our inquiry in that they bring to the fore a tension between two, somewhat opposed modes of essayistic reflection that Godard has to negotiate as his approach becomes increasingly politicized—one mode that is more activist in its orientation and another that is more resolutely speculative. As we shall see, this is a tension that has the issue of citation at its crux. I pointed out in chapter 1 that Debord stands as a significant pioneer of the essay film in its most politically engaged mode. His films look ahead to, and participate in, the revolutionary ferment that comes to preoccupy the activities of several essayistic filmmakers by the late 1960s, Godard included.

In several of his underground writings of the period, Debord fulminates against Godard's work, exposing what he believes to be the sheer myth of its inventiveness. Debord's claims come down to a charge of plagiarism. He argues that Godard's "collage" method is in fact nothing more than an ersatz, co-opted version of the Situationist practice of *détournement*, albeit a version whose political utility has been compromised. *Détournement* roughly translates as "hijacking," "rerouting," or "turning-aside." For Debord, it describes the citational process of appropriating and transforming any cultural artifact—magazine ads, newspaper clippings, cartoons, popular films—in order to put forth a critical point of view contrary to, or at the very least in addition to, its intended purpose. As Debord explains this process and applies it in his own films, it is a procedure of *immanent critique* whereby he seizes and reworks the most degraded material churned out by the very capitalistic system of domination he opposes. With this repurposing, he looks to provoke an engaged response and bring into existence alternative, liberating forms of social life.[22]

In two unsigned Situationist articles probably co-written by Debord, "The Role of Godard" (1966) and "Cinema and Revolution" (1969), Godard's integrations of found materials are at the center of criticisms.[23] For *détournement* to be productive, the authors stress, it must rigorously negate and repurpose the annexed material; and in doing so, it must also manage to communicate a coherent message or idea to the audience (i.e., it should be didactic). In their

A Critical Poetics of Citation   *81*

view, Godard's collage lacks a *negating* component, it parades the bourgeois education he shares with his equally retrograde admirers, and it presents not arguments so much as a muddled, equivocating subjectivity that doesn't seem to know what it thinks, what it wants, or what its principles are (*Situationist International*, 228). Even after Godard's *Le Gai Savoir*, which drastically moves away from anything like commercial cinema and altogether scraps cinephilia in its series of dialogues enacted by two Marxist-Leninist investigators, Debord and the Situationists persist in calling Godard a purveyor of "pretentious pseudoinnovation," a charlatan whose "deconstructive style" is taken right out of Debord's own playbook, minus the underlying intelligence. The authors contend that it will be up to Debord's adaptation of his own text *The Society of the Spectacle* (1967) to show the way forward for a cinema of revolutionary critique (*Situationist International*, 378–79).

My purpose in dredging up this venomous commentary on Debord's part is not to enter a fray in which it is necessary to determine which director is the more "original" and which is the better practitioner of a cinema geared to revolutionary struggle.[24] I take these criticisms and the comparison they entail to be a useful backdrop against which to weigh Godard's transition into his middle period and the political stakes of this shift for his essayistic practice, his techniques of citation included. To be precise, there are three connected matters of rhetoric and expression that require our attention here.

1. *Spectator address.* An essential difference arises between the filmic approaches of Debord and Godard where tones, moods, and manners of address to the spectator are concerned. We saw in the first chapter how Godard's hushed voiceover in *2 or 3 Things* tentatively and indirectly tries to recruit the viewer into being his accomplice; nowhere does he boldly declaim an argument that sees itself as definitive. In Debord's films, which extensively use voiceover, one finds a heightened pose of authoritative knowledge. If Godard tends to bewilder and frustrate, Debord tends at times to talk down to an audience he regards with contempt, expressing little faith in the viewer's capacity to understand him or catch his *détournements* without him having to emphasize them indelicately in quotes. This hectoring of the spectator, which reaches its pinnacle in Debord's *In girum imus nocte et consumimur igni* (1978), comes with a certain haughtiness that differs in spirit from the relative modesty not just of Godard's essaying but also that of Marker, Resnais, and Agnès Varda (tonally, it more closely dovetails with Georges Franju's examples). There is little in Debord's style that could be said to partake of Montaigne's unpretentious claim to "speak as an ignorant questioning man. . . . I am not teaching; I am relating" (II.2: 909).

2. *Didacticism.* Debord's essayistic discourse amounts to a lecture in a way that Godard's discourse more typically avoids, even during his militant years. The instructive confidence of Debord's narration rarely wavers in his essay films. Transcriptions of his commentaries hold up as literary polemics in their own right, and the films themselves privilege the word above the

image. In his "lateral montage" between vocal commentary and image, the image track, when it isn't excluded through white-outs and black-outs, is often made to illustrate and allegorize an argument that is primarily lexical. In Debord's film version of *The Society of the Spectacle* (1973), still photographs and moving images that portray police brutality, military combat, colonial empire, placid nude models, bourgeoisie watching television, and ceremonial meetings between state officials are made to *index and indict* a mass-mediated, commercialized regime of systematic oppression insofar as they supplement Debord's commanding verbal disquisition. I don't mean to argue that his films are without visual wit and playfulness, only that his spoken commentary ultimately holds sway over what is onscreen. At the end of *The Society of the Spectacle*, by jumping between film clips of the U.S. cavalry on the charge in John Ford's *Rio Grande* (1950), Gregory Arkadin charming his guests at his masked ball with the tale of the frog and the scorpion in Orson Welles's *Mr. Arkadin* (1955), and documentary shots of the May 1968 revolts in Paris, Debord's cinematic *détournement* argues for the need to unmask and short-circuit spectacular society. But here again, the image matter is shorn of ambiguity as it forcibly sums up the foregoing oration.

There are salient contrasts between Debord's didacticism and what Serge Daney refers to as Godard's "pedagogy." Remarking on Godard's move away from commercial filmmaking and his radicalization up to and including *Ici et ailleurs* (co-directed with Anne-Marie Miéville, 1976, a work we will inspect below), Daney writes that Godard, just before and certainly during his stint with Jean-Pierre Gorin and the Dziga Vertov Group, disavows his cinephilia and clings to a revised conception of cinema as a site of schooling:

> For the most radical fringe of filmmakers—those farthest to the left— one thing is certain in 1968: one must learn how to leave the movie theater (to leave behind cinephilia and obscurantism) or at least to attach it to something else. And to learn, you have to go to school. Less to the "school of life" than to the cinema as school. This is how Godard and Gorin transformed the scenographic cube into a classroom, the dialogue of the film into a recitation, the voiceover into a required course, the shooting of the film into a tutorial, the subject of the film into course headings from the University of Vincennes ("revisionism," "ideology") and the filmmaker into a schoolmaster, a drill-master or a monitor. School thus becomes the good place which removes us from cinema and reconciles us with "reality" (a reality to be transformed, naturally).[25]

School, unlike cinema in this formulation, is a "good place" where there is no urgent pressure to resolve fully one's confusion about things, words, sounds, sights, and ideas: a place where there is time to study and reflect. For Daney, Godard's role as "drill-master" consists not of instilling messages, or

A Critical Poetics of Citation

imparting knowledge gained from experience or from his research. Instead, his role entails the elaborate, at times arbitrary-seeming orchestration of *given* materials and discourses that attract his interest (as a robustly topical, "barometric" filmmaker)[26] in large part because they already exist. Daney contends that Godard's pedagogy doesn't concern itself much with where these things come from or what lends them weight, but busies itself with a search for what might possibly countervail them:

> [Godard's] approach is the most anti-archeological there is. It consists of taking note of what is said (to which one can add nothing) and then looking immediately for the *other* statement, the other image which would counterbalance this statement, this sound, this image. "Godard," then, would simply be the empty place, the blank screen where images, sounds come to coexist, to neutralize, recognize and designate one another: in short, to struggle. More than "who is right? who is wrong?" the real question is "what can we oppose to this?" The devil's advocate.[27]

Godard's pedagogy in this stage of his career, as Daney explains it, is thus characterized by what is, for many, the Situationists included, a maddening undecidability of position, even in cases where Godard agrees with the "proper" discourses he channels (e.g., Marxist-Leninist teachings).

All this is to say that Debord's reflective approach is *apodictic*—assured of its own authority and mastery—whereas Godard's, for the most part, is not. If Debord mobilizes the essay film as a polemical tract, then Godard is more at home as an artist and thinker when his inquiries are more openly sketch-like and self-critical, when his arguments are more teasingly oblique and offered in a tentative fashion.[28]

3. *Iconoclastic cinema.* Valuing the word and the voice above the visual image, Debord's anti-spectacular attitude is spiteful toward the image track itself. Martin Jay positions Debord squarely in a post–World War II trajectory of "anti-ocular" thought in French critical theory, a tradition in which a deep distrust of the visual and of human vision persists as a dominant trope.[29] Debord's first film, *Howls for Sade* (1952), is infamously "a black-and-white sound film *without images*," made up of white screens, black screens, and commentary by five voices. His later films strike the image track for shorter intervals, still expressing an aversion to it as though it has been hopelessly tainted by spectacle, which, in its tersest Debordian definition, is "*capital* to such a degree of accumulation that it becomes an image."[30]

There is no denying that Godard's work goes through a comparable stage of iconoclasm (in the literal sense of the term, from the Late Greek word *eikonoklastes*, "the act of destroying images") in the years leading up to and including his collectivist projects with the Dziga Vertov Group. His repudiation of his cinephilia and his departure from commercial narrative cinema result in a sharp attenuation of the depictive and dramatic functions of the image, as well as in a newly motivated exploration of acoustic expression. There is no more exemplary scene of this shift than the ending of *British Sounds* (1970), with its abstracted series of fists, clenched in the gesture of solidarity, bursting through Union Jack banners from the back. The banners are flush with the film frame, so this gesture reads as an assault on the image track itself, its inducement of passivity, its collusion with a state-sanctioned system of class domination.

This change of tack in Godard's middle stage has extreme consequences for the citational methods we have seen at play in his New Wave films. Gone are the enchanting and invocatory visit-to-movie-theater scenes. His reflexive animation of film style as an implicit exercise of film criticism gives way entirely to social criticism and commentary, or, to put it better, his vaunted reflexivity now has as its model the Maoist protocol of *autocritique* whereby one's tactical errors in an ongoing class struggle are recognized and dealt with, at the interface of theory and praxis, as a guard against complacency. With this lapse in cinephilia comes a profound instrumental reconfiguration of the film medium for the sake of discourses that have become the deferentially narrated scripts of his work: Karl Marx and Friedrich Engels's *The Communist Manifesto* (1848) in *British Sounds*; Louis Althusser's "Ideology and Ideological State Apparatuses" (1970) in *Struggle in Italy* (1971); and the litany of Maoist slogans that echo across all of these films, in voiceover or handwritten title cards. Daney's account of Godard's pedagogy loses its traction where these films rattle off sectarian mantras.

Godard's years with the Dziga Vertov Group shaped his development as an essayist in lasting ways. The experience cemented an ethic of resistance that never entirely subsides in his later work,[31] and the formal innovations of the films—especially the complex editing methods used to dissect and critique mass-mediated information—equip him with tools he goes on to use in later undertakings.[32] That said, the Vertov Group films at times descend into a suffocating dogmatism that runs counter to essayistic thought. Those productions, no less than Debord's, are audacious, still-relevant examples of the interventionist essay-tract, but at many turns they proceed too firmly from an apriority of knowledge. The exhortative "what to do" intertitles in *Wind from the East* (1970) tellingly omit a question mark.

The Godard project from this turn-of-the-decade moment that most faithfully sustains the non-dogmatic character of essayism is *Le Gai Savoir* (*The Joy of Learning*), even as it breaks with his earlier films in many presentational respects. The film consists of late-night dialogues between two young Marxist-Leninist investigators, a filmmaker named Emile Rousseau (Jean-Pierre Léaud) and a maven of revolutionary theory who has lost her job on account of her activism, Patricia Lumumba (Juliet Berto). This couple of sorts hold their nocturnal meetings on a barren, darkened television soundstage, their bodies exquisitely traced in light. (As James Roy MacBean rightly notes, the look of these scenes calls to mind the dark interlude between the principal couple in Godard's earlier *Alphaville* [1965] where Anna Karina's character begins to learn the definition of love.)[33] By cross-cutting between their discussions and highly fragmented collages of documentary film footage, photographs, book covers and excerpted pages, drawings, and newspaper and magazine articles (materials on which Godard has handwritten additional phrases in marker), the film articulates a radical project of "starting from zero," that is, of making a fresh beginning that has as its modus not just a questioning of all presumed truths, however self-evident or sacred they might be, but also an attempt to forge a new expressive language liberated from the ideological constraints of popular narrative cinema, as well as from those found in agitprop filmmaking (fig. 2.4).

Emilia and Patricia are both immersed in the protocols of Maoism and design their plans accordingly, but above all they are students and critical spectators invested in relearning how to read, listen, and observe. To this end, the film delights in breaking down ("dissolving," they call it) words into phonemes and portmanteau pieces, and images into colors and gestures laden with signifying attributes. The abstract dark space they inhabit and cast their gazes around is nothing other than a depiction of the conjunctive space between one image and another, between images and sounds—the

Figure 2.4. Patricia and Emile cast their attention offscreen: *Le Gai Savoir* (Godard, 1969).

86   Chapter 2

space where phenomena cross and relationships arise. In this way, the students stand in both for Godard and for ourselves as we watch.

In this film that is everywhere more about learning than it is about teaching, what keeps things in the register of the essayistic, as Harun Farocki observes, is a feisty "provisionality" that tempers the play of ideas.[34] This is nowhere more evident than at the end of the film, where we hear the disembodied voice of Godard comment in an almost shrill whisper, "This film has not wished to, could not wish to, explain the cinema or even constitute its object, but more modestly to offer a few effective means of arriving at that point. This is not the film that ought to be made, but it shows how, if one is to make a film, one would need to follow some of the paths traveled here." This "modest" non-ending thus suspends finality and focuses on the generative process of one's reeducation of the senses.

This provisional tone is accompanied by ambiguity, noise, and interferences that impose themselves in the director's reflective discourse. Hints of Godard's presence mark the film—his voiceovers that break in erratically, photos of himself, and a still from his previous film *La Chinoise* (1967) that appear transitorily—but these traces of his authorship aren't in the service of a Debord-like thesis that emanates from and confirms his authority. At most events in this film, the transmission signal of Godard's voice is neither clear nor direct (hence the acoustic signature of the film, the electronic drones and squelches that make it difficult for us to hear the verbal content). In short, though *Le Gai Savoir* may set the course for the Vertov Group films to follow, it also foretells where Godard's essayistic style will go after the collective disbands. I agree here with Vinzenz Hediger, Roland-François Lack, and Michael Witt that *Le Gai Savoir* is formally and conceptually a prototype of Godard's late video essays, in particular *Histoire(s) du cinéma*, which we will take up soon.[35]

Thinking of That Again: Enter Miéville, Enter Video

The most thoroughgoing critique of the Dziga Vertov Group and its methods issues from within Godard's own corpus. A key transitional endeavor, *Ici et ailleurs* (*Here and Elsewhere*, completed in 1974 but not released until 1976) marks the end of his involvement with Gorin and the launch of a new partnership with Anne-Marie Miéville. *Ici et ailleurs* presents itself as a critical duet, with voiceovers contributed by Godard and Miéville as they revisit and inspect footage from a never-finished film that Fatah (at the time, the chief faction of the Palestine Liberation Organization) had commissioned Gorin and Godard to make during their visit to Jordan and Lebanon in 1970. Constructed on and with the material ruins of the prior, faulty work, *Ici et ailleurs* sets out to unmake the Dziga Vertov Group film that was to be titled *Until Victory* and to test an approach that remains leftist and polemical, but with a newly restored tentativeness.

A Critical Poetics of Citation 87

Ici et ailleurs bears testament to Godard's evolution as an essayist by breaking with the programmatic methods of his collaborations with Gorin. It is significant, not just for Godard's corpus but for the cinematic essay at large, that this move into a post-militant phase coincides with and critically benefits from Godard's adoption of video technology. His use of the video mixer in *Ici et ailleurs* opens up new inquisitive possibilities at the levels of material citation, multi-image comparison, and a fledgling shift into historiography. Moreover, the film begins the process whereby he self-critically maintains and comments on his expanding oeuvre through revisions of his past efforts. In his films with the Vertov Group, Godard suspends his habit of alluding to his own work—a decision mandated by the group's collectivist mentality and his own desire, which he states often in interviews of the period, to embrace anonymous production and leave behind the "glorification of the individual" in Western bourgeois thought.[36] Godard's habit of inscribing his authorial subjectivity in body and/or voice also ceases, or is strictly curtailed, in his Vertov Group productions. (We could perhaps count the image of his own bloody hand near the close of *British Sounds*, inching across a snowy battlefield and hoisting a red flag, as self-inscription insofar as the scene represents his sacrifice for the sake of the revolutionary struggle.) If Godard returns in *Ici et ailleurs* as an inscribed author, this is so that he and Miéville can take his earlier approach to task. Handling *Until Victory* as found footage, they materially sample the film and expose its procedural missteps.

Godard and Miéville's film is thus a palinode on his part—but one in which her voice is the more trenchant. The idiom of dueling and duetting narrators, one male and the other female, can be found in some of the Vertov Group productions (e.g., Vladimir and Rosa in *Pravda* [1970]), but *Ici et ailleurs* frees this dually voiced idiom from the drawbacks of an ideology-first approach. What Miéville notices as she and Godard sift through *Until Victory* is Godard and Gorin's imperceptive grafting of a teleological narrative of Marxian struggle onto events that they staged more than caught. A young girl recites a resistance poem by Mahmoud Darwish, but Miéville points out that the shot is too theatricalized and that the girl performs a ritual of public protest on loan from the 1789 French Revolution. Fedayeen soldiers discuss, as Godard puts it, "how to combine revolutionary theory and practice." Miéville objects by remarking that the men speak about something far simpler, namely a feeling of connection to the soil when they prepare their trenches. A woman expecting a child tells the camera in direct address that she is proud to give her son to the Palestinian revolution, but Miéville reveals that the woman is not pregnant, that she is an actress cast for her beauty. Further, Miéville faults Godard for not showing himself, as the scene's director. We only hear his offscreen voice tell the woman to adjust her pose and clothing, a command that *Until Victory* would have concealed in its finished state. Now, in *Ici et ailleurs*, a black screen recognizes that a countershot of the director ought to have been present then. Such a refusal to show "the one who commands," coupled with a pretense of frankness, is, as Miéville argues, akin to the concealments of fascism.[37]

For Godard and Miéville, what most calls for a turn to an alternative manner of working is that in the interim between the filming of *Until Victory* and the editing of *Ici et ailleurs*, a lack of foresight has become tragically apparent. The fedayeen fighters that Godard and Gorin filmed in 1970 were all killed soon after in the events known in the Arab world as "Black September," when the Jordanian armed forces, acting on King Hussein's orders, launched a full-scale offensive against the PLO and its strongholds in the city of Amman. The Palestinian death toll, which included civilians, ran well into the thousands. Photographs attesting to the grisly results of the massacre are reiterated throughout *Ici et ailleurs*, each time asking for a reckoning. The severest charge that *Ici et ailleurs* levels against Gorin and Godard, a claim made poetically through intertitles and voiceover, is that they failed to discern warning signs of this disaster: charged "silences" in the images they captured were stifled by the "too loud" rhetoric from the West that they blindly projected onto this situation. As Godard says over a shot of a hand (his own) entering the dates of past and longed-for revolutions—1789, 1917, 1936, 1968—into a calculator, "Adding hope to our dreams may have impaired our addition." For Godard and Miéville, who are now "thinking of that again," as an intertitle phrases it, this failure of vision and thought necessitates research into new forms of investigating images and their possible links and ramifications.

It is with this goal in mind that Godard and Miéville use the video mixer.[38] The device brings with it operations of simultaneous linkage within single frames—wipes, patchy dissolves, multilayered superimpositions—that are texturally distinct from film editing. The co-directors press these techniques into the service of reworking of both found and newly shot material and seeking relations between them, not just affinities but differences and discordances. In the words of Michael Witt, this way of processing and analyzing a broad array of sampled matter ushers in an early, primitive mode of Godard's "videographic thinking."[39]

The key expressive figure in this procedure is the "AND"—a figure of both conjunction and contrast that most explicitly appears, in the body of the film itself, in the guise of two, what look to be wood-carved letters that have been set on a pedestal and filmed under a flashing light. Gilles Deleuze, who singles out this "method of AND" as a pivotal innovation in the ongoing adventure of modern cinema, interprets it as a means of breaking free from the linear chain of succession that inevitably constrains the film medium and of practicing in its stead a reflective form that makes discernible the gap—the "interstice," to use Deleuze's term—between images. Deleuze insists that this procedure is "not an operation of association, but of differentiation," in that it refuses to traffic in simple analogies.[40]

To study this videographic process in action, let us go back to the passage where Godard types revolutionary dates into an adding machine and admits

A Critical Poetics of Citation

to the false calculations of his and Gorin's prescriptive regard. In the same section, we see a series composed according to the raised-hand gestures in photographs of Vladimir Lenin, Adolf Hitler, Léon Blum (who appears in a large group with other members of the French Popular Front), and Golda Meir, the prime minister of Israel at the time of *Ici et ailleur*'s making. By associatively connecting the hands in and across each of these photographs through wipes and superimpositions, Godard and Miéville entertain a rather controversial trajectory of relationships and antagonisms. This compression of imagery entangles both French and Russian Communism with National Socialism, by way of an eerily continuous choreography of gesture and an attendant, questioning emphasis on the word "popular," which spans these contexts in blinking onscreen text and which registers sonically in fragments of a crowd singing a Soviet anthem and Hitler ranting at a public rally.

This sequence has attracted a fair amount of critical debate on account of the argument it seems to proffer, namely that the modern state of Israel, born in the wake of the century's most horrible atrocities committed against the European Jews, became in time a brutal persecutor in its own right. In Godard and Miéville's ensemble, the word "Palestine" forms onscreen with letters reused from "Israel," flashing as if emerging from Meir's lips. Meir's vertical hand, through its juxtaposition in the same riven frame with Hitler, is made to evoke and echo the Nazi salute. Richard Brody and others have read this moment in the film as blatant, undeniable proof of Godard's anti-Semitism, cloaked as a criticism of Israeli national politics.[41] There is indeed something "monstrous" about the linkage between Meir and Hitler, which doubtlessly means to shock and offend.[42] I have no intention of overturning the criticisms it has received, yet it must be said that those who have responded with outrage to this sequence and branded it mere propaganda have typically not examined it very closely. By zeroing in on the one juxtaposition of Hitler with Meir, such reactions tend to oversimplify Godard and Miéville's critical gesture here and to misconstrue the "AND" method at work in the sequence as crudely establishing false equivalences.[43]

This single conjunction must be grasped as it emerges within the unfolding sequence as a whole. Interspersed with Godard's voiceover, the sequence expressly denies the kind of thinking that neatly draws analogies on the basis of a fixed, sectarian outlook. "Too simple and too easy to simply divide the world in two," he says while arranging photos (Richard Nixon, Leonid Brezhnev, the My Lai incident, the Soviet invasion of Prague . . .) around the recurring "AND" insert. The verve of Godard and Miéville's reflection is certainly polemical, but it is more interrogative than declarative. They make no secret of their sympathy with Palestine (and this vision of history is something that Godard will take up again, with his "law of stereo" exercise in *JLG/JLG: Self-Portrait in December* [1995]). However, the "AND" between National Socialism circa 1939 and Israel circa 1974 *is not a direct equation* (such an association or equivalence doesn't entirely "add up," we might say). Occurring within a knotted series of provisionally constructed relations between and across divergent histories, it engages in a mixture of similarity and difference while prompting the viewer to consider whether a graphic correspondence points to a historical one. The question this conjunction most emphatically provokes is this: how, without descending into doctrinal allegiance and vilification, can one think and understand the relationship between the nation of Israel's brutal othering of Palestine and the history of the Jews as a brutally othered people? By weaving into the ensemble a shot of a grotesquely burned Palestinian casualty from the massacre at Amman, and by having this body resonate across historical contexts with a sound clip of a Hebrew-language lament reading out the names of Nazi death camps, Godard and Miéville suggest that this open question, however problematic, cannot go unconsidered.[44]

But there is still a larger question being posed by the sequence as a whole, one that has to do with the rhyming hand gestures across these contexts. The speculative thought that drives the ensemble of photographs asks whether the inclusive spectacle of "popularity," of a unitary body politic, be it in the form of the revolutionary mass or fascist crowd, must of necessity have as its remainder (and as its very confirmation) the spectacle of massacre and catastrophe visited on the excluded and the adversary. Said another way, must the preservation of one's collective identity, strength, interests, and well-being be built upon, and continually shored up by, evidence of one's nemeses and rivals being vanquished? Another layer of the sequence complicates matters further by insinuating that this disposition of violent antagonism is reinforced by the essentially fascistic imperatives of capitalism and by the international Cold War-era alliances that have been set up to protect its dominion (the film's critique of Israel's national conduct is inseparably bound up with an objection to the U.S. empire of capital). These are the questions the photo of the incinerated Palestinian corpse urges the spectator to consider each time it resurfaces. To neglect these larger political and reflective dimensions of the sequence, while fixating on one incendiary moment of linkage, is to give short shrift to the overall essayistic thrust of Godard and Miéville's work as it chips away at dogmatic thought.

Ici et ailleurs looks ahead to Godard's later essayistic ventures not only through its combinatory forms afforded by video, but also through its dark vision of history as a tragically repetitious series of catastrophes that results, in large measure, from a failure to break down and overcome self-other hostilities. There are two remaining points that need to be stressed apropos of what I have defined as a post-militant and post-filmic mode of the essayistic that Godard embarks on with Miéville. First of all, Godard's essayistic tendency to invoke the viewer, through his handling of characters in the fiction, returns in *Ici et ailleurs*. Throughout the film, and during the sequence just explored, there are interspersed shots of a contemporary French family in their home. A thinly developed narrative concerns a factory worker who has lost his job and is not seeking employment because he spends his

A Critical Poetics of Citation　　　　　　　　　　　　　　　　　　　　　　　　　*91*

time (futilely, the film suggests) at revolutionary meetings. This French family embody the "here" relative to the "elsewhere" of the events in the Middle East, and, more to the point, they figure as viewers within the film, as we frequently see them watching a television set in their living room. But they are not simply TV viewers misled by the sensationalistic news reports on the conflicts in the Middle East; they are also edited into the flow of Godard and Miéville's reflection in such a way as to indicate that they are spectators *of the same videographic compositions that are presented to us*. The film often cuts from a shot of the family gazing to a shot that is not of the content on their TV screen but instead, a shot of the multilayered configurations of cited material that Godard and Miéville achieve using the video mixer (figs. 2.5 and 2.6). It is as if the family studies the videographic spectacle offered to us. When the co-directors highlight in a flashing title the goal of "learning to see / not to read," this goal applies both to these characters in the fiction and to the viewers of *Ici et ailleurs*, who are, in effect, being invited into the film's investigation through the use of these characters as their rough surrogates.

Second, Godard's essayistic tendency to inscribe himself returns in *Ici et ailleurs*, not just in voice but in body as well. Although there are no shots of either his or Miéville's face, the film integrates several brief inserts of their hands as they tend to such tasks as adjusting the volume on sound equipment

Figure 2.5. The French family of spectators: *Ici et ailleurs* (Godard, Miéville, 1976).

Figure 2.6. Superimposition contemplating "popularity" between contexts of the Soviet revolution, the Third Reich, and the French Popular Front: *Ici et ailleurs*.

or shuffling through a stack of paperback books. It is his hand that is shown entering dates of past revolutions of into the adding machine; just as significantly, it is her hand that is shown turning down the volume. This sparing form of authorial self-inscription, which is similar to Marker's gestural insertions in *Sans soleil* (another major instance of post-militant essaying that benefits from newly available video technology and the expressive strategies it furnishes), is a critical gesture of "self-implication," to borrow an apposite term from Thomas Elsaesser.[45] Instead of serving narcissistic reflexivity, this showing of the hand is in part Godard's way of acknowledging his artistic responsibility—his gesture bears the trace of a personal history wherein he, not unlike some of the figures with their hands raised in the mix of photographs, stands at fault. As we have found, his film with Miéville is nothing if not a manifest exercise in self-reproach.

Miracles of Our Blind Eyes: Citation as Historical Montage

Having examined the decisive changes—aesthetic, political, technological—that inform Godard's evolving practice of material citation, we are now in

A Critical Poetics of Citation

a position to understand the directions it takes during his late period, particularly in his seminal *Histoire(s) du cinéma ((Hi)story(ies) of Cinema)*.[46] Released in increments and continually crafted by Godard from 1988 to 1998, the eight-part, four-and-a-half-hour experiment is the centerpiece of his late work and, as a number of critics and theorists have argued, a supreme example of essayistic thought unfolding in audiovisual terms.

Given our interests in this chapter, and in this book as a whole, the series is of paramount significance. Not only does it rethink Godard's own corpus by distilling the revisionary process that shapes it over time; the video series also combines and tries to reconcile the practices of material citation we have been tracing. *Histoire(s)* is the apotheosis of Godard's search for a critical form wherein sound and image comment directly on sound and image. Its citation-driven procedure brilliantly realizes what he described as "film criticism in its own right" in 1965. And yet he could not have succeeded without video, without having tinkered with and mastered the combinatory and critical maneuvers that video makes possible.[47] Godard's feat in the series is not just technical and critical but political, since it also brings to a head what I have called his post-militant mode of essaying. My purpose in what remains of this chapter is to illustrate how the videographic montage of *Histoire(s)* carries out a number of important tasks by functioning as a historically minded, politically conscious manner of open-ended investigation that invites and *needs* the contribution of a diligent viewer.

Over all eight of its episodes or "chapters" (Godard's sectional use of this term compares to Montaigne's), *Histoire(s) du cinéma* consists predominantly of material Godard has drawn and reshaped from other sources: Hollywood and European cinema, both narrative fiction films and documentaries, art films and mainstream films, cartoon animations, and pornography. As such, the series satisfies Godard's own previous call, in his debate with Kael, to "bring in the evidence." But these clips—far from being traditional extracts like those offered in, say, *A Personal Journey with Martin Scorsese through American Movies* (1995) or Thom Anderson's slightly more daring essay film *Los Angeles Plays Itself* (2003)—are substantially adjusted in their texture, color, acoustics, velocity, and duration, and rather densely recombined with reframed details of photographs, paintings, sculptures, and frescoes. These newly devised ensembles are disturbed at quick intervals by black screens and further punctuated by videographic measures that have only loose filmic equivalents, from rhythmic, stop-started motion to rapid iris-ins and iris-outs between graphic layers that are superimposed. What is more, there are aural samplings of classical and popular music, as well as a barrage of literary citations that shifts between high and low genres and asserts itself through titles and vocal commentary. Adding another level of intricacy is the polyglot breadth of languages involved at any given moment: French, German, English, Italian, Latin, Greek . . . , only a portion of which is translated by subtitles on DVD releases of the video series.

94   Chapter 2

Intermittently in each episode, Godard foregrounds his authorial presence, both vocally as a narrator and corporeally as a character, a somewhat ludic version of himself absorbed in a variety of activities in his studio/library/laboratory—reading, writing, remembering the past, daydreaming, mingling with clips through superimposition. In Sam Rohdie's description, "there are many Godards" in *Histoire(s)*, assuming multiple roles and attitudes, "being angry, reflective, comic, dressed, half-dressed, pensive, aggressive, shy, crude, lyrical . . . and to each of these are attached different voices." The onslaught of citations can be viewed "as so many impersonations by Godard issuing from his memories and associations as various as moods and the characters he plays."[48] At heart, *Histoire(s)* is a self-portrait of a changeable, multitudinous entity inclined toward a total rejection and effacement of any *singular* identity that would claim him, and yet at the same time, Godard is indeed Godard in the series, the essayist composing the montage and reflecting on it simultaneously, a figure who remains, if not centered and stable and entirely cohesive, then at least particular—an individual authorial subject with a personal history and an oeuvre that constitutes a significant piece of the larger "(hi)story(ies) of cinema" he recounts. If the citations muddle and empty out his individual subjectivity by forcing him to speak and see through numberless others, they also testify to the resilience of his own expressive sensibility by virtue of the fact that he has carefully selected and reorganized them.[49] On this score, we should also bear in mind that Godard's own films make up a weighted percentage of the sampled clips in the series. By citing himself and his earlier output, the director unfolds a running commentary on the history of his career, a point to which I will return.[50]

In episode 1A, Godard makes his first appearance, seated at an electronic typewriter and wearing a white lab coat, as befits his role as experimenter. He speaks out loud to himself and also keys clipped phrases—mostly allusions to films or texts—into the typewriter, which, at the push of a button, clatters out the phrase over and over to a staccato rhythm (the machine has a mnemonic setting). As if a conjuring trick, this act generates flashes of montage. At times, the sampled scenes visually overlay where he sits and appear congruously in the space between two of his desk lamps. For instance, as he types and mutters "rules of the game"—a glancing nod both to Jean Renoir's 1939 masterpiece and Michel Leiris's literary self-portrait of the same title—a still from Chaplin's *Modern Times* (1936) portraying Chaplin as the Tramp sitting in a field with and adoring Paulette Goddard, superimposes itself within this pictorial nook between lamps in the composition. It is striking that a number of these film citations at the outset of the series bring together and "couple" men and women, whether this occurs in successive or simultaneous combinations. We should remember this organizing trope of coupling, as it will later be of prime importance. For now, Godard is only hinting at the "rules of the game" about to commence, his game and ours. So far, he has mostly checked and tuned his instruments, like a musician readying for a performance.

A Critical Poetics of Citation

After a costume change to a dress shirt and blazer, Godard is ready to begin, as is implied further by the studio microphone that swings into position at his desk. He puts a blank page into his typewriter, puffs on his cigar, and types out additional phrases. He says in voiceover: "*Histoire(s) du cinéma*. With an 's.' All the histories that might have been, that were or might have been, that there have been." He lifts one hand to adjust his eyeglasses, then, just as a string quartet (the adagio from Beethoven's tenth) emerges musically, he looks upward, casting his stare beyond the frame. This physical gesture triggers a montage of clips that begins with a rapid succession of axial cuts between increasingly tight close-ups of a young woman's intense eyes, aglow with blue light.

The montage presents clips for our comparative inspection, without disclosing where they come from; it falls on us to catch and interrelate them. In this stirring sequence, spanned by the staggered titles "the cinema substitutes / for our gaze / a world / more in accordance / with our desires" (a reference to the complicated pseudo-Bazinian opening of Godard's *Contempt*),[51] we see Mephistopheles materialize in flames in *Faust* (F.W. Murnau, 1926), Fred Astaire and Cyd Charisse dancing a number in *The Band Wagon* (Vincente Minnelli, 1953), the beaters scene from Renoir's *Rules of the Game*, the distressed merchant's wife in *The Crucified Lovers* (Kenji Mizoguchi, 1954), a young woman learning to swim in *People on Sunday* (Robert Siodmak and Edgar G. Ulmer, 1930), an upscale social gathering in *The Public Enemy* (William Wellman, 1931), Lillian Gish in a deserted street in *Broken Blossoms* (D. W. Griffith, 1919), group gaiety in a western saloon in *Rancho Notorious* (Fritz Lang, 1952), the grand ball in *The Leopard* (Luchino Visconti, 1963), and the Teutonic Knights in *Alexander Nevsky* (Sergei Eisenstein, 1938) robotically jabbing their opponents, an attack that Godard amplifies with videographic pauses and repetitions. Equally relevant, the vocal dialogue that joins these shots is from *Last Year at Marienbad* (Alain Resnais, 1961), a scene in which a man tries to convince a woman of an exchange of looks and gestures they had a year earlier.

Notably absent from the soundtrack here is Godard's voice. We are given nothing like an explanation as to how these clips go together. In a way, the montage is atypical of the series as a whole in that Godard doesn't entwine the citations with videographic gestures. Aside from some minimal cross-dissolve work at the start between *Faust* and *The Band Wagon*, the editing is limited to sharp intercutting and the insertion of rhythmic black screens, and only Eisenstein's film has been altered in terms of rhythm. The structure of the sequence is asyndetic, refusing to supply the conjunctions for us. It is as if Godard has followed Montaigne's example by "piling up" citations without developing them, leaving it to the viewer to explore their meanings and "pluck them apart with a bit of intelligence" (I.40: 281–82).

The sequence indeed holds together, on the basis of the content freighted by the clips and despite extreme differences between generic, national, and

96   Chapter 2

historical contexts. *Faust* belongs with *The Band Wagon* insofar as Minnelli's musical turns on a pompous stage adaptation of the Faust myth that flops with the public. *The Public Enemy* resonates with *The Band Wagon* insofar as the scene from Minnelli's film is a pastiche of the noir gangster genre. Together, these citations play off of each other through shared motifs and conflicts (for instance, ritualistic community versus lonely isolation). In another connection, the massacre by the Teutonic soldiers—originally meant to rouse indignation against Nazi Germany, which was set to invade Russia at the time of the film's making—becomes in *Histoire(s)* a shot that evokes, through comparison, the cruel and treacherous subjugation at the crux of *The Leopard*, a film that unmasks the politics of national "unification." More still, the aristocracy in *The Leopard* embody an eclipsed social order, a motif that also extends to *Rules of the Game*.

One could go much further in examining this sequence (knowing where to stop in one's analysis of the series is a serious challenge), and other scholars, most significantly Daniel Morgan, have done so with insightful results.[52] But I would like to return to the initial citation in this sequence, a clip whose relevance has not been given its due—the spasmodic shots of the young woman's glowing eyes. This fragment comes from Brian De Palma's *The Fury* (1978), a horror, science fiction, and espionage film that may seem out of place in this parade of canonical films but whose form and narrative content are richly suggestive of certain ideas in the sequence. Godard cites another clip from this film later in *Histoire(s)* (in episode 2B), and the fragment he uses here channels forth in memory the whole from which it has been removed. *The Fury* revolves around two teenagers—a boy and a girl—who possess profound telekinetic and telepathic abilities. The boy is stolen away from his father by an unfeeling agent (John Cassavetes) working for a clandestine U.S. intelligence organization which then subjects the boy to grueling research/torture. Meanwhile, the girl begins to discover and harness her power, which includes a sensitivity to what one of her clinicians calls the "bioplasmic universe," a virtual inventory of "every human impulse, word, and deed, of lives past and lives to come." She has mental access to a temporal order wherein past, present, and future events interpenetrate. In the course of her visions, which show the horror of the boy's testing, she acquires a strong desire to collapse the distance between them. One of the tragedies of the film is that the boy and girl meet only at the moment of the boy's death, when he transfers his rage from his eyes to hers. The close-ups Godard reuses, those of her eyes blue with fury, appear at the end of the film, when she deploys her power so intensely that she causes the Cassavetes character to burst into pieces (an explosion Godard cites in 2B).

I have summarized De Palma's film because its original concerns resound thematically with Godard's rules of the game. The sampled shots of the girl immediately follow the shot of Godard at his typewriter. There is a direct link, and a visual rhyme, between Godard's upturned gaze and the girl's

A Critical Poetics of Citation

active stare. This relay, which couples Godard with this female figure, tropes on the idea of cinema offering a form of second sight, rendering sensible the interconnectedness of disparate events across vast distances and histories outside of chronological time. After all, the sci-fi premise of a bioplasmic universe in *The Fury* has as its complement in Godard's opening episode not only his assertion regarding "all the histories" that were *and that might have been*, but also the temporally unhinged conversation from *Last Year at Marienbad* about an incident that may, or may not, have occurred in the past. More to the point, if the young girl's eyes sampled from *The Fury* rhyme with Godard's self-inscription, they also act as an apostrophic inscription of and invitation to Godard's spectator. At no point in the episode does Godard engage in "direct address"; he speaks as if only to himself in private and seems absorbed in reflective thought, but throughout the video series he makes appeals to the viewer's activity, this invocatory insert from De Palma's film being one of the earliest (figs. 2.7 and 2.8).

The Fury carries further citational meaning for Godard's sequence in that its narrative shows that this extrasensory gift isn't understood by those who have it, that this capability can bring things and people together but is potentially dangerous and violent, and that it is under threat by villainous forces intending to abuse it for nefarious ends. This story adumbrates what soon emerges as a central premise on which *Histoire(s)* founds itself: Godard's claim for the revelatory power of cinematic montage, its unsurpassed ability to make evident relationships to which viewers would otherwise be insensitive. The citations of *The Fury* in effect represent this extraordinary power, its potentialities and its fate.

The circuitous logic of Godard's argument as he reflects back on cinema of the twentieth century is this: what distinguished the medium was its enigmatic, astonishing power to bring into view, through montage, linkages between things, people, and events—relationships that could be observed together in the communal darkness of the theater. For Godard, this power was first and foremost an operation of thinking through and with images. But the medium, he argues (and this is where the near-oppressive melancholy of the series comes in), failed to make adequate use of this power when it was most urgently in need, that is, when it found itself confronted by the century's most appalling injustices, the Holocaust being the most atrocious of all and, thus, the site of cinema's most unforgivable failure. As Godard puts it succinctly in voiceover in chapter 3A, the "flame" of cinema's calling as a form of thinking and vision "was extinguished at Auschwitz." This mournful argument at the heart of the series, however, is counterpointed by Godard's own use of montage, which does far more than illustrate his verbal thesis. The videographic style he animates doesn't quite show us what cinema once was, in the terms of his argument. Nor does it quite recapture that cinema in its communal splendor (his experimental video is well removed from the massive audience of popular cinema). Rather, his process unfolds as a heightened

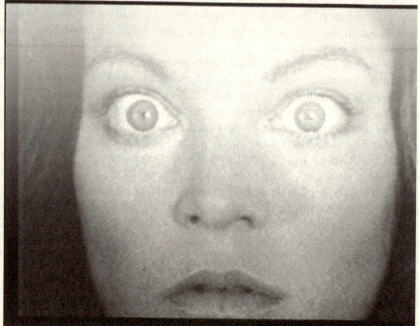

Figures 2.7–2.8. Godard with eyes raised, followed by the young woman's entranced stare from *The Fury* (De Palma, 1978): *Histoire(s) du cinéma* (Godard, 1988–98), episode 1A.

A Critical Poetics of Citation

version of *what cinema could have been* if its power of montage had been properly grasped and put to the test. There is not just regret in this conceit but a trace of enduring hope, albeit within a different, more essayistic circumstance of reflection and reception.[53]

This bid to rekindle montage as a form of thought bears an attendant emphasis on ethical responsibility. Fragments from *The Fury*, for instance, are in both cases braided with the same scene from Murnau's *Faust*. Godard's suggestion is that to practice montage is to summon a mysterious force, here incarnated by Mephistopheles, that can radically alter the course of human events, but that in answering to its summoner's desires ("a world more in accordance with our desires"), it can be used just as readily and profoundly for destructive goals. This is Godard's cautionary admission that to engage in montage, whether as filmmaker or spectator, is to expose oneself to the risks and temptations of a potentially dark art.

A specific poetic conception of the image lies at the basis of Godard's videographic process in *Histoire(s)* as he calls on the power of montage. He derives this guiding conception from Pierre Reverdy's "The Image" (1918), a poem he quotes with regularity in his work and interviews of the 1980s and 1990s:

> The image is a pure creation of the mind.
> It cannot be born of a comparison but of the *rapprochement* of two more or less separate realities.
> The more distant and just the relation between these realities that are brought together, the stronger the image will be—the greater its emotional power and poetic reality.[54]

From this text, Godard adapts a montage-based method that he enlists in *Histoire(s)* as a way of detecting and weighing relationships between "distant" phenomena. He carries this principle of the image over into history, using it as a critical device.[55]

To be specific, there are three salient dimensions of this Reverdy-inspired poetics at work in the series, all of which inflect Godard's essayistic reliance on citation in newly substantial ways. Indeed, this poetics enables a key adjustment and refinement within the career-long series of trials we have been tracing.

First, at this stage in his oeuvre, an "image" for Godard is not to be confused with a mere standalone "shot" or "picture." An image is comprised of *at least two elements* that are brought into fleeting convergence. It is a *composite formation*, an "ensemble-being," as Nicole Brenez words it, that is suffused with dynamic tension and, if the effect comes off, a provocative sense of accordance.[56] To speak of an image in this way is thus already to speak of montage. This is why the technique of superimposition is privileged in *Histoire(s)*—it gives material shape to the sense of *rapprochement* adapted from Reverdy. There is perhaps no more interesting case of this principle in action than the much-discussed moment in episode 1A where a clip of a young Elizabeth Taylor sunbathing on a lakeshore with Montgomery Clift in *A Place in the Sun* (George Stevens, 1951) is interwoven and superimposed with documentary footage (also captured by Stevens) of victims at Auschwitz and Ravensbrück. This composite image entails, as a third component, a reworked detail of Giotto's fresco *Noli me tangere* (1304–06). Taylor's hand seems to reach out to the death camp victims *and* to rhyme visually with the outspread hands of Giotto's Mary Magdalene, who, in Godard's 90-degree rotation of the religious fresco, dips down into the videographic frame like an angel (the extended hand of a resurrected Christ is just discernible in the bottom right corner). Taylor's gesture becomes one of assistance, as if saving the camp victims from their horrendous fate. Over this striking ensemble, Godard's voice says in a half-whisper, "O how marvelous to be able to look at what one cannot see! O sweet miracle of our blind eyes!" The image then disintegrates, layer by layer, leaving a black screen.[57]

This image, this *rapprochement* of distant elements, is offered not as mere formalism but as evidence of robust historical connection—a bond discovered in and through the act of montage. It is also an eloquent expression of Godard's desire to make amends for cinema's most unpardonable failure to confront and document the real. The director attempts to redeem, as it were, the neglected critical and intellectual vocation of cinematic montage itself, by having his videographic version of it broodingly reckon with the Holocaust. The Christian undertone of this composite image isn't, in fact, theological in Godard's usage. As Michael Witt argues, Godard evinces a quasi-spiritual faith in the transformative and revelatory capabilities *of cinema*, a faith that stems from a worldly, secular sense of hope and only takes recourse to Christian ideas in order to appropriate them.[58] In the light of our present inquiry in this chapter, Godard's adoption of this Reverdian poetics also testifies to his renewed belief in the value and utility of the image, in the wake of what I have called his iconoclastic militant work.

Secondly, an image in *Histoire(s)*—no matter how affecting or emblematic it appears at any one stage—is *always at some level unfinished* and open to still further division and synthesis, still further thought. If an image comes to pass in crystallized form as a superimposition, it still needs to be seen as a cumulative sensory event, with a buildup and aftermath. It must be said, after all, that comparatively few of the ensembles in the series are rounded off as cleanly and poignantly as the Elizabeth Taylor/Auschwitz example, which serves more as a highlight than a perfect encapsulation of Godard's entire method. Indeed, if one isn't careful, discussing his montage in Reverdian terms can lend a thin impression of how *Histoire(s)* actually looks, sounds, and *moves*, since relations generally take shape in torrential buildups that allot the viewer little time to reflect; it is not as if each link halts this intensity and joins only two things at once. The task, then, is to observe how images

A Critical Poetics of Citation

gradually begin, coalesce, disperse, and recur in new guises within an unfolding sequence, as Godard varyingly figures persistent motifs. There is another important literary reference at play here, one that complicates the principle of Reverdian *rapprochement*. At a number of points in *Histoire(s)*, Godard invokes Samuel Beckett's single-sentence short story "The Image" (1959), citing it as an irised page onscreen. Instead of a methodical means of staging convergences, this story suggests a chaotic and arduous activity of *striving* to form an image, a restless struggle occurring in and through a convulsive language ("now it's done I've done the image," Beckett's narrator finally, exhaustedly, states at the text's end).[59] We will see in a moment that Godard reflects on this difficulty characteristic of the image-forming process, doing so through the montage itself.

A third attribute of Godard's montage-based notion of the image in *Histoire(s)* is that an image is at some level *a mental construction*, "a pure creation of the mind," in Reverdy's words. No doubt the videographic process effects the impression of combinatory thought on the move, of a searching, contemplative mind borne along by the associative pulls of memory, the pangs of melancholy, and the prospect of revitalizing neglected and mishandled potentialities that were once cinema's province. This operation of thought isn't something that is represented on the screen in its entirety, or something the audience evaluates from a distance. If an image, in its Reverdian sense, is a mentally constructive activity, this goes not just for Godard but for his spectator as well. This thought process immerses us in its dynamic contortions and connective leaps. And yet the images at stake in our encounter *are not restricted to those that assume material shape on the screen*. Our task is essentially twofold. As arbiters, we must weigh the ensembles on display and determine whether Godard has indeed seen something, whether his montage discloses a relationship of historical import. But in addition to this, we must respond imaginatively and constructively to the gaps in the sequences he organizes—we must do the connective work when his process breaks off and digresses, falling short of its goals. *Histoire(s)* seeks our involvement in both of these capacities. Implicit here is the notion that *the viewer must become a skilled montagist also*. The act of *rapprochement*, which Godard literalizes through superimpositions, is something that *we* may have to do on our own, through a mental imagistic exercise adding our thought to the series.[60]

In order to see how this combinatory poetics is brought to bear and essayed, let us turn to a passage in the series that is less tidily composed than the Elizabeth Taylor/Auschwitz example. I want to show how the Reverdian notion of an image is itself subjected to scrutiny in the series, instead of serving as a formula for montage. Godard's videographic style is too versatile and impulsive to be subsumed under one method, oscillating as it does from sequences that come to us with the citations precisely ordered by ideas, events, and claims, to sequences that seem half-willed, half-accidental, and that operate more in a lyrical register of feeling and imagination. In examining this passage, I also

102   Chapter 2

want to more carefully consider how Godard's montage indirectly addresses and takes into account his audience.

The sequence I have in mind is a remarkable example of the way in which the content *of* the montage in *Histoire(s)* is made to signal and critically comment on what Godard is trying to achieve *with* the montage. This sequence unfurls at the start of episode 1B, "A Solitary History." Right after a close-up of a page from Beckett's "The Image," titles profess, "cogito ergo video" ("I think therefore I see") and Godard, reciting an aphorism from Robert Bresson's text *Notes on the Cinematographer*, expresses in voiceover: "Be sure of having used to the full all that is communicated through immobility and silence." From the start of the episode, then, we find already underway a reflection on the image as an instrument of investigation and as a tool by which Godard tries to communicate with others—albeit communicate through "immobility and silence" as much as he does through sensory plenitude, it being advisory for the filmmaker not to say or show things too forcefully or coercively. Godard soon makes clear that he is thinking of his role as director and of his own place in the history he recollects: "For me, my story [*histoire*], what have I got to do with all this? All this light? All this obscurity?" His voice echoes, lowering in pitch artificially while having to compete with the loud squawks of a crow that are recycled from his own work (it is a recurring disruptive sound in his late films). A still of the witch from Disney's animated *Snow White and the Seven Dwarfs* (1937), with her hand raised, reestablishes the trope of montage as a kind of sorcery that demands responsibility.

These thoughts lead into a stream of montage ruminating on the needs and difficulties of the image-making process. We see a three-part composite of a black-and-white still of Vivien Leigh from *Gone with the Wind* (Victor Fleming, 1939), a reeling strip of celluloid placed over her right cheek (appearing and disappearing twice, speeding to a colored blur and then slowing just enough for us to make out the frames, which show men with drawn pistols in *Rio Bravo* [Howard Hawks, 1958]), and a shot of Jean Marais as the titular poet in *Orpheus* (Jean Cocteau, 1950), searching with his hands around Leigh's mouth as if trying to grasp the evasive strip (fig. 2.9). This ensemble-image springs from a growing chain of associations that Godard triggers a few moments earlier, when he shows Glauber Rocha at the crossroads between politically militant cinema and aesthetic "adventure" in Godard and Gorin's *Wind from the East* (1970), to Rocha's right an added, superimposed film strip (of Ricky Nelson and Angie Dickinson in *Rio Bravo*) that vanishes to reveal a woman approaching. Godard, now riffing on the first sentence of Marcel Proust's novel *In Search of Lost Time* (1913), mutters in voiceover, "Sometimes at night someone whispers in my bedroom. I shut off the television but the whispering continues. Is it the wind or my ancestors?"

This line gives rise to a "history of wind," as titles announce while quoting Joris Ivens's *A Story of Wind* (1988), a frame of which appears onscreen. We hear a strong current blowing and see Lillian Gish assailed by a dust storm

A Critical Poetics of Citation

Figure 2.9. Cocteau's Orpheus grasping at the screen's surface: *Histoire(s) du cinéma*, episode 1B.

in *The Wind* (Victor Sjöström, 1928), then a disconsolate Dorothy Malone hurling a stone into the river in *Written on the Wind* (Douglas Sirk, 1956). Godard's titles shift from "written on the wind" to "gone with the wind," which leads into the still of Leigh. When the reeling strip appears, it figures as a tenuous and volatile stream that Orpheus can't quite embrace as he inspects the surface of the screen (the superimposed film strip replaces, while still evoking, Cocteau's mirror-entrance to the Zone).

So much thought is compressed in this short sequence. First of all, Godard's personal *histoire* as a director is bound up with this history of wind through his cinephilic attachments to his "ancestors" (Hawks, Sirk, and Cocteau) and through citations of his own films at notably different stages in his career. After he mentions the nocturnal whisper in his bedroom, he says that he had the actor who plays the chauffeur in *Orpheus* (François Périer as Heurtebise) speak the same line in a film called "A Place on Earth," the subtitle of Godard's *Keep Your Right Up* (1987). The sequence also features a slowed, apocalyptic clip from Godard's *Week-end* (1967), and the episode later splices in scenes from Godard's *Contempt*.

Yet the montage acknowledges that this history of wind is potentially our history as well, as viewers. Godard does this by repeatedly interspersing a still he takes from Ingmar Bergman's *Prison* (1949), a two-shot of a man and young woman, side-by-side behind a film projector and focused on the spectacle before them. Godard subjects this recurring citation to a number of intensive formal alterations: he at times splits the two-shot into singles of each figure, decorates it with the metamorphic titles "Histoire(s) du cinéma," modifies its coloration, and layers it with shots of a film strip winding through the bobbins of an editing console. But most importantly, he integrates this still in such a way as to stress this couple's spectatorship and *to make it seem as if they are studying the same images he is in the midst of showing us*. The couple, indeed, appears to be watching *Histoire(s) du cinéma* from the inside-out. Godard repeatedly cuts to these inserts as if they are point-glances and reaction shots that underscore this couple's point of view (fig. 2.10). This curious effect is similar to how Godard depicts himself as a viewer embedded within the video series who readies his gaze just before a flurry of montage occurs.

Godard invokes the spectator in one way or another throughout the video series, in part through wordplay with the cyclical French intertitle "toi" ("you"), which reminds us that we ourselves are included in the "his-*toi*-re(s) du cinéma" he recounts, through the act of our viewing, by dint of our own

Figure 2.10. Whirring film strip superimposed onto the couple of viewers from *Prison* (Bergman, 1949): *Histoire(s) du cinéma*, episode 1B.

A Critical Poetics of Citation

cinephilic memory and imagination.[61] Such a rhetoric of address is nothing new to Godard's corpus; we have already seen that his citational tactics consistently incorporate surrogate viewer-figures. But in this history of wind in *Histoire(s)*, this tendency becomes newly configured, serving a more particular demand of his montage process: what I would like to call, expanding on Daniel Morgan's use of the term in reference to Godard's late work, a condition of "twoness."[62]

By "twoness" I mean to define a dyadic, interpersonal bond, a circumstance of intimacy that Godard accentuates in the episode through the theme of romantic coupling. The spectating couple from Bergman's *Prison* is made to embody an intimate relationship that is vitally at stake in Godard's own videographic style—a sense of *seeing together*. Because Godard alone cannot confirm the strength and validity of his findings through montage (a fact he bluntly confesses elsewhere in his late stage),[63] the process he animates must appeal to the perceptual acuity and critical judgment of the audience. Reflecting on this basic requirement, the "history of wind" segment implies that *at least two viewers*, sharing in the perception of an affinity, are needed to decide if Godard has in fact seen something, if a revelation has opened to sight. In this way, the "twoness" required of an image is at once formal and spectatorial. An image, in order to qualify as such—in order for it to be "just," as Reverdy puts it—must not only be made of two or more material layers; it must also bring together a minimum of two observers who, for the moment, mutually discern its significance. In other words, the *rapprochement* should exert a conjunctive force on those who take in the series, *if* a genuine image comes to pass.[64]

In Bergman's *Prison*, this scene of coupling, between an alcoholic writer and a prostitute, is one of respite, since these two characters, while watching a projection of a silent film on an attic wall, find temporary relief from their bleak predicaments. This citation ties in with a motif of coupling spun throughout the episode, as part of a reflection on cinema's historical fascination with stories about sex and death. (Very soon after the "history of wind," Godard reworks the last scene from *Duel in the Sun* [King Vidor, 1946] where Jennifer Jones writhes toward Gregory Peck, each fatally injured by the other's hand, their passionate embrace serving, at one level, as a figurative expression of the connective force of montage: "the image / will come / oh time! / of resurrection," declare the intertitles.) Godard, through his passing appearances in the episode, weaves himself into this motif of coupling by associating himself with the male character in the *Prison* still. This happens visually through cross-fades as well as through a play of onscreen text whereby the fragment "his" is drawn from "his-toire(s)" and imprinted on the male figure (this of course entails a linguistic change from French to English).

Godard refers to himself and his montage process in still another respect: Cocteau's poet, Orpheus, stands in for Godard, an avatar of the montagist, searching with his hands for a flux of images that proves ungraspable. This is Godard's reflexive way of facing up to the challenge of his project: how to conduct a historical inquiry with an elusive substance (images that come and go in perpetual variation) *and* how to discover and present a revelatory combination that will, in turn, bring together at least two viewers. This is the basic procedural problem around which the "history of wind" sequence revolves. And Godard's self-inscription implies that *he* can be one of these two "viewers." Again, the motif of coupling organizes this reflection: the sequence unfolds through several male-female pairings that momentarily form and then disperse, as if blown by the wind. This focus on the couple is central not only to *Histoire(s)* but to Godard's late period in general, and I will return to this theme in our next chapter where I will discuss how it speaks to Godard's collaborative partnership with Anne-Marie Miéville, whom the female character in the recurrent still from *Prison* evokes, with a spirit of optimism, as if coupling stands to "counter the despair" that saturates *Histoire(s)*.[65] For now, I just want to emphasize how this key motif figures forth the relational intimacy that Godard hopes his montage will inspire with another thinker and perceiver in addition to himself. This motif expresses the importance of twoness and conveys how the image, in its robust sense, fundamentally aspires to be a vehicle of relationship, between and for its viewers, between Godard's thought and ours.

What I am calling twoness—or better still, *at-least-twoness*—is a requisite condition of the montage in *Histoire(s)*, but nothing intrinsic to the process itself or Godard's discourse on it guarantees such an outcome. Two viewers becoming bound in and through their sharing of the manner of seeing that Godard promotes—this is a possibility that must be *sought*; it cannot be taken as a given. This all-important feature, however, has gone unobserved by even some of the most sagacious criticisms of the series. Jacques Rancière, over a number of articles that turn to *Histoire(s)*, dismisses the series and its citational montage because of what he sees as its sheer formalism and spurious construction of community. Where some have made the argument that nothing ever quite coheres in the series,[66] Rancière objects to how, in his view, everything *is made to cohere* by the beguiling forgeries of the montage. He ascribes to the series an "inter-expressive" poetics: each shot or document is removed from its original context so as to become a "pure presence," a "pure sensory block" shorn of the designs and meanings initially attached to it; this fragment then becomes a "metamorphic" element that relinks with other such purified potentialities within a boundless continuum.[67] What irks Rancière is the way in which this poetics insinuates a connection between "artistic forms" and "shared forms of life." He argues that Godard fabricates a sense of "co-belonging" at once formal and communal, imposing a sensation of shared experience where none exists. He traces this dubious method back to early German Romanticism, in particular Friedrich Schlegel's concept of "progressive universal poetry," which both composes new, modern poems from the reworked fragments of ancient poems and "ensures that the

A Critical Poetics of Citation 107

speeches and images of art are interchangeable with the speeches and images of common experience."[68]

It is this framing of collective life through a logic of pure, endlessly recombinable image matter that leads Rancière to take the video series to task. He goes so far as to label *Histoire(s)* a *Gesamtkunstwerk* ("total work of art," in the Wagnerian sense of the term), his argument being that its montage fosters a consensus-oriented community through its rhythmic ability to weave each and any element into an ecstatic totality.[69] Setting his critique in the context of Godard's overall career, Rancière regrets that the "dialectical clashes" of collage that distinguished the director's more admirably politicized work of the mid- to late 1960s have been "swallowed" by this late-phase method of montage that falsely spins the heterogeneous materials and histories it cites into a seamless, harmonious fabric.[70]

The problem with Rancière's account is that for all the rigor and erudition of his thesis, he misconstrues the dynamics by which Godard's montage operates. His claim that the clips are utterly divorced from their original contexts for the sake of formalist relays is amiss (we saw above how *Histoire(s)* adaptively plays on the narrative content of the films it samples in its very first moments, e.g., the citations from *The Fury*). Rancière nowhere pays heed to how Godard inhabits the series by inscribing himself as an investigator whose visions and conjugational formations *must be judged* by others who encounter them. Rancière ignores the coupling motif and its rhetorical appeal to an attentive audience. His nostalgic embrace of "collage" over and against "montage" in his summation of Godard's oeuvre is also misguided for reasons I will soon make evident. And Rancière fundamentally miscasts the Schlegelian poetics of the fragment that he maps onto *Histoire(s)*.

Jacques Aumont and Vinzenz Hediger have each demonstrated that the Jena school of the German Romantics, and Friedrich Schlegel in particular, indeed compare tellingly with Godard's late videographic style. Aumont entertains the comparison in the midst of situating *Histoire(s)* as a "cinematographic essay on cinema" that weds poetic and scientific principles,[71] and Hediger claims for Godard's evolving practice a "strategy of continuous inception," an impulse to perpetually start anew, abandon schematism, and maintain for his work-in-progress a sense of open-ended futurity.[72] When Rancière turns to Schlegel in his critiques of *Histoire(s)*, he puts aside such traits, screening out the essayistic verve of Godard's montage and ignoring entirely the way in which the process *tries* the combinations it sets forth. Rancière writes that Godard orchestrates what Schlegel terms the faculty of "wit" (*Witz*), a faculty in and through which the poet can discover affinities between outwardly incompatible elements.[73] This faculty thrives in unruliness, in contradiction, wielding its revelatory power in sudden flashes, like bursts of lightning in a night sky. What Rancière overlooks, however, is that for Schlegel, as well as for Godard, each link is provisional, the poetic-experimenter has only limited sway, and there is a rather high risk of chaos

108 Chapter 2

and incoherence at each juncture. The fraternal tides and rhythms of the combinatory process can be disturbed at any instant by what Schlegel calls "the glimmer of error and madness."[74]

In stripping *Histoire(s)* of its essayistic bent, Rancière also leaves us with a cynical and reductive description of the role of the viewer. Even as his own close readings of certain parts of the video series would suggest otherwise,[75] he posits a bewitched, naively submissive audience whose only function is to be drafted into a mendacious sense of community that Godard presents. I hope to have made it clear that *Histoire(s)* encourages a more keenly sensitive kind of viewing experience, one in which seeing together and realizing the condition of twoness can come about *only* as a contingent, hard-earned result. Godard, to be sure, wants his montage to astonish us, to strike us as "miraculous," but whether the formal linkages are legitimate and "just" hangs on our judiciousness.[76] Let us put it this way: unless a mutually constitutive rapport between at least two viewers sharing in the constructive labor takes shape—unless Godard is indeed able to share the perception of an affinity—then there is no montage at all, but merely virtuosic collage in which ensembles fail to detect historical relations. Throughout the series, Godard cites cinema's power to shore up communities at the level of whole nations, but the social bond he seeks to initiate through his own procedure entails a more intimate and concertedly pensive circumstance of togetherness. *Witz* is more germane here than Rancière allows: its special power to reveal and instruct, according to some of its Jena exponents, works at its peak intensity *with and for a small audience*, best of all between "friends."[77]

The purely formalist and/or ideological manufacture of co-belonging is precisely the type of necromancy Godard stays on guard against throughout *Histoire(s)*, as he subjects his own principles to scrutiny. To neglect this is, moreover, to fail to grasp how the intricate notion of the image that Godard openly essays in the series amounts to a critical revision within his long and diverse career and within his dependence on citation—a revision of which *Histoire(s)* is deeply mindful. With a view to taking this chapter to its end, let us briefly return to a charged moment in the "history of wind" segment in which Godard brings in a scene from his and Gorin's *Wind from the East*. The original scene in this Dziga Vertov Group production is literally (and not coincidentally) a crossroads moment. A young woman, visibly pregnant and carrying a film camera, approaches the Brazilian director Glauber Rocha at an intersection of dirt roads in the countryside and remarks, "Excuse me for interrupting your class struggle, but could you tell me the way towards political cinema?" Rocha, his arms out like a scarecrow or road sign, tells her that one path leads to an "unknown cinema, the cinema of aesthetic adventure," whereas another leads to a more politicized cinema devoted to practical matters of production, distribution, and training with the aim of combating imperialist oppression. The woman starts off down the second path that Rocha identifies, describes in much greater detail, and seems to

A Critical Poetics of Citation

endorse, but then she turns back and wanders along the path of "aesthetic adventure," only to deviate from this course as well by heading into a dense thicket of trees. In her quest for political cinema, she appears dissatisfied with the paths available to her, as does the Godard of 1970.

I take it that Godard's point in revisiting this scene in the late 1980s, when he composed episode 1B, is to reaffirm that this choice between paths was and remains a false one—that this distinction was never precisely an either/or question for his enterprise. By doubling back to this crossroads, *Histoire(s)* doesn't imply a complete break and transition between his middle and late phases, but instead asserts that his late, post-militant work concerns itself with the political in a different way, through a restyled approach where aesthetic adventure is a part of his still-vigilant but tempered political consciousness. With *Histoire(s)*, then, Godard doesn't withdraw from the realm of politics but rather adapts his essayistic practice to a new situation, in the long fall-out of his disenchantment with militant filmmaking, a situation in which it seems no longer sensible to postulate in advance, and take for granted, an entire collective subject waiting to be goaded into revolution by the proper political discourse. Through his videographic montage, he reinstates a speculative mood, colored by hesitation, uncertainty, and suspense, and he does this working to build from the ground up a collaborative relation between initially just two persons (this is plenty difficult enough to achieve). His concept of the image is, at heart, not a recipe for concord, but a process of *continually retesting* the principal grounds whereby twoness may take hold, ensemble after contingent ensemble.[78] This is why Godardian citation is so often a matter of repetition: certain citations, both within and across his projects, become repertorial, appearing again and again in newly exigent compositions.

I will make one final point regarding how citations figure in this essayistic process as it concerns both Godard and potentially ourselves. I noted earlier that Godard cites the work of others as liberally and tortuously as he does in part to confound any singular authorial identity one might affix to his practice. I also noted that in spite of this complication, his very selection and handling of citations indexes the presiding agency and interiority of a specific individual, albeit an inconstant one. Now that we have seen how his montage in *Histoire(s)* contemplates its own powers and limits through a thematics of coupling and a fundamental condition of twoness, I want to suggest that Godard's poetics of citation hinges on an imperative to keep in check, and if possible shed, one's narcissism.

In the movement from singularity to twoness there is not simply an addition but a kind of splitting of the one into two, a rivenness of monadic subjectivity as one enters into intensities of becoming-other. Colin MacCabe well captures the spirit of what I am trying to define when he writes: "While Godard was resolute in his defence of art as a privileged site of individuality, that individual is constantly produced as dividual, the divided site of traces, quotations, relations which refuse any unity, as the artist is made and remade

110 Chapter 2

in a ceaseless flow of meaning."[79] Such a turn from individual to "dividual," and from self to other: is this not at stake at every juncture in and with the citational montage of *Histoire(s)*?

I don't mean to suggest that the video series has as its corollary the *absolute* fracture and deletion of the subject (Godard is too much of a Romantic and a modernist for that). After all, the series' tropes of responsibility and self-implication are asserted in terms of individuality. What I wish to suggest is that in our encounters with the folds and vortices of *Histoire(s)*, we, along with Godard, are meant—but are not coercively made—to lose and rediscover ourselves not as unitary beings but as "dividuals," in MacCabe's definition of the term. Godard says many times in his late interviews that what he found during the making of *Histoire(s)* is that without cinema, he would not have learned that he had a history and that his personal history is enmeshed in certain larger histories.[80] The video series grants that this cinephilic view of having a history applies to us as well: whether our memories match up with Godard's, we, too, are of course the living repositories of voices, gestures, and events we have taken in and processed as film viewers—"traces" that have become ambiguously fused with our own experiences and thoughts. Further apt here is Michael Witt's observation that the videographic montage evokes "the idea of the inscription of films in the human psyche, and of the inhabitation and animation of individuals by half-remembered clips."[81]

I suspect that if studies of the cinematic essay have tended to give the question of citation short shrift despite its pivotal role, this is because the question draws out a dispersive, multiplicitous sense of essayistic thought that doesn't fit well with the convenience of focusing on first-person subjectivity. Theodor Adorno writes in "The Essay as Form" (1958):

> In the essay, concepts do not build a continuum of operations, thought does not advance in a single direction, rather the aspects of the argument interweave as in a carpet. The fruitfulness of the thoughts depends on the density of this texture. Actually, the thinker does not think, but rather transforms himself into an arena of intellectual experience, without simplifying it.[82]

As the styles of Godard and other essay filmmakers can attest, if we transpose Adorno's striking description of the literary essay onto its cinematic counterpart, then it must be added that this "carpet," this "arena," is thoroughly encroached on and textured by thoughts and voices and sentiments that are not the essayist's own, by myriad impressions that filter in from an outside.[83] Godard's citation-dense work faces up to this existential fact, urging that we do the same. To miss this point is to ignore his fondness for citing Arthur Rimbaud's extraordinary claim, "I is another." It is to turn a blind eye to his rebuttal to Descartes in 4A of *Histoire(s)*: "The 'I' in 'I think' is not the same as the 'I' in 'I am.'"

Chapter 3

✦

Refiguring the Couple:
Love, Dialogue, and Gesture

I don't believe that I exist, I don't believe that you exist; I believe that we're a movement materialized of movements, of forms that pass between us.

—Jean-Luc Godard

Togetherness, you know what I mean?
—Roger O. Thornhill, *North by Northwest*

One is in the other, the other is in the one, and these are three persons.
—Anne-Marie Miéville, *The Old Place*

I began this book by proposing to reframe the evolution of the essay form in cinema along two separate yet related paths—the "essay film" as a more or less distinct genre, and then, more broadly, narrative films that make use of essayistic operations. If we take a moment to revisit the examples I adduced to mark the emergence of these two directions in post–World War II modern cinema, a curious point of overlap reveals itself. Couples, or male-female pairings, recur as prime expressive elements across both kinds of films, whether as voiceover narrators in Varda's *Ô Saisons, ô châteaux* (1957) or as dramatis personae in Franju's *Hôtel des Invalides* (1952), Rossellini's *Voyage in Italy* (1954), Resnais's *Hiroshima mon amour* (1959), Antonioni's *Eclipse* (1962), and, of course, Godard's *Contempt* (1963).

One could expand this set of examples. Several of Marker's essay films turn on dyadic male-female relationships in elaborate ways. Take the Plato's cave segment from *The Owl's Legacy* (1989) that I referenced in the preceding chapter, a segment in which the intellectual argument is conveyed through a layered montage of male-female interactions. Marker's *Sans soleil* (1983) unfolds as a series of intimate dispatches by Sandor Krasna (one of Marker's authorial proxies in the film) addressed to an unnamed woman

111

who in turn provides the film's spoken narration. Marker's two essayistic fiction films, *La Jetée* (1962) and *Level Five* (1997), revolve around amorous couples. The former film, as part of its meditation on traumatic history and its citational reworking of Hitchcock's *Vertigo* (1958), regards the couple, or the hero's *desire for* coupling, as a persevering force that somehow facilitates "rationally impossible" trips through time.[1] *Level Five*, which has as its main setting or hub a cluttered multimedia workstation (Marker's actual apartment in Paris), features a woman, Laura (Catherine Belkhodja), who assumes the task of finishing the production of her deceased lover's video game about the Battle of Okinawa. The film consists of video diaries she addresses to her lost partner as she simultaneously copes with her grief, wrestles with technological difficulties, feels her way into the nonlinear capabilities of digital media, and pieces together a more thorough account of the fate of the Okinawan civilians, thousands of whom committed suicide because of a cultural ethos against surrender. When Laura hits a stumbling block, she calls upon a close friend and collaborator, Chris (played by Marker himself in voice only), an "ace of montage" who lends a helping hand by showing Laura—and by extension the viewer—how to make clever, inventive use of historical material gleaned from archives.

The respective approaches of the essay films and essayistic narrative films we have touched on so far clash in certain respects, but this thematic reliance on coupling that bridges them is not just a coincidence. There are three basic ways in which this affinity emanates from the very crux of essayistic reflection in modern cinema. First of all, forms and scenarios of coupling—romantic or otherwise—furnish the filmmakers in question with a fecund means of adapting and playing with the dramatic codes of popular cinema (*and* art cinema). As we've already witnessed, film essayists often engage with narrative cinema idioms even while exploring alternative approaches with varying degrees of resistance and critique. Second, this thematic emphasis on the couple is connected to how essay filmmakers express *and test* the interpersonal dimensions of essayistic thought. Third, in several of the films at issue, coupling thematically entails a reflexive component concerning the directors themselves. In some of the works I named above, the male-female pairings reflect the personal, collaborative relationship between the director and lead actress: Rossellini and Ingrid Bergman in *Voyage in Italy*, Antonioni and Monica Vitti in *Eclipse*, and, in a more platonic manner, Marker and his recurrent muse, Belkhodja, in *Level Five*.[2]

Godard's essayistic oeuvre here again stands out in intriguing ways. He is a "director of the couple," to borrow an epithet he once bestowed on Hitchcock (*GG*, 53). All through his career the couple takes on reflective importance in his work in multiple and interrelated senses. His films, television series, and video projects approach the couple as a focal point of tireless and intensive research into the linguistic, perceptual, bodily, and affective vagaries of interpersonal dialogue and exchange—an endeavor at once quasi-scientific and

Refiguring the Couple

aesthetic, with Godard reconceiving practices he takes from popular cinema as well as from art cinema. Furthermore, there is an indisputable personal element to much of this research. The French-Swiss director's different career stages can be (and frequently have been) divided up according to his personal and artistic partnerships, all of which insinuate their way into the porous worlds of his films: the early, New Wave stage (with Anna Karina); his leftist radicalization (which starts with Anne Wiazemsky); and his move to Switzerland and shift into his late work (with Anne-Marie Miéville), which runs well into the new century and makes up his longest, most prodigious stage.

As part of the auto-retrospective turn of his late phase (i.e., his tendency to reflect back on his career vis-à-vis the history of cinema), Godard has endorsed such a couples-based organization of his oeuvre but with a certain arc in mind. Consider the photomontage he contributed to the last two pages of the biographical "roman-photo" compiled by Alain Bergala as an introduction to the publication of *Jean-Luc Godard par Jean-Luc Godard* in 1985. On the verso page are photographs of his first wife, Karina (from *Band of Outsiders*, 1964); Wiazemsky (from *Wind from the East*, 1970); and Myriem Roussel (from *Prénom Carmen*, 1983). A caption describes these three as women who "played a role in films." On the adjacent recto side is a solitary close-up of Miéville, her hair tumbled around her shoulders, the grain and contrast modified to produce a more painterly portrait. A caption demarcates her as a woman who "played a role in life." That Godard grants a privileged position to Miéville in this gallery of past female collaborators is unmistakable. And if "playing a role in life" is marked off from "playing a role in films," this is because with her he has taken part in a unique artisanal relationship in which love and work, life and cinema, and creation and critical inquiry all coexist.[3]

Since *Ici et ailleurs* (1976), Godard and Miéville have carried on a partnership whose closest parallel among filmmakers with essayistic inclinations is perhaps the creative relationship between Jean-Marie Straub and Danièle Huillet, which lasted from the early 1960s until Huillet's death in 2006. But with Straub-Huillet—as many scholars who explore this comparison have noted—the division of labor is less difficult to figure out: Straub (much like Godard, the public spokesperson for the couple) has often explained that he directed the shooting, while Huillet handled the editing. As can be observed, however, in Pedro Costa's *Where Does Your Hidden Smile Lie?* (2001), an engrossing portrait of the couple at work in their editing room, the most miniscule formal choices were made mutually, if after much debate and sometimes terse argument. Costa's film is a valuable document of their joint creativity, their shared rhythm, their comic and touching old-couple repartee as they weigh the pressures and tensions that shape every single cut. Through Costa's own symbiotic, gently reflexive approach, the film captures elemental forces of coupling that circulate between the film they are cutting and the space of their worksite: seated at the editing console in the dark, Huillet inspects each frame and relations between frames while Straub wavers in the doorway, restless, backlit by light from the hall as he aphoristically remarks on the demands of their practice, that is, until a decisive cut calls for two sets of eyes and ears. Costa's portrait of the couple is a study of edges, borders, instants, and intervals—a study that shows and to some extent mirrors the couple's acute weighing of these very factors.

Godard-Miéville's partnership has involved a greater variety of projects, from jointly directed productions to performances in one another's work (e.g., Godard's extended recital of a passage from Hannah Arrendt's *The Origins of Totalitarianism* [1951] in Miéville's feature film *We're All Still Here* [1997]). There are also very strong motivic and aesthetic correspondences between films and videos they have made independently, Miéville being a skilled director in her own right. Godard himself once memorably distinguished his and Miéville's relationship from that of Straub-Huillet by declaring: "The Straubs work in tandem, on the same bicycle, him in front, her behind. We have two bicycles."[4]

Despite Godard and Miéville's public reticence regarding their collaborations, Jerry White, Catherine Grant, Michael Witt, Colin MacCabe, and Richard Brody have each provided insights into the specific nature of the French-Swiss couple's dynamic, with attention to the institutional factors that pertain to the small, peripheral production companies that they have set up together, most importantly Sonimage.[5] These studies, however, have not considered at length how Godard's work with Miéville shades into his essayism. In chapter 2, we saw how Godard-Miéville ignite properly non-doctrinaire essayistic thinking in *Ici et ailleurs*, and how in *Histoire(s) du cinéma* their couplehood serves implicitly as an example of "twoness," of shared inquisitive work that stands in for the dialogical intimacy *Histoire(s)* looks to establish with its viewer. My objective here will be to expand further on the ways in which this creative couple deploys the theme of coupling itself as a means of both practicing essayistic investigation and striking a rapport with the viewer in the process.

To this end, I am going to examine a reflective arc over five of their dual engagements from the late 1970s to the end of the century: their TV series *France/tour/détour/deux/enfants* (1977); their jointly edited feature film *Every Man for Himself* (Godard, 1980); their diptych of feature films *Hail Mary* (Godard, 1985) and *The Book of Mary* (Miéville, 1985); their made-for-TV video *Soft and Hard* (1985); and, finally, *The Old Place* (1999), their video essay on cinema history, ethics, and modern art-making. Tracing this arc will, in the first instance, highlight the couple's abiding investment in the study of human gestures—a tendency that not only links their work to Godard's earlier films, but also expands to include a self-reflexive account of *their own gestures* as artists, as montagists. In addition, looking at these five collaborations will allow us to fathom how the concept of love informs their essayistic thinking—not erotic love, I will argue, so much as love founded on friendship.

Refiguring the Couple

My concern will not be to unearth how Godard-Miéville distribute their responsibilities but to study in detail how their films and videos allude to, inscribe, and allegorize their partnership. I eventually want to show how they embody a certain revised practice of cinephilia that mediates conceptually between their feature films and shorter video essays, as they explore major themes running through Godard's late phase. We will see that love, understood as *philia* instead of *eros*, figures as the binding force in and of their work together as essayistic filmmakers—a force that enlivens their address to the spectator as well.

The Study of Gestures

Godard's dissections of the heterosexual couple have long subtended his critical regard for, and research into, the relational and affective intensities of gestures. In his early films, problems of language and communication consistently plague his couples, but in some instances a window of potential for more meaningful interaction opens up where ordinary, verbal dialogue breaks down. *A Married Woman* (1964) features tableaux in which the main couples caress one another in shots that fragment their bodies and evoke, but in essence differ from, the kitschy eroticism of magazine lingerie ads. In a film that otherwise cynically underscores a dearth of understanding between its amorously linked characters, these artful, Beethoven-accompanied scenes hint at something more charged with possibility through their unusual tenderness. A more hopeful, rapturous instance of such a scene happens in *Alphaville* (1965), namely the interlude in which Lemmy Caution (Eddie Constantine) teaches Natacha (Anna Karina), or rather sparks off her process of becoming able to feel, a definition of "love," a verboten term in the film's dystopian world. Her "lyric illumination," as Chris Darke calls it, transpires through stylized choreography: Natacha and Caution, captured up close in gently flashing, modulating light, strike measured poses, dance in a circle, gaze back at the lens, gesture in arcing patterns as if spellbound, and stroke each other's faces.[6] A soft ensemble of strings (as opposed to the strident horns that score the film elsewhere) envelops them, as Natacha, in voiceover, recites lyric verses written by Paul Éluard, her changed tenor suggesting the gradual onset of an epiphany: "Increasingly, I see the human form as a lover's dialogue." The scene is striking for the way it cordons off this "lover's dialogue" from the daytime event that surrounds it (police are descending on Caution) and from the dehumanizing reach of Alpha 60, the supercomputer that reigns over the technofascist state. What begins as a failed interrogation in Caution's hotel room, as his questions come up against Natacha's insensitivity, veers for the moment into a gestural and lyrical register that proves more effectual. The scene conveys a mutually enacted sense of love that promises the rehabilitation of a deadened, indoctrinated woman, an official "seductress" assigned to

116   Chapter 3

Caution by the state. It instigates what becomes Caution's successful rescue mission, and a rare upbeat conclusion in Godard's early period.[7]

In Godard's later work with Miéville, a focus on gesture returns but in a different light. As I illustrated in my above analysis of the controversial sequence in *Ici et ailleurs*, the montage turns on a comparison of raised hands that rhyme across photos drawn from different historical and political contexts. In the same film, we also repeatedly see the hands of the two filmmakers themselves, which alternatingly enter the frame either to adjust the volume on a piece of sound equipment (more frequently her hand) or to type numbers into a calculator (his hand). Gestures, for Godard-Miéville, act as important circuits of montage. And this study of gestural associations extends from the contexts they engage to the sense in which they inscribe *their own*, interactive gestures as a creative couple of filmmakers.

This attentiveness to gesture already shows up in their first projects together, yet it takes on increasingly elaborate dimensions in their work over time. Let us begin with the twelve-part series *France/tour/détour/deux/enfants* (*France/Tour/Detour/Two/Children*) which they co-directed for French television in 1977. Each episode includes a portion in which Godard, in the guise of a reporter whom we hear from offscreen but never see, poses bewildering questions either to a young girl, Camille (Camille Virolleaud), or to a young boy, Arnaud (Arnaud Martin). The episodes include recurrent segments in which scenes of these children doing routine tasks, or of crowds trudging through the cityscape at rush hour, are slowed down and analyzed through the strange technique of video stop-starts, with the tape speed adjusted so as to render each recorded motion a jagged series of constituent parts. In addition, the questionnaires and "altered motion" experiments[8] are reviewed and discussed in dialogues between Betty (Betty Berr) and Albert (Albert Dray), television "presenters" who figure as approximate stand-ins for Miéville and Godard (fig. 3.1).

Here, then, as in many of their dual efforts, dialogue and the inspection of gestures run together. A shared purpose links these two features in *France/tour/détour* (and lends Godard's preoccupation with human gesture a stronger political valence). As Michael Witt has shown in his examination of the series, Godard-Miéville, in an effort that engages with trends in French poststructuralist thought of the same decade (Michel Foucault, Jean-François Lyotard, Gilles Deleuze, and Félix Guattari), work to reveal the social forces that constrain and condition both common knowledge and seemingly natural, quotidian gestures. The episodes, each of which is organized around a juxtaposition of terms that loosely names the focus (e.g., "Dark/Chemistry," "Light/Physics," "Disorder/Calculus," "Violence/Grammar"), suggest that the daily routines to which both Camille and Arnaud are subjected—at home, at school, and en route between—are geared toward taming them into "docile bodies" (Foucault's term) in the efficient service of the capitalist economy. School comes to denote a carceral environment, less a site of actual

Refiguring the Couple

Figure 3.1. Betty and Albert discuss an altered-motion exercise: *France/tour/détour/deux/enfants* (Godard, Miéville, 1977), episode 4.

learning than a training ground, the regimentation of which corresponds to the regulatory schemas of both the urban landscape and TV programming.

The interviews and the altered motion sequences function in the series as interdependent means of interrogation and reflection that permit Godard and Miéville to ascertain the extent to which Arnaud and Camille have already submitted to this debilitating process of social control. Godard's questioning is by turns intrusive, ludic, and callously difficult as the children struggle to provide answers; but it intriguingly draws out their ingrained views regarding properties of time and space, light and dark, day and night, as well as accepted-as-natural incongruities of capitalism. As for the use of decelerated motion, Witt astutely argues that Godard-Miéville "conduct a kind of videoscopic ultrasound of the calibrated body" and "cast into relief the work of the micro-powers in producing human docility-utility."[9]

The TV series introduces into Godard's work, which is now Miéville's work as well, a new visual texture: not "slow motion" but variable, jerky motion. This videographic process evokes an old resource of the film medium—frame-rate manipulation, which figures such as Dziga Vertov, Jean Epstein, and Walter Benjamin praised for its revelatory power—without replicating it. Godard and Miéville's use of "saccadic" motion, as Witt and

Constance Penley have properly defined it,[10] reanimates the old avant-garde aim to open to sight the complexities of movement that escape our habitual and unassisted glance at the world.

If the procedure succeeds in revealing where gestures fall in line with disciplinary forces, it also gives form to a corporeal presence onscreen that differs sharply from the fluid bodies we find in the cinema of Vertov or the French Impressionists. Decomposed, the gestures oscillate between laminar and turbulent motion. As Albert says in a voiceover passage that accompanies a visual analysis of Camille "preparing her body for the night" (undressing before bed), the irregular jumps between speeds lend the sensation of "uncovering a secret, then covering it back up." Godard and Miéville have been criticized for the sensuality this disrobing scene entails, given its emphasis on a juvenile actress.[11] However, as Jerry White maintains, this use of altered motion avoids eroticism, indulging neither a voyeuristic nor an exploitative gaze. The segment calls attention to an analytic method that balances intimacy and critical distance. White contends that it reworks a motif of domesticity from European painting (young "women at their toilette") while urging the viewer to interpret the dissection of Camille's mobile figure as part of a larger study wherein such gestures, once broken down, reveal the work of forces extending between domestic and public spheres.[12]

This procedure may seem self-contradictory in that Godard-Miéville's use of the device, however well-intentioned, puts into effect its own regime of control, perhaps with deterministic themes elected in advance. Yet Godard's public remarks suggest a more complex process. In an interview around the release of *Every Man for Himself* (1980), his narrative film that uses roughly the same videographic effect, he looks back on *France/tour/détour* and points to the technique's sense of play and discovery:

> [W]hen you change the rhythms, when you analyze the movements of a woman, even moments as simple as buying a loaf of bread, for instance, you notice that there are loads of different worlds inside the woman's movement, whereas the use of slow motion with the boy was much less interesting. We would stop the image, and between each image was always the same directing line. But with the little girl, even when she was doing extremely banal things, you'd go suddenly from profound anguish to joy a split second later. They were real monsters . . . And I, in my guise as a scientist who knows certain theories, had the impression that they were particles [*corpuscules*] and different worlds, galaxies that were different each time, and between which you could travel via a series of explosions.[13]

The experience Godard recalls is that of he and Miéville reviewing footage in the editing stage, but this sense of experiment and surprise still informs what

Refiguring the Couple

119

the completed work offers the viewer. Although intent on capturing how the gestures of their young subjects have been culturally molded and habituated, the co-directors find themselves astonished by these "monstrous" screen bodies whose slightest motions, Camille's in particular, open onto entire "galaxies" of expression one could not otherwise see, vectors of meaning and emotion that change by the millisecond, one video step-frame after the next. The device enables us to perceive a body that *evades* determinations by hinting at different potentials and trajectories.

One last point bears mention here. The altered motion segments in *France/tour/détour* not only examine gestures within the footage. They also render conspicuous Godard-Miéville's creative gestures *upon and with* the footage. The viewer cannot fail to notice the intrusiveness of this effect, the rhythms it forcefully inscribes and the way in which it *sculpts* the motions of the children as much as it traces them. This isn't to revoke my previous point. Far from imposing a choreography, Godard-Miéville's manipulations amount to an essayistic version of what Vilém Flusser regards as "the gesture of searching"—a scientific or quasi-scientific procedure in which "one does not know in advance what one is looking for."[14] Improvisational at least in part, these gestures by the co-directors enact a testing out of the videographic process.[15]

For Flusser, "the gesture of searching" is additionally "a gesture in search of others" who might share in the discovery,[16] a notion that resonates with the goals of essayism as they extend from the side of production to reception. Godard and Miéville's appeals to the audience come across through Albert and Betty's exchanges and news anchor-like moments of direct address. If these characters stand in for the two filmmakers, their observations and commentary often seem tentative, as though meant to prompt a more rigorous examination that never occurs within the program itself. As Betty puts it in an explanatory line Godard recycles in his interviews of the period, "With our questions, we seem as though we're always trying to have the last word when in fact it's the first word that concerns us; and, if the second word rarely follows, this is because we're alone in doing this kind of work."

This "first word" invites an essayistic mode of reception, one at odds with conventional television. From its altered motion sequences to its political arguments, *France/tour/détour* radically reimagines television as a medium favorable to exploratory research and dialogue. Its pedagogy of looking and listening tries to countermand the institutionalized schooling that produces the automata we see slogging to the cadence of the workday and tuning in as television dictates—subjects stripped of spontaneity and of the ability to envisage an alternative. Where essayistic reimaginings of television are concerned, Godard and Miéville's effort (here and in their prior series *Six fois deux/Sur et sous la communication* [1976]) is matched in inventiveness only by Alexander Kluge's programs.

A Shared Activity, Not Just at Night

The themes and questions in Godard and Miéville's essayistic collaborations of the 1970s do not go away, even as the two directors, working independently or together, venture into new directions, tones, and production modes during the next decade. Godard's triumphant return to feature filmmaking in 1980 with *Every Man for Himself* sets a basic agenda for his reflections of the era through its study of a modern couple failing to reconcile the demands of romantic love with those of work. In doing so, the film, while featuring more of a fictional narrative than anything Godard had crafted since *Tout va bien* (co-directed with Jean-Pierre Gorin, 1972), picks up and carries forth certain key threads from his earlier undertakings with Miéville, from their use of altered motion and close attention to gesture to their interest in domestic life. The opening titles against a cloud-streaked blue sky acknowledge this new project to be another collaboration: while they read "a film composed by Jean-Luc Godard," Miéville is credited for the "scenario," and the names of both artists appear under "montage."

The film's drama and Swiss setting would seem to encourage biographical interpretations insofar as the lead couple, Paul Godard (Jacques Dutronc) and Denise Rimbaud (Nathalie Baye), roughly call to mind Godard and Miéville's relationship through contrasts as much as superficial resemblances. Paul Godard is a filmmaker who, as many critics have noted, bears his namesake's cigar, spectacles, and style of dress. Denise Rimbaud works for a television station, where Paul is also employed, but she aspires to write a novel once she relocates to the more serene countryside. (We will see in our analysis of *Soft and Hard* that Miéville figures in the couple's dynamic in a way that aligns her with verbal expression; given the underlying themes of *Every Man for Himself*, I take Denise's surname to conjure up Rimbaud's famous line in *A Season in Hell*, his 1873 prose poem, that "love needs reinventing.")[17] It is not that this fictive couple replicates Godard and Miéville's partnership. Rather, Paul and Denise's unsettled disagreements point up the problem of love in a reflexive sense that comparatively refers to Godard-Miéville's work and life together, allowing it to hover around the edges of the fiction.

That Godard and Miéville's essayistic research from their earlier engagements continues into *Every Man for Himself* is most apparent in the altered motion scenes that punctuate the film. On fifteen occasions, shots abruptly change tempo and movements take on a staggered look and rhythm—an effect achieved through step-printing, which closely resembles the video analyses in *France/tour/détour*. In *Every Man for Himself*, this similar technique, as Robert Stam writes, often inspects "relations between the sexes. Godard probes the formulaic nature of conventional movie slaps, kisses, embraces," showing how these "usually stereotyped actions" in fact contain "a vast multiplicity" of nuances.[18] In this respect, Godard deploys the device to mine and comment on emotional ambiguities that remain after Paul and Denise

Refiguring the Couple

decide to separate. In one such scene, slowed and fitful motion happens as Paul leaps across a kitchen table and wrestles Denise to the floor. While his outburst is without question a violent act of aggression, there are steps in which their "embrace" evokes love more than hostility. Once they reach the floor and continue to flail about, what we see is more indicative of lovemaking. The electronic musical score that coincides with this event is replayed from an earlier scene at a train station where a woman is slapped (also in step-printed motion) because she refuses to choose between two men. This link keeps hints of affection in check. And yet, the kitchen scene complements another slowed instance from earlier in the film where Denise and Paul lovingly embrace outside their workplace, this time with much calmer, more ethereal musical scoring.

France/tour/détour uses altered motion in order to scrutinize figures either in isolation (the two children) or en masse (the rush hour crowds), but here, the study of physical gestures takes up a couple who have reached the end of their companionship.[19] We find, as in several of Godard's earlier films, not least *Contempt*, a charged spatial interval between characters who feel their love fading. Launching Godard's late stage, *Every Man for Himself* reintroduces the question of love, or more specifically *lasting* love. A resentful conversation between Paul and Denise, filmed as a long-held two-shot at a café bar in Nyon, clues us in to the reasons for their breakup and indicates how love is under threat in the world they inhabit.

> PAUL: Buying a bike and going to the mountains won't change your life.
>
> DENISE: It's none of your business now.
>
> PAUL: Yes, but I have eyes, and I see what's what.
>
> DENISE: You always wanted love to come from work . . . something we could do together, not just at night. Our nights should grow out of our days, you said. Not vice versa.
>
> PAUL: It's not me. That's how people live. We both agreed love couldn't survive without a little bit of work. Otherwise it's just bursts of passion—nothing that lasts.
>
> DENISE: It's too hard when it lasts. I want to stop defining things and just do them. Call that what you will.

This all-important need to synthesize love and work, to practice a shared activity "not just at night," reverberates throughout much of Godard's late work as it intersects with Miéville's. In *Every Man for Himself* the very prospect of achieving and continuing a romantic relationship is in dire peril, the film suggests, due to capitalism's rigid division between work time and leisure time, which sections off love from labor and superficially relegates the

122   Chapter 3

former to a "nighttime" activity, sexual intimacy alone. Without an integration of love and work, the film's characters are left with "bursts of passion" lacking duration (and what counts as "passion" is up for debate in many lines of dialogue in the film). It is nothing new for Godard to portray sexual relations as corrupted by the logic of capital, but this perennial theme has its most degrading rehearsal in the third part of *Every Man for Himself*, titled "Commerce," in which a businessman dictates an elaborate orgy with two female prostitutes and one of his employees, impassively organizing the event according to a sequence of sounds and gestures. The film's placement of a floral bouquet in the pictorial space between the businessman and Isabelle (Isabelle Huppert) underlines the blockage of any emotional connection between these characters.

The film poses the problem of the utter debasement of what might be termed—again after Flusser—"the gesture of loving" in late twentieth-century life under capitalism.[20] How to reinvent a genuine, mutually beneficial sense of love in the face of its clichéd, abusive manifestations? And how might one combine love with work so that they become coextensive? What gestures perhaps already attest to this possible synthesis, and how might we nourish them to our advantage? How might cinema, or for that matter video, awaken its viewers to these possibilities and make them graspable? In his subsequent projects, Godard revisits these questions in a variety of ways. They often fuel his essayistic thinking during "the Miéville years" of his career, and, as we will see, they eventually lead him to reference their creative partnership as an extension of this evolving concern with love and its perilousness.

En ce temps-là

Godard's solo-directed feature films *Passion* (1982), *Prénom Carmen* (1983), *Keep Your Right Up* (1987), and *Nouvelle vague* (1990) all explore the interwoven themes of love, dialogue, coupling, and gesture in sophisticated ways at the levels of both form and subject. Any of these films could lend support to our present inquiry, in particular *Nouvelle vague*, whose nearly obsessive reiteration of the central couple's hands clasping against a blue sky and verdant backdrop figures as one of the most distinctive pictorial signatures of Godard's late period.

But a still more relevant narrative film to the arc of essayism I am tracing is Godard's *Hail Mary*, which in 1985 featured as the second part of a diptych with Miéville's shorter film, *The Book of Mary*. Although Godard and Miéville directed these films individually without their conjunction in mind, *The Book of Mary* and *Hail Mary* display a number of thematic and formal parallels (albeit with distinct aesthetic sensibilities), and Godard insisted that they be shown in immediate succession as a double bill. Indeed, the transition from her film to his is fluid: a black screen (a device already extant

Refiguring the Couple

123

in *The Book of Mary*) soon becomes an intertitle that both initiates *Hail Mary* and recurs throughout: "En ce temps-là" ("at that time," or "in those days"). This intertitle, in part, continually alludes back to Miéville's film and serves to reaffirm a close bond between the two parts of the diptych. Granted, Godard's film right away makes use of more captivating imagery and sounds, with squawking crows from offscreen that declare his film's beginning. But "at that time," notwithstanding its biblical and fable-like mood, is a kind of variation on "ici et ailleurs" ("here and elsewhere"). It implies that the films share temporal and conceptual if not diegetic boundaries.

Hail Mary is a modern-day, set-in-Geneva rendering of the Annunciation and Immaculate Conception. Jerry White argues persuasively that *The Book of Mary*, while less overtly a version of the religious tale, shares with Godard's film the project of bringing the Marian narrative down to earth through a serene, unornamented approach that is both Protestant and specifically Swiss in its fixation on the quotidian.[21] The "Marie" in Miéville's film isn't the virgin mother but a clever, Baudelaire-reciting eleven-year-old girl (Rebecca Hampton) who copes with the bitter separation of her parents, the reasons for which are not spelled out beyond her mother's built-up resentment over the routinized domestic role in which she has been cast as her husband freely comes and goes in accordance with his job.

By way of a shrewdly chosen citation, Miéville's treatment of this circumstance brings into play Godard's earlier output. In a poignant scene, Marie sits on the living room floor and watches Godard's *Contempt* on television, as her mother, shown in the background, repairs the cord to a lamp (a subtle nod to the significance of lamps in Godard's scenes with couples across his work) and as the father walks back and forth gathering his belongings before he moves out of the house. We can see the television monitor at the bottom-left corner of the frame. Marie is viewing the lengthy apartment scene from Godard's film—the moment where Paul slaps Camille after she insults him. We hear this clip before seeing it: Paul's voice accompanies a shot of Marie's mother as if his question, "Why don't you want us to go to Capri?" is directed at her. Stronger than just a reference, this cited scene from *Contempt*, with its articulate depiction of a disintegrating married couple no longer able to communicate, is woven tightly into the fabric of Miéville's fictive world and made to describe its elemental conflicts. Marie shifts her gaze from the television to the domestic situation around her, the citation reinforcing her position as a spectator interpreting an opaque disagreement. The citation also imports a spirit of melancholy through *Contempt*'s musical score, which builds and fuses with the diegesis as grippingly as do the Chopin and Mahler compositions elsewhere in Miéville's film.

On a first impression, it may seem that little in *The Book of Mary* continues from Godard and Miéville's earlier undertakings together, apart from a stress on everyday life in the domestic sphere, which now provides the only setting for the film's events. But in fact the film highlights performance gestures with subtle emphasis, observing them with a certain reserved curiosity as Marie adjusts to her altered family dynamic. A nimbly expressed gestural contrast distinguishes her time spent with each parent after their breakup. She exchanges gentler caresses of affection with her mother, and, with her father, more angular gestures that trope on sexual difference in a manner that escapes her (the archetypal blade and chalice symbols her father demonstrates with his hands, as if they relate to her geometry homework and the definition of an intersection). At home by herself in a climactic scene, she dances with abandon to the mournful adagio movement of Mahler's Ninth Symphony. As Ellen Draper puts it, Marie "transforms the living room space that was the scene of the initial quarrel into a performance space. The shot of the lake that first registered the different views of her mother and father becomes the backdrop . . . with the doorway serving as an ad hoc proscenium."[22] This dance is a cathartic release for Mary, but her feelings and thoughts remain ambiguous. In each of these scenes, performance gestures take on an air of mystery exceeding their psychological legibility.

White finds that one crucial link connecting Miéville's film to Godard's in their Marian diptych is a joint commitment to showing, or rather to *suggesting*, that the divine and the earthly, the metaphysical and the physical, are enmeshed. He rightly attributes to both films a realist yet modernist style, with different inflections in each case, that evokes, in the midst of the everyday, spiritual forces that cannot be directly or fully represented, this forming part of the Bressonian legacy that marks both films.[23] Gestures have a vital place in this approach for both Godard and Miéville, who appear invested in theological concepts insofar as they amplify the perceptual and ethical concerns of their secular enterprises. They rework religious dogma, redirecting the belief and wonder it elicits onto daily, immanent relationships and gestures that are no less enigmatic. (Godard says as much in his 1983 video essay *Small Notes Regarding the Film "Hail Mary"* through the aphoristic instructions he offers Myriem Roussel, the young woman who will play his Marie. While she irons a dress, rehearsing a scene in what looks to be Godard's own home in Rolle with Miéville, he asks her to contemplate the degree to which her everyday gestures evoke a potentially transformative play of spirit.)

Hail Mary indeed rethinks the tale of Mary, Joseph, and the birth of Christ primarily for the purpose of bringing its spiritual components into inseparable convergence with the physical, the carnal, the material, and the earthly. "At that time," we might say, Godard's Marian project responds to *The Book of Mary*'s drama of embittered separation with one of Mary and Joseph's miraculous reconciliation, which is achieved, in the film's most pivotal scene, through a mutual redefinition of the gesture of loving, a scene I will turn to shortly.

Hail Mary alternates between two couples: Marie and Joseph as they struggle to endure the exceptional situation into which they are thrust; and

Refiguring the Couple

an adulterous affair between a Czech science professor, exiled for his unconventional ideas about intelligent design, and a female student, Eva. *Hail Mary* links and contrasts these two narrative strands and their couples through a reflection on concepts of origins, creation, and the body and soul. "At that time," the film also digresses sporadically to evoke, through beautiful natural landscapes, the miracle of the virgin conception. Far from being a single, contained, and distinct happening, this event is widely dispersed across sounds and sights of the natural world, gestures of daily living and work (Joseph is a taxi driver, Marie a gas pump attendant). This event is manifested, if at all, as a mysterious commingling of atmospheric forces and events: sunlight on rippling water, gusts of wind in the grass, spates of birdsong, mutters of thunder, flare-ups and fade-outs of both secular and sacred music, seasonal shifts into winter and spring, an airliner soaring over bare tree limbs and power lines, a relay of spheres linking Marie's stomach and organic rhythms to the sun and moon. However much the film alludes to a divine presence, which Marie identifies—"The hand of God is upon me, and you can't interfere," she instructs Joseph—it inscribes the miracle firmly within the mundane details of this couple's difficulties.[24]

The film's main focus falls not on the miracle of Christ's birth and subsequent deeds, but instead on the gradual, awkward, trial-and-error steps toward restoring love between Joseph and Marie, a fragile achievement that *Hail Mary* deems equally miraculous. Everything builds toward the scene where Joseph, alone with Marie in her bedroom, must overcome his incapacitating doubt and distrust (he has suspected she has been unfaithful) as well as his sexual frustration, in order to learn how to declare *and* how to demonstrate, through a gesture of proper intensity and direction, "I love you." Sitting on the bed in front of Marie, who is stripped from the waist down, wearing just a tank top, Joseph at first touches her too assertively, too possessively, and this provokes the sudden appearance of the angel Gabriel, who fiercely throws Joseph to the ground. Trying again, now with Marie's verbal guidance ("No . . . No . . . No . . . *Oui*"), Joseph begins to gesture properly, which is to say *receptively*, by withdrawing his hand from her bare stomach, rather than applying it. He learns in this moment, despite his earlier retort that "miracles don't exist," to acknowledge the mystery of her condition, to live with it and engage her body without sexual intent foremost in mind. "Je t'aime," he says, redoing the gesture successfully. "Oui," Marie affirms, as an aural montage of a Dvořák cello concerto and a Bach toccata celebrates their reunion. The film also cuts to a sky with deep blue clouds, then to fields of wind-rustled flowers, so as to remind us that this miracle is an event at once interpersonal and cosmic.[25]

Godard arranges the scene in such a manner as to grant the spectator sudden visual access to the space where the gesture is discovered. At first the camera, placed low, takes what looks to be an inopportune angle, from a medium distance. A straight-backed chair in the foreground interferes with the

126   Chapter 3

camera's, *and with our*, vantage of Joseph's actions; the chair also impedes the pictorial space between characters, who are shown in a profile two-shot. But then, prompted by Joseph's upward glance at Marie's face, the film cuts to a striking close-up (but notably not a point-of-view shot) of her side-lit stomach, as his hand tentatively enters and exits the frame. This shot change gives *us* an intimate and unimpeded look at the gesture making contact (figs. 3.2 and 3.3). His tactile and verbal discovery in the scene has as its correlate this closer, "clearer" angle, which is shared by the camera and spectator; it is as if the film wants the exhilaration of this moment of interconnection to be ours, too.[26]

Significant here is the fact that in this collaborative situation, it is Joseph, the male, who must learn, through the guidance of a more enlightened female character. One can understand this scene as a critical restyling of the interlude in *Alphaville* (noted earlier) in which the central couple enter into a lyrical trance that teaches Natacha to begin to grasp what the banned word "love" means. In *Hail Mary*, the body language of gesture once again rivals speech and carries a transformative function, but in a reversal of Caution guiding Natacha, it is Marie—who already embodies acceptance in the face of mystery—who directs Joseph's actions until the two of them realize a condition whereby they share this acceptance.

What does persist from *Alphaville*, and from much of Godard's earlier output, is a certain profound suspicion, even denigration, of erotic love. *Eros*, to paraphrase Antonioni, tends to be sick in Godard's oeuvre, doing more to hinder than to conduce meaningful, mutually favorable interaction. Joseph learns in the bedroom scene that saying and meaning "I love you" entails not just the acceptance of mystery but also rigorous suspension of the possessive drives of his egoistic individualism, which love ought to keep in check. This suspension is what the gesture he learns enacts. Repeatedly in late Godard, amatory couples either go through a version of this dual realization or wither beyond recovery.[27] His work shows that in order to be and remain lovers, *eros* must cede priority to a kind of love for which friendship, what the ancient Greeks called *philia*, is a more suitable term (more on this below).

Not unlike *Every Man for Himself*, Godard's Marian diptych with Miéville also explores the question of love's endurance, its sustainability. In *Hail Mary*, this becomes evident very soon after the two-pronged miracle of the couple's restoration and the virgin birth. At the film's end, Joseph's offscreen voice invokes the final words of Robert Bresson's *Pickpocket* (1959): "Oh Marie, what a strange road I had to take to reach you." Godard's invocation of Bresson's film and its ambiguous ending is richly significant. Despite the embrace between Michel and Jeanne on either side of prison bars in the film's uplifting finale, the causes and effects that bear on the protagonist's "strange path" remain far from apparent. We cannot pin down what has led Michel to this point of union with Jeanne, nor does the film give a sense of the couple's future. As Susan Sontag remarks, "we do not see love lived. The moment in which it is declared terminates the film."[28] In Godard's film, the Bressonian

Figures 3.2–3.3. Marie teaches Joseph the gesture of loving: *Hail Mary* (Godard, 1985).

128   Chapter 3

line, while freighted with associations of grace and conversion, is immediately followed by Marie's offscreen voice, asking, "Now what's wrong?" This question calls attention to the *aftermath* of transformation. She and Joseph have become reunited by a strange path; Christ has entered the world. But where to go from here? The final scenes of the film mark the couple's return to convention, in all its ordinariness, as their brash child, "Junior," now twelve years old, leaves home to tend to his heavenly father's business. This denouement, which doesn't quite settle the film's conflicts, underlines the practical travails of what Bresson's film leaves unstaged: "love lived."

A Song of Two Humans

The questions raised around love and coupling throughout the Miéville years of Godard's oeuvre build circuits of reflection that run between his narrative films and his video experiments of the same stage. Godard's essayistic thought, in spanning these different production modes and intertwining with Miéville's thought, reconfigures love not as a mere theme so much as a core self-reflexive dynamic through which his process of investigation opens onto the company and input of an intimate other. The critical conjunction of love and work, the problem of love's endurance, the emphasis on friendly love above the erotic, the place of gesture in the constitution or furtherance of dialogue: these key questions and motifs find, if not solutions, then at least cogent provisional responses in the co-directed videos of Godard and Miéville during the 1980s and 1990s, two cases of which warrant attention here.

Produced for Britain's Channel Four Television in the same year as their adjoining Mary films, *Soft and Hard* (1985) stars Godard and Miéville as "themselves," a duo engaged in daily activities in and outside of their modest residence in Rolle. If they appear physically in some of their earlier projects (she more sparingly than he), *Soft and Hard* offers their first conspicuous double self-portrait. The video begins with their overlapping and competing voiceovers, which accompany titles on a black screen and the opening of the slow, hymn-like third movement of Beethoven's fifteenth string quartet. Their words speak to the historical juncture of the video's making and frame their lives against a global set of current affairs: technological advances, goings-on in professional tennis, economic changes, sustained military conflicts with civilian casualties. Implicitly regarding the "triumph of private television" as a culprit, they paint a dire situation for reflective intelligence, in an age when it appears the days of cinema are numbered ("the time of the last picture show"). "More than ever it was a time when all the water in the sea could not wash away the stain of intellectual blood."

The simultaneity of their voiceovers almost disguises the fact that Miéville, who begins to speak after Godard, repeats the same words but gives them a softer, subtly different reading. Like chamber instruments, their two voices

Refiguring the Couple 129

incline toward harmony but relish their separateness. They say they are "still looking for the path to our language," but lately have been "talking less and more slowly." Meanwhile, the text onscreen reports the more complete title of their video: "Soft Talk on a Hard Subject between Two Friends." Even before an image appears they have raised the central problem of finding a productive way to share language, and therein bring their views and practices into alignment.

The early, episodic scenes of *Soft and Hard* portray these "two friends" through a focus on the quotidian, domestic, and gestural, continued from their earlier ventures. They carry out their chores individually, make business-related calls (Godard), work at a writing desk or flatbed editing bench (Miéville), arrange a bouquet of flowers (Miéville), and record ideas and perhaps "dreams" in a notebook while on the fringes of sleep (Godard). They also recite passages from anterior sources (e.g., Godard's reading from Hermann Broch's *The Death of Virgil* [1945]) without signaling these quotes as such; and thus several of their utterances make obscure the distinction between original and appropriated speech. At one point, Miéville stands ironing a skirt as Godard enters the room with a tennis racket. He then practices his backhand, jumping into the air. This is the first scene in which they both inhabit the same shot; and their gestures are caught and studied with video freeze-frames, as he states in voiceover:

> In dreams different directors have a hand. One mixes action and vision, the other contrasts them. To the first, the self and things are identical. To the other, they're just objects. One sprays the eye onto the phenomenon. The other captures the phenomenon. One looks with his eyes shut, the other with his eyes open. On the one hand, a monologue on the inner stage. On the other hand, a dialogue.

This cryptic distinction between types of filmmakers serves to define the approach taken in *Soft and Hard* as one that sets vision in contrast to action, staging a dialogue in which they study with "eyes open" the phenomena they capture. Miéville's voice now takes over as the shot dissolves to a still from *Gone with the Wind* (Fleming, 1939), Scarlett and Rhett entwined in a dramatic kiss. "The northern dreams are paler and all the more violent because they make the images explode," she says. "When it comes to the image, half a turn in the south is more significant than a movement in the north." How, we are left to wonder, does Miéville's comment follow from Godard's? What is this business about northern and southern dreams? What are these motifs of coupling and dialogue working to achieve? I take it that the videographic pauses are in concert with the sort of vision that Godard's remark delineates. They seem to be in search of a relationship between these two figures, instead of representing one already found—that is, we are made to sense the potential of interconnection without seeing it realized. As for Miéville, her response

130   Chapter 3

modulates Godard's words on two types of directors by drawing a contrast between northern and southern dreams. A gentle half-turn in the south carries much greater significance than the "explosive" movements in the north. We can thus perhaps read the "south," in this vaguely territorial formulation, as a counterpart to the inquiring, perceptive regard that Godard approvingly identifies in the preceding passage (and the north as the action-based Hollywood "dream," represented by *Gone with the Wind* and its classically perfect kiss). But it is rather far from evident why "north" and "south," and why a contradictory reference to the U.S. Civil War, are necessary terms for this point.

This early segment is worth noting precisely because of its ambiguities, its poetic twists of association that border on being abstruse. The couple, as authors and actors, are acclimating the spectator to the expressive manner of their search for a shared language, which comes with a refusal of forthright and easily digested meaning.

The next scene reverses the camera angle in the same room and focuses on Godard as he does a comic pantomime of a tennis player serving (*in the direction of the viewer*) and taking a rest between games. Miéville enters the shot in a different floral dress and, smiling, shakes his hand as if she were an opponent meeting him at the net. This is how *Soft and Hard* sets up their friendly partnership, which will be one of contention as much as accord. The tennis conceit is more than a reference to Godard's personal fondness for the sport. Several of his films invoke the bi-directional interaction of a tennis match as a trope of dialogue.[29] Montaigne, we might add, refers to the sport in a similar way as a metaphor for linguistic exchange and the essayist's interplay with the reader on the other side of the net: "Words belong half to the speaker, half to the hearer. The latter must prepare himself to receive them according to such motion as they acquire, just as among those who play royal-tennis the one who receives the ball steps backwards or prepares himself, depending on the movements of the server or the form of his stroke" (III.13: 1235).

These early moments in *Soft and Hard* lead to an extended conversation scene between Godard and Miéville in their living room—the main event of their video, which begins in medias res. How they situate themselves may seem simple, but there is much to notice. Their dialogue is shot from one camera setup, as if to present one side of a shot/countershot interchange, but without ever cutting to a countershot.[30] They sit on separate couches whose edges almost touch to make a right angle, Miéville on the left, Godard on the right. The camera is static and placed behind Godard's head and shoulders; we can't see his face but have a relatively straight-on view of Miéville. A white lamp, its shade glowing with a pale orange light, dominates the leftmost portion of the frame and graphically takes up as much room as their two conversing figures. This desk lamp isn't needed to light the scene—the light pouring in through the windows is ample—but it boldly marks a field of interaction. This setup visually suggests that the space between them is just

Refiguring the Couple

as significant as the words passing back and forth across it. And if the lamp also divides the couple, the framing discourages us from reading the object as somehow obstructing their communication (a cliché of melodramatic *mise en scène* that, as we saw in chapter 1, Godard tinkers with in *Contempt*; as we saw above, he does something similar with the chair in the two-shot of love's gestural discovery in *Hail Mary*).

Their self-positioning within the frame denotes a shift in relation to Godard and Miéville's previous dialogical setups, in particular those in which Godard physically appears. In *Six fois deux*, he faces the camera head-on in interview segments as his interlocutor remains offscreen.[31] In *France/tour/détour*, we hear him ask questions, but he does not occupy the frame in body. In *Soft and Hard*, with his back to the camera—a position he repeats with variations in subsequent video dialogues conducted with Woody Allen (*Meetin' WA*, 1986), Michel Piccoli (*2 x 50 Years of French Cinema*, 1995), and Serge Daney (episodes 2A and 3B of *Histoire(s) du cinéma*)[32]—he shares the frame, and his address to Miéville is considerably more open and receptive. He thus assumes a position more conducive to reciprocal exchange, with the stress falling on neither him nor Miéville so much as their interspatial field.

Their setup also reasserts their critique of television. In graphic terms, their arrangement with respect to one another and the camera is designed to counterpose the position and mode of address embodied by a TV news anchor shown in clips that fleetingly disturb their conversation. As a comparison of these shots (figs. 3.4 and 3.5) reveals, the clearing or physical interspace between Godard and Miéville takes up the same area of the frame as does the newscaster's frontal figure. Whereas the newscaster, edged to the left to make room for a keyed-in picture window, has his back to the image while delivering his monologue, Godard is edged to the right with his back to the camera, making room for a balanced exchange and facing images that arise between himself and his partner. Periodically during their conversation, through the use of video cross-fades and superimpositions, images materialize in their intercorporeal field and are tightly framed by their heads, their gestures, and the lampshade (a tactic Godard reuses in the self-inscriptive library scenes of *Histoire(s)*). For instance, as Miéville relates how as a child she projected images on her bedroom wall by putting a light inside a shoebox and sliding negatives of family photos through an aperture (one thinks here of Proust's magic lantern scenes), a stilled shot of Marie taking a bath in *The Book of Mary* fades in as a superimposition. Miéville's hand gestures while she talks to Godard uncannily enfold the young girl's head, which, in the original shot, is already being caressed by her mother's hand (fig. 3.6).[33]

Soft and Hard, in this way, evokes and reconfigures the use of the lampshade in the tense apartment scene in *Contempt*, but here, the spatial interval between the couple, instead of being studied with a mobile shot that ferries between lovers who fail to communicate, becomes the site for composite linkages that convey quite the opposite. If the layering resonantly includes the

Figures 3.4 and 3.5. The two directors in conversation, versus the format of television news: *Soft and Hard* (Godard, Miéville, 1985).

Figure 3.6. A stilled shot from Miéville's *The Book of Mary* (1985) materializes: *Soft and Hard*.

co-directors themselves, this is to suggest that these ephemeral images spring from and spirit along their friendly, generative dialogue; texturally, they register onscreen as mental images speaking to the momentary entwinement of their subjectivities.

In this central discussion scene, however, Godard and Miéville rarely reach an agreement because of differences in their creative sensibilities. Almost reprising her role in *Ici et ailleurs*, Miéville assumes a critical stance toward Godard's work, in particular his treatment of couples. Speaking mainly of *Détective* (1985), she argues that while he excels at presenting a complex modern world with which characters cannot find peace, something is missing in his quieter scenes of intimacy with couples. She says he should "go further" in those scenes, instead of relying on what comes easiest to him and recycling formal constructions from one film to the next. Godard responds to her criticism by saying that he has *to see things first* and that scripting dialogue isn't his strong suit, whereas he believes it comes to her more easily.

Godard's comments elevate the visual over the verbal aspects of his practice, while Miéville, who professes greater humility about her own work in film, gravitates more closely to the expressive resources of the word. Godard says he values in the cinematic image precisely what she finds limiting—its "inaccessibility," its lack of concreteness. He defines himself as a "father" of

134   Chapter 3

images instead of children, and goes so far as to boast that he could make a
film equipped with merely a pencil and a box of matches. For her part, she
casts doubt on the image's ability, whether filmic or televisual, to provide any
sort of truth. She implies that his image-focused approach would do well
to explore more delicately the possibilities she locates in the "voice."[34] She
admits that she finds it difficult herself to preserve in audiovisual production
the soft and fragile "sliver of a voice," which the image can "endanger."

What keeps the two aligned is their animosity toward television, which
Godard, as he does throughout his late stage, describes as an oppressive
empire in its reign over the public (the keyed-in graphic shown in back of the
TV news anchor reads "Catastrophe"). Their discussion comes to an abrupt
end as Godard extols the capacity of cinema to enlarge and *project* the "'I'
toward others, toward the world." Television, he maintains, inherently lacks
this element of projection; it rather reduces and subjugates its spectators.
"You become its subject, like the subject of a king," he says. With this critique, *Soft and Hard* transitions into a more formalized finale. In a long take,
the camera slowly zooms in on a television on the floor of their home, its
screen changing channels through ads and various sorts of programs. After
its screen (now, almost flush with the video frame) goes black, it shows the
famous opening of *Contempt*, the shot of Raoul Coutard and his camera
crew dollying alongside a young woman as she reads a script on the vacated
studio grounds of Cinecittà. The video camera moves up and away from the
television screen, panning over to a blank white wall, which is soon lit up
by a projector beam. There, we see the same scene from *Contempt* projected
on film. Miéville and Godard extend one arm apiece into the video frame,
from the left edge, creating gray shadows that superimpose onto Godard's
earlier film. "Where has it gone, these projects to grow, to be enlarged into
subjects? *Where has it gone?*" he asks. She responds, "It is hard to say." He
then responds in turn, as if processing her words aloud: "Hard to say." Now
a musical fragment from the third movement of Beethoven's sixteenth string
quartet, which has been building up gradually in this parting scene, crescen-
dos, and the projection of *Contempt* vanishes, just as Coutard's camera in
Contempt turns to face the viewer.

The resonance of this ending defines Godard's relationship with Miéville
in a number of ways that not only bring *Soft and Hard* to a touching chord
of reconciliation, but also underscore their joint characterization as essayists.
First of all, this finale elegantly reopens and readapts the dramatic themes of
Contempt through this crafty citation. It isn't just that Godard and Miéville
figure as a new kind of modern couple wrestling with problems of language,
love, and alienation. What also resurfaces from the 1963 project is an anxiety regarding cinema's fate. "Where has it gone?" intertextually reasserts the
melancholy that *Contempt* raises around this question. In Godard-Miéville's
intermedial juxtaposition of television, video, and film, it is significant that
only video remains at the end. Video is not cinema, but it serves in their

Refiguring the Couple

hands as an instrument that allows for a dissection and diagnosis of cinema's possibilities. As with many of Godard's open endings, the mood here is both sad and hopeful: it bemoans cinema's defeat by television but also gestures toward possible renewal.

This equivocal mood has as its figurative embodiment the "lover's embrace" that the two filmmakers perform together. Their overlapping gestures nearly evoke (intentionally or not) the tableaux of caressing lovers in *A Married Woman*. Their pose also recalls the nocturnal interim in *Alphaville* articulating "the human form as a lover's dialogue." Godard-Miéville's physical gestures mediate between the light source and its destination: the projector beam hits the wall at an angle as their silhouettes converge and constitute a new form, a spectral ensemble that emanates from their solid bodies.

This *rapprochement* of their gesturing figures allows for a temporary solution to their disagreements. The phrase "hard to say" suggests a way forward. Throughout *Soft and Hard*, they have playfully allied the term "soft" with Miéville, femininity, and the word (written or voiced) and "hard" with Godard, masculinity, and the image. "Hard to say" declares uncertainty regarding cinema's future *and* effects a reconciliatory alignment of opposing terms: cinema's plight is hard to assess in words, but the *rapprochement* of the verbal and the visual, "soft" and "hard," her work and his, might offer a place to begin. And as part of this reconciliation, Godard acknowledges that his artistic sensibility is wanting where hers is strong.

The video thus ends by bearing out the sentiments compressed in its title. The scene entails one last jab at television. Several of the clips from TV shows and commercials that have disrupted their dialogue (vapid couples kissing, caressing, smiling) illustrate that expressions of love have, in the age of television's dominance, been reduced to a multitude of banalities. This "erotic" imagery issues from a defeated, *occupied* territory of representation. In Godard and Miéville's alternative form of coupling, "soft" and "hard" keep *eros* in play but sublimate its energies into the critical and creative labor on which their friendship is based.

This friendly conjugation of a woman and a man strikes an important chord of revision in the history of the essayistic. When Colin MacCabe considers Godard in relation to Montaigne, he notes a fundamental discrepancy:

> Montaigne, in order to carry out his own intellectual project, constructed at the centre of his castle a huge library—a physical refuge from the world, a place to which he could withdraw and think, a place which he named his "arrière-boutique," his back room. But this arrière-boutique was explicitly masculine. It was a place from which his wife and daughter were excluded—"ni femme ni fille." Over the past twenty-five years, Godard has constructed his own arrière boutique in the small Swiss village of Rolle, but he has constructed it with a woman, and it is unthinkable without her. It is Miéville who rescued

136   Chapter 3

him from the political and aesthetic dead-end in which he found himself in the early seventies. The strategic use of their company, and its investment in its own equipment, was crucial to that rescue.[35]

To be sure, *Soft and Hard* affirms Miéville's vital importance to Godard's late stage, but let us push further with and refine this comparison between essayists along the lines of friendship. I pointed out in the introduction to this study that the late-sixteenth-century author of the *Essais* conceives of friendship as a motive force of essayistic thought, a pivotal condition without which his work would be impossible. Not only does Montaigne view his project as a sustained dialogue with an ideal friend, Étienne de La Boétie, whose death has left him devastated. He also casts the reader—a "diligent" reader—in the role of a living, surrogate friend who will contribute by following his divagations, attending to things half-said or not said, and expanding the ideas the text abandons midstream. "O my friends, there is no friend!" Montaigne declares in a famous quotation of an apostrophe attributed to Aristotle (I.28: 214). It seems the "friends" invoked are at once present and absent for the essayist, there to be counted on and not. If this paradox reflects the difficulty Montaigne has in defining the exact character of his friendship with La Boétie, it also has to do with his address to the reader-friend of the *Essais*. The second part of the sentence doesn't fully undo the vocative aspect of the first. The capacity to call on *potential* friends is affirmed *in spite of* the uncertainty that looms over this relationship.

Godard and Miéville, as we have seen, also present friendship as a crux of their essaying, but they differ from Montaigne's example insofar as they place male and female figures on an equal footing. Montaigne's exclusion of women from his "back room" has its complement in his (initial) claim, following the ancients, that women in general are not suited to the demands of sustaining a productive friendship over time (I:28: 210).[36] At issue here, beyond a revision of this gender-based privilege, is the integration of difference into friendly love, and with it, the distance and conflict required for debate. Montaigne poetically describes his relation with La Boétie as an *indivisible* union: "In the friendship which I am talking about, souls are mingled and confounded in so universal a blending that they efface the seam which joins them together so that it cannot be found" (I.28: 211–12). He maintains that he and this perfect friend lost themselves in one another. The individual "will" of the one "plunged into" and became that of the other and vice versa: "we kept nothing back for ourselves: nothing was his, nothing was mine" (I.28: 212). As for Miéville and Godard, they intimately couple, and their bond is no doubt a check against egoism, but they do not constitute such a state of "universal" cohesion. They make allowance for the separateness of their ideas, their beings, their aesthetic approaches— even as shared epiphanies of their work bring them into momentary coalescences.[37]

Godard-Miéville's essayistic friendliness acts as a response to Godard's body of work. Their performance in *Soft and Hard* relates to Godard's films of the same decade by evincing a kind of partnership that satisfies the conjunction of love and work. Their friendly dialogue as co-authors embodies precisely the kind of shared activity, "not just at night," that the couple in *Every Man for Himself* lack. The tacit claim on offer is that filmmaking brings work and love together in uniquely valuable ways; but here one finds a key change within Godard's corpus. Part of the reason why *Soft and Hard* makes allusions to Godard's prior career stages is to remind us that his companionship with Miéville marks a different sort of collaboration. Godard fused love and work in his marriages with both Karina and Wiazemsky, but both of those relationships were predicated on a muse-like, unbalanced twoness between actress and auteur.[38] *Soft and Hard* asserts that with Miéville, Godard of necessity makes room for a more even and *reciprocal* dialogue with a prominent female voice—a fellow filmmaker with a strong say in all technical, creative, and philosophical matters.[39]

Earlier I claimed that Godard and Miéville's conception of love privileges *philia* above *eros*. We are now in position to see the aptness of this term *philia* and the stakes it carries vis-à-vis their particular elaboration of the essayistic. A deep-rooted term in the history of Western philosophy (its cognate, *philos*, of course resides in the very name "philosophy"), *philia* imprecisely translates as "amity" and "affection." Empodocles, among other pre-Socratic thinkers, construes the term in a cosmological fashion: *philia* is a force of attraction that creatively combines both like and unlike matter in a constantly shifting universe; it acts as the dualistic opposite of *neikos* ("strife"), a force of repulsion and fragmentation.[40] For Aristotle, *philia*, specifically the type of friendship founded on virtue rather than pleasure or utility, becomes an ethical humanistic paradigm upon which to construct the larger community of the polis. In the *Essais*, Montaigne takes from debates around *philia* in Greek and Roman antiquity while implicitly addressing the necessity of friendship in his contemporary context of civil war. In Montaigne, and later in Friedrich Nietzsche, who indirectly refers to Montaigne's chapter on friendship when he reworks Aristotle's contradictory invocation of absent friends, the prospect and function of the *potential* friend are transferred in part onto the textual relationship between the writer and future reader—a relationship suffused with daring and risk. In his account of *philia* as a wellspring of philosophical adventure reaching from Nietzsche to Gilles Deleuze, Gregory Flaxman shows that such *philia* between thinkers emboldens both parties to move and experiment well beyond the precincts of convention. "What is a friend, if not the one with whom we dare to think otherwise?"[41]

The connective, social, and adventurous aspects that *philia* has harbored for philosophers find eccentric expression in and through Godard-Miéville's essayistic cine-*philia*. With this term, I point to something more than the love *for* films that cinephilia is traditionally taken to define, and to something

138   Chapter 3

more than the French heritage of cinephilia that in many ways has stayed with Godard since his early years as a critic.[42] Godard and Miéville certainly express the sentiments of aggrieved loss and nostalgia that have been common to cinephiles of their generation in the face of a newer media climate ("*Where has it gone?*"). But what I have in mind is a sense of *philia* constituted and sustained by way of an abiding, lived belief in the mysterious capacity of cinema to bring people together, building social bonds through the material circumstances of production and reception. As Godard will maintain in a later interview, "There is no film without love, love of some kind. There can be novels without love, other works of art without love, but there can be no cinema without love."[43] Godard-Miéville, in their self-described "double solitude" in Rolle,[44] use thier loving friendship to reanimate, however faintly, this endangered power of cinema, in and for their essayistic video practice.

The structure of *philia*, it must be acknowledged, is selective in that it marks off a field of intimacy from a broader sphere. The expressive logic— esoteric and incomplete—of *Soft and Hard* is addressed to fellow thinkers who are to some extent already conversant with their work so far. Friendship, however, isn't just the privilege of insider status. Its pleasures and rewards are attained over time, through a generous commitment that entails—beyond familiarity—patience, work, trust, critique, forgiveness of mistakes, and risk, a willingness to have one's thoughts contested and pressed by those of the friend beyond the bounds of habit and convention. Time is of the essence, in friendship and in shared essayistic investigation alike. Both unfold as tryingly long-term affairs.[45]

Godard-Miéville are not alone among audiovisual essayists in their use of friendship in this rhetorical light. Marker and Varda exhibit analogous gestures of address.[46] One also thinks of Farocki's description of his style in *As You See* (1986) as effecting the tortuous, hypothesis-driven feel of a drunken discussion between friends.[47] In *Soft and Hard*, friendly love tacitly accords a share to the observer. Godard's mimed tennis serve into "our court" indicates that we have a role in the dialogue and the cine-*philia* it espouses. It is not for nothing that he will later, upon the release of *Histoire(s) du cinéma*, affectionately describe his and Miéville's audience as "100,000 friends around the world."[48]

Exercises in Artistic Thinking

I want to turn to one more Godard-Miéville collaboration where love, coupling, dialogue, and gesture intersect. *The Old Place* (1999), a co-directed video essay commissioned by the Museum of Modern Art in New York, resembles the look, feel, and citational texture of Godard's *Histoire(s)* and enlarges on that work's concerns, but it has met mostly with mixed reactions by critics. Colin MacCabe, who produced the video, is in the minority when

Refiguring the Couple

he claims for *The Old Place* a central position within Godard's late period, defining it as an elegiac "poem" that encapsulates the director's partnership with Miéville.[49] Jerry White writes, on the contrary, that *The Old Place* suffers from incoherence and a defeatist attitude that curb any note of lyricism or hopefulness the video expresses. Most damning is his claim that the production is only "superficially engaged with meaning or communication," which suggests that Godard and Miéville make at best a half-hearted attempt to execute their work and encourage the viewer's involvement.[50]

My reading of *The Old Place* is more favorable. A tremendous melancholy imbues the video, but it is not all-consuming and doesn't quite prevail in the end. MacCabe's take on *The Old Place* as a poem is instructive. Embracing the poetic element should not be seen as an apology for the abstractness or the unyielding obscurity of the video. Let us remember that Friedrich Schlegel (and Georg Lukács in his wake) conceived of the literary essay as an "intellectual poem," due to its mercurial synthesis of poetic and scientific thought.[51] *The Old Place* indeed merits such a description on account of its poignant play of ideas at the limits of mutual understanding. The poetic turns, associations, and ellipses in its argument are not signs of a fatigued enterprise. I want to demonstrate that they are rather part of a still-vibrant method that tries to spark our critical contribution through the use of puzzling, unfinished structures.

Subtitled "Small Notes Regarding the Arts / At Fall of 20th Century," *The Old Place* is an intellectual poem offering many things: a defense of figurative art over abstraction; a meditation on the ethical demands of art-making in relation to history; a lament for the demise of cinema as Godard-Miéville know it; a reflection on aging; a confrontation with the problem of the audience where both film and fine art are concerned; and a resumed, less tumultuous elaboration of the poetic sense of the image that animates the montage of *Histoire(s)*. More ambitious in scope than *Soft and Hard*, and more densely citational, *The Old Place* composes its ideas through fragments taken from the overlapping histories of cinema, painting, sculpture, literature, photography, and philosophy. Godard and Miéville, again through alternating voiceover passages, weave through heterogeneous materials, articulating a jointly authored dialogue. Their agile work together in the video effectively stands as a finale to the arc of essayism we have been tracing in this chapter.

The Old Place starts with an acknowledgment of its own essayistic status. The opening titles, over a black-and-white photograph of a young woman on a swing interlocking glances with a man below, define the project as a dually composed "film / essay." The photo's amorous scene invokes the couplehood of the filmmakers themselves. Additional titles then declare that their video will be organized into "twenty-three exercises / in artistic thinking." In actual fact, there will only be fourteen such segments, this being part of the video's incompleteness. This notion of "exercise" is of the utmost importance, suggesting as it does that what *The Old Place* presents to the viewer is a series of

140   Chapter 3

trials that have a preliminary function—exercises to be repeated in order to hone "artistic thinking" through practice.

Their conversation is much less casual than in the living room scene of *Soft and Hard*. They make only a single, fleeting appearance, which I will examine shortly, but the video still abounds with subtle indices of their authorship. Clips from their own films find their way into the montage—for instance, his *Germany Year 90 Nine Zero* (1991), her *We're All Still Here* (1997)—and there are many occasions, after the initial photograph, in which paintings and juxtapositions of shots that couple men and women allude to Godard and Miéville. The repeated intertitle "at that time" reemerges from their diptych of Mary films, taking on a novel purpose in the video's reflections into montage and history. Although the co-directors make us mindful of their creative partnership, they also, through vocal citations that are not clearly signaled as such, make it difficult for us to know for certain if they are, at any given instant, speaking in their own words or recycling the words of others.

A consistent premise links together the exercises, namely that during the twentieth century, modern art-making unforgivably turned away from its responsible engagement with the real—away from the century's many horrors and catastrophic injustices, and thus, away from the cry of human suffering. Godard and Miéville find fault with the artistic methods of Marcel Duchamp, Kazimir Malevich, Francis Picabia, Andy Warhol, and Pierre Soulages. They argue that painting committed "suicide" when it became too preoccupied with medium-specific mischief, conspired with advertising to the point of forgoing its ontological separation, and descended full tilt into abstraction. The directors are particularly troubled by art practices that expunge the human figure. Hence their critique of Christian Boltanski's installation methods of gathering and piling up used clothes so as to evoke the memory of the Holocaust. Miéville calls this "an artistic crime committed by a public figure." Her claim is that this exhibitory logic uncritically resembles that of an upscale clothing boutique; worse still, this means of expression, despite the artist's intention, does more to mimic the Third Reich's orderly elimination of bodies than it does to oppose it.

These criticisms move Godard and Miéville to describe their own artistic practice through vivid contrast. A number of their exercises, however abstruse they might be, orient the spectator to the turnings and remit of the aesthetic they have aspired to—an aesthetic that not only responds to historical atrocities and conflicts but also retains and carefully studies the human figure, out of what they now define as ethical consciousness. *The Old Place* puts forth this multifaceted approach through three related motifs:

1. *Charitable attention.* Scenes of cruelty and suffering drawn from wide-ranging historical situations populate the montage: civilian casualties of bloody wars, prisoners undergoing torture, ignored refugees, deprived children in "underdeveloped" parts of the world. Such imagery is less preponderant here than it is in other late video essays by Godard (such as *The*

Refiguring the Couple

Origins of the 21st Century [2000]), but it still gives the observer pause. White interprets these scenes as integrating an iconography of horror and "dehumanized violence" that undercuts the video's lyricism through its "sense of defeat."[52] This claim is not entirely wrong, but a more complicated project is afoot than White notes. If these scenes of suffering show the kind of historical events that Godard-Miéville take certain modern artists to task for ignoring, they also give the co-directors occasion to reflect back on the political and ethical trajectory of their own work together.

In back-to-back exercises titled "Photos of Utopia" and "A Prisoner in Love,"[53] the video recalls the revolutionary aims, struggles, and defeats of the radical Left in the wake of May 1968. We see shots of a multitude of French demonstrators marching peacefully through the streets of Paris with large, billowing red flags. This footage is taken from Chris Marker's *A Grin without a Cat* (1977, 1993) where it documents a funeral procession in honor of the Maoist activist Pierre Overney, who was murdered by a security guard while he was giving out leaflets at the gate of the Renault factory in Billancourt. Godard-Miéville next incorporate a slowed shot of a victim from Godard's short video essay *Je vous salue, Sarajevo* (1993), a mortally wounded man in the siege of Sarajevo whose extended arm and fist here evokes through association the raised-hand gesture of leftist resistance.[54] Another, overhead shot of the red flags from Marker's film appears and slowly dissolves, with a graphic match, into a field of red poppies painted by Monet. This gives rise to a curious passage in which Godard-Miéville reflect on newly filmed views of poppies gathered along the roadside in rural Switzerland. Their voiceovers and the politicized music they sample personify the flowers as living tributes to the fallen spirit of leftist revolution. Consigned to the edges of the landscape, these "last artists," as Miéville calls the poppies, "still organize a small demonstration, but only for love."

Obliquely self-implicating, this sequence adumbrates Godard's middle period of Maoist militancy, the eventual defeat of which is connected here to the death of the New Left that Overney's funeral betokens. At the same time, the poetic riff on red poppies—with its transition from the Paris streets to the Swiss countryside—refers in part to the shift he has undertaken with Miéville. The concept of "love," which once again figures crucially in relation to their *couplage*, describes not an about-face so much as an altered form of resistance in which the rhetoric of 1968 has given way to a humanist perspective granting ethics, or more particularly a concern for the other-in-need, an elevated role. A subsequent exercise, "Blind Love," comes back to this reflection on their output. Godard's voice, reciting a celebrated passage from Henry James's 1893 story "The Middle Years," remarks: "We work in the dark, we do what we can, we give what we have. Our doubt is our passion and our passion is our task. The rest is the madness of art." In James's story, a dying novelist speaks these lines to an ideal reader who is very nearly the double of himself. The novelist's words pass judgment on his own literary

142   Chapter 3

legacy and reaffirm with sadness that there is no "second chance" after the ink has dried. Godard, fond of end-of-life parables about artists, restyles this passage so that it becomes a comment on *his* life's work. It isn't quite a mea culpa for his commitment to Maoism, but the words suggest he was laboring "in the dark," prior to public disclosure in the West of the brutal reality of Mao's Cultural Revolution. At the same time, the lines from James's fiction describe Godard-Miéville's creative dialogue as fueled constructively and passionately by doubt. The exercise develops further with a cut to a shot of Auguste Rodin's bronze sculpture *The Thinker* (1904). We then cut to a scene inside a museum gallery where two visitors, their faces not shown, searchingly inspect the bodily contours of another Rodin statue. Godard-Miéville iris the frame, and, as a quiet piano-with-cello piece comes in on the soundtrack, Miéville's voice says: "This reminds me of my old philosophy teacher Mr. Brunschvicg. One is in the other, the other is in the one, and these are three persons."

I will come back to this aphorism, which Miéville credits to Léon Brunschvicg. For now, let me just remark that this scene further defines the co-directors' ethical vocation: it proposes a dynamic of interconnectedness that extends from their partnership to others drawn into the orbit of their art. It isn't friendship that underpins this sense of relation at this point, as was the case in *Soft and Hard*, but the less exclusive ethical principle of love for one's neighbor.

For Godard-Miéville, this principle raises a problem. Given their remote life in Rolle and their withdrawal from activism, how can they claim to have an ethically minded practice? Where in their work does an observance of this principle emerge? Their exercise "Destiny of Things" offers an answer. Reciting, with slight changes, Paul Valéry's reflective fragment "A Charitable Attention," Miéville says in voiceover:

> So many things you have not even *seen*, on this street you travel six
> times daily, in this room where you spend so many hours a day! Look
> at the angle the edge of the furniture makes with the windowpane.
> You have to reclaim it from banality, from the unseen visible. You
> have to *save* it. You give what you can, through imitation and the
> shortfalls of your sensibility, to any sublime landscape, sunset, storm
> at sea, or any artwork in a museum. Those are ready-made views.
> But give to this poor person, to this place, to this insipid moment and
> thing, and you will be awarded a hundredfold.

The montage illustrating this moving recitation consists of both details from religious paintings (isolated body features) and shots of what appear to be the furnishings of Godard and Miéville's home (wooden chair, lamp, table on which books are stacked, Persian rug, open window). This exercise also cites two stunning natural landscapes from Godard's earlier *JLG/JLG:*

Refiguring the Couple

Self-Portrait in December (1995), which examines his Swiss home and environment with equal acuteness.

Through this use of Valéry's reflection, *The Old Place* sketches out an ethics of attention to quotidian detail—one to be applied intensively to works of art, one's ordinary surroundings, *and* one's direct or mediated encounters with suffering and neglected others. What Valéry refers to as "charitable attention" is close to Simone Weil's principle of "creative attention," which selflessly directs its contemplative and constructive energies toward the afflicted other, in pursuit of justice and to restore human dignity where it has been deprived.[55] Miéville's handling of the passage heightens this affinity through her addition of "poor person" to Valéry's object-based reverie. The exercise advocates a mode of attentiveness that rescues places, phenomena, events, and human subjects from obscurity. The indication is that this creative, effectively loving gesture of attention brings into perception something that was absent beforehand, filling in where there was a dearth. The montage by Godard-Miéville that goes with the recitation illustrates a *combinatory* way of seeing. Notice how a resonance arises between a detail in the Persian rug and, in the next shot, folded hands extracted from a religious fresco. This shows that the task is to explore possible relations through the associative conjunction of different elements (once again, Godard's late work insists that no element encountered should be weighed in isolation from others). And the second-person address—the "you," retained from Valéry's text—suggests that this way of perceiving should guide the artist and spectator alike.

2. *The image as constellation.* This endorsement of montage is further informed by a curious astral motif running through *The Old Place*, from a reference to Van Gogh's *The Starry Night* (1889) through to kitschy cosmic drawings and a clip from *The Empire Strikes Back* (Irvin Kershner, 1980). This motif anticipates the directors' turn to Walter Benjamin's venerable notion of the image as a "constellation," which occurs in their "Logic of Images" exercise.[56] In one of the video essay's few instances of attribution, Godard mentions the German-Jewish philosopher by name and reads from the epistemological *Konvolut* of *The Arcades Project*, its account of the image as a phenomenon by which the past and present briefly interpenetrate in a lightning flash "to form a constellation."[57] Much has been written on Godard's affinities with Benjamin—their use of citations, reliance on montage as a device of historiographical recuperation, notions of catastrophe, appropriation of theological discourse, and so on.[58] Certainly the reiterative title in *The Old Place*, "at that time," takes on a Benjaminian tone, as a rough analogue to Benjamin's concept of "now-time," the short-lived and unpredictable moment—occasioned through the intervention of an artist, or revolutionary intellectual—when a historical image is "blasted" out of the continuum of chronological time and becomes readable within and for the present.[59] Having said all this, Godard-Miéville's turn to Benjamin in this instance is highly idiosyncratic, more than a surface borrowing but somewhat fast and loose.

"This image that you are, that I am, that Benjamin speaks of . . . ." Godard's remarks seem to indicate that he and Miéville aren't just spectators and orchestrators of images in this Benjaminian sense: they are themselves integral, existential components of the very makeup of such images. As Godard says this, we are shown a clip from Hitchcock's *To Catch a Thief* (1955), the famous kissing scene between Cary Grant and Grace Kelly, which is here decelerated videographically. Just as their lips converge, the video cuts to an explosion of fireworks in the night sky (this is an altered version of the original scene). These entwined lovers, these two "stars," are in this way made to figure forth the principle of montage as a constellation—its momentary spark where the past and present collide (figs. 3.7–3.9). Godard reuses this clip from episode 4A of *Histoire(s)*, where it embodies the Pierre Reverdy-inspired poetics of *rapprochement* that underwrites Godard's montage. Here in *The Old Place*, the repetition of this clip correlates the Reverdian and Benjaminian components of Godard-Miéville's videographic style.[60]

How does this cinematic citation relate to Godard's contention that he and his partner are *intrinsic to the montage*? To answer this question, we must engage another citation that occurs a few seconds later, another scene of "stars" combining in a riff on this concept of montage. Godard and Miéville sample the planetarium sky show from Nicholas Ray's *Rebel without a Cause* (also 1955). Re-editing the original, they intercut between James Dean and Natalie Wood, marking them as a couple of viewers gazing up at the visualization of the catastrophic end of the planet in a burst of fire and gas.[61] While these shots echo the explosive scene from Hitchcock's film, Godard-Miéville now stress spectatorship. This is all to express that a constellation entails not just a relationship among its luminous points; it also fundamentally involves *the very perceptual event of its observation*. After all, constellations in the sky are formed in and through our constructive perception of them. Their patterns do not exist independently in nature; they are, in large measure, the product of our earthbound gaze.

Godard-Miéville reflect on their own couplehood through these citations, describing themselves as viewers as much as artists, inquisitive beings who do not take in a constellation from the outside but are inscribed in the explosive flash they perceive. This reminds us that montage, in addition to constellating diverse elements, is a practice that can bring together its viewers. Godard-Miéville's partnership attests to and ardently cultivates this faculty, for themselves and for viewers whose interaction they invite. It is therefore fitting that right after the clip from *Rebel without a Cause*, they contemplate in greater detail their "approach" and its interpersonal stakes, doing so as they work from simple to more involved kinds of links. They begin with shot/countershot (in the form of a tennis match!) and then fan out toward larger, more complex historical relationships.

This definition of montage as a constellation names a crucial essayistic operation that puts assorted materials, histories, and people into contact

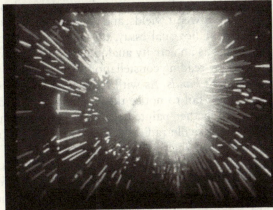

Figures 3.7–3.9. Hitchcock's lovers evoke the combustive spark of montage in the "Logic of Images" segment: *The Old Place* (Godard, Miéville, 1999).

146   Chapter 3

across vast intervals and that discloses to the perceiver coordinates of the sensible that commonplace modes of seeing obstruct. Godard-Miéville deploy this process and reflect on its capabilities simultaneously. In the overall context of *The Old Place*, they show how it carries out the mission of "charitable attention." And late in the video they pose this constellational montage as a possible remedy for a profound sense of disorientation in modern life at the turn of the century, a tragic condition of rootlessness that needs repair. "We are lost not only in the universe," Godard asserts, "but in the depths of our minds." Miéville responds, over a clip of Lillian Gish in a sandstorm in *The Wind* (Sjöström, 1928, the same clip used in 1B of *Histoire(s)*), that humankind used to have a "yardstick," or "an index finger in the wind," but "now we are lost even when we think we know where we are. Either there's no path home or we don't have a homeland worth returning to." We can surmise that montage is a navigational tool that grants a fallen humanity a way to reacquaint itself with the world, to regain and rethink its relational bearings. Such is the recuperative power it wields, and the redemptive function it bears. (In the context of the audiovisual essay, this exercise begs comparison to Kluge's idea of montage as an activity analogous to the way in which Odysseus charts his voyage by reading constellations.)[62]

3. *Thinking with one's hands*. As with *Histoire(s) du cinéma*, the viewer of *The Old Place* cannot fail to notice the emphasis accorded to hand gestures in the montage, whether painted, sculpted, photographed, or filmed. Indeed, if Godard and Miéville radically object to sheer abstraction in art, this is surely in part because the gesturing human body is vital to their work, figuring both as an object of analysis in its own right and as a basis of comparison that sparks flights of associative montage across different contexts and media. The "Logic of Images" sequence hinges on rhyming hand gestures: for instance, a photograph of Sharon Stone waving on the red carpet at the Cannes Film Festival leads to and rhymes with a photograph of smiling schoolchildren who are all enacting an eerily similar Nazi salute from a half century earlier.

In the same exercise, as soon as Miéville passionately details "the endless dialogue between imagination and work" on which her rapport with Godard is founded, an intertitle appears that refines their embrace of montage still further, a phrase that viewers familiar with Godard's late stage will recollect from elsewhere: "to think with one's hands." This notion perhaps most memorably factors into chapter 4A of *Histoire(s)*, prefacing and qualifying Godard's segment on Hitchcock's "control of the universe," which the British-American auteur achieved through his unsurpassed mastery of montage in a popular art, so contends Godard.[63] "To think with one's hands" ("Penser avec les mains") is the title of a 1936 essay by the Swiss writer/cultural theorist Denis de Rougement. In the chapter of *Histoire(s)* in question, an unseen male narrator quotes cobbled-together passages from the manifesto-like essay, which meditates with urgency on questions of individual

Refiguring the Couple

creative thought (as "manifested" through actions for which a thinking subject is answerable) and friendship, in response to brutal interferences of the state (de Rougement's main cause for alarm is the ascendance of National Socialism). During this recitation, shots of hands recur and highlight the work of joining and dividing. These shots also describe the act of montage as an ethical gesture in and of itself. That is to say, the gesture of montage figures reflexively in the episode as "a hand held out," an "act of love for one's neighbor," a creative thought extended into action. It harbors the power to transform, mending damage done to human relationships by abstract ideologies, as well as by "laws born of the abandonment of thought," but this power is itself violent and potentially dangerous, even to the person who uses it. This recitation of de Rougement's essay tempers the ensuing segment on Hitchcock's films by broaching questions of love, compassion, and artistic responsibility. A recurring photo of Hitchcock, with one hand raised, comes to signify not merely demiurgic creativity but public accountability for what is created, for the power the artist commands. In fact, one of the underlying points of the episode—and this is missed by readings that view it as a wholly approving, unambivalent tribute—is to show, through both documentary and fictional scenes of starvation, negligence, and violent cruelty, the stark disparity between de Rougement's urgent plea for compassion and the immense, "universal" connective potential that Hitchcock's montage taps. In *Histoire(s)*, Hitchcock is characterized in part as an artist whose work fails to sufficiently realize its ethical possibilities.[64]

The Old Place picks up this thread by again portraying montage as an act of "thinking with one's hands" and by applying the concept, even more self-consciously, to the gestures of Godard and Miéville. A cross-dissolve that links a photograph of a film editor to a photograph of another man sewing red communist flags makes the filmic tenor of this motif more explicit (and recognizes the centrality of montage to the history of left-wing revolutionary cinema). We also see a cross-dissolve between a photograph of Glenn Gould playing Bach's *Goldberg Variations* and a production still of Conrad Veidt inspecting his hands in Robert Wiene's *The Hands of Orlac* (1924), a German horror film whose plot follows a concert pianist who loses his hands in an accident, receives a surgical transplant (the hands of a man executed for committing murder), and worries that his new hands have dark designs of their own. The montage compares Gould's virtuosic absorption in the act of playing his instrument with the film's horrifying premise of losing control over one's own gestures, of one's deeds and thoughts being at radical variance.[65]

Here again *The Old Place* thematically oscillates from horror and catastrophe to scenes more suggestive of possibility, with the co-directors drawing creatively from the reservoir of theological discourse. "Thinking with one's hands" becomes, in the same digressive exercise, what titles describe as the "baptism of montage." The phrase appears over a gritty black-and-white

148   Chapter 3

photo of a double baptism being performed in a river. With a cross-dissolve, we then move to a baptism scene from Pier Paolo Pasolini's *The Gospel According to St. Matthew* (1964). The questions arise: how does this motif of baptism relate to the preceding reflections on historical constellations; and why do Godard and Miéville, as "non-believing" intellectuals, affiliate the most cherished device of their practice with so specific a religious custom?

As ever, pictorial details matter tremendously. It is clear enough that the baptism theme re-confers a gestural status onto montage. But Godard and Miéville are doing something more complex here than forging a simple parallel. The first still shot in question already expresses an *internal* enactment or figuration of montage, with the two immersed bodies standing in for discrete shots, and the body administering the ritual standing in for the montagist. The still supplies an *intra*-shot complement to what Miéville-Godard are in the midst of doing themselves with multiple images in their grasp. Subtly, the still from Pasolini's film reintroduces the question of the audience, through its public gathering of onlookers. In Christianity, baptism is a symbolic ordinance that indicates a liberation from sin and the fate of an unredeemed humanity; it is a public affirmation of faith initiating one into a body of believers founded on the mutual reception of the Holy Spirit. In Godard-Mieville's secular, essayistic appropriation of this custom, they endow montage not just with intimations of rebirth and liberation, but with an *initiatory* power to induct those who come into contact with its powers into a heightened form of perceiving the world and its historical relationships. And yet an intense melancholy, expressed by the Tomasz Stanko trumpet piece that goes with this part of the exercise, suggests that this promise of montage has been irrecoverably squandered. Details taken from Masaccio's 1423 fresco of Adam and Eve's expulsion from Eden—first a "two-shot" of the couple together, then a single of Adam covering his eyes in shame, then a single of Eve with her eyes shut and head thrown back in pain—trope on the original event that necessitates baptism in Christian doctrine. Godard-Miéville rework this scene, splitting it into fragments to impart visually a broken-up couple. They displace its aggrieved context onto what they view as the equally disastrous neglect and misuse of montage in the modern era.

In sum, through their intellectual poem in *The Old Place*, Godard-Miéville take stock of the themes and questions at the evolutionary basis of their work together. The historical constellations they explore reach allusively back through their own previous ventures together, following the end of Godard's Maoist phase. This perspective enables them to put forth, as a consequence of their twosome, an ethically and historically minded practice of montage that takes into account the ramifications of their own gestural deeds as artists. In this way, they characterize themselves as still-engaged artists "thinking with their hands" in an alternate manifestation of resistance. It remains for us to reckon more conclusively with how their dynamic as a couple brings the viewer into the workings of their process. This question is inevitable if we follow where the hand imagery in *The Old Place* directs us: its relays tumble into the sensuous realm of reception, through scenes such as the aforesaid shot of museum visitors caressing a Rodin statue in tandem, or a cropped detail from Georges de la Tour's *St. Sebastian Attended by St. Irene* (circa 1645), which directs attention to the torchlit hands of a female onlooker at the site of Irene's restorative act of charity.

In the co-directors' sole appearance in *The Old Place*, they portray themselves in the act of viewing. Through a superimposition, we see them seated behind a wheel-based film projector of sorts, their bodies in thick shadow except for one eye apiece (fig. 3.10). A cut to a shot from their point of view suggests they are watching a video projection, with its content (the curator/producer Dominique Païni talking enthusiastically about video installations finding a home in gallery space) reduced to vague eddies of blue, green, and red. In this segment on "technologies of the future," which continues motifs of loss and disorientation, Godard-Miéville reference the passing of cinema by placing themselves in the same side-by-side position as Ingmar Bergman's film-viewing couple in *Prison* (1949), a two-shot that, as we saw in the previous chapter, Godard cites in *Histoire(s)* and other late works in order to reflect on cinema's special capacity to bring its spectators into meaningful, contingent, and

Figure 3.10. Double self-portrait of Miéville and Godard: *The Old Place*.

150   Chapter 3

restorative convergence. The co-directors' allusion does not show confidence that this power will be preserved, let alone nourished, in the years ahead.[66]

Spectator involvement returns thematically to center stage in the video's last exercise, which, like many of Godard's endings, mingles mournful and inceptive moods. Miéville recites a story that concerns a mystical creature known as the "A Bao A Qu." This creature dwells inside a remote tower from which a traveler who reaches the top of a winding staircase can gaze out onto "the loveliest landscape in the world." According to the story, the A Bao A Qu lies in a dormant, all but invisible condition at the lowermost step. When a visitor enters and ascends the stairs, this creature follows close behind and gradually assumes a more conspicuous shape, with its tentacles now giving off a bluish glimmer. The creature achieves its fullest potential at the top of the stairs, becoming able to see with its whole body. But as soon as this visitor goes back down the staircase, the A Bao A Qu slinks back into nothingness. It is said that only a spiritually evolved person can reach the top and bring the creature to its most brilliant and complete existence, an event that has occurred just once in the course of centuries. When Miéville finishes relating this seemingly out-of-place legend, Godard cuts in to declare that they are ending with it because it "perfectly" illustrates the video's main theme.

The source from which this obscure parable is borrowed is Jorge Luis Borges's *The Book of Imaginary Beings* (1976). Co-written with Margarita Guerrero, the text is a playful encyclopedia of creatures imagined in literature and folklore from around the world. The A Bao A Qu, one of the most metaphysical of creatures in this bestiary, appears as the first of more than one hundred entries. When we watch *The Old Place* for the first time, Godard's claim concerning this story's relevance perhaps seems obnoxiously withholding and cryptic, like his "no comment" title at the end of *Film Socialism* (2010). However, I take his comment here to be an earnest and particularly fitting one: the tale indeed sums up the video by allegorizing the very relation the co-directors hope to build with the diligent viewer through their "artistic thinking," which is to say, through their essayistic montage.

The Borgesian legend, as Godard and Miéville make use of it, comments on the mutually constitutive relationship between themselves *and the spectator*—or rather, the "visitor" their work attracts. The legend is one of endless repetition and the "Sisyphian" task involved therein.[67] This affirms the essayistic sense of repeated trial inherent in the concept of "exercise," while extending this act of constant rededication to the share of the viewer. The story entails both the prospect of revelation ("the loveliest landscape in the world") and the frank acknowledgment that this joint process of exploring connections through montage is replete with difficulties and is threatened by encroaching forces. Clips in the exercise, from the "no trespassing" sign from Welles's *Citizen Kane* (1941) to an actual sign in rural Switzerland that reads "property of the state," remind us that there are larger powers out to obstruct and suppress this work. The content of the montage itself suggests

Refiguring the Couple

151

figuratively that these forces have fenced off the tower, preventing interaction between visitors and the lonely, diminished creature inside.

What we have in this fanciful, semi-disguised apostrophe to the spectator is a longing for contact and dialogue. "The creature suffers when it cannot come to completion," Miéville states, "and its moan is a barely audible sound, something like the rustling of silk." The tale serves as a parting summary and distillation of the two essayists' *need* to secure the viewer's role as a ternary extension of the binary relationship that they embody as a couple. The final exercise, in this way, revisits the mysterious aphorism heard earlier: "One is in the other, the other is in the one, and these are three persons." As we are now in position to see, that line prefigures what the A Bao A Qu tale holds out as a fading but still realizable possibility of interconnectedness, through shared work and its mutually grasped revelations.[68]

The co-directors' adaptation of this tale sets forward a dynamic of intimacy that comes with obstacles imposed not just from without but also from within. The parable holds that not all visits (and not all viewer-visitors) are equal to the task, and that only once has a climber excited the A Bao A Qu into its full radiance. This isn't a snobbish stance but a return to what Godard-Miéville file under friendship in *Soft and Hard*, what I have called their cine-*philia*. Their partnership, far from catering to a self-congratulatory club of devotees, asks the viewer to take part in a long-term relationship wherein the basic grounds for jointly held convictions and practices are ceaselessly confronted and tested anew. Of course, our interaction can only occur through mediated visits. But if we repeatedly engage in the process of judging the combinations they offer, if we daringly exercise our constructive thought by sketching in the structures they leave open, and if we do all this with a careful eye to their evolution in and across multiple efforts over time, then we are in fact the "friend" their essaying solicits: we are, in concert with their deepest aims, doing our part of love's work.

Chapter 4

To Show and Show Oneself Showing: Essayistic Self-Portrayal

> Elsewhere you can commend or condemn a work [*ouvrage*] independently of the author [*ouvrier*]; but not here: touch one and you touch the other.
> —Michel de Montaigne

> I need to talk and show me talking, to show and show me showing.... I need to have a philosophical talk on the technical aspect and a technical talk on the philosophical aspect.
> —Jean-Luc Godard

> I don't believe in the solitude of an artist and the auteur with a capital A.
> —Jean-Luc Godard

Over the course of his career, Godard has been a serial self-portrayer, making and revising images of himself in a wide variety of roles. From cameos in *Breathless* (1960) and *Contempt* (1963) to his more self-interrogatory appearance in *Camera-Eye* (1967), through to later performances in *Numéro deux* (1975) and the "Jean-Luc" episode of *Six fois deux / Sur et sous la communication* (1976), he has practiced self-inscription as a vital component of his ongoing research into the capabilities of his craft.[1] Particularly in his films and videos since the early 1980s, he has fashioned an indelible screen persona, either playing burlesque versions of himself as a rambling, incomprehensible fool, as in *Prénom Carmen* (1983), *King Lear* (1987), and *Keep Your Right Up* (1987), or donning relatively more sincere autobiographical roles, as in *JLG/JLG: Self-Portrait in December* (1995), *Notre musique* (2004), and *Message of Greetings: Swiss Prize / My Thanks / Dead or Alive* (2015). Indeed, the pervasiveness of the aging director in his work of the period is such that the phrase "late Godard" brings to mind his physical characteristics: his unshaven face and wiry, half-receded hair, his

153

154   Chapter 4

increasingly granular voice, his thin smirk beneath horn-rimmed glasses and cigar smoke.

The activity of inhabiting one's own productions as a filmmaker encompasses a rich legacy of practices of which Godard is well aware. Through affectionate citations in *Histoire(s) du cinéma*, he pays tribute to several directors who, in one way or another, performed the double task of appearing onscreen and experimenting with the codes and resources of the film medium: Georges Méliès, Charlie Chaplin, Buster Keaton, Jean Cocteau, Jacques Tati, Alfred Hitchcock, Orson Welles, Jean Renoir, and John Cassavetes. If these references indicate Godard's knowing contribution to this varied history, they also signal a key point of separation. What distinguishes his work, I am going to show, is the acutely essayistic sense in which his self-inscriptions aim to provoke and sustain a critical rapport with the spectator he addresses, that is, a dialogue premised on the possibility of shared thought and vision.[2]

Self-depiction is a common feature of the cinematic essay. Many leading practitioners show up in their films with regularity, achieving an audiovisual equivalent of what Montaigne terms the "consubstantial" relation between himself and his *Essais*: "a book of one substance [*consubstantiel*] with its author, proper to me and a limb of my life" (II.18: 755). The multifariousness of the essay is such that directors go about this in different ways and to various ends. Some documentarians who have been classified as essayists assume a rather direct and conspicuous persona in their projects (such as Ross McElwee in his autobiographical meditations, or Michael Moore in his more brashly self-assertive interventions),[3] whereas others grace their reflections with a sense of reserve. There are some who drastically play down their authorial presence by decentering it, disguising it, or limiting it to short intervals. Take Chris Marker's habit of appearing in his work—if at all—as hands in the frame sorting through collected materials or using production technology (e.g., *The Last Bolshevik* [1992] and *Level Five* [1997]).

The most inventive essayistic portrayers of themselves fall somewhere between these extremes. Agnès Varda occupies her nonfiction films as a sharply delimited autobiographical subject, her roles as character, narrator, and director allied by her use of a first-person voice. But she also takes measures to undercut whatever impression of vanity such a practice might suggest. *The Beaches of Agnès* (2009) is a case in point. In the opening scene, she looks into the lens of the camera and affirms that her self-portrait will be primarily interested in other people, "others who intrigue me, inspire me, make me ask questions, unsettle me, fascinate me." Barefoot on a windy beach with a team of assistants, she directs the improvised assembly of a mirror maze in which her screen image is doubled, diffracted, and displaced onto the surrounding sand and surf that, as she words it, form her subjective lining: "If we opened people up, we'd find landscapes. If we opened me up, we'd find beaches." The marine landscape, in its manifestations across her body of work, thus arises as the prime motif around which Varda organizes her remembrance of her

To Show and Show Oneself Showing

past artistic achievements and the meaningful relationships she forged with countless collaborators along the way. Balancing self-inscription with genuine self-effacement, *The Beaches of Agnès* unfolds as a self-portrait keyed to interpersonal experience, as we come to learn how her creativity across media has been made possible by a large group of friends and relatives; and this communal aspect is made to extend, at least rhetorically, to the congenial bond she insinuates with the viewer. Here, as in her other late self-portraits (*The Gleaners and I* [2000] and the television miniseries *Agnès from Here to There Varda* [2011]), Varda elegantly enacts the "I-You" structure of direct address that, according to Laura Rascaroli, functions at the very core of the audiovisual essay and testifies to its dialogical inclination.[4]

With Godard's essayistic self-portraits, however, we encounter a more complicated series of experiments that exert greater pressure on both the authorial "I" and the spectatorial "you." Like Varda, Godard tends to appear in body and voice and to deflect attention onto other figures, contexts, and histories, but he does this through a rather oblique and obscure screen persona that is less open and relaxed with autobiographical details, less lucid in explaining his ideas and arguments, and *less direct* in his address. The constitution of dialogue with the viewer is equally pressing in his examples, but he submits the discursive agency and privilege of his "I" to greater critical scrutiny, and he dramatizes the inherent difficulty of achieving and maintaining dialogue, rather than taking it as a rhetorical given.

In view of this comparison to Varda's warmly engaging work, one might be inclined to say that Godard's self-portraits embody precisely the abstruseness, *the lack of willingness to communicate*, that his detractors find so vexing about his late phase in general. In this chapter, I intend to show, on the contrary, that this opacity speaks to just how crucial the possibility of dialogue is to his self-portraiture, so crucial in fact that dialogue must not be assumed in advance or reduced to neat representations of its smooth functioning. Implicit in Godard's efforts is the notion that deep-seated problems of language, thought, and perception need to be confronted and dealt with if anything like meaningful dialogue between two or more beings—or more specifically, between essayist and viewer—is to transpire.[5] Moving in chronological order through a series of his late projects—*Scénario du film "Passion"* (1982), *JLG/JLG: Self-Portrait in December*, *Histoire(s) du cinéma*, and *Notre musique*—I am going to examine how, and to what purposes, he dedicates his body and voice to reflective pursuits in which the prospect of dialogue turns on the viewer's capacity to learn forms of seeing and thinking that Godard either demonstrates or gestures toward with virtuosic command. I will illustrate that these four late endeavors do not simply affirm a general condition of dialogism that inheres in human relations and artistic expression. They make strenuous demands on our sensory and cognitive aptitudes so that dialogical interaction *might* begin.

Carefully examining Godard's self-portrayals will lead us toward an appropriately complex account of authorial subjectivity and spectator

156   Chapter 4

address as they play out in an unfolding essayistic inquiry. In particular, I
want to grapple with three tendencies that the filmmaker displays across these
late projects. First, his self-sketches betray certain ambivalences concerning
his legendary renown as an auteur. They waver between, on the one hand,
Romantic declarations of his singular talent and significance in film history
and, on the other hand, a more self-abnegating mood that understands his
authorial singularity as a problem to be overcome. In his late period, Godard
finds himself largely at odds with the auteurist perspective that served to
launch his career. This indeed is a central theme that he voices in several of
his interviews of the era. "Auteurs aren't important," he tells Serge Daney
in 1988. "Today we supposedly respect the man so much that we no longer
respect the work."[6] Repeating this revised outlook at the end of episode 3B
in *Histoire(s) du cinéma*, an episode titled "Une vague nouvelle" ("A New
Wave," or "A Vague Bit of News"), he says in no uncertain terms, "Not the
auteurs, the works!" His self-portraits put forward a similar viewpoint, but
we will see that even in moments where he stages the "death" of himself as
author, an irony surfaces, in that the profundity of this gesture recuperates
the special status it means to revoke.

The second, when Godard appears in these late projects, he tends to blur the
usual division of roles and responsibilities between artist and observer—
between a producer of images and sounds on the one hand and a consumer
of them on the other. We will see that his screen presence often intertwines
authorial and receptive duties—even (and especially) when he depicts himself
in the middle of his work. This habit of course inflects his dialogical appeal
to the viewer's constructive involvement, but it bears with it a rather indirect
style of address that has not yet been adequately explained in the context of
the essayistic.

The third, associated tendency I want to consider has to do with Godard's
extravagant use of citations. What I argued in chapter 2 will hold true here,
namely that through his citational procedures, Godard orchestrates two
potential dialogues at once: one with the viewer and a second with other
authors, whether living or deceased, whose thoughts, affects, and images he
inventively recycles. To participate in the former dialogue, we have to sift
through the intricacies of the latter. Besides testing our competence, this twofold process attunes us to the kind of subjectivity that his self-inscriptions
figure forth. He embodies a sense of essayistic selfhood defined largely in
terms of other voices that reverberate through "his own" expressions. I am
ultimately going to show that he tries to become a cinematic medium in
his own right. Inspecting the ways in which he sets about this conversion
will not only allow us to understand more deeply and carefully how he
maneuvers as an essayist; it will also give us traction on some of the most
pivotal concerns of his late stage as a whole, from his rethought methods
of political engagement to his use of montage as an instrument of historical
investigation.

The Work to Be Done Is Seeing

Scénario du film "Passion" arguably contains the most absorbing and memorable scenes of Godard at work during his late period. Made for Swiss television to correlate with the theatrical release of his then-latest feature film, *Passion* (1982), the project might seem a minor, peripheral addition to his body of work, but it centrally attests to his intensified experimentation with video technology.[7] More to the point, it initiates what will emerge as something of a pattern in the late self-portraits I have singled out—an attempt on the director's part to extend to the viewer notions of thought and perception that underlie his approach.

"Friends and foes, good evening," Godard says in the opening scene, smoking and facing the camera head-on, in a pose of direct address that he will soon abandon and complicate. He tells us that the video he is about to present is an exercise in envisioning the scenario of *Passion*, his feature film, *before it is written*. "I think we see the world first, then we write," he explains. "The world described in *Passion* had to be seen first—to see if it existed before being filmed." He frames what follows as a preliminary draft of *Passion*, but in fact he has already made the feature and he integrates its scenes throughout the *Scénario*. His video is thus an oddly fantastic reenactment in which the images on view belong to multiple, overlapping temporalities. They refer at once to a film he would like to make, the video he is in the midst of making, and the film he has just recently made.[8]

Through this contrivance, *Scénario* offers itself as an adventure in seeing-on-the-spot. "The work to be done is seeing," Godard says. Still alone in his studio, he stands at a panel of controls in front of a large white screen, his back to the camera, his figure in silhouette. From this position, he calls the screen a Mallarméan blank page, "a beach in a blinding sun." He instructs, "You want to see, re-cei-ve [*re-ce-voir*]. A blank page confronts you. A dazzling beach. But there's no sea. So, you invent waves, I invent waves. You imagine a wave."

At that instant, a stilled shot from *Passion* materializes onscreen, gently fading in and out as Godard dictates from his video panel. This visual effect is striking. The "wave" drawn from *Passion* appears to be projected from a point physically internal to where Godard has positioned himself, but its contents overspill the borders of the inset screen. "Just a murmur. Only a vague idea, but already there is movement," he says (now punning on the two senses of the French word *vague*, "wave" and "indefinite"). "I have a vague idea: a woman running with flowers, a young woman in the flower of youth. Here, just a faint disturbance, which the film will make a storm. A wave. It comes, it goes. Just an echo." To visualize this sensation of an emergent image, Godard is, in fact, enlisting video cross-fades: the screen in front of him remains blank as the scenes from *Passion* are superimposed videographically onto the entire shot of his figure. There are two monitors, one on either side of the inset screen, in which he can check and observe his actions in real time, relative to the composite images shown to us (fig. 4.1).

If the complexity of this self-inscriptive setup bears witness to Godard's fascination with the textural affordances of video—its layering effects and "process orientation"[9]—it also drives home the point that such measures are needed to estrange us from our viewing habits, thus clearing the ground for what Godard terms "seeing first"—seeing prior to the imposition of spoken words or written texts. In *Scénario*, this setup is defined in stark opposition to the television news broadcast, a monological, verbocentric format that Godard detests because the news anchor values speech above pictures that have only a cheaply illustrative link to the information being relayed. To mark this difference, Godard shows us a clip of a German-speaking announcer with a keyed-in photograph behind him. "In television," Godard maintains, "they see nothing because they turn their backs on images instead of facing them. The image *sees them*. So do the people manipulating the images."

Against this format, Godard draws on the structure of address peculiar to the self-portrait in painting—the scene of the artist looking at himself looking, while in the process of making an image of himself. *Passion* itself probes the relation between cinema and the European heritage of painting, and in the *Scénario*, Godard in effect reimagines the play of mirrors intrinsic to the

Figure 4.1. Godard demonstrates how to receive images: *Scénario du film "Passion"* (Godard, 1982).

self-portrait. As Michael Fried has demonstrated with particular insight, self-portraiture from the late Renaissance forward often acknowledges—whether blatantly or implicitly—the painter's use of a mirror. Resourceful artists from Annibale Carracci and Caravaggio (a key reference in Godard's late period) to Gustave Courbet and Henri Matisse (these, too, are oft-cited painters by the director) foreground this reflective technology by craftily elevating it to a matter of intellectual curiosity and by inviting the spectator to bear in mind the actual, material conditions of the artwork's execution. For Fried, these open acknowledgments have to do not only with the artist's negotiation of a corporealized relationship with the canvas produced, but also with the self-portrait's implied relationship to its viewer.[10]

Godard's twin video monitors make for a comparable mirror effect and disclosure of his instruments. We see the artist seeing himself as an image, seeing and showing this image as he renders it. And we see him seeing—from a position *within* the image—what we concurrently see from the "outside," on what we might term the master screen, the screen that includes the others. Only after showing us this apparatus does Godard move into tighter shots of his shadowed figure against the screen in front of him, its edges now flush with the master screen.

From this point on, *Scénario* consists primarily of Godard moving his hands like a conductor over superimposed scenes taken from *Passion*, calling attention to formal patterns and associations that he claims constitute the basis for the film's plot, which must be seen before it is committed to text. A chord of despair tempers his performance. He says that during the filming of *Passion*, neither the crew nor the actors were able to learn this all-important principle of seeing things first. Over cross-fades between footage of his earliest meeting with the production team and a photographic print of Tintoretto's *Bacchus and Ariadne* (1576), Godard recalls, "I was trying to tell them that we had to set out from an image that was yet to be made. I told them traces already existed. The film would show great moments of humanity using great painters." He recounts that he showed his collaborators the Tintoretto as inspiration for a possible love triangle in *Passion*, but they merely "saw a finished image, whereas I hadn't reached that stage yet." Lacking the imagination, the sense of discovery on which he hoped to depend, they could only conceive of final, reified images. "It was difficult," he says, seeking our sympathy. "I'd talk of something I could see but they mostly saw themselves and what the audience would say about them. . . . I always ended up here alone, before this purity, this beach without a sea."

This aggrieved flashback stresses that Godard's self-portrait is geared toward orienting the viewer to that initial, *substrative* point of the image-forming process that his collaborators proved incapable of accessing. That is to say, *we* have a chance to succeed where his cast and crew failed. "Audience," he says, appealing to our contribution (these words rework the first stanza of François Villon's autobiographical poem "Ballad of Hanged Men,"

160   Chapter 4

in which the speaker braces for his execution alongside other criminals and proclaims kinship with all of humanity), "don't harden your hearts against me. If you pity me, poor soul, God will have pity on you. Thank you." The video's dialogical quest becomes clear in this moment, but what we have in *Scénario* is not quite an "I-You" structure of interaction between the essayist on one side and the viewer on the other.

Vocally, bodily, Godard inhabits the video in ways that confound the difference between directorial and spectatorial roles, between the "I" referring to him and the "you" referring to us. For instance, when he delivers the citational line imploring us not to harden our hearts against him, his back is turned to the camera and his statement is directed as much inward as outward, *as if he is speaking to himself and we happen to overhear him*. Throughout his exercise in front of the screen, he assumes the position of a spectator himself, alternating freely between first- and second-person pronouns and verb forms as he mulls his process. "See and you find. I find myself and I find myself seeking. You find yourself confronted with the invisible." "You want to see, *re-ce-voir*." "So you invent waves, I invent waves." Such vocal ambiguities have as their complement Godard's back-viewed silhouette, his self-portrayal as a *Rückenfigur* of sorts: a shown-from-behind beholder figure within the work whose task doubles up with and stands in for that of the viewer (this, too, is a motif of self-portraiture that Godard in part takes from the history of painting).[11] His performance thus slips between registers in a compound drama of creation and reception, of making and perceiving. In view of these material factors, it is misleading to call his style of address "direct." Although his use of second-person is directive and longingly inclusive, a certain obliqueness imbues this relationship such that neither the "I" nor the "you" has a stable assignment.

Connected to this point, another feature of *Scénario* needs to be emphasized, namely that what enables Godard to depict himself in such an elaborate fashion is the device of videographic superimposition. We will see shortly in this chapter, in our account of *Histoire(s) du cinéma*, that this technique takes on immense importance in Godard's self-portraiture as it conspires with his spectator address and attendant conception of montage. In this earlier project, the videographic superimposition of Godard's figure onto the scenes he inspects from *Passion* texturally produces what I am calling, after Montaigne, a *consubstantial* merger with his work in progress. His body is made to fuse with the multipart images he orchestrates—it cannot be located "this side" of the clips, or rather the "waves," that claim him as an integral element. From this position, he lovingly and attentively traces his hands over graphic contours, discerning certain resonances of form and movement. On two occasions (once with Jerzy Radziwilowicz, then later with Isabelle Huppert) he caresses and kisses the faces of his players; his wraith-like figure, in mingling with the images that take shape, itself falls into pictorial patterns that seem fortuitous. He attends the meeting site of outstretched hands, or nestles into open nooks of the *mise en scène*, such as the space between a couple conversing. Though

To Show and Show Oneself Showing   161

the emphasis is on seeing, Godard's demonstration suggests that this pursuit
goes beyond ocular vision and entails a gestural, embodied interaction with
the forms and ideas that emerge.

This is also to suggest that, in Godard's entanglement of authorship and
spectatorship, *our* merger with the work is under negotiation as well, and
with certain stipulations attached. To enter into a relationship of intimacy
with the work requires that we embrace as valid, and strive to attain ourselves, the skill of "seeing first" that he defends by example. One of the major
themes around which *Passion* revolves is the relationship between love and
work. In *Scénario*, Godard tells us that he first needed to see, through conducting "research," if gestures of labor in a factory bore some affinity to
the gestures of love he had in mind for the film. Again using cross-fades, he
comparatively inspects a documentary shot of a seamstress, a shot of Isabelle
Huppert as a factory worker in *Passion*, and Tintoretto's *Bacchus and Ariadne*
(itself a scene of three figures intersecting: Bacchus offers a ring to Ariadne as
Venus glides overhead, crowning Ariadne). With his shadowy hand, Godard
declares a resonance among these three pictures, on the grounds of their
rhyming gestures. "You can see that love and work . . . it isn't just Jean-Luc's
usual ravings. It's something that exists."

Godard's assertion here—and this will be true of his montage in *Histoire(s)*
as well—is that in bringing these disparate fragments together, he has not
fabricated a link between them so much as he has brought one to light. As
he explains it in this earlier video, the process he tries to share is a matter of
looking for "movements and gestures that look for themselves"; it involves
successfully finding two or more elements that are, despite their perhaps great
contextual differences, disposed to combine.

Critics have tended to discuss *Scénario* as a self-aggrandizing project that
displays Godard's singular, matchless powers of vision and creativity,[12] but such
a perspective misses how his self-portrait is at pains to make his process communal. He highlights his failure to do this during the production of *Passion*
precisely because he hopes to avoid reliving that earlier outcome, which left him
in bitter isolation. What *Scénario* attempts to establish isn't simply the screenplay of his feature film but the generative basis for a rapport with the viewer: a
"friend," rather than a "foe," as Godard's opening apostrophe words it.

What Cinema Can Do with Godard

That interaction with others is vitally at stake in Godard's late self-depictions
is in further evidence in *JLG/JLG: Self-Portrait in December*. Released in
1995, the film is mostly comprised of scenes of the filmmaker reading, writing,
and thinking in and around his actual home in Rolle, Switzerland. Though
the film, to some degree, revels in Godard's public image as a melancholic
hermit radically withdrawn from the social sphere, a close inspection of his

162   Chapter 4

performance reveals, on the contrary, that the dialogical aims of his *Scénario* remain in effect, albeit with added layers of significance and complication.

In interviews around the release of *JLG/JLG*, Godard explains his title in ways that distill his ambitions and preempt the accusation of egoism. He insists that his "self-portrait" should not be confused with autobiography or "what one calls in French *un examen de conscience*." He relates that he opposed Gaumont's plans to distribute the film in North America as "JLG by JLG" and thus supplant the slash. "If there is a 'by,' it means it's a study of JLG, of myself by myself . . . which it is absolutely not." He argues that a "self-portrait," by contrast, has no firmly situated subject at its center, "no 'me,' " and although the genre exists "only in painting, nowhere else," *JLG/JLG* attempts to transpose its workings to the cinema.[13] Enlarging on this key intermedial comparison, Godard frames his undertaking as a self-portrait specifically "in the sense that the painters have practiced this exercise; not by narcissism but as an interrogation on painting itself."[14] Put another way, the "self" on display is less a locus of insight mined from the inside-out than a pretext for a testing of the powers and limits of the medium used. The slash is needed, Godard says, because it indicates a level of remove from oneself, "JLG in the mirror," and what the film portrays is not merely his body but a thinking process for which he serves as the conduit more than the source. "*JLG/JLG*," he summarizes, "is an attempt to see what cinema can do with me, not what I can do with it."[15]

As befits this description, the film begins by expressing an uneasiness about the authorial "I" that Godard will perform. In a dark, cramped interior streaked by bluish natural light coming in through a window, a series of shots cautiously approach a framed photograph of a young boy (Godard himself). These shots pair with the cacophonous sounds of children playing on a shore, and we also hear Godard's whispered, apprehensive voiceover (almost as if reprised from *2 or 3 Things I Know About Her*) review a list of tasks he must carry out if his project is to be "a success" rather than a "failure." A spectral male figure (Godard?) leans into the shot and briefly obstructs the photograph, but his identity is suppressed. Once the photo comes to fill the entire film frame, Godard's voiceover changes, becoming wearier and much gruffer. "He possessed hope," Godard says, reflecting back on his childhood in the third person, "but the boy didn't know that what counts is to know by whom he is possessed, what dark powers are entitled to lay claim to him."[16] The film, in sync with the shrilly disruptive scream of a child, cuts to an exterior view of Lake Geneva, its waves lapping against the shore, the Alps looming in the distance, the wind whistling through the brush, a dog barking somewhere offscreen. The voiceover and this landscape imply that *JLG/JLG* will concern itself not solely with an individual—a subject in possession of unique qualities, experiences, insights, and so forth—but with the forces that encroach and impress upon this subject from the outside.[17]

The film's opening positions Godard obscurely and dispersively, as a man divided between the past and present, youth and maturity, light and darkness,

To Show and Show Oneself Showing

an interior and the exterior. The rest of *JLG/JLG* follows suit by distributing "JLG" across multiple filmic registers. He surfaces in and through a voiceover track that wavers between tones (and between left and right audio channels); in allusive intertitles written on notebook paper in his own cursive hand; in references to several past and discarded projects (there are nods to his other late-period films, and *La Chinoise* [1967] can be glimpsed on his television set at one point); and in some of his public remarks as recalled, oddly enough, by a scantily dressed housemaid who seems to be a manifestation of his sexual fantasy.[18] At times we can see JLG reflected in windows, his body decentered in the frame. When he does show up more "directly," he tends to be filmed from the side or from behind while absorbed in thought at various stations inside his home, backlit either in warm lamplight or in cool, overcast daylight. Here again, then, he inscribes himself as a tenebrous being, his address to the viewer constitutively oblique.[19]

The film's beginning also puts into play a salient theme of death and mourning. Repeated strains of a tolling bell lend the scene a funereal mood. Moreover, the scene musically samples a plangent cello composition by David Darling, as well as the "Entombment" movement from Paul Hindemith's aptly named symphony *Matthias the Painter*. The latter piece accompanies a passage in voiceover suggesting that the death in question is, in fact, Godard's. "I was already in mourning for myself, my sole and unique companion," he states, his voice still hoarse. "I suspected that my soul had stumbled over my body, and that it had left without offering a hand." It is hard to know how to read this line, in part because Godard also insinuates that he *eagerly* expected his death at earlier times in his life. "But death never came," he says, as if disappointed. "Neither on the streets of Paris, nor on the shores of Lake Geneva."

At one level, this theme reflects Godard's heightened awareness of his own mortality. The seasonal dimension of the subtitle refers to the winter stage of his life and oeuvre. He would turn sixty-four the year of the film's release, and while *JLG/JLG* refuses any brief synopsis, we could do worse than to call it a reworking of Montaigne's claim that "to learn how to die" is a philosophical necessity (I.20: 89–108). Kaja Silverman explains in her analysis of the film that the theme of death speaks most pressingly to Godard's need to kill off, as it were, a certain institutionalized sense of authorship that he considers a hindrance: "The mortal event to which Godard refers" in the film's early moments "is clearly the death of himself *as an author*."[20] For Silverman, the film pursues nothing less than the director's "authorial suicide." That is, it acts out his attempt to "divest" himself of authorship on the order of production and to install, in its place, a transformed conception of himself as "a pure receiver, receptacle, and reflector of stimuli."[21] Silverman rightly notes that this "death" has played itself out before in Godard's work (e.g., his turn to a collectivist ethos with the Dziga Vertov Group, after the "end of cinema" signaled by *Week-end* [1967]). What *JLG/JLG* contemplates is whether he can sustain himself *"in the mode of dying."*[22]

The film indeed links the theme of mortality to the director's ambivalence about his status as an auteur filmmaker. A recurrent intertitle, "I am legend," at once comments on his venerated place in cinema history and nods to Richard Matheson's 1954 science fiction/horror novel. The intertextual suggestion is that JLG's renown has landed him in a predicament not unlike that of Matheson's protagonist, the lone remaining human in a world that has suffered a pandemic of vampirism.[23] No doubt Godard relishes the tale of a man condemned to live out his final days in solitude, but at least for JLG as portrayed in the film, this is not a desired state. If the film has a guiding logic, it unfurls as a series of exercises through which he weighs his possible movement back toward the world, toward some measure of togetherness with other thinkers and perceivers, this being the sought effect of his auteurial suicide. Thus, the possibility of JLG sloughing off his legendary identity has interpersonal stakes. His death is less a motif than the goal, the pursuit of which forms the film's circuitous build, its steps between sequences that may seem—on a first or second viewing—only arbitrarily connected.

That the self-portrait has sociality on its mind is hinted at periodically by scenes in which JLG interacts with other people. He exchanges words with two housemaids; a "wet nurse"; two "film center inspectors" who appear, like emissaries from the world to which he has become an outlier, to make him answer for his past deeds; a young blind woman he hires to help edit a film he has just finished shooting; and an elderly, Latin-speaking woman in a black shawl, whom he meets in the snow-covered forest near his house. We also see him in a strangely edited match of doubles tennis: he participates on both sides of the net, first playing a point while teamed with a young boy, then a point while teamed with a young woman, his attire changing colors (from red to navy blue) to correspond with that of his partner.[24] These encounters alternate with segments in which JLG ruminates aloud while well removed from the physical company of others.[25] But these moments continue a dialogical aspect insofar as they rely heavily on quotation, with the director drawing on the ideas of others. More still, these reflections pertain not just to JLG but also to the spectator whose involvement he indirectly invites. They point up snarled problems of perception, language, and thought that will have to be wrestled with, by JLG and by us, if his auteurial death is to come to pass successfully.

One such sequence involves what JLG describes as the "law of stereo" and its destructive consequences in history. At his writing desk—with just his hands visible in the frame—he reads two short passages from Ludwig Wittgenstein's *On Certainty* (1969), a compilation of notes the philosopher composed during the final months of his life. Specifically, Godard recites fragment 121 ("Might we say that where doubt is lacking, knowledge, too, is lacking?") and then 125 ("A blind man asks me, 'Do you have two hands?' Looking at my two hands would not reassure me. Yes, I don't know why I would trust my eyes if I were in doubt"). He then replaces the text with Denis Diderot's *Letter on the Blind for the Use of Those Who See* (1749) from which he rehearses an account of a young woman, a friendly acquaintance of Diderot's, who considers her blindness an asset, since it defends her against the charms of attractive men. Without pause Godard then recites a statement by the same woman, which comes later in the original piece: "Men of geometry live most of their lives with their eyes shut."[26]

This juxtaposition of texts challenges simple faith in habitual ways of seeing and knowing the exterior world relative to oneself. The lines from Wittgenstein import a tenor of questioning with respect to the grounds against which one's beliefs are tested and confirmed. For Godard, the accent falls on doubt as a practice necessary to any epistemic system, and the interplay of sight and touch initiates a crucial trope, as will later become clear. The lines from Diderot, in turn, extend this spirit of interrogation by way of their essayistic inquiry into the sensory particulars of blindness, which Diderot holds up as a corrective to those who arrogantly presume their sight is adequate and thus found their deepest convictions on it.

In Godard's film, the mention of "men of geometry" is a rebuff. It follows from Diderot's critique of the religiously tinged "geometrizing of the universe" of Cartesian philosophy—its installation of a sovereign subject for whom the exercise of reason unclouds the world before a well-positioned and exacting gaze.[27] This leads JLG to offer a geometry lesson of his own, a kind of counterproof he tries to verify in historical terms. Still seated at his desk (the segment consists of just one shot), he diagrams what he calls the rule of "stereo," as in stereography. He takes a blank sheet of paper and draws two triangles that interlock to form a hexagram. Each triangle, he says, is a vector of "projection," thrown from a subject position toward the world and others. "In history, the history of history, there was Germany, which projected Israel. Israel reflected this projection, and Israel found its cross." Courting controversy, the lesson thus suggests that the Star of David, which adorns the national flag of Israel, bears the geometric impress (and logic) of this historical dynamic according to which the victims of a monstrously inhumane aggression became, in time, aggressors in another dogmatic conflict with another people: "And the law of stereo continues," JLG states. "Israel projected the Palestinian people and the Palestinians, in turn, bore their cross. That is the true legend of stereo."

Godard has drawn reproach for this demonstration, which recycles a line of argument we dealt with in our study of *Ici et ailleurs* (1976) in chapter 2. Richard Brody, for instance, reads this scene as conspicuous evidence of Godard's anti-Semitism. JLG's description and use of the Star of David is indeed disturbingly terse, but Brody doesn't take into account the Wittgenstein and Diderot citations that come before it, and he reductively treats the scene's place in the film as a whole.[28] The point of the lesson exceeds a simple critique of Israel as a perpetrator of fascist violence. Thunder peels on the soundtrack, and a trousseau of keys gleaming on JLG's desk in a pool of light hint that there is something deeper at stake.

166 Chapter 4

Considered in the intellectual context of the Wittgenstein and Diderot quotations—and in the light of what I have said Godard is out to achieve in the self-portrait—the lesson serves in the main as a continued critique of presumed knowledge and vision, with the director now exploring the horrific ramifications that spring from such a perspective. The stereo diagram takes on a host of erroneous, to-be-avoided sentiments that motivate what he calls "projection"—an antagonistic regard for the other that wears away doubt with doctrinaire surety and sets in motion a relentless cycle of violence, with one adversarial projection/reflection inspiring another, then another, and so forth. I should note that JLG arcanely recognizes how his personal history intersects with this larger history and its problems when he says, just before he sketches the hexagram, that "stereo" rhymes with "Jeannot," his nickname as a child. This line, I take it, refers to his upbringing in a French-Swiss Protestant family in which pro-Vichy and anti-Semitic attitudes were a staple, and in which he was encouraged to root for Nazi forces during the war.[29] Now, in *JLG/JLG*, a film set in the landscape of his youth—and a film marked by fleeting but weighty allusions to the Shoah and to Resnais's *Night and Fog* (1955)—he reflects back on this regrettable chapter from his past and takes his family's misguidance to task.

The main purpose of the stereo lesson is to critique a pernicious type of self-versus-other hostility that JLG wishes to circumvent while on his anticipated path back toward the world and sociality. The lesson implies that in order to avoid being such presumptuous "men of geometry," we, like him, must subject our limited vision to radical scrutiny.

Hence the very next sequence, which continues and modulates this strand of reflection as we find JLG reading in bed, again in heavy shadow. Neither his face nor the jacket of the book is legible as he reads aloud: "He was stupefied but, strangely enough, had no desire to dwell on the point. A thing is not what you say it is. It is much more. It is an ensemble in the largest sense. A chair is not just a chair. It is a structure of inconceivable complexity— atomically, electronically, chemically, etc." He turns his head and the film cuts on his glance to a shot of a chair, its wicker seat smashed in. In a different verbal register (lower, more guttural, closer-miked; we cannot make out his lips but it seems to be voiceover), he says: "Therefore, thinking of it simply as a chair constitutes what Korzybski calls an identification. And the totality of these identifications produces nonsense and tyranny" (figs. 4.2 and 4.3).

The book from which JLG reads, with slight changes, is A. E. van Vogt's maligned 1948 science fiction novel *The World of Null-A*. The passage is an epigraph from a chapter where it is attributed to "Anonymous." The reference adds to Godard's self-characterization as a loner hero familiar to dystopian speculative fiction (Vogt's protagonist embarks on a quest to learn his true identity and discovers that he exists in multiple bodies and has astonishing mental and neural abilities, which he uses to combat a repressive galactic empire whose machinations he never quite unravels). More apposite here is

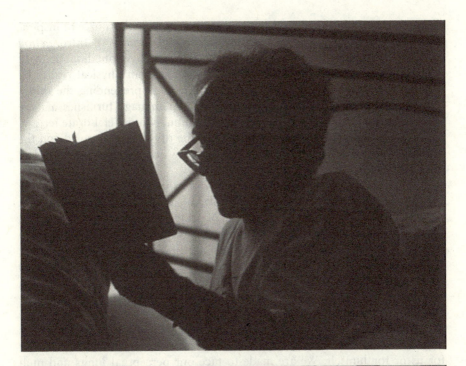

Figures 4.2–4.3. JLG reads in his bedroom and studies a damaged chair: *JLG/JLG: Self-Portrait in December* (Godard, 1995).

the matter of "identification." Vogt's fiction has as its main source of inspiration Alfred Korzybski's 1933 treatise *Science and Sanity: An Introduction to Non-Aristotelian Systems and General Semantics*. A founding claim of Korzybski's is that we are unavoidably separated from physical reality by our perception of it, and that language, far from apprehending the things it names and describes, at best approximates. Language furnishes a mere "map," as Korzybski puts it, for what is an infinitely more elaborate terrain. The error of "identification" happens when the things of the world and the language that references them are taken to be one and the same, when we act as though this is the case.

In *JLG/JLG*, this reuse of Vogt's novel introduces another dire mistake the director wants his work and our involvement with it to mindfully avoid. "Identification," not unlike the dynamic of projection, consists in misreading the phenomenal world because of an imposition of language assumed to be proper to its object. The chair JLG examines isn't a "chair" but a whirling dance of electrons, the nature of which outstrips the name assigned to it, as well as the shot the film shows of it. To our eyes, the object is unremarkable, apart from its damaged seat (which discourages the ascription of preconceived utility). Vogt's hero acquires, through training, the ability to observe and synthesize his mind with the subatomic energy at play in apparently inert objects. Godard's scene, however, holds out no such fantastical hope either for us or for himself. We are made to face our perceptual limits and mull the possibly grim consequence of not facing them. If projection fosters brutal enmity toward the other, identification produces "nonsense and tyranny" (Godard's added terms to the cited passage).

These lessons prepare us for a later exercise near the film's end that brings this reflection full circle, with the force of an epiphany regarding the film medium itself. In this segment, JLG hires a female editor to assist with his not-yet-finished feature film, *Oh, Woe Is Me* (1993), and the young woman, to his surprise, is blind. "A shady business [Une ténébreuse affaire]," reads an intertitle,[30] after which JLG proceeds to work with her at a table near the editing console, using two spools of film, just his hands shown in the frame. He removes his eyeglasses and lays out the task of combining two shots from a scene in *Oh, Woe Is Me* (where the main couple, Simon and Rachel, discuss an amorous incident that may or may not have occurred). As per JLG's guidance, the blind assistant mimes the required steps and then makes a cut, doing so as a flourish of violin music underscores a feeling of revelation.

Of course, the motif of blindness, together with the emphasis on touch, arches back to the Wittgenstein and Diderot passages from earlier. What occurs next continues the use of Diderot's essay (sans attribution) even further. JLG, with his assistant, restages an interaction that Diderot has with the young blind woman he profiles. Following Diderot's account verbatim, JLG tells his editor from offscreen: "Mademoiselle, imagine a cube."

To Show and Show Oneself Showing

EDITOR: (*while facing a bright window as if looking outside*) I see it.

JLG: Imagine, in its center, a point.

EDITOR: It's done.

JLG: From this point, draw straight lines to the angles. Into what have you divided the cube?

EDITOR: Into six equal pyramids, each having as its base one side of the cube, and a height equal to half of its height.

JLG: This is true. But tell me, where do you see it?

EDITOR: In my head, as you do.
(*Cut to black leader, as the violin sonata briefly returns.*)[31]

This dialogical exercise does several things at once. The sonata by Paul Hindemith repeats from *Histoire(s) du cinéma*, where it accompanies the passage in which two lovers from *A Place in the Sun* (Stevens, 1951) cross with Nazi death camps, bearing forth a redemptive "miracle of our blind eyes" (see chapter 2). In *JLG/JLG*, a mood of discovery arises in the blind editor segment.[32] Her capable "vision" stands in contradistinction to the missteps of projection and identification outlined previously in the film. Issuing from ocular blindness embraced as an advantage, this perceptiveness owes to the image-forming faculty of the mind, through a delicate interplay of touch and listening and imagination. In this self-conscious scene, the film medium (or more precisely, the procedure of montage) both facilitates this exchange between JLG and the woman *and* extends their shared revelation to us, as a third party. The black screen lets us see more distinctly "in our heads" the subdivided cube that they both see in theirs.

This isn't to say that the exercise calls for reliance on the mind's eye alone, or a retreat inward. The tactile experience of cutting Godard's scene at the editing station inspires the blind assistant to reflect on being constitutively in touch with her surroundings as well, by means of a body-world connection she calls "flesh," reciting Maurice Merelau-Ponty's *The Visible and the Invisible* (published posthumously in 1968):

> If the visible has a relationship to itself that goes through me and becomes me as I watch, watching this circle which I do not create, but which creates me, then this winding of the visible can traverse, animate other bodies, as well as mine. And if I could understand how this wave is born in me, how the visible over there is simultaneously my landscape, then I can understand that elsewhere, too, it closes on itself, and that there are landscapes other than my own.[33]

In the midst of her reverie, an "I am legend" intertitle reappears, as do shots of crashing waves on the banks of Lake Geneva. Thus, as the lesson in seeing

170   Chapter 4

the invisible moves into a meditation on the unseen but substantial "flesh" of the world that enfolds, becomes, and circulates through the perceiver, the film turns back to the problem of how to carry out JLG's authorial demise—a process that, as we have seen, the film conceives as a movement toward the social world and some form of co-involvement. Having criticized pitfalls of perception and reflected on certain alternatives that spring from a deep acknowledgment of blindness—instead of from an egocentric and logocentric presumption that one's manner of seeing and knowing is accurate—JLG finds himself in position to culminate his death.[34]

His voice taking over from the editor's on the soundtrack, the director cinematically pairs Merleau-Ponty's concept of "flesh" with a sense of language that immerses the subject in a supra-individual stream of expressions. We believe that our utterances "express the individual," JLG says, when in fact they describe "the universal." The film has already put language under suspicion, but at this juncture, language factors in differently—not as an a priori and routinized mechanism of "identification," but as a token of one's humble connectedness to others. To speak or write is to enter, wittingly or not, into a milieu of co-belonging. Illustrating this point, JLG says: "'I am cold.' It is I who says 'I am cold' but it is not I who am heard. I disappear between these two moments of speech. All that remains is the man who is cold, and this man belongs to everyone." Yet a further aspect of relatedness colors this remark, as JLG is actually citing Brice Parain, the philosopher of language who appears in an important dialogue scene with the heroine in *My Life to Live* (1962).[35] Citation thus serves here, as it has throughout the film and Godard's late period in general, as a willful dispossession of the singular "I," a critical abdication of the myth of individual, auteurial expression. As Christopher Pavsek puts it, "this expression of a self through citation passes into an emptying of the self, a dispersal into citability in which all belong to him and he belongs to everyone."[36]

In its final moments, the film eloquently renders this disappearance and dispersal on the part of the director. Somewhere between shots of winter and springtime landscapes—a passage marked by the turning of blank notebook pages—JLG, whom we last glimpsed walking into the snowy forest outside his home, vanishes. Only to resurface, however, in the last, long-held shot of the film, in the form of shadows (of clouds) sweeping across a green field toward the horizon (fig. 4.4). His voice resurfaces, too. Paired with David Darling's sonorous cello, it intimates the meaning of this parting gesture:

> I said I love. That is the promise. Now, I have to sacrifice myself, so that through me the word love means something, so that love exists on earth. In return, at the end of this long undertaking, I will end up being he who loves. . . . A man, nothing but a man. No better than any other, but no other better than he.

Figure 4.4. The culmination of JLG's authorial death: *JLG/JLG*.

The last sentence, spoken over a black screen, completes, or at least figures out for the time being, JLG's movement from solitude toward dialogue, here expressed as a gift of love requiring self-sacrifice. Quite fittingly, the utterance is not his own but a citation of the closing, lapidary sentence of Jean-Paul Sartre's 1964 literary self-portrait *The Words*: "A whole man, composed of all men and as good as all of them and no better than any."[37] Sartre (as Godard surely realizes) was already involved in a game of revision with regard to precursors. His last sentence revises the comment that opens Jean-Jacques Rousseau's *Confessions* (1782): "Simply myself. I know my heart and understand my fellow man. But I am made unlike anyone I have ever met; I will even venture to say that I am like no one in the whole world. I may be no better but at least I am different."[38] Where Rousseau professes the singularity and originality of himself (and of his book, which "has no precedent" and "will have no imitator"), Sartre declares a leveling of himself among others, and a hard-won sense of community into which his words have at last thrust him.

JLG reworks Sartre reworking Rousseau, in order to ascribe stakes to his own self-portrait that are more than private. The voiced words are both his and not his, or not *only* his, and his use of them affirms a condition whereby his work and thought are the work and thought of others as well. Visually, verbally, intertextually, the expiration of the auteur that this ending dramatizes is on the order of death and transformation (hence the winter-to-spring shift in the *mise en scène*). What *JLG/JLG* ultimately shows us is not simply a demise but a diffraction of an authorial self in three directions at once: into the very texture of the film and its processes, into the "flesh" of the verdant landscape, and into citation as a medium of exchange.

Godard, not unlike Sartre in *The Words*, expects his dramatic parting claim to be valid only to the extent he has earned it through the previous reflections, only on the condition that he has vacated his legendary status, passed into public discourse, merged receptively with the flesh of the world and with the sounds and sights his film conducts, and has avoided (and moved us to avoid in turn) the delusions of both "projection" and "identification." Far from simply portraying a disaffected filmmaker in lonely retreat, *JLG/JLG* undertakes a mission of "making love mean something" on the grounds that these endeavors succeed.

Some detractors of the film have been unmoved by JLG's suicide, which they deem a Romantic act of authorial reaffirmation and thus no "sacrifice" at all.[39] Such a view neglects the essayistic stipulations and the film-long series of investigative exercises that lead up to and bear upon this ending, but there is indeed an interesting tension here between Godard's self-effacing and self-elevating impulses, a tension common to essayistic self-portraiture. What better example than Welles's oration before the Chartres cathedral in *F for Fake* (1975)? He exalts the collective force of art and the "anonymous glory" of the premodern Gothic architecture. And yet, the style, the eccentricity of his vocal delivery, combined with elegant superimpositions emphasizing less the cathedral itself than a way of looking applied to it, render the scene another testament to Welles's distinctive persona and command of his medium. His fading last line, "Maybe a man's name . . . doesn't matter . . . all that much," paradoxically makes the scene an anthology moment in his own authorial body of work. One finds a similar paradox in Godard's self-portraiture, but this testifies not simply to residual egoism. The "Godard" who remains and returns in future experiments is a figure who repeatedly stakes his historical significance as an artist on his capacity to strip away the myth of individual creative genius, clearing the ground for the collaborative thought to which his essaying devotes itself.

Hoc opus, hic labor est

The challenging, essayistic appeal to dialogue that colors both *Scénario du film "Passion"* and *JLG/JLG* returns in *Histoire(s) du cinéma*, which to date is Godard's most ambitious self-portrait. As a many-voiced narrator, character,

To Show and Show Oneself Showing

participant in a conversation with the film critic Serge Daney, and orchestrator of mostly repossessed sounds, images, and texts that assail the viewer in highly complex and rhythmic ways, Godard seems almost omnipresent in the series, his "phantom"-like role distributed even more broadly over the work's surfaces than in *JLG/JLG*.[40] As the essayistic magnum opus of his late period, *Histoire(s)* retrospectively comprises and reconsiders each of his earlier phases through acts of citation from within his own corpus. Using video superimpositions, he stages historical encounters between "Godard" and "Godard" at different moments in his career, as when episode 1B samples the last shot of *Contempt* (1963) in which Fritz Lang films Ulysses saluting an invisible Ithaca: we see, in a composite image, Godard light a cigar in his study, circa 1988, while he appears alongside the younger Godard who plays Lang's assistant.

As I explained in chapter 2, *Histoire(s)*, at its crux, is an argument for and intensive demonstration of the power of montage to bring into sight relations between things, events, and people—*otherwise undetectable relations*, the shared observation of which brings people together in turn. This, for Godard, is what gave cinema its calling. Yet he also argues that the medium failed to harness this capacity when it was most needed—namely, in the face of the twentieth century's most horrific social injustices and catastrophes. His videographic montage does not try to revive this power *as it once was*, in the full span of cinema's communal bearings (which would require a popular framework of reception from which the video series is well removed). Rather, it presents an intensified expression of *what cinema might have been*, had its resources of montage been better understood, applied, and tested. It is through this *subjunctive* approach to the cinematic past that Godard retains for his video project—all its melancholy notwithstanding—a lingering sense of possibility as he tries to share a way of perceiving with the viewer. His performance in the series and his manner of address are conjointly keyed to this task.

My earlier reading of *Histoire(s)* showed how Godard reflexively comments on the binding force of montage through a motif of "twoness" that extends to the video's reception: the dazzling links he displays, in order to count as revelatory findings, must bring together *at least two viewers* who share the perception of a historical affinity. I illustrated how this plays out in the form and content of the series itself through images of coupling that rhetorically stand in for the spectators required for this intimate relational process. What I would like to take up here is the way in which Godard figures, through self-portraiture, as one of the two viewers in question, the other being the co-investigator his practice invokes.

From the outset, the video series solicits and characterizes our encounter. Episode 1A opens with titles (in Latin) warning that the task at hand is arduous: "hoc opus / hic labor est" (this is the task / this is the toil).[41] The first clip shows James Stewart as Jeffries in Hitchcock's *Rear Window* (1954), his

174   Chapter 4

eyes shifting behind his telephoto lens at a slowed, uneven rate.[42] More titles assert that we will have to "negotiate" for ourselves the relations among the manifold fragments since Godard—now citing a Robert Bresson aphorism in voiceover—will refrain from showing us "all sides of things," leaving a "margin of indefiniteness."[43] Our role is alluded to in Hitchcock's vigilant and imaginative Jeffries—a spectator who constructs a fuller picture from the transient and ambiguous details he spies from across the courtyard (while obsessively projecting his desires and anxieties onto them). In this way, the series indicates that our charge as participants goes beyond critically weighing the combinations Godard presents. Because *Histoire(s)* burdens us with its incompletion, and because no implicit logic of *pars pro toto* (the part representing the whole) points us toward a grand unity, our role also consists in creatively responding to gaps and blind spots in the open-ended ensembles we are shown.

Godard's reuse of Hitchcock's protagonist is further apt in that Jeffries, a photographer by trade, is something of an artist, an image-maker, in addition to being a spectator. A similar, more deeply self-conscious marriage of creative and receptive roles informs Godard's self-portraiture in *Histoire(s)*. The key scenes in this respect are those set in his library/study, where he typically assumes one of two positions—seated behind his typewriter or standing by his crowded bookshelves. These recurring scenes, interspersed across the eight episodes, appear, on the surface, to correspond to the director-at-work shots that appear in many essay films. Consider the foregrounding of the editing station in examples as disparate as Welles's *F for Fake* (1975) and Farocki's *The Expression of Hands* (1975).[44] These moments can be seen as counterparts to the passages in Montaigne's *Essais* where the self-studying essayist makes his reader aware of the physical setting, the circular library, in which the composition of his work happens. In many of Godard's late videos, most dramatically *Scénario du film "Passion,"* we see him using the basic tools of his art. But in *Histoire(s)*, for all its emphasis on montage, there are no shots of him technically at work (unless we count the collaborative blind editor segment he recycles more than once from *JLG/JLG*). The library scenes instead show him writing short, evocative phrases—mostly citations—on his mnemonic typewriter, a machine that, with its staccato clacking, substitutes for the technical apparatus of cinema. Just as often, Godard removes a text from his bookshelf at random (a contrivance, of course), says its title, reads from its pages, or uses its cover for visual purposes. These acts trigger videographic streams of montage that issue forth abruptly as if from his cinematic memory and imagination.

These scenes in Godard's library cut to the heart of *Histoire(s)* and its montage-based effort to build a critical bond between essayist and viewer. Like the interludes with Welles at his Moviola in *F for Fake*, they return us to the nucleus from which the film's reflection unfolds, but, as I have said, Godard's filmmaking utensils are nowhere in sight. Even as his appearance affirms his quasi-corporeal connection to the work he composes, these scenes depict him less as a filmmaker per se than as a writer, reader, and, most importantly, spectator. In these scenes, he often turns his eyes upward just before the montaged images arrive, as if to cast his gaze onto a screen somewhere out of frame. At other times, he holds his eyeglasses in place with one hand, staring raptly ahead and looking inside-out from superimpositions of which he is a constitutive feature. He receives images from a frontal position, as in *Scénario*, but no longer with his back to the audience. These visions materialize somewhere between him and ourselves. Unlike the titles that accompany them, they seem not quite inscribed on the picture plane; more delicate, they take shape as though projected onto the smoke rising from his cigar (fig. 4.5).

Godard's synthesis of authorial and spectatorial roles adapts the Montaignean tradition of the essayistic. Montaigne's self-portrait performs a constant overlap of writing and reading (and of rewriting and rereading). He thus functions as what Jean Starobinski calls "the first reader" of the *Essais*, a figure who models particular strategies of reading that he aims to pass on.[45] In *Histoire(s)*, Godard depicts himself in the role of what I wish to call the "first viewer," that is, a character who boldly incarnates, within the video series itself, the form of seeing he tries to share. In this account, we are the "second viewers."[46]

Figure 4.5. Video superimposition as sally of the mind: *Histoire(s) du cinéma* (Godard, 1988–98), episode 1B.

176   Chapter 4

In the context of debates on the essay film, this might not sound like a fresh claim. It might seem to have recourse to the "I-You" scheme of direct address and interactivity theorized by Rascaroli, which I have already shown Godard eschews. After all, in her interpretation of Farocki's *Images of the World and the Inscription of War* (1989), Rascaroli comparably maintains that Farocki inhabits the film's investigation less as an author than as a "researcher" and "spectator" who is "practically on the same level as the audience," an audience the film continuously and directly "interpellates," summons into action.[47] But my argument for Godard as the "first viewer" entails a stranger, more radical fusion of roles that renders murky the border between the essayist's inquisitive seeing and ours, between his thinking and ours. At stake in this relationship is a more intricate conception of the image and its shareability.

As we saw in chapter 2, the video montage in *Histoire(s)* abides by a poetic definition of the image that Godard borrows from Pierre Reverdy: the image as a "pure creation of the mind," its construction owing to the *rapprochement* of "two more or less distant realities," two apparently unrelated materials that converge to yield an unexpected resonance. This means that for Godard, an image is as much a mental process as something concretely filmed. By portraying himself as a spectator/reader removed from the gadgetry of image production, and by shifting the emphasis, within his conception of montage, from issues of making to *viewing*, the scenes of Godard in his study reassert the point not just that the image is a psychic operation, but that the "second viewer" must become a skilled montagist as well.

Video superimposition is a cardinal device in Godard's elaboration of this dynamic, bearing forth as it does the pensive, combinatory spirit of *rapprochement* while mediating between his role in the series and ours. The library/study scenes enlist the optical device somewhat in line with its use in certain French impressionist films of the 1920s—as a means to exhibit a process of thought that oscillates between the "inner life" of a character and the sensuous world outside. The composite images that integrate Godard's ruminating persona do not grant us a window into his individual subjectivity so much as they portray the opening of his exploratory thought onto external forces, onto otherness. And if the feel of these images is such that their emergent strata hover at the very boundary of the screen, this is because we, as second viewers, are among the others to whom this process invitingly offers itself.

Doing our part as second viewers means that, beyond examining the ensembles shown to us, beyond thinking in stride with the videographic process (which, as often as not, outpaces us), we contribute where the material discourse breaks down, where connections between fragments are missing, where obscurity resounds, where "a margin of indefiniteness" requires our creative addition. Godard links superimposition to the form of spectatorship

To Show and Show Oneself Showing

177

he models precisely because it is not the exclusive province of a filmmaker but a combinatory process we can enact, too, albeit mentally. In his interview with Youssef Ishaghpour, Godard says that he uses the optical device "not all the time, but to remind, to show that it's there."[48] Godardian superimposition is an ongoing interplay between the visible and the invisible, the patent and the implied: it portrays a thought process that is not restricted to material coalescences on the screen.

It is during one of Godard's library scenes, in episode 3A, that he first applies the phrase "a form that thinks," which some scholars have glossed as a shorthand for the essay film in its generic entirety.[49] For Godard, this notion of a thinking form develops through an intermedial comparison between cinema and painting. What prompts his use of the phrase is his memory of George Bataille's claim that the women in Édouard Manet's portraits seem to be saying to the beholder: "I know what you're thinking." *Histoire(s)* shuffles between several portraits of women (prints of works by Leonardo da Vinci, Johannes Vermeer, and Jean-Baptiste-Camille Corot). This happens as Godard's voiceover, now drawing on André Malraux's argument, contends that prior to Manet's extraordinary female portraits, the attitudes of the depicted subjects evoke narcissism—the women "say *me, me*. The rest of the world comes after that." Conversely, Manet's work shows "the interior world" in the midst of its becoming enmeshed with "the cosmos." The barmaid from Manet's *A Bar at the Folies-Bergère* (1881–82) fades in and out as Godard says that Manet, through this innovation, ushers in modern painting. And, for Godard, this means that Manet prepares the ground for cinema as well: "That is to say, the cinematograph. That is to say, forms making their way toward speech. To be exact, a form that thinks. The fact that cinema was initially made for thinking was soon forgotten. . . . The flame was finally extinguished at Auschwitz."

For Godard, "a form that thinks" is, more than a generic label for the essay film, a power of expression and engagement that he claims modern painting historically bequeathed to cinema, where it came into its own, only to be squandered, "forgotten." This is a form, moreover, that departs from egoism, orients itself toward exteriority, and embroils the viewer in a drama of thinking that opens the "interior world" onto the "cosmos." We can also deduce in the light of the overall context of episode 3A—which is a plea for resistance to state tyranny and violence—that this form harbors a vital ethical and political charge. The reference to the Holocaust reminds of us of this calling (as does a clip recycled from the "legend of stereo" lesson in *JLG/JLG*).

Folded into this reflection are views of Godard puffing on a cigar in his study, with most of his body engulfed in shadow. "I was alone, lost in my thoughts," he comments, while looking off to our right. His frontal figure rhymes with (and via superimposition overlaps with) a series of the sampled paintings, making it clear that *his* system of address is under consideration here, too.

178   Chapter 4

The portrayed women vary, in their relationship to the viewer, between direct address and absorption, between lively and deadpan countenances—between figures who return our gaze and others who cast their attention inward or elsewhere. As for Godard, at no point does he look into the camera or speak in a way that recognizes his audience. He appears oblivious to our presence, and yet the discourse of the montage signals the necessity of his movement toward, and thinking with, others. A title coinciding with his claim of solitude declares, "1 thought." Seconds later, however, a new title reads, "1+2 thought." (This expression has two possible permutations: either a bond formed between "first" and "second" viewers; or Godard's thought ["1"] as assayed and confirmed by that of at least two other viewers ["2"]. We might also read this addition as riffing on the key aphorism from *The Old Place* [1999] we addressed in chapter 3: "One is in the other, the other is in the one, and these are three persons.")

Delimiting as it does a process of putting one's thought in porous contact with the world and with the thought of others, "a form that thinks," in Godard's sense, does not simply sum up the essay film as an already existing genre. It designates the highest dialogical ambition toward which his practice strives without assurance of its fulfillment. The movement from "1" to "1+2," from solitude to thinking together, isn't a recipe but an always uncertain and laborious push. At the end of episode 3A, a staggered title repeats, "a form / that thinks" (in contradistinction to "a thought / that forms," which Godard adversely aligns with the coerciveness of fascism and "bad films").[50] As is the essayist's wont, he reinscribes a motif of coupling as he ponders the possibility of achieving this "1+2" relation. A photograph of a contemplative Pier Paolo Pasolini pairs with a detail of a feminine onlooker from Piero della Francesca's fifteenth-century fresco *The Legend of the True Cross*. And this leads to a charcoal drawing of a man and woman, a couple in what appears to be eighteenth-century western European attire, gazing in the same direction. The "+" in Godard's arithmetic is, to be sure, a call to intimacy with and between fellow observers. But we sense this call through its indirect address, through its portrait of the essayist immersed in "the task, the toil" that the video series partially assigns to us.

Given this coupling motif, the visual apostrophe that opens *Histoire(s)* and associates us with Jeffries in *Rear Window* takes on added dimensions, already implying, through citation, a necessary move from solitary to dual perception. Jeffries, a flawed, immobilized, and initially uncompromising character, requires the intervention of Lisa (Grace Kelly), whose thought and sensitivity prove more instrumental than his in uncovering the mystery. Hitchcock's film thus offers no simple valorization of spectatorship but an example of spectatorship crucially made companionable. Godard, supplementing his own warnings and disclaimers, also brings into play Hitchcock's reflexive notion that spectatorship can be a potentially perilous affair—both Jeffries and Lisa nearly pay for their inquisitiveness with their lives.

I Was That Man

Given the many roles Godard plays in *Histoire(s)* and the vast array of others he "impersonates" through citation,[51] how can we even identify "Godard" as a specific, coherent subject? How are we to reconcile his identity as an essayist with the alien presences that infiltrate his persona? And how are we ultimately to understand where he himself fits within the (hi)story(ies) of cinema he recounts?

To respond to these thorny questions, we need to take up how the video series, similar in this respect to *JLG/JLG*, achieves a kind of "becoming medium" on Godard's part—an intensive and dispersive passage of himself into citation, into the sounds and sights that comprise his work, and into the way of seeing he upholds from the position of a viewer. Let us consider the end of chapter 4B and, hence, of the series as a whole. In a gesture culminating a chapter already dense with references to his earlier films,[52] Godard inscribes himself as a figure trying to seize hold of something irretrievable, something that faintly glimmers in the work of artists and poets before him. He does this through the use of cited material that itself evokes variations on this objective. Following a reworked shot of the blind editor executing a cut in *JLG/JLG*—the shot now mixes with Mischa Auer peering through his magnifying glass in Welles's *Mr. Arkadin* (1955), and also with the razor-slashing of the woman's eye from the prologue of Luis Buñuel and Salvador Dalí's *Un chien andalou* (1929)—we hear Ezra Pound reading from his *Cantos*. Pound's voice is made to coincide with a clip of Orson Welles as Othello, spying on Desdemona while she walks through a dark, labyrinthine interior, throws open curtains, and then stares back at the eye of the camera. Already in play here are associated motifs of adapting, recovering, optical detection, blindness, and (potentially) perceiving anew. Where Welles's film adapts Shakespeare's tragedy, Pound creatively retranslates (from an older Latin translation into archaic English) Homer's *The Odyssey*—specifically the *nekyia* scene from book XI, in which Odysseus and his crew summon souls of the dead and interact with the "pitiful spirit" of their fallen friend, Elpenor.

On the heels of the Welles and Pound citations, there appears a shot of a yellow rose that fleetingly couples with the title "machine of dreams" (a subheading gleaned from Jean Epstein's text *The Intelligence of a Machine* [1946]). The flower is from Godard's own *Germany Year 90 Nine Zero* (1991), but where the flower is white in his earlier film to express mourning for the execution of Sophie Scholl, a German student beheaded in 1943 for distributing anti-Nazi leaflets (the name of her intellectual resistance group was The White Rose), here its color has changed, through videographic tinkering, to yellow. An intertitle, "Jorge Luis Borges," alerts us to the relevance of this switch. Godard's gruff voiceover now intones, "If a man . . . If a man . . . If a man wandered through paradise in his dreams and kept a flower to remind himself of where he'd been and on waking discovered the flower in his hands . . . What's to say, then? I was that man." As Godard speaks this last line, a photographic portrait of himself in dark sunglasses materializes in two consecutive ensembles: first, in a rapidly pulsing alternation with the yellow flower; then, in a superimposition with a print of Francis Bacon's painting *Study for a Portrait of Van Gogh II* (1957), a near-abstract landscape scene in which an artist figure seems to melt into his own deathly shadow (fig. 4.6).

This valedictory sequence in *Histoire(s)* displays Godard's videographic montage at its most acutely palimpsestic, the notions of memory, revision, and layered repetition already infusing the texts he gathers. The story of a man waking from a dream of paradise with a flower in his hands comes from Borges, who was already rephrasing a notebook entry by Samuel Taylor Coleridge, who, in turn, was reshaping a passage written by Jean Paul. The allusion to Borges here is itself multiple, pointing as it does not just to his essay "The Dream of Coleridge" (1952) but also to his related short stories "The Other" (1975), in which the elderly Borges converses with his younger self in a dream of indefinite origin, and "The Yellow Rose" (1960), where an aging poet who was once heralded as "the next Homer and the next Dante" is given the titular flower on his deathbed and has an epiphany

Figure 4.6. Godard's parting, citational act of self-portraiture: *Histoire(s) du cinéma*, episode 4B.

To Show and Show Oneself Showing

of seeing it "the way Adam must have seen it in Paradise" (hence the switch to yellow in *Histoire(s)*). These minutely reconfigured associations attest to the fact that Godard has chosen and rearranged the concluding fragments of his video series with utmost care. Collectively the citations traverse a liminal realm between hell and paradise, between the living and the dead, between dream and waking, between horror and beauty, between fiction and document, between cinema and other media.

The montage hints at a potential for astonishment, but running through these scenarios of authors drawing on their precursors, there is also an undercurrent of failure and remove, a sense of irretrievability despite the proof of passage suggested by the flower. These ghostly re-creations depart from the sources on which they are based. Bacon's canvas only distantly evokes the spirit (and empties out the sanguine mood) of Van Gogh's autobiographical *The Artist on the Road to Tarascon* (1888), the original of which is believed to have been destroyed by Allied planes in the bombing of Magdeburg in 1945.[53] In Pound's recitation of his own *Cantos*, we have an effort to channel—from antiquity into a high modernist poetics of citation and commentary—the force of Homer's epic verse so that it might describe the present and future. Godard's use of montage, however, negates Pound's effort by asking us to judge the undeniable lyricism of the poet's verbal recitation in the light of the despicable cultural aims and pro-fascist view of history toward which the *Cantos*, here invoked here at its germinal root, would soon work.

"I was that man." This poignant statement at once affirms for Godard a singular status in the history he narrates *and* ambiguously stitches him into the multiauthored web of that history, in effect dividing and pluralizing an "I" that can know itself only via the intensive mediation of others. The content of the montage and the music that goes with it—a calm piano solo by Ketil Bjørnstad—lend a funereal overtone to this conclusion. To some extent, Godard replays the last moments of *JLG/JLG* by again turning his concerns to his mortality and by venturing a dramatic claim upon posterity. But the statement "I was that man" carries a more specific valence than "a man, nothing but a man" does in the earlier film. It is unclear whether Godard allies his project with one of the artists and writers involved in the passage more than the others, but the "dream" in question, we can be sure, pertains to the cinema ("machine of dreams") and to the particular conception of the medium that Godard remembers and looks to reanimate even while conceding the impossibility of its full recovery.

Godard claims to have been "that man" who participated firsthand—as a spectator, critic, and filmmaker—in the lived experience of a cinema that enabled people to see things, histories, and complicated relations between them, a cinema that bound people together in the process of discerning these relationships. The rose he retains from his dream is a vestige of the reality of a cinema of shared vision and thought on which *Histoire(s)* premises itself retrospectively. But the meaning of this borrowed parable also bears

182   Chapter 4

on present and future engagements with Godard's work by fellow observers. Whether he *remains* "that man," we might say, depends on how convincingly he effects a more intimate, inquisitive, and revelatory form of this kind of cinema through his videographic montage—it depends on his ability to make this form of seeing our own. Nothing guarantees this outcome. The repeated, conditional "if" that begins his parting lines insinuates as much.

The Essayist as Obscure Pedagogue

Across the examples of Godard's self-portraiture that we have focused on in this chapter, three essayistic features have stood out. First of all, it should be apparent that the director inhabits his work in a fashion that shows little concern for representing himself as a personality or as a subject steeped in conventional signs of psychological interiority. Autobiographical traces make their way into these late works, but what Godard portrays isn't "himself" so much as his method, a method to which he devotes his voice, body, and thought because it is vital to his (and to our) engagement with certain aesthetic and conceptual problems. His method, which we can generally encapsulate as exploratory montage, is not a static protocol. The method of "seeing first" that he exemplifies in *Scénario du film "Passion"* anticipates his approach in *Histoire(s)*, but in both instances, what we see in action is an experimental method that he subjects to continual change and recalibration in the midst of its use. Moreover—and this is the second feature I want to stress—the reflective method he exhibits in these efforts isn't reserved for technical image-making; it is the potential province of the viewer, too, as a mental and perceptual exercise. These self-portraits are nothing if not attempts to "educate the image-making medium within us."[54] Third, although this essayistic approach situates Godard as a figure who models—or in his parlance, "shows"—a process that he intends to transmit, we typically have to meet him more than halfway. Our share in the reflection comes down to our *acquisition* of the method on display, but Godard invariably makes this a trying affair by heaping obstacle upon obstacle, layer upon layer, giving us little in the way of forthright guidance.

I want to bring this chapter to a close by attending to one final example, another late work of self-depiction in which Godard's aim of extending a method of inquiry to the viewer becomes more manifest and urgent. *Notre musique (Our Music)* features the director again in the role of "himself," and his performance nearly condenses all of the main themes and conflicts of his self-portraiture I have emphasized. Judged alongside our earlier examples in this chapter, what is most immediately striking about *Notre musique* is that it portrays the older, white-haired Godard released from his Rolle hideaway and returned, temporarily, to public life. What seems to have drawn him out is a call of artistic and intellectual responsibility in the wake of a disastrous

To Show and Show Oneself Showing

event, the siege of Sarajevo. Within the film's narrative, he travels to the war-scarred Bosnian city to take part in an annual European Literary Encounters conference and deliver a lecture entitled "Text and Image." To be precise, the film presents a reenactment of the lecture he gave when he in fact participated in the conference in 2002, two years before he completed *Notre musique*.[55] On the face of it, this social circumstance might appear to indicate Godard's reinvigoration as a politically committed and didactic filmmaker. His lecture indeed preoccupies itself with political matters and with their historical ramifications, but we will see that the form it takes and the mode of address it employs remain consistent with the post-militant, more markedly speculative style of essayism that has been in force in his work since *Ici et ailleurs*.

To make sense of Godard's lecture scene, we need to recognize its place within the film's overall, essayistic ravel of semi-fabricated narrative, meta-critical consciousness, and historically informed argument.[56] *Notre musique* consists of three successive parts distinguished by Dantean intertitles: "Kingdom 1: Hell," "Kingdom 2: Purgatory," and "Kingdom 3: Paradise." The "Hell" segment that begins the film is a videographic montage that resembles the look and character of *Histoire(s)*—it takes clips from fiction films and documentary footage and weaves them into new, sometimes clashing and sometimes harmonious combinations. The motif linking these fragments is one of imperial (and genocidal) conquest as the montage intertwines atrocities of the twentieth century, events that are echoed by the content of fiction films caught up in the mix—films varying in genre from the Hollywood western and the film noir to European art cinema. The "Hell" segment also invokes the history of the essay film itself. Footage of camp victims reappears from *Night and Fog*. Godard's (more sparing) use of a tranquil female narrator brings to mind both Marker's *Sans soleil* (1983) and Farocki's *Images of the World and the Inscription of War*; and his appropriation of westerns and combat films recalls Guy Debord's *In girum imus nocte et consumimur igni* (1978).

If Godard's eclectic montage muddles the distinction between fiction and documentary, it also drives home a well-nigh apocalyptic view of history as an endless succession of skirmishes and annihilations. The Bosnian War blends in with a gamut of other conflicts around the globe that, for all their contextual variances, seem to replicate one another in terms of their outcomes if not also their root motivations. If the musical accompaniment—a medley of tracks from Hans Otte's wistful solo piano work *The Book of Sounds* (1984)—plays on with little disruption and without competing noise, which is not typical of Godard's sonic tendencies, this is because it, too, lends the events recounted in the montage a feeling of inevitable perpetuation (by dint of the repeating arpeggios and the accented notes within them that Godard coordinates with military offensives). An unnerving graphic correspondence between a mortally wounded civilian woman from Sergei Eisenstein's *Battleship Potemkin* (1925) and an actual female death camp victim being dragged

184   Chapter 4

off to a mass grave suggests not just another repetition but the failure of leftist revolution and of cinema in its name to prevent or reverse this history.

At one point the music pauses and the female voiceover intrudes, concurrent with a black screen, to offer a rephrased line from the Lord's Prayer: "Forgive us our trespasses as we forgive those who have trespassed against us. Yes, *as we forgive them* and no different." This statement introduces a baseline ethical perspective counseling charity toward the other, the suggestion being that our salvation hangs on it. We cannot, after all, neglect the fact that the horrors multiplied before us result from one or more prevailing dogmatisms—nationalistic empire, racist mythology, theistic entitlement, or geopolitical doctrines cemented around the Cold War—as they authorize cyclical aggression toward the Other whom they necessarily designate as their foe, their inferior, or their unequal. We are not far here from the "stereo" lesson in *JLG/JLG*. The underlying point of the "Hell" montage, as it transitions into the "Purgatory" section, isn't just to identify and condemn the guilty parties, but also to raise—rather modestly and without an already settled-upon course of action—the questions of how to resist this violent paradigm, how to install genuine dialogue in its place, and how to use the cinematic medium to this end. *Notre musique* thus begins by longing for the *discovery* of a rhythm of togetherness, an "our music" that rejects these militaristic and fraternal worldviews and founds itself on a humble embrace of alterity.

Godard's lecture takes place in the "Purgatory" part of the film, which revolves around the literary conference and the European intellectuals who have voyaged to Sarajevo to participate in it. In the plot, his lecture occurs immediately after a scene where a young Israeli female journalist (who narrates the "Hell" opening) interviews the Palestinian poet Mahmoud Darwish. This order of events is significant in that the interview prefigures the lecture, along the lines of both subject matter and form. Godard stages their discussion with odd breaks in continuity, utilizing only the light from a window, the characters mere silhouettes at times. The scene treats their dialogue not as a given fact of interpersonal exchange but as a fragile, trying ordeal. At one juncture, Godard subtly uses a technique that will function as the conceptual basis of his lecture, shot/countershot cutting, but already, he makes the device strange by using it within coordinates of time and space that are unstable and irrational.

The lecture itself is a kind of attempted dialogue (likewise marked by an interplay of light and darkness) between Godard and a small, mostly young audience, through the intermediary of a woman translator. It begins as Godard sits down, snaps open his briefcase, and launches into a divagating series of questions and provocations raised by photographs. The first portion of his lecture concerns quandaries of perception—the identification of buildings ruined by war, the identification of the Virgin Mary—when there is only one picture, viewed in isolation, cut off from comparative contact

To Show and Show Oneself Showing   185

with other pictures. He challenges those in attendance to correctly identify
a bombed-out cityscape in a grainy, black-and-white photograph, and after
their wrong guesses—"Stalingrad," "Beirut," "Sarajevo," "Hiroshima"—they
are surprised to hear him reply: "Richmond, Virginia. 1865."

Throughout the scene, the use of sound is just as meaningful as the
photographs. It allows Godard's vocal address to shift in tone, vector, and
orientation, thereby distinguishing between two groups of receivers: the
attendees of the lecture and the viewers of *Notre musique*. That is to say, his
voice does not stay in one register but erratically changes, now sounding as
though it fills the entire lecture hall, now sounding softer and more internal
as though it is a voiceover passage that the audience *of* the film can hear
while the audience portrayed *in* the film cannot. It is with this latter nuance
of voicing that he arcanely remarks, "Yes, the image is joy but beside it lays
the void. All the power of an image can only be expressed through it."

This aphorism, which suggests that the power of an image owes not to its
integral content but to expressive forces at work in the voids surrounding it,
prompts Godard's camera to track laterally back and forth over the small
crowd, continually adjusting its speed and proximity and focal range as an
introspective piano score emerges. Godard tells the audience: "Try to see. Try
to imagine. In the first case, you say: 'Look at that.' In the second, you say:
'Close your eyes.'" The camera comes to a halt on a young woman with her
eyes shut. Precisely at the moment she opens them, Godard says, "The shot
and countershot are basics of film grammar." Before he finishes this line, a
cut (anticipated by a flare of light and a short-lived black screen) reverses the
camera's angle, so that we are now gazing back at Godard. This shot, in fact,
is a countershot, in line with the vantage of the woman just shown.

These sensory details within and between shots matter precisely because
they—as much as Godard's spoken queries and statements—are the carriers
of thought at play in this roundabout lecture prompting us to reconsider the
utility of a device that is ordinarily, at least in traditional narrative cinema,
constricted to the back-and-forth representation of characters speaking to
one another. Godard—now a blurred, shadowy figure in the background—
refers to two successive shots he has taken from Howard Hawks's romantic
comedy *His Girl Friday* (1940).[57] The shots appear as photographic stills in
the immediate foreground, as two hands compare them through juxtaposition and alternation. There are, in fact, two different members of the diegetic
audience who handle these photos, their bodies offscreen except for their
limbs: one holds a shot of Cary Grant while someone else, in an adjacent seat,
wields the corresponding countershot of Rosalind Russell (fig. 4.7).

We have observed many times in this book that Godard uses images in a
manner whereby the relationships they express, the happenings they stage,
have a reflexive bearing on the kind of relationship he seeks to build with
the viewer. In such moments, the events shown onscreen at some level allude
to and comment on the conditions of our requested engagement. The shot in

Figure 4.7. Rethinking the principle of shot/countershot: *Notre musique* (Godard, 2004).

the lecture scene that makes use of the stills from *His Girl Friday* is another instance of this. The complexity of its staging is such that three different relational fields converge and overlay at the same time: one between Godard and the audience depicted *in* the film; another between the two attendees holding the stills; and yet another between Godard and the implicit addressee of *Notre musique*, that is, the viewer. As we closely study the example of shot/countershot from Hawks's film (which is itself a figure of interpersonal exchange), we are pressed to keep in mind multiple other fields of interaction that converge around Godard's use of it—fields that visually intersect in the frame beneath the ceiling lamp that hangs just to the side of Godard's head and supplies an air of mystery with its chiaroscuro accents.

Still speaking from the background, Godard contends that the shot/countershot from *His Girl Friday* in essence shows "the same thing twice." As such, it also shows that "the director is incapable of seeing the difference between a man and a woman." This criticism initially seems tangential, but it holds a key to what Godard is out to achieve through his lecture in the overall context of *Notre musique*. I take it he disagrees with Hawks's traditional shot/countershot on two related grounds—because it manufactures sameness where we ought to discern difference (the shots of Grant and Russell talking on the phone to each other indeed mirror one another with regimented

To Show and Show Oneself Showing

symmetry) *and* because it imposes a narrative-based, talk-driven sense of continuity as an a priori matter of course. Hawks's contrivance is not just that it conceals and therein degrades otherness, but that it programmatically assumes—*instead of seeking out*—a continuous relationship between the elements it juxtaposes.

Godard calls attention to these problems with a view to rethinking the applicability of this device beyond the routine syntax of popular narrative cinema. As becomes evident as the lecture goes on, he recasts shot/countershot as a principle of comparative and differential observation, a form of seeing that always deals with a minimum of two shots at once and that ignites—for the viewer as much as for the filmmaker—exploratory and imaginative thought. He thus turns to the device in response to the problems of perception that set his master class in motion, and starts to use a modified version of it himself in the hope of extending its function, its potential efficacy, to the audience he engages.

Having redefined the formal procedure, Godard guides us through a series of "shots" and "countershots" that are more political in character. He holds up two photographs that reveal opposing sides of the same moment in 1948: a vibrant color "shot" of Jewish refugees walking from the sea onto the shore of a newly established nation of Israel; and a black-and-white "countershot" of Palestinians "walk[ing] into the water to drown," as Godard puts it.[58] This provocative juxtaposition insinuates an affinity with the perspective of Darwish in the preceding interview scene, namely that "the truth has two faces," a line uttered by Darwish, now repeated by Godard as if from memory.[59]

In the circuitous logic of the lecture, then, the concern for safeguarding difference (which is first indicated in terms of gender) leads to an ethically minded consideration of disastrous self-versus-other hostilities that affect entire cultures (which returns thematically to the beginning of the film and its hellish montage of unending cruelty). It is certainly the case that Godard sympathizes with the Palestinians as he does elsewhere in his corpus, but this isn't a simple act of side-taking that holds to a predetermined view. At a more basic level, his retooling of shot/countershot works to break down the doctrinaire non-thought that has prolonged this territorial, religious, ethnic, and political dispute. A pivotal moment on this score occurs just before the 1948 comparison, when Godard's voice pauses and we cut between two young audience members who are investigating photographs—a young woman associated with a photo of an emaciated camp inmate, this picture inscribed with the word "Jew"; and a young Arab male who is linked with a different photo of a death camp victim, this one inscribed with the word "Muslim."[60] With this shot and countershot between viewers embedded in the diegesis, Godard recalls that in the Nazi camps and at Auschwitz in particular, the German term *Muselmann* (Muslim) was used for those who had declined to such a condition of abject suffering as to be ignored even by their fellow inmates.[61] As is frequently the case with Godard's references to

188   Chapter 4

Israel-Palestine, the purpose of this history lesson is to decry the methodical oppression of displaced Palestinians by the Israeli regime and to address this injustice, however troublingly, with regard to the earlier persecution of the European Jews, an atrocity whose magnitude Godard's thought nowhere plays down. But the spirit of this moment of the lecture is more searching than it is declarative. Godard uses shot/countershot as a provisional way of detecting and traversing a field of relatedness between two beings who nevertheless retain their respective otherness to one another, without otherness figuring as a menace and thus as grounds for aggression. What this cinematic gesture acts to articulate is a shared mortality—a commonly felt and lived substrate of vulnerability that dogmatic positions on the conflict have made it their business to efface. And given that the "Muslim" and "Jew" featured in the scene are being taught the same investigative process that we are, the film endows this process with the potential not merely to uncover hidden connections, but also to initiate the collaborative "we" that welcomes, and in fact needs, otherness.[62]

The lecture comes to an unresolved end with a shot of a lamp swinging diagonally across a black frame (I would call this insert non-diegetic were it not for the ceiling lamp shown earlier in the scene).[63] Godard's voiceover, vying with murmurs from a crowd that has grown restive, offers a charged if obscure mantra: "Shot and countershot. Imaginary: certainty. Reality: uncertainty. The principle of cinema. Go towards the light, and shine it on our night. Our music." After this insert, a brief question-and-answer session takes place, consisting of a single question. Someone offscreen asks Godard if the new digital cameras can "save the cinema," and Godard sits mutely in the shadows, opting not to respond.[64]

Even *Notre musique*'s most sedulous viewer will have many questions for Godard at this point. What final claim or message are we to take away from all this? How, and in what sorts of circumstances, are we, as viewers, supposed to apply the operation of shot/countershot that he demonstrates? If everything turns on our acquisition of this means of comparison and analysis, then why does he teach it so abstrusely? If Godard hopes to inspire a critical dialogue with his addressees, then why does he disregard the question he is asked? Why does he take elaborate measures to emphasize the relational space between himself and his audience—and to stress interaction more generally on ethical as well as perceptual grounds—only to refrain from lucid communication, leaving that interspace a chasm? And what, in the end, are we to make of this essayistic filmmaker's insistence on portraying himself as obscure, in both the semantic and pictorial senses of the term? How does this tendency on his part resonate with the cinematic essay at large and its evolving history?

Much of this interpretive confusion can be cleared up once we elucidate, in sharper detail, the divided structure of address at work in the lecture—the way in which the scene differentiates between its diegetic and extra-diegetic

To Show and Show Oneself Showing

audiences. I have already pointed out that Godard's vocal delivery shifts throughout the scene, at times sounding softer and more internal, as if conveying thoughts to which only the extra-diegetic viewer of the film is privy, as a sort of eavesdropper. As the scene unfurls, the audience *in* the film becomes restless, laughing and whispering to each other during some of the lecture's most enthralling moments. Even before Godard ignores the only question he is asked, the scene shows a failed attempt at dialogue.

Rascaroli interprets this breakdown as Godard's amusingly self-conscious affirmation that in "essayistic communicative negotiation," success isn't guaranteed. If Godard had "answered the question," she argues, "he would have closed down the dialogue. . . . Faithful to the content of his lecture, and to the rhetorical structure of his entire film, he chooses instead to let the question hang."[65] For Rascaroli, what is most important is this "ethos" of open-endedness and the scene's dramatization of "direct address" itself.[66] Her analysis, however, makes too little of the important fact that a certain way of seeing, shot/countershot, is being demonstrated for the viewer's critical procurement. It seems to me that Godard is silent during the question-and-answer session precisely because the question put to him, which is strictly technological in nature, has nothing to do with this process and thus brings home the fact that his lecture has been in vain. Rascaroli's account assumes that Godard's manner of address to the attendees of the lecture is essentially the same as his manner of address to the film's audience, but this isn't so.

Once the diegetic audience begins to stir and disengage, Godard alters his address to the spectator *of* the film. From this point on the scene predominantly focuses on his side of the lecture hall, with the camera much closer to his figure and the crowd before him a blurred mass. For instance, the 1948 Israel-Palestine juxtaposition rounds off with a tight medium close-up of Godard from the back, the camera just behind his semi-dark head and shoulders as he compares the two photographs with his hands, doing so with the pictures turned away from the crowd and toward the extra-diegetic viewer, that is, *toward us*. Indeed, he handles the photos so that we can spy them clearly above his right shoulder (fig. 4.8). This oblique mode of address pursues a more intimate, co-investigative relationship with the film's viewer than the format of the public lecture allows. Dispensing with direct address, which proves futile in the diegesis, Godard appeals to our complicity, our judgment, through subtle insinuation.[67]

We have witnessed this move before in Godard's self-portraits. He frequently holds up the reflective power of the method he intends to share while making us conscious of a past or parallel circumstance in which it failed to work for others besides himself. He does this with what he calls "seeing first" in *Scénario*; with a montage-based principle of seeing together in *Histoire(s)*; and now with a modified version of shot/countershot. The failed transmission and reception dramatized in the film's diegesis serves to accentuate, through contrast, the stakes riding on our own attempt to make sense

Figure 4.8. Over-the-shoulder view of Godard's lecture: *Notre musique*.

of Godard's lecture and to acquire the method at its crux. This discrepancy between audiences also emphasizes the mentally constructive labor asked of us. After all, the stakes of the lecture hang on Godard getting through to a spectator who must, in order for this interaction to succeed, become able to animate the process of shot/countershot herself as a means of perceiving and thinking her way through a multiplicity of encountered images and histories. This point is key, for the essayistic resides not simply in the gesture of address to the spectator, but in the possibly shared exertion that follows from it. In this film, Godard gives a name to this striven-for condition of seeing together: "our music."

This brings us to Godard's pedagogical place in the ongoing history of the cinematic essay. His master class in *Notre musique* and indeed his instructional aims in each of the self-portraits we have taken up remain consistent with what I described earlier, in chapter 2, as a post-militant direction of the cinematic essay. This change in direction happened as a number of essayistic directors who had once devoted their practices to an all-out bid for leftist revolution turned, in the extended fallout of their disappointment, to more tentative approaches that grant the viewer a more imaginative role in the apprehension *and furtherance* of a thought process whose claims and forms remain at some level incomplete. For Godard, as well as for others in this group

To Show and Show Oneself Showing

such as Marker and Farocki, a leftist attitude still suffuses their late work, but without adherence to a script of Marxist-Leninist teachings, and with greater uncertainty regarding the effect of formal strategies on the audience.

In this post-militant context, the closest essayistic counterpart to Godard's repurposing of shot/countershot in *Notre musique* is Farocki's use of "soft montage" in his video installations, an exhibition format that confronts us with two (or more) screens simultaneously and obliges us to think constructively in the gaps between them. The interplay between screens entails both serial and concurrent linkages that carry out a variety of doublings, refrains, side-by-side weighings, and relays of motifs (not to mention the black screens and titles that disturb but also rhythmicize the flow of imagery). The montage is "soft" in this formulation because its ensembles, while they may be robust, have a provisional feel, as if relations are still being essayed. "More trial, less assertion," Farocki explains.[68] If this method is less stridently didactic than other methods Farocki enlists in some of his earlier, more agitational projects such as *Inextinguishable Fire* (1969), it also increases the share of the viewer, refusing to call attention too coercively to meanings and links that have already been squared away by the filmmaker.[69] Farocki's most germane example of this format is his first video installation, *Interface* (1997), an edifying self-portrait of Farocki at work in which he introduces and historicizes this method while recutting scenes from his own past efforts. At one and the same time, he recounts his trajectory as a politically conscious filmmaker, transposes the *dispositif* of the video editing console to the space of the art gallery, and implicitly shows the viewer how to think in such combinatorial terms herself.

Farocki defines soft montage as a heretical derivation of shot/countershot syntax that came to him while tinkering with material at the video editing station, which involves two monitors arranged adjacently. He also cites as a formative influence Godard's earlier, daring experiment with video integrating several frames simultaneously in *Numéro deux*.[70] Farocki's style isn't identical to Godard's. He is more of a forensic documentarian and his essaying, though not averse to flights of fancy, is less inclined to take poetic license with the historical record when he handles either found or newly shot material. Even so, his soft montage holds to a principle of essayistic style that also deeply characterizes what Godard is out to achieve in his self-portraiture. For all the changes to their approaches over time—and for all the perplexities and convolutions their essays present—these two directors remain, in a fundamental sense, pedagogues. I say this not because they teach through the lucid transmission of arguments that we absorb and consider chiefly at the level of ideational content, but because they both model, in and through their montage, a sharpness of perception and a sinuosity of thought that they aim to impart to us, while placing our habits of viewing under strain.

Said another way, the late essayistic works of Godard and Farocki are nothing if not perceptual training exercises.[71] Over and above the goal of delivering a thesis to be accepted or refused, these directors aim to improve our intellectual agility, to stretch and strengthen what Alexander Kluge—another kindred essayist on this score—calls the "muscles" of perception.[72] They go about this task by attempting to instill a detail-driven means of cinematic rumination, proportionate in its intensity to the one they exhibit and retest.

Indeed, theirs is a pedagogy of critical repetition, of continual reassessment of the sounds, images, texts, and techniques that enter into their webs—a pedagogy of repeated acts of scrutiny. No surviving branch of modern cinema depends more vitally on the elicitation of repeat viewings and on the prospect of making the spectator an agile montage-based thinker in her own right. The hope held out by Godard's reinvention of shot/countershot is that we might learn *and then repeat in other viewing situations* the inquisitive method on offer.

The melancholy Godard's late stage exudes is due not only to the calamitous histories and injustices he recalls, but also to what he laments as a lapse of cinematic vision in an altered media landscape, dominated by television and telecommunication networks (which, in Godard's view, amounts to a repressive "occupation"). His screen pedagogy responds to this predicament by retraining the image-forming abilities of the spectator on whose nimble cooperation he relies. We can detect a related mission in Farocki's soft montage, for it, too, reimagines a cinematic form of editing in order to resist and counter what his work pinpoints as a widespread cultural deadening of human perceptual labor.[73]

Pertinent to this pedagogical mission is a distinction that Serge Daney once put forward between "the image," which he associates with the (imperiled) power of cinema to articulate and rouse critical thought, and the "visual," by which he means an opposing, increasingly dominant televisual circulation of sights and sounds. Although Daney doesn't have the essayistic in mind specifically, Farocki quotes at length this distinction in a diary regarding his own work,[74] and it is no stretch to claim that Daney's argument is inspired by Godard's montage-based notion of an image as a composite *and mental* structure:

> The image is always located at the forefront of a conflict between two energy fields, it is doomed to bear witness to a particular otherness, and something is always lacking even though it invariably has a hard center. The image is always both more and simultaneously also less than what it is in itself. . . . So as not to complicate my life further I have decided to clearly differentiate between the "image" and the "visual." The visual I understand to be an optical verification of a purely technical function. The visual knows no reverse shot [*contrechamp*], it lacks nothing, it is complete within itself, a closed circuit, a little like a pornographic spectacle that is nothing more than an ecstatic verification of the functioning of the organs.[75]

To Show and Show Oneself Showing

193

What Daney calls "the visual" is a logic of automatic transmission and confirmation, a purely technical relay of audiovisual matter that asks of the recipient only "optical verification." The very idea of a countershot is irrelevant, since there is no lack, no offscreen, no "otherness" to be acknowledged or admitted, so this logic deceptively implies. On the other hand, "the image" bears no such ruse of completion and self-sufficiency. It figures relationships that are robust and resonant, yet always alerts us to the fact that still further thought is needed. One of Daney's main points here is that in a world where "the visual" reigns, the viewer, if critical thought is her goal, is obliged to perform her own montage, by mentally supplying "countershots" where they fail to find material expression.[76]

Godard's essayism during his late period—in particular his portrayals of himself and their attendant pedagogy—can be said to reclaim and animate the critical power of "the image" in the face of "the visual." The glancing but important mention of "otherness" in Daney's passage is of course further appropriate to Godard's enterprise as we have seen it in action. Arguably, no other preoccupation of Godard's late stage more forcefully entwines the aesthetic, ethico-political, and dialogical aspects of his work than does his embrace of alterity where shared, essayistic thinking is concerned. Understood within the series of his late self-portraits that we have traced, this open regard for otherness stems primarily from a philosophical disposition that keeps a vigilant check on the social, epistemic, and perceptual pitfalls of narcissism, on ways of thinking and being that deal with alterity either by violently exorcizing it or by incorporating it falsely into the order of the same. Conceptually, the nemesis that Godard's self-portraiture foils is perhaps best defined, in the end, as the imperious projection of the "I." His montage-based practice values irreducible otherness precisely because it throws into doubt one's routine ways of organizing, interpreting, and mastering the world.

We have seen that Godard's presence in these self-portraits is always a catalytic element in a larger play of forces and positions that is far more complex than a desire for personal self-representation. With this in mind, I want to close by addressing his willful obscurity, which can easily be (and often has been) dismissed as unnecessary abstruseness or, little better, as a self-martyring commentary on his public persona as a past-his-prime artist.[77] Self-deprecating humor indeed leavens his work at times, but this shouldn't distract us from the fact that he portrays himself as obscure for critically exigent reasons central to his role as an essayist. His penchant for dark lighting schemes when he shows up onscreen needs to be understood as a figural strategy in pursuit of dialogue with the diligent viewer. I read this choice in part as citational, in that it echoes pictorial traditions he is fond of referencing (expressionism, film noir, and painterly chiaroscuro effects created by Rembrandt, Caravaggio, and Georges de la Tour). This aspect of his self-depiction is part of a general expressive economy in his late stage that conceptualizes the drama of light and shade in a variety of ways and further extends to his

194   Chapter 4

wordplay (e.g., the repeated title "response from the darkness" in *Histoire(s)*
and the intertitle "a shady business" in *JLG/JLG*). One might further note
along these lines the director's occasional (and sly) shading of photographs
with a black magic marker, so that they fit more congruously with the montage he interweaves (e.g., the darkened photo of Hitchcock, with an upraised
hand, in episode 4A in *Histoire(s)*).

Through its predilection for shadows, this aesthetics of obscurity enables
Godard's figure to fluctuate indistinctly between the capacities of filmmaker
and viewer and back again, this being, as we have witnessed, a carefully
enacted manner of indirect address aimed at achieving intimacy with the
spectator—even as it results in a frustrating paucity of conclusiveness. Godard
"makes dark" the essayistic scene of inquiry and his own place within it not
merely because he addresses his thoughts to followers who already know his
idiolect by heart, but because he leaves an ample "margin of indefiniteness"
proper to essayistic work, which potentially becomes our work, too, by way
of the attunement his self-portraiture offers.

Coda

✦

Stereoscopic Essays for the New Century

Over the preceding chapters, I have teased out a Montaignean practice of essayistic thought that materializes in cinematic terms—a tradition in which the director doesn't just make discrete essay films in line with generic dictates, but constructs a body of work in an essayistic fashion over time, conceiving his oeuvre as a ceaseless series of experiments in which essential ideas and methods are reconfigured and tried again and again. Godard has served as our leading example of an essayist because of the striking sense in which his corpus not only corroborates but also demands this diachronic perspective. As we have seen, his output, especially in his late stage, addresses itself to a repeat audience that is deeply acquainted with his evolution as an artist and thinker. I have made the case that there potentially develops in and through this rapport between director and viewer a rare form of mediated intimacy, of cinematic togetherness that needs to be viewed not just as dialogical but as verging on the order of "friendship."

In what remains, I would like to expand my arguments still further through a study of how Godard's essayism has continued to evolve in the twenty-first century. More specifically, I want to examine how he has taken part in a more general trend in the quasi-generic purview of the essay film. In the 2010s, certain essay filmmakers have responded in imaginative ways to the resurgence of 3D that has occurred in popular narrative cinema on the heels of *Avatar* (Cameron, 2009) and other box office triumphs. These essayists have done this by fashioning elaborate 3D spectacles in their own right, enlisting the stereo format for reflective purposes where fiction and documentary intersect. If this marks a new direction in the cinematic essay's history, it continues a long-standing tendency among its practitioners to engage the forms and devices of mainstream cinema with a mix of fascination and critique.

Granted, some essay filmmakers in the past have regarded stereo cinema with extreme disfavor. In Guy Debord's film version of *The Society of the Spectacle* (1973), a photograph of a 3D audience from the 1950s illustrates precisely what Debord's project takes dead aim at and tries to negate: the passivity of a pubic in thrall to the spectacular machinations of late capitalist society. But in recent years, essayistic filmmakers and media artists from Ken

195

Jacobs and Werner Herzog to Peter Greenaway and Lucy Raven have forayed into stereoscopic imaging in one format or another in order to reconfigure its sensory enticements and explore its aesthetic and intellectual possibilities, through modes of address that situate audiences between the competing pulls of immersion and distance. Jacobs's *Seeking the Monkey King* (2011) does this with an abstract, flickering 3D image field, an undulatory play of light and metallic texture (now warm and magma-like, now cool and glacial) paired with equally jolting stereo sound and titles that articulate a brooding anticapitalist tirade. Greenaway's short film *Just in Time* (2013) deploys 3D video to stage a layered compression of history while a virtual camera roves through the nooks and furrows of the Palace of the Dukes of Braganza in the Portuguese city of Guimaraes. Working in a less ostentatious register, Raven's video installation *Curtains* (2014) craftily uses an old-fashioned anaglyph form of 3D to comment on documentary footage of cheap laborers immersed in the process of converting 2D images into 3D for major Hollywood studio releases. We see these cubicled workers staring at screens across a variety of locations (Beijing, Chennai, London, Mumbai, Toronto, and Vancouver) while Raven splits her frame into shifting blue and red panels, each an iteration of the same shot, that play on our desire for them to merge and hold, thereby stabilizing the 3D impression of depth and solidity. This is how the installation leads us to question the ethics of this practice of outsourcing, an exploitative labor process at the root of the very effect of three-dimensional imaging.

Herzog's *Cave of Forgotten Dreams* (2010) is an even more accomplished demonstration of essayistic cinema in 3D.[1] The film uses a low-budget, makeshift digital 3D format to capture and study in "hyper-haptic detail" Paleolithic cave paintings discovered in Chauvet Cave in southern France.[2] Given the film's verbal and bodily inscriptions of its director, its clever estrangements of traditional documentary, its playful reuse of existing film imagery (Fred Astaire's "shadow dance" from *Swing Time* [1936]), and its reflection on prehistoric and contemporary technologies, including stereoscopy itself, *Cave* more than satisfies received classifications of the essay film.[3] What I find most intriguing about Herzog's film is the way in which its stereoscopy lures us into the reflection by appealing to a sense of closeness and touch: we are drawn *toward* what the screen displays, drawn *into* an exploratory process, and at the same time, urged to reflect on the film's means of exerting these pulls and of achieving its effects. As Miriam Ross writes, "the stereoscopic film provides the viewer with an intensified proximity to its expressive consciousness, but we remain aware of its material body that enacts this expression."[4] Ross also admires how the film subtly uses negative parallax effects (objects and volumes extending into our viewing space) to faithfully render contours of the paintings and other geomorphic formations in the cave.[5]

Throughout this book, I have focused on the ways in which essayistic filmmakers work to build a critical dialogue with a spectator they implicitly, if not always directly, address. Herzog's first, and so far only, foray into 3D innovates along these lines: its tactile and textural attractions enliven such an attempted dialogue by compounding the sensorial aspects of the film's rhetorical invitation. Herzog's cinematic cave serves as a kind of laboratory of perception within which we are meant to become attuned to ancient, shamanic ways of observing and experiencing the world, that is, to the contemplative mindset that led to the paintings' creation. Herzog singles out a prehistoric visitor to the cave who can be identified by handprints that chart a route through the labyrinthine interior. Each time this handprint turns up, including its appearance in the film's ultimate shot, it doubles as an index of the person who made it *and* as an inviting reference to the film's viewer. It is as though the visitor has prefigured our own excursion within a layered temporality of aesthetic experience that reaches from 30,000 BC to the moment of our viewing. This handprint, traced in rust-red paint, nearly looks as if it marks the surface of *the screen*. It functions throughout, and most poignantly at the end, as a gestural, tactile emblem of the film's essayistic address (fig. C.1).

With questions of address and spectator experience chiefly in mind, I want to look at the two essayistic exercises in 3D that Godard has made to date, his short video *The Three Disasters* (2013) and his partly narrative feature *Goodbye to Language* (2014). Despite his claims in interviews to have had little artistic interest in 3D and to have only used it in order to show its uselessness,[6] I will argue that Godard reimagines and estranges stereoscopic cinema to a degree of complexity unparalleled in the history of the essayistic,

Figure C.1. Essaying the tactile affordances of 3D: *Cave of Forgotten Dreams* (Herzog, 2010).

and that he does this while remaining faithful to *and* convoluting the dialogical vocation of the essay, its bid for reflective intimacy with the viewer. In making this argument, I will need to consider how these works contribute to Godard's oeuvre as a whole. *The Three Disasters* and *Goodbye to Language* are every bit as self-critical and self-retrospective as *Histoire(s) du cinéma*. We cannot grasp their excursions into 3D unless we think them through in this cumulative and comparative light. Both projects in fact engage us hoping we will do just this.

Histoire(s) du cinéma Redux

The Three Disasters premiered at the 2013 Cannes Film Festival as part of a triptych of unrelated 3D projects in which the Greenaway video named above was also included. Despite its spare running-time of just under seventeen minutes, Godard's video broaches enough ideas for seven or eight films and displays an arsenal of essayistic tactics, from digressive montage to stark authorial self-inscription. It also samples sounds and sights from earlier efforts directed by Godard, some of which were already reused in such a manner in *Histoire(s)*, whose style *The Three Disasters* echoes.

The Three Disasters in effect expands *Histoire(s)* into a stereoscopic form, adding to the multiple editions of the series already released across different media. By title, *Histoire(s) du cinéma* technically names not a single text but the VHS tapes (1998) and DVDs (2007) put out by Gaumont, the four art books published in Gallimard's esteemed Blanche Collection in 1998 and reissued in 2006 (the books consist of stills and text in a recto-verso arrangement that differs from the video edition), and the box set of CDs released by the label ECM in 1999, which features just the soundtrack. Gaumont also commissioned Godard to make a 35-mm abridged version of select moments from the series, *Moments choisis des Histoire(s) du cinéma*, which screened at the Pompidou Center in Paris in 2001 and 2004, and is a rethought work in its own right. Michael Witt sees yet another extension of *Histoire(s)* in Godard's 2006 installation at the Pompidou Center, *Voyage(s) in Utopia, JLG, 1946–2006: In Search of a Lost Theorem*, which recomposed "shards of many of the series' constituent ideas, arguments, sources, and references within the three-dimensional space of an art gallery."[7] *The Three Disasters* does this, too, its added dimensionality springing from volumetric 3D imagery, which remediates *Histoire(s)* while staking out new critical directions.

From the beginning, with a grainy, dark shot of someone's hands rolling three dice on a wooden table (this is a pictorial pun on 3D in French: "trois dés," and hence "trois dés/astres"),[8] Godard initiates a reflexive commentary on stereoscopy. His use of the format makes itself felt in sharply stacked and delimited layers of colored titles and still and moving imagery. *The Three Disasters* thus organically continues Godard's poetics of superimposition in

Histoire(s). Godard samples scenes from mainstream 3D releases, all treated with ridicule: a young woman with her hair caught in a boat propeller in *Piranha 3D* (2010), a teenage girl bursting into smithereens in *Fright Night* (2011), and a young woman shrieking in pain while a laser sears her eye in *Final Destination 5* (2011). Godard's criticism goes beyond a dismissal of this relegation of 3D to crassly visceral attractions and computer-generated effects. I take it that the violence we see visited upon the human body, a female body in every instance, evokes in a drastic sense what Godard feels mainstream 3D cinema does to its spectators, as embodied perceiving subjects, a point I will enlarge on below. A few of Godard's newly made 3D compositions are stunning (e.g., a scene of four hands playing a piano, overlaid with a churning seascape). The video twice discloses Godard's humble 3D rig of two digital single-lens reflex cameras placed side by side, which we see at one point as the cameras record themselves in a mirror. The video approvingly cites a fragment from Herzog's *Cave of Forgotten Dreams*, which it intercuts with Godard's engagement with western European painting in *Passion* (1982). And in its last seconds the video takes a jab at James Cameron by insinuating that the director of *Titanic* (1997, converted to 3D in 2012) and *Avatar* stresses "depth!" without in fact understanding what a dimension is and how best to handle it cinematically.

One refrain continued from *Histoire(s)* is that of the couple, which here finds expression in several overlapping iterations in Godard's montage of appropriated material. As in much of his late projects, this motif of the couple expresses a conceptual investment in love, a condition of togetherness and co-belonging offset from, *and implied to be under severe threat by*, the oppressive abuses and encroachments of the state. Prompted by the numerical designation "3D," Godard speaks to this conflict with what we might call an aphoristic arithmetic that ambiguously yokes together political, philosophical, and technological frames of reference. A sonic clip of dialogue, from a film that Godard doesn't show visually, argues that "nothing is more opposed to love than the state," and this hooks in with the video's roundabout intimation, through the voices of Godard and others, of a "universal war" in which capital reigns by reducing subjects to "zeroes" (a trope resurfacing from a blackboard demonstration in *Ici et ailleurs* [1976]) and by withering away the mathematical probability of love, charity, and genuine communication between human beings.[9] Godard brings technology into the mix by asserting in voiceover that "the digital [*numérique*] will become a dictatorship," an empire of 1s and 0s with little tolerance for what I have defined in the preceding chapters as dialogical twoness.

Godard considers this situation while picking up loose strands from a number of his earlier films and videos. There returns from *The Old Place* (co-directed with Anne-Marie Miéville, 1999) and *Dans le noir du temps* (*In the Darkness of Time*, also co-directed with Miéville, 2002) a Blaise Pascal-inspired lament regarding a dearth of meaningful acts of charity in the world.

And there returns from *Film Socialism* (2010) the sentiment of "facing a kind of zero" as "an impossible history lies ahead" (itself a modified iteration of what "back to zero" describes in *Le Gai Savoir* [1969]). In *The Three Disasters*, this lament becomes a trying matter of finding one's way between "infinity and zero" (and this is an allusion to *Le Zéro et l'Infini*, the French title of Arthur Koestler's 1940 novel *Darkness at Noon*, which allegorically deals with the corruption of Soviet Communism under Stalin, who is "Number One" in the plot). These and other references in the video contribute to a theme of human suffering amid an ever-present, yet shadowy, totalitarianism. This context also brings to mind a lapidary statement we hear in *Notre musique* (2004), a quotation ascribed to the German student and activist Sophie Scholl, who was beheaded in 1943 for handing out antifascist leaflets: "The dream of the state is to be one, but the dream of the individual is to be two."

Hence, the fitting reuse in *The Three Disasters* of the still from *Prison* (Bergman, 1949) that Godard reshapes throughout *Histoire(s)*, the two-shot of a man and woman viewing a film together in a moment of respite. Godard inserts this shot, tinged green, precisely as he states in voiceover that "the digital will become a dictatorship." For good measure, he splices into this rapid montage a clip from *Captain Blood* (Michael Curtiz, 1935), an American swashbuckling epic about a slave uprising in the context of colonial empire, and then a clip from *Apocalypse Now* (Francis Ford Coppola, 1979) showing the U.S. air cavalry after they have decimated a Vietnamese village. Godard incorporates the *Prison* still twice in this segment, and its second iteration singles out the woman on the right side of the frame, who is then linked to the woman whose body explodes into 3D shards in *Fright Night*.

In chapters 2 and 3, I showed how Godard reuses this shot of a spectating couple in part to reference his companionship with Miéville. *The Three Disasters* repeats this tactic, which becomes evident when Miéville's voice marks the soundtrack (and when we see a short clip of the young girl looking through a camera viewfinder in the intro from Godard-Miéville's television program *France/tour/détour/deux/enfants* [1977]). Miéville's inclusion here is such that she enters into a certain iconography of the feminine. I pointed out above that *The Three Disasters* is starred with disturbing scenes of violence directed at women. Indeed, the suggestion of apocalyptic tyranny has as its complement a motif of suffering and dying females; and this motif is further tied, in an ulterior fashion, to a musing on the death of revolutions (early in the video Godard cites an anonymous woman's death in November, then asserts that "the revolution, too, was sinking into winter"). This nest of citations and motifs will resurface in *Goodbye to Language*, a then in-progress production whose images sporadically appear in this video (*The Three Disasters* is a sort of warm-up and teaser trailer for the impending feature). Godard prepares the stage more than he begins to work through each of these matters and their interconnection, but already he makes it clear that

Stereoscopic Essays for the New Century   201

coupling—vis-à-vis his twosome with Miéville—remains at the heart of his cinematic thinking and his thinking about cinema. Godard shows up three-quarters of the way into the video, in a rather unflattering extreme close-up of his bearded lips and blackhead-stippled nose, and this appearance underlines not himself as an individual so much as *a loss or deficiency of two*. Speaking into the camera, his narration addresses the history of negative numbers and their introduction by the Hindus, and the algebraic equation he offers us, "$x + 3 = 1$," tellingly specifies, once we solve for x, "negative 2." When Godard uses mathematical expressions in his oeuvre, they are usually poetic in their meanings, defying mere computation. In this instance, we can read his math as a suggestion that stereo cinema colludes with the "oneness" of the state when it rules out the existential conditions of twoness. This is why the close-up of the filmmaker leads into a somber clip from Joseph L. Mankiewicz's *The Barefoot Contessa* (1954), which shows the Count in a rainstorm, holding his wife, a star actress he has murdered. This clip overlaps in a flashing montage (the effect evokes lightning) with one of the editor bench sequences from Dziga Vertov's *Man with a Movie Camera* (1929)—a shot of the hands of Elizaveta Svilova (Vertov's wife) holding a film strip above a light-emanating work surface (fig. C.2). This composite of clips recurs from 4A of *Histoire(s)* and again contemplates the dreams and failures of Soviet Communism (and its revolutionary cinema), while using these clips to sketch a larger history in which Godard's image practice has a potentially redemptive relevance. What this all adds up to is a mood of intense despair as Godard circles around the historical, political, and interpersonal stakes of his upcoming 3D feature.

Figure C.2. Through superimposition, Vertov's editing bench scene crosses with Mankiewicz's tragic death scene: *The Three Disasters* (Godard, 2013).

However, after the woman is blown apart in *Fright Night*, Godard interjects something of a hypothesis—a hint of a potential "key" to reversing the oppressive state of affairs to which the video points. Playfully, he introduces this new element in combination with a fragment from Maya Deren's dreamlike avant-garde film *Meshes of the Afternoon* (1943), a shot of a young woman (Deren herself) pulling a metal key from her mouth and extending it enticingly toward the camera, hence toward the audience.[10] The key leads to an introductory shot of a character who will have a central role in *Goodbye to Language*: this is not a human but a dog, a lurcher mix that is initially shown jaunting through a 3D landscape littered with fallen autumn leaves. In voiceover, Godard recites (without disclosing this book by title, of course) a passage from Clifford D. Simak's science fiction novel *City* (1952), a series of loosely linked futuristic tales editorially framed by a race of pacifist, hyperintelligent dogs who recount a downfall of human civilization, an apocalypse of loneliness and isolation that could not be averted by technological progress. Godard reads the "editor's preface," which is narrated by a dog and addressed to an audience of dogs, in an age when humans have vanished from the earth and their cultural ways have become the stuff of myth—so much so that the dogs need to be given detailed definitions of "war," "killing," and "city." They are incredulous when told that beings with a central nervous system did such things.[11]

The dog in Godard's video essay, who will be credited as "Roxy Miéville" in *Goodbye to Language*, is more than just an intertextual figment inspired by Simak. On a personal level, he is Godard and Miéville's actual pet. Each time he appears (the dog is male despite his feminine-sounding first name) we are reminded of a certain biographical dimension that carries weight both in *The Three Disasters* and the ensuing feature. But more to the point, the dog, as I will show in a moment, acts as a kind of guide, almost like an emissary sent from the future world Simak depicts, to warn us about where we are headed. This dog cannot speak, but Godard treats him as a numinous and philosophical being who is poised to show by example how our powers of sight, love, and dialogue have been treacherously reduced.

An Essayistic Love Story, Twice-Told

Comprised of voiceover by the director, recycled fictional and documentary material, and a peregrinating argument, *The Three Disasters* agrees with taxonomic classifications of the essay film, but *Goodbye to Language* is a thornier case in that it also has a duplex fictional plot.

In this book, I have argued for a conception of Godard's essayism that does not, as is the custom, sharply divide his "essays" from his narrative projects. I have used Godard's own voiced account of himself as an essayist to support my claim that he avoids such a neat distinction from his early to

Stereoscopic Essays for the New Century

late career stages. His endlessly relevant statement, from the early 1960s, that he makes "essays in novel form or novels in essay form," is many times reaffirmed in his late period by the works themselves. As he states in a 2000 interview, "I have always been divided between what is commonly called the essay and what is commonly called the novel."[12] Godard doesn't precisely alternate between "essays" and narrative fiction films. Rather, even in his narrative undertakings, an essayistic sensibility emerges where he suspends the choice between two generic alternatives: either staging a drama or carrying out a critical inquiry. Godard explores both in the same work, without limiting his practice to what is "commonly called" the essay.

In Godard's late stage, which *Goodbye to Language* summates, this dividedness between novel and essay imbues the films themselves. At the start of *Nouvelle vague* (1990), as the opening credits appear on a black screen, a bodiless male voice laments, "But I wanted this to be a narrative. I still do. Nothing from outside to distract memory." This line sets off a montage of natural landscapes forcing the film, be it essay or narrative, to confront the outside world. The enduring *wish* for narrative, which arises from an alienated subjectivity or *sensus internus* in the guise of the voiceover, thus introduces a paratactic series of sounds, views, and textures that calls for a reflective encounter with the sensuous world onscreen. The exhilaration of this passage results from generic undecidedness. Instead of plying a narrative logic from the outset, *Nouvelle vague* commences with an essayistic priming of perception, opening its thought and ours onto the presence, rhythm, and noise of an atmospheric exteriority that doesn't necessarily submit to narrative syntax or an already determined chain of causes and effects.

Godard's mosaics of narrative and essay in his late period can be fruitfully compared to Roland Barthes's description of Proust's *In Search of Lost Time* (1913), a text that, for Barthes, gains its aesthetic and intellectual power from its "indecisive" shifting between "the way of the Essay (of Criticism) and the way of the Novel." Neither strictly a novel nor an essay, Proust's text engenders what Barthes calls a *"third form,"* an indeterminate, disjointed mix of essayistic and novelistic aspects that "abolish[es] the contradiction" between them.[13] This fusion of genres on Proust's part opens the door to a highly creative *"disorganization"* of both narrative teleology and autobiographical chronology, keeping elements of story and the writer's life in play but in a webbed orchestration of discontinuous "correspondences" and "reappearances." The book thus moves freely between different orders of time and renders the "I" of the narrator ambiguous—a displaced, discoursing variant of the author, one of his doubles.[14]

Goodbye to Language is a cinematic *"third form,"* its essayistic and narrative attributes so chaotically intermingled as to deny their separation. In discussions of the film, the term "essay" is common, but it has generally served as a tag that does little to explicate how the film unfolds. Critics have tended to invoke the term in reference to the film's ideational content alone,

204   Coda

as if the essay must be filtered out from the story about two couples that it competes with and interrupts. But it is precisely this elaborate, *inseparable* conjugation of dramatic and (meta-)critical features that is so distinctive of Godard's temperament as an essayist and that qualifies this 3D film as yet another of his "essays in novel form or novels in essay form."

The impulse to oversimplify when confronted with this initially opaque, multi-leveled beast of a work is understandable. It is tempting to concentrate on, say, *just* the use of 3D, *just* the theme of coupling that underlies the fictional narrative, *just* the melancholic recollection of the history of modern Europe and its traumas, or *just* the elegy for miscarried revolutions on the Left. But these approaches would all miss the film's surprising coherence, how these elements interdepend. Our mission, should we choose to accept it, lies in keeping track of the film's thematic and cogitative build in and across segments as its philosophical citations, fictional episodes, essayistic claims, and 3D aesthetics go hand in hand. Critics before me—Nico Baumbach, David Bordwell, James Quandt, Blake Williams, and James S. Williams—have taken strides to explain the film's formal strategies: its logic of doubles and repetition, its tinkering with stereo optics, its references within and in excess of Godard's corpus.[15] Yet we still lack a thorough reading of how an essayistic spirit presides over and permeates *Goodbye to Language* as a whole, encompassing both dramatic and noetic operations.

In the film's press kit, Godard, no doubt anticipating the confusion this film would cause, offers a poem-like synopsis in his own handwriting:

> the idea is simple
> a married woman and a single man meet
> they love, they argue, fists fly
> a dog strays between town and country
> the seasons pass
> the man and woman meet again
> the dog finds itself between them
> the other is in the one
> the one is in the other
> and these are three persons
> the former husband shatters everything
> a second film begins
> the same as the first
> and yet not
> from the human race we pass to metaphor
> this ends in barking
> and a baby's cries

While this skeletal outline is accurate, it almost comically plays down the film's convolutedness. Even on a second or third viewing, it is extremely hard

Stereoscopic Essays for the New Century

to follow the precise unfolding of events and the logic of their arrangement. Reiterated titles, "1 nature" and "2 metaphor," seem to mark two strands of narrative and the fraught interactions of two similar-looking couples respectively. But Godard's digressive style ensures that much of the story and its upshot escapes us. Periodic black screens, indistinct commotion in offscreen space, boldly discrepant textures of sound and image, spliced-in documentary footage and clips from fiction films, abrupt and jarring switches between left and right channels of stereo sound, sudden shifts in the seasons of the year, erratic fluctuations between color and grayscale footage, disembodied voices oddly peripheral to scenes they haunt, a storm of (mostly occulted) citations from a daunting array of texts, fields, and media, truncated framings that withhold the identities of characters—these and other Godardian touches see to it that we receive the work not as continuous episodes but as elliptical fragments that pique our curiosity and demand our constructive participation.

What we are given to pore over is less a fully realized story of two couples than uncanny repetitions and parallels that crop up "vertically" between the enumerated divisions; and we are challenged, moreover, to work out how this "simple" domestic fiction set on the Swiss banks of Lake Geneva folds in with a citational play of arguments as regards such matters as the diverted goals of revolution, self-other relations as figured in French phenomenology, and the persistence of despotism at the core of Western democracy.

Commenting on the film's bifurcated composition in an interview, Godard claims to have relied on "Hitchcock's theory" that "when you want something to be understood" by the audience, "you say it at least twice."[16] What, then, do the reprises in *Goodbye* mean for us to comprehend? Our first task is to notice how the film's focus on two couples arises in the context of—not as a retreat from—the larger social crises dealt with in the film's opening sequences. As Bordwell has shown, *Goodbye* commences with two prologues that occur in succession, each set in a different public spot in Nyon but enacting a version of roughly the same event.[17] A somewhat weathered philosophy professor called Davidson (Christian Grégori) converses with other minor characters including two students—Marie (Marie Ruchat) and her unnamed male companion (Jeremy Zampatti)—and an older woman, Isabelle (Isabelle Carbonneau), who only appears in the first prologue. These talks are interrupted by a mustachioed, German-speaking businessman (Daniel Ludwig) who emerges from a Mercedes sedan and accosts his wife at gunpoint. The wife's noncompliance sends him away; then a male stranger approaches her, pledging: "I am at your command." Both main couples pair up in this way: Josette (Héloïse Godet) with Gédéon (Kamel Abdeli), and Ivitch (Zoé Bruneau) with Marcus (Richard Chevallier).

The dramatic action in both prologues coincides with a swift accretion of ideas vocalized by Davidson and his interlocutors. The first scene, which takes place at a bookstall across the street from a cultural center, references at length a 1945 journal article by the French polymath and philosopher Jacques Ellul, titled "Hitler's Victory?" Recitations of this text shade in a historical backdrop for the film's general concerns. Ellul's central thesis is that Hitler, despite his army's defeat, must be remembered as having achieved a decisive political victory insofar as each of his conquerors put in place more stable and cunningly veiled schemes of mass control, guaranteeing the state absolute authority while granting its subjects only illusory freedoms. According to Ellul, the seeds of this sinister plot were sown well before the Third Reich by such innovators of deceptive statecraft as "Machiavelli, Richelieu, and Bismarck," but Hitler's coup (and lasting legacy in liberal democracies) was to have machinated a system wherein the people *demand* the exercise of unrestrained state power over every aspect of their lives.[18]

Godard's scene complements this thesis with notions borrowed from Ellul's 1954 treatise *The Technological Society*. The extension of this manner of governance into the twenty-first century registers as a comprehensive takeover of daily existence, an "occupation" of our very gestures and thoughts, economies of attention, and interpersonal dynamics: a takeover procured through ever-more ubiquitous and proficient technology. Hence, the use of smartphones in the first prologue and Davidson's ominous comment—with a punning nod to the French "Little Thumb" fairy tale—that "the Ogre takes us by the hand, *all* of us." Expanding on Ellul's claims, Davidson reminds his two pupils that Hitler democratically became chancellor in the same year that Vladimir Zworykin invented television, the suggestion being that these events launched analogous, and linked, schemes of domination.

These dual prologues set the stage both dramatically and discursively, establishing that the characters reside in a twenty-first-century world that confirms Ellul's dystopian vision. Additional, harmonious nods to A. E. van Vogt's *The World of Null-A* trilogy of novels, in which a technocratic, intergalactic empire programs the brains of its earthly citizens, confer on this grim setting a sense of science fiction become fact. (Vogt's first installment in the trilogy has certain thematic affinities with Godard's own *Alphaville* [1965], and, as we saw in chapter 4, Godard reads from Vogt's fiction during a key scene of *JLG/JLG* [1995].) *Goodbye* (as does *The Three Disasters*) features shots of the cover of the French-language edition of Vogt's *Null-A Three* (1985), so as to define its own diegesis intertextually in this light (to be exact, Godard has altered the original design of the book jacket, adding a picture of a totem).

That Ellul serves as a prophet of doom is an intriguing choice, given the other pioneering Continental philosophers of modern technology Godard might have cited to similar ends (such as Martin Heidegger, Herbert Marcuse, and Jürgen Habermas). Ellul's role in *Goodbye* owes partly to biography and nationality: as a onetime leader in the French Resistance during World War II, Ellul accords with Godard's focus on the political past of France. Furthermore, the "technical milieu" that Ellul delineates—a world in which all

Stereoscopic Essays for the New Century

human activities (social and economic) are organized by a techno-rationalist quest for maximum "efficiency" at the utter expense of spontaneity, intuition, and creativity[19]—squares with the American science fiction of the postwar era that Godard cites, principally Vogt's novels. What most vexes Godard, it seems, is the noxious impact of this milieu on interpersonal relations. In *Goodbye*'s plot, the brutish, gun-bearing husband character (a banker in the first story, an "events planner" in the second) overtly connects the film's drama to a history of violent oppression that is also in line with the financial and technical schemes identified by Ellul. But Godard's essayistic thinking on this score extends to aesthetic matters as well. This is why the film everywhere enjoins us to scrutinize the 3D compositions on view, their sensual textures, their choreographies that impart an enticing sense of mystery.

The initial prologue is a case in point. Godard's almost musical staging of rhythmic action around the bookstall carefully emphasizes physical interactions between characters *and the spatial intervals their movements traverse*. The canted framing omits faces and rivets our attention on hands and on used paperback books, whose covers are just legible to us onscreen. Accents of orange-red mark resonances between different planes in the image, from the USINE-A-GAZ bannered fence of the cultural venue and the headwear of an extra in the background, to Marie's curly hair and the large umbrella above the bookstall in the foreground. ("Usine-à-gaz" translates as "gas factory," although in French, as Godard's wordplay recognizes, this term idiomatically refers to a system of extreme, distressing complication.) The painterly use of color assigns special emphasis to one of the paperbacks that passes between different figures in the scene. The slow-building reveal of this orange-red book's title notably culminates with a shot that both condenses and enlarges on motifs adapted from Ellul. At the bookstall, Davidson and the male student exchange and toy with their iPhones as Marie, seen in the more immediate foreground, picks up and flips through the book in question. The *mise en scène* thus stages a contrast between old and new media and the gestures they require, that is, between the handling of the book in the foreground and that of the smartphones in the background. Then, at the precise moment that the husband's Mercedes makes its first, menacing appearance by passing through the background in the space between Davidson and the male student, Marie rotates the book so that we can make out the text on its cover: it is Emmanuel Levinas's *Time and the Other* (1947). A stereoscopic effect of subtle negative parallax further stresses this object, making it appear as if within our reach, too (fig. C.3).

Borrowings from Levinas's thought occur within many of Godard's late works, perhaps most saliently *Notre musique* (2004). There, the Jewish philosopher's book *Entre Nous: Thinking-of-the-Other* (1991) is cited visually during a reflection on self-other dynamics that spark imperial aggression and sustain tragic antagonisms between whole cultures. A momentous figure for the ethical turn of French philosophy in the aftermath of May 1968, Levinas

Figure C.3. As Marie picks up Levinas's book, the businessman coasts through the background: *Goodbye to Language* (Godard, 2014).

is less a guide for Godard than an interlocutor whose views lend nuance to the director's own, at times dissenting quests.[20] The impetus for *Time and the Other* traces back to the notebooks Levinas wrote while interned in a Nazi labor camp for prisoners of war.[21] *Time and the Other* consists of provisional lectures putting forth a "phenomenology of alterity," an account of the subject stripped of the assimilating power of the transcendental ego by virtue of a disruptive encounter with something, or someone, absolutely Other. The lectures ultimately negotiate an "I-Thou" sociality that respects the "mystery" of the other person, maintains the distance between subjects, abandons self-serving impulses toward "possession," and welcomes what Levinas articulates as the onset of an unknowable future.[22]

In *Goodbye*, the 3D foregrounding of this text is complexly allusive and a hint as to what Godard is out to achieve through his own endeavor. It isn't that the film cites specific passages from *Time and the Other*. More generally, this reference, appearing as it does on the heels of the film's engagement with Ellul's dystopian prophecy, brings into the tangled web of associations a strand of philosophical inquiry that offsets, decries, and *militates against* the all-pervasive reach of state authority. Levinas's humanist thought here represents a (post-Holocaust and post-Heidegger) phenomenology of the interpersonal encounter wherein, as Levinas puts it, an ethical "metaphysics precedes ontology."[23]

As the first prologue continues, Levinas's philosophy of the encounter inspires Godard's stereoscopic *mise en scène*, in particular the way in which each shot calls attention to the spaces of interplay between characters, to rhythmic to-ings and fro-ings portrayed crosswise in the frame, as well as along the "z-axis" between background and foreground. At one point, the intersection of bodies, forces, and citations is marked by a slatted chair in the frontal plane: an object that, not unlike the used paperbacks displayed earlier, appears tangible, as if jutting into the space of our viewing (fig. C.4). As intellectual content and 3D cinematic form intermingle, the film's appeal to our engagement here comes with two insinuated questions. To what extent are these interactions conditioned by "Hitler's Victory"? And where, if anywhere, might we spot interhuman connections removed from and resistant to that scheme?

This concern for what arises in the very spaces between characters, in relation to larger cultural forces that impress on their quotidian lives, is of course nothing new to Godard's work: it reaches back to the recitation of Élie Faure's lines on the late style of Velázquez at the start of *Pierrot le fou* (1965) and continues well into Godard's late period. Here, this concern takes on a more philosophical cast, albeit without rigorous adherence to an existing tradition or text. The nod to Levinas is certainly weighted, and it is reinforced by an aphorism from the philosopher's *Totality and Infinity* (1961) that we hear later in the film, when a male voice remarks over a shot of what seems to be a vision exam (a solitary white dot in an otherwise black frame) and then a subsequent shot of Roxy the dog, playing outside: "Only free beings can be strangers to each other. They have a shared freedom but this is precisely what separates them." Nevertheless, in the referential weft of *Goodbye*, Levinasian lines and gestures vie with citations of a host of other authors, from

Figure C.4. A chair juts out where planes converge and characters cross paths in the 3D image: *Goodbye to Language*.

Paul Valéry to Jorge Luis Borges, that speak in different ways to linguistic, perceptual, and ethical dimensions of self-other proximity.

The thread of reflection that the introduction of Levinas sets in motion continues into the film's second prologue, which more overtly situates philosophy as an activity of investigation (this is why Davidson and Ivitch wear private detective trench coats and fedoras). As we see a variation on the same narrative event unfold again, now around a bench facing the lake, there occurs a voiceover recitation from a book that clashes radically with Levinas's outlook, Jean-Paul Sartre's *Being and Nothingness* (1943): "Philosophy [*la philo*] is a being such that in its being, its being is in question, insofar as this being implies a being other than itself." The unnamed male student cites this line, which coincides with two trembling, vertiginous shots that examine the body and limbs of a tree.

This is not a faithful quote. "Philosophy" has taken the place of "consciousness" in the original, and Godard's change is telling. Levinas's clash with Sartre's phenomenology comes down to what Levinas calls the latter's "reduction of the other to the categories of the same" and Sartre's inability to consider otherness except as a "threat," a "degradation" of the "I" and its freedom.[24] The term Godard replaces, "consciousness," is the very notion Sartre calls on to bring about what Levinas views as a totalizing and self-oriented synthesis of different forms of being, namely "the for-itself and the in-itself, the self and the other-than-self."[25]

Formally and discursively, Godard's delicate work in the scene suggests an ousting of this egoism, this ontology that, according to Levinas, institutes in the interpersonal realm a corrosive autarchy of the "I," even as it pretends to secure personal liberty. At an ulterior but crucial level of the film's intertextuality, *Goodbye* approvingly integrates Levinas's suspicion that Western ontology (Heidegger and Sartre) is guilty of a deep-seated egoism that allies itself, wittingly or not, with state tyranny.[26] To be sure, once the film turns to its domestic dramas with its newly formed couples, it will pursue a notion of individual subjectivity that is more radically unfixed, through interactions with others and with the external world. The student's revised quotation of Sartre is disrupted by offscreen sounds—a boat horn and lapping waves—that trigger a cut and force his voice into a more abstract register; and the camera's caress of the tree departs from the viewpoint of any character in the scene. It is also suggestive that the casual abbreviation of philosophy as "la philo" rids the word of its assuming attachment to knowledge (*-sophia*) and moves the accent onto loving (*philo-*). In this way, the prologues of *Goodbye* set up and contextualize the following scenes as sustained reflections on a philosophical problem: the possibility of attaining a kind of love that prioritizes the freedom of the other above that of the self. Additionally, the shots of the tree and the acoustic disturbances from offscreen alert us to the fact that we will have to attend not just to interpersonal relations but to an insistent world outside.

Eros Is Sick: Roxy as Intercessor

Godard's handwritten summary of the film reports, at least of the first couple, that "they love, they argue, fists fly." But where is "love" depicted? The scenes in the "1 nature" and "2 metaphor" sections portray not romance so much as its ruin, as the two couples, in states of undress, lounge and shift about a remote house while at cross-purposes (it is, curiously enough, the same house in both sections, Godard's actual residence in Rolle). It appears that somewhere between the vows of allegiance by Marcus and Gédéon in the two prologues and these later interactions, love has begun to wither.

These scenes could perhaps be said to respond to Levinas's discussion of erotic relations in both *Time and the Other* and *Totality and Infinity*, but Godard's treatment of the matter is far less optimistic. The bulk of the repetitions that compare his two main couples reveal an impasse of communication. In one reprised scene set in the bathroom, the female character protests against the inequality of the couple's dynamic (one should note that "égalité" and "liberté" are recurring, freighted terms in their dialogue, invoking the clarion call of the 1789 Revolution and the eventual motto of the French Republic), but her partner, while using the toilet in a bit of deadpan humor, replies that "equality" has its only authentic expression in the act of defecating, where all assume the same task and position, that of Rodin's bronze statue *The Thinker*.

His line at least responds to hers. What usually prevails in the spoken dialogue between either couple is an absence of continuity. Their exchanges are recitations of philosophical aphorisms that riff on the need to embrace otherness, yet they deliver these lines without appearing to realize their reflective application, and they seem unaware that their words come from antecedent sources. Language itself seems a stumbling block, as tends to be the case in Godard's fictions. "With language, something is happening. Something awkward about our relation to the world," Marcus says to Ivitch at one point, or rather, he asserts this aloud in her presence, both of them naked. "It acts against pure freedom. I am speaking: subject. I am listening: object." As he utters these sentences and makes two trips across the room to retrieve Ivitch's trench coat and then a bouquet of flowers, the film deploys its most spectacular and disorienting optical effect. One of the two side-by-side digital cameras used for shooting in 3D stays focused on Ivitch, who sits at the left perimeter of the frame. The other camera, however, pans to follow Marcus, and the shot suddenly pulls apart into two overlapping views, producing a superimposition, one in which each layer depicts "the off-screen space of the other," as Nico Baumbach well puts it. Baumbach also points out that when this effect happens, the viewer is temporarily granted the option of forming his or her own shot/countershot alternations: if we close one eye, we see a shot of Ivitch by itself, and if we then shut that eye and open the other, we see a countershot of Marcus.[27]

Whatever we make of the cleverness of this moment—its combination of montage with a dual-layered long take and a tracking camera, its destruction of stereo cinema's illusionist power and so forth—we need to observe the multifaceted work it does with regard to the philosophical concerns of the scene. The thrust of this audacious superimposition is to study the charged space between these characters—and to disclose *for the spectator* a field of interconnectedness, one that confounds the problems of spoken language and the rather "awkward" subject-object binary that Marcus complains about. At the same time, it's clear that the characters themselves remain blind to their interconnectedness along these lines. In some of Godard's late films, such as *Hail Mary* (1985) and *Nouvelle vague*, the couples at odds are able to reconcile, establishing some chord of togetherness based on reciprocity, an achievement conveyed through a tender dialogue of gestures as much as through speech. But in this case what Godard's technical maneuver shows us is an interpersonal gap within which love fails to materialize. There are shades of *Contempt* (1963) and its tinkering with a cliché of melodramatic staging: the placement of conspicuous things in the space between two arguing lovers so as to suggest their mutual alienation. Here the superimposition conducts a jarring collision between a lamp and an equally prominent vase of flowers. It is not that *Goodbye* urges *us* to see these interlying things as obstacles. Rather, this convention of staging, as Godard makes eccentric use of it, highlights the insufficiencies of the dramatis personae, their inability to access and share the kind of vision and thought toward which the intricate composition draws us. Granted, this superimposition does as much to baffle and distress our binocular gaze as it does to enhance it. Our vision, it is fair to say, fails at this juncture, too.

Enter Roxy. In the light of these human failings—both ours and the couples'—we can begin to understand how the stray dog, first seen in *The Three Disasters*, comes to the fore as a central character, a kind of hero through which *Goodbye*'s reflective project deepens and takes on added significance. Godard's poetic synopsis, his complex arrangement of stills in the press kit, and his statements in interviews all designate Roxy as an intercessor, as "a link, between two people,"[28] a figure who mends lines of communication. This seems to imply that the dog goes from person to person, somehow assisting an improved form of dialogue, but the film depicts nothing of the sort. Roxy, in fact, never physically occupies the same shot as a human being. Both of the couples take him in, but in the rare moments when they interact with him, the film reduces their presence to voices from offscreen, and what they say to or about this animal underlines their lack of awareness of his mediating role.

What this 3D film actually expresses, then, is Roxy's intervention in and for the film's essayistic relationship with the spectator. This becomes apparent in the intermittent scenes in which Roxy, unleashed, explores natural landscapes using perceptual abilities that, according to the voiceover narration, surpass those of humans. These scenes are interludes in which the film becomes more deeply ponderous, the barrage of ideas and references slows, and we are given a bit more time to contemplate the motifs and questions running through the film as a whole. This shift in mood, which is signaled by musical transitions from Tchaikovsky's dreary *Slavic March* to the more hopeful second movement of Beethoven's Seventh Symphony, is one in which a feel of possibility surfaces, putting us on the cusp of something transformative. The film aesthetically comes alive in these interludes, heightening our sensitivity to the environments that Roxy surveys, their vivid colors, their 3D-rendered volumes that defy the boundary of the screen. Handheld shots of the sky and of ponds mirroring the forest work as seductive emblems of reflection. These recurring interludes are further fascinating for the sense in which they exhibit a rough, glitchy texture of mediation. Part of their strikingness comes from their pixilated compositions produced by technical flaws and interferences in the low-grade digital video registration and playback—a look that Godard welcomes even as it conflicts with the pristine HD imagery shown elsewhere in the film (fig. C.5).

The film's other characters are absent from these abstracted promenades, but it would not be accurate to say that Roxy is alone. His intermittent looks-to-camera stare back at the audience *and* betray an intimate familiarity with the person filming him (Godard himself operates the handheld camera in these scenes, though the film makes no direct reference to this).[29] These returned gazes address the spectator and flout the convention of the fourth wall, configuring the screen as less a barrier than a threshold. This also happens through 3D protrusions of Roxy's exploratory muzzle, as though he is sensing clues or curiosities on our side of the screen (fig. C.6). Further,

Figure C.5. Roxy roams a pixilated landscape: *Goodbye to Language*.

Figure C.6. Roxy's protruding snout in 3D: *Goodbye to Language*.

Godard often films Roxy at close range and from the back, framing him as a *Rückenfigur* staring into the recess of the shot or past its borders. Roxy thus figures as a seer within the film whose conduct has a bearing on our own engagement.

This isn't to argue that Roxy serves as an unqualified stand-in observer with whose abilities we become aligned. These interludes complicate and faze our involvement as much as they induce it. At one point, Roxy's back-viewed silhouette figures in a charming illustration of his capacity to see "metaphors," that is, connective forces between disparate places (Godard plays on the Greek word *metaphora*, meaning "transfer," or "transit," hence the train that Roxy observes in this scene as the cross-cutting situates him both in the city and countryside at once). During another of Roxy's jaunts, an unidentified male voiceover addresses the dog's importance:

> It is not animals who are blind. Man, blinded by consciousness, is incapable of seeing the world. What is outside, wrote Rilke, can be known only through an animal's gaze. And Darwin, citing Buffon, maintains that the dog is the only living creature that loves you more than it loves itself.

These lines attribute to Roxy a power of amplified vision that is bound up with and animated by his propensity for selfless love: he embodies an unsparing kind of *friendly* love—a joyful regard for the other that is unrivaled among other species. Implicit here is the idea that he can perceive and love in this way precisely because he lacks the egocentric and verbocentric tendencies

Stereoscopic Essays for the New Century

215

that blunt human perception and diminish interhuman relationships. *Goodbye* thus delimits Roxy's powers as falling beyond our reach, and yet the line from Rilke's eighth *Duino Elegy* allows that even as we have no direct access to what Roxy sees and contemplates, his gaze, his cinematic figure, can still somehow act as an opaque medium that lets us indirectly apprehend "what is outside" and take it into account. The stage of references is already crowded, but I must note that Roxy's figural role also resonates with Montaigne's thoughts regarding animal intelligence, dogs included. The observation of animals, for Montaigne, curbs human pride by requiring us to face the shortfalls of our wisdom, perception, and communication (II.12: 506–41).

What, then, are we to make of the rhetorical gestures noted above by which the film pulls us close to this creature? If, being humans, comparatively blind and unloving, we are barred from his aptitudes, then what work are these moments doing? Roxy, it turns out, is less a surrogate for our spectatorship than both a lure and an absolute limit. Godard's stereoscopic style and address draw near to this superior vision without quite matching it. *Goodbye* unfolds a utopian conceit around this animal: namely, that if the couples in the narrative (and if we ourselves) *were* capable of seeing and thinking in the manner that he does, then their (and our) relationships with one another and with the world at large would conceivably undergo an ecstatic transformation of a *revolutionary* magnitude, to the point of countervailing, or at least resisting, the effects of what Ellul diagnoses as Hitler's victory.

Through this characterization of Roxy, several of the film's reflective strands—spanning its plot, citations, and 3D aesthetics—converge. Roxy's role reinforces the parallels between Ellul's argument and the dystopian postwar science fiction of Simak and Vogt. While Roxy is modeled roughly after Simak's post-apocalyptic dogs, his faculties are closely akin to those of Vogt's two-brained protagonist who harnesses his telepathic and telekinetic gifts to fight against a tyrannical empire. Godard, as I have shown, works Levinas into this weave for the sake of a critique of revived totalitarianism. By embodying an inquisitive, joyous sensitivity to alterity that improves on human shortcomings, Roxy comes forward as a fulfillment of the ethical potential the film raises through the use of *Time and the Other*. Of course, it is well known that Levinas omits nonhuman animals from his own ethical framework. Godard's use of Roxy is a stark revision, yet we might also read this canine hero as an allusion to a late essay in which Levinas himself appears to amend this exclusion: his fond memory of a mongrel dog, "Bobby," who wandered into the Nazi POW camp where he was held captive and restored his and his fellow Jewish inmates' sense of humanity.[30]

We are still left with the question of the stereoscopic significance of Roxy's promenades as they respond to and bridge these references. My sense is that the dog's performance works in step with Godard's ravishing yet glitch-ridden and at times painfully off-kilter use of 3D by compelling us to reckon with the fact that we perhaps see very little and that we love even more poorly. The creature figures in concert with the 3D imagery to test and rattle our perception regarding two domains of alterity—the between and the "outside," or what the film's idiolect calls "the forest." This is why Roxy's walks happen in a pattern of oscillations from the couples' house to the wooded exterior.[31]

These forest promenades transpire within a "Zone" of sorts, to borrow the concept from Marker's exemplary essay film *Sans soleil* (1983), which itself appropriates the conceit from Andrei Tarkovsky's essayistic science-fiction film *Stalker* (1979). Indeed, *Goodbye* seems to allude to Marker's and Tarkovsky's respective Zones through certain shots of Roxy (figs. C.7–C.9). In *Stalker*, the Zone, where a mysterious dog appears,[32] names a forbidden and mystical territory formed in the wake of a global catastrophe, its borders patrolled by state authorities. Purportedly those who journey to this landscape and negotiate its snares and difficulties will see their wishes granted. In Marker's rendition, the Zone becomes technological—a realm of near-abstract imagery opened up by manipulations of archival film footage using a video synthesizer. One of Marker's personae in *Sans soleil*, Sandor Krasna, embraces this form of imaging after becoming disillusioned with militant filmmaking, due to setbacks and betrayals on the Left after May 1968. "If the images of the present don't change," the film's narrator reports, reading one of Krasna's letters, "then change the images of the past." Krasna's last-ditch gambit is keyed to the hope that this intensive alteration of past scenes, such as those documenting the political unrest of the late 1960s, might recapture utopian energies to be developed more advantageously in the future. This is the anxious wish that Marker's electronic Zone may or may not grant.

If Roxy guides us through a stereoscopic Zone, Godard's version likewise comes with a double-edged sense of hope and desperation. We feel the promise of discovering new ways of perceiving and thinking—the promise of revitalization at once aesthetic, political, and ethical. But *Goodbye* never quite achieves this transformation for us; and with equal force, the film anarchically confounds our vision and understanding. I find it necessary to remove my 3D glasses periodically, giving my eyes and brain a rest. If at some crucial moments, Godard's use of stereoscopy augments our perceptual acuity, at others, it presses our thought and vision to their limits, underscoring the fact of our *not yet* seeing. A line heard in voiceover during one of Roxy's promenades, a line Godard takes from Marcel Proust but accredits to Claude Monet, touches on this aspiration of his project: the narrator, after describing a river shrouded in fog, remarks, "At that spot of the canvas, paint not *what* we see, for we see nothing. Nor what we cannot see, for we must only paint what we see. But paint *that we do not see*." The last part of this vocal recitation joins two landscapes that are beautifully shot through a car windshield in a rainstorm, the wipers activated. This vehicular framing motif is repeated elsewhere in the film (and resurfaces from other late Godard works, such as *In Praise of Love* [2001]), but here, the car is notably stationary, not moving

Figure C.7. The Stalker and a mysterious dog rest, deep within the Zone: *Stalker* (Tarkovsky, 1979).

Figure C.8. A dog rests on the seashore in the electronic Zone: *Sans soleil* (Marker, 1983).

Figure C.9. Roxy in the forest, detecting what a narrator calls "the revolutionary force of signs": *Goodbye to Language*.

218   Coda

ahead. In the second shot, washer fluid spurts on the glass, as if to give us a clearer view, but only further obfuscates. These shots through the windshield reflexively comment on the cinematic screen itself and our confrontation with it, while Godard all but revokes the stereoscopic sensation of depth. By painting the realization *"that we do not see,"* these rain-streaked landscapes bear out the motif of human perception and consciousness falling short at a threshold (it is a typical late Godard paradox that images acknowledging a state of blindness should still be so striking and have the feel of an illumination). The film thus offers itself as an impressionistic portrait of vision being held largely in check, at the transition between the visible and invisible, the inside and outside.

Remembrances of Essays Past

For the characters in the film's fiction, Roxy's intercession is to no avail. After the double-tiered narrative ends in disaster with the vicious murders of the men in each couple, presumably at the hands of the former husband, a coda takes place in which the mood lightens and a third, much older couple emerges—though they remain mostly outside the image track as their voices debate, for instance, the content of Roxy's dreams. This occurs at the same time that Godard's authorial and biographical role in the reflection becomes more apparent (though we are given nothing like the close-up of his lips in *The Three Disasters*). Twice in a short stretch, he inscribes himself in this coda. First, as a hoarse narrator, he recounts the conception of the novel *Frankenstein* when Mary Shelley and Percy Bysshe Shelley summered on Lake Geneva, the two writers figuring as a creative couple enmeshed in revolutionary politics. Godard intrudes a second time, in a dialogue with an unseen woman who listens to his esoteric point about fitting "flatness into depth," which he tries to illustrate using black ink on graph paper, with just his hands in the shot (notice that his inkwell reappears from the historical scene featuring the Shelleys).

Identities at this juncture are tenuous at best, but the older couple invokes Godard-Miéville. This aspect of the coda is in fact a culmination of half-hidden traces of Godard's life and work that run through the film, spanning his career stages. There are citations from and allusions to his start as a film critic, his New Wave years, his Maoist militancy (e.g., a reiterated shot of blood draining from a shower recalls the Dziga Vertov Group's *Pravda* [1970] where a similar shot links up with a relay of red-hued references to the brutal oppression of the working class), and his productivity thereafter, with and without Miéville. A shot of a couple awkwardly tussling in the shower together restages a moment from *Prénom Carmen* (1983). Building on this layer of recollection, there is a reenactment of the bedroom scene in *JLG/JLG* (see chapter 4) where JLG reads from Vogt's science fiction, although

Stereoscopic Essays for the New Century

in this variation, an actor substitutes for Godard and reads a later novel in Vogt's *Null-A* trilogy. The coda is set in the same house shown earlier—again, Godard's home in Rolle. As I have noted, Roxy is the director's pet with Miéville, and so the promenade scenes have a built-in personal element. Godard's footsteps can be heard in these scenes, crunching on the forest terrain from offscreen.

The spectator conversant with Godard's work will notice distinct echoes in this coda of his joint undertakings with Miéville (whose voice graces the soundtrack one point),[33] in particular *The Old Place*, which is the tonal prototype of this final section. A shot of two red poppies swaying in the wind along the roadside returns from a lyrical exercise in *The Old Place* (see chapter 3) that recounts the losses of past revolutionary struggles and admires how these poppies still organize a demonstration for "love" instead of violence. These retrospective touches help to bring threads of *Goodbye* into convergence as we are pressed to consider the stakes of Godard's latest experiment in the context of his overall corpus.

The quietly poignant coda of *Goodbye* turns attention to the very cruxes and motivations of Godard's essayism, from its penchant for endless revision to its bid for dialogue that extends to the spectator. We have seen how Godard's couplehood with Miéville has long worked as a reference for his essaying. Once again, their collaborative rapport bespeaks the possibility of achieving, through cinema, an essayistic modality of shared vision and thought—one that fuses love and work, retests its methods and convictions habitually, allows ample room for dissensus, and continues to advocate ethical and political resistance, but in a gentler vein of reflection than Godard practiced during his Maoist years.

There is a correlation between Roxy's faculties and what Godard and Miéville's embodiment of twoness potentially stands to offer: an antidote to Hitler's victory. But given the elegiac feel of this "goodbye," one also senses that Godard's twoness with Miéville has *expired* and become the stuff of history (a situation to which *The Three Disasters* alludes through motifs of imperiled couples and fading women, implicitly among them Miéville).[34] The montage that takes the film to its unfinished end at once intimates something of their egress as a couple and invites the spectator into the relational dynamic for which they have stood. We witness—in addition to another shot of Roxy looking back at us—a series of unpeopled scenes that nevertheless convey shared experience: *two* vacant place settings at the kitchen table, one angled diagonally toward us, the frame alive with shadows of trees from outside; *two* empty chairs facing a television screen busy with electronic snow; and the *two* scarlet poppies from *The Old Place*. If these parting shots refer to the elderly couple in the coda's fictional narrative, and to Godard-Miéville, they also apostrophize our potential involvement (fig. C.10).[35]

The weary but still intact utopian attitude of *Goodbye* leaves us with a brief coda to the coda in which the ghost of revolution is summoned one last

Figure C.10. Spectatorship evoked as a (failed? potential?) matter of coupling: *Goodbye to Language*.

time. Over end titles, we hear a galvanizing, folksy Italian-language protest song circa 1968 ("Always united we win / long live the revolution!"), a tune that, in fact, returns from both *Histoire(s)* and one of Godard's productions with the Vertov Group, *Struggle in Italy* (1971). There is nothing sarcastic about this musical appeal to revolutionary action, which resonates with Godard's comment in an interview that Roxy carries the torch for the third estate of France and thus intercedes for "the common people" and still-unmet demands for political equality.[36] Be that as it may, the tail end of the film, mixing as it does elegiac and optative sentiments, does not simply interpolate us into an already achieved movement. It expresses a deep longing for a condition that—within the bounds of the film's own rhetoric—cannot be currently claimed or pictured. With a blacking-out of the visual field we hear a duet of a dog barking and a baby's cries (the soundtrack is sampled from a popular, Lumière-like YouTube video, "Husky Sings with Baby"). The film thus gestures toward a threshold beyond its current reach, toward the dawn of a new perceptiveness—the birth into the world of a language keyed to the potentialities that Roxy incarnates. But there is a tension, not a neat groove, between this song of two creatures and the Italian protest anthem that comes after it. Rather than a "we" postulated in advance as an entire collective, Godard pursues a friendly "we" of just two, starting provisionally from there, and he forces us to confront the ethical challenges of its foundations. His stereoscopic essay is such that revolution remains imaginable only on the other side of a black screen—a night of the senses that obliges us to think through the very limits of our not-yet-seeing.

Stereoscopic Essays for the New Century

I would like to end this book with one last point as regards what I earlier called Godard's aphoristic arithmetic. His synopsis for *Goodbye* declares: "One is in the other, the other is in the one, and these are three persons." At some level, this aphorism activates our memory of essays past, reappearing as it does from *The Old Place*. In that prior work, this declaration is ultimately associated with the A Bao A Qu, the Borges-supplied "imaginary being" around which the final segment of the video is focused, a mystical animal whose role allows for a partly bleak and partly buoyant reflection on the interpersonal stakes of Godard-Miéville's work together. As I argued in chapter 3, their treatment of this radiant creature serves to comment tacitly on the tripartite relationship between themselves and the especially diligent viewer or "visitor" they seek to attract. *Goodbye* redoes this reflexive gesture, with the slightly less abstract dog replacing the A Bao A Qu. The aphorism isn't a clarification of the film's plot, but rather a thought that adumbrates the sensitivity to between-ness and alterity that Roxy enacts—a sensitivity we might begin to understand through the observance of his performance.

In interviews Godard has framed this aphorism as a citation that relates back to Montaigne. The statement, he claims, is taken from the philosopher Léon Brunschvicg's book *Descartes et Pascal: Lecteurs de Montaigne* (1944).[37] Timothy Barnard, however, has discovered that this remark actually comes not from Brunschvicg's book but from a passage in Blaise Pascal's *Pensées* (1669).[38] The fragment originally refers to the Holy Trinity as an analogy for the spiritual and bodily connection between believing members of a community and the body of Christ. For Pascal, the statement defines a social atmosphere in and through which authentic subjectivity, self-giving love, and thought can be most beneficially realized.[39] Godard's creative misattribution of this quote to Brunschvicg gives the expression a secular turn. In an interview with *Le Monde* given around the release of *Goodbye*, Godard again cites Brunschvicg as the source, admiring how this aphorism strikes a balanced ensemble of three thinkers who embody different guiding views or impulses: Descartes ("I know"), Pascal ("I believe"), and Montaigne ("I doubt"). Godard finds it "very alive, this feeling of three," and then he obscurely relates this feeling to cinema and its resources of montage.[40]

From Godard's use of this aphoristic line, we can extrapolate a number of affinities with his own essayistic practice. If the state dreams of being one, and the individual dreams of being two, then doesn't the essayist dream of being two, shadowed by a third co-investigator to come? The move from two to three is in the direction of community, a small, modest community built around the condition that all knowledge and belief *must be squared with doubt at each turn*: not the pseudo-doubt Descartes raises as a pretext for an inevitable, overriding display of certainty, but the resilient kind of doubt that stokes Montaigne's inquiries.

This aphorism, in its Godardian turn, is not an adage but a dare to think differently. I read in this "feeling of three" a conception of interrelatedness that compels us to reimagine the human ties at stake in his image practice. To answer the call of his essayistic work is to find ourselves party to a convoluted crossing of thoughts, memories, and perceptions in which individual subjectivity becomes so porous and dispersive as to lose its monadic grounding. In and through this process, we become more than just interlocutors who interact with the forms on display, more than secret sharers invoked by the filmmaker's rhetoric. It is more precise to say that we become the essayist as the essayist in turn becomes us.

Becoming isn't being. We *are* not Godard, he *is* not us, and the technical media that let us interface with his thought also keep us at a remove from it. That said, his essayistic style opens up dialogical vectors of becoming between his thought process and ours—vectors whereby we become partially seduced, possessed, populated, and transfigured by so many alien intelligences. We swing between active and passive roles, between being the critical arbiter and becoming a medium through which the reflection streams. If risks come with this replayed encounter—a loss of individual agency and subjectivity up to a point—there are also uncommon rewards. Godard's daringly experimental style, at its most brilliant, at its most hopeful, short-circuits the machinery of narcissism, suggesting how thought, vision, and feeling with and for others can begin to break beyond it.

NOTES

Introduction

1. See Elizabeth A. Papazian and Caroline Eades, introduction to *The Essay Film: Dialogue, Utopia, Politics* (London: Wallflower, 2016), 1–11.

2. Phillip Lopate, "In Search of the Centaur: The Essay-Film," in *Beyond Document: Essays on Nonfiction Film*, ed. Charles Warren (Middletown, Conn.: Wesleyan University Press, 1996), 243–70; Nora M. Alter, "The Political Im/perceptible in the Essay Film: Farocki's *Images of the World and the Inscription of War*," *New German Critique*, no. 68 (1996): 165–92; Paul Arthur, "Essay Questions," *Film Comment* 39, no. 1 (2003): 58–62; Laura Rascaroli, *The Personal Camera: Subjective Cinema and the Essay Film* (London: Wallflower, 2009); Michael Renov, "The Electronic Essay," in *The Subject of Documentary* (Minneapolis: University of Minnesota Press, 2004), 182–90; Christa Blümlinger, "Lire entre les images," trans. Pierre Rusch, in *L'Essai et le cinéma*, ed. Suzanne Liandrat-Guigues and Murielle Gagnebin (Seyssel: Champ Vallon, 2004), 49–66; Timothy Corrigan, *The Essay Film: From Montaigne, After Marker* (New York: Oxford University Press, 2011).

3. Rascaroli, *The Personal Camera*, 1–18.

4. Ibid., 95–103.

5. Ibid., 15.

6. See, for example, Lopate, "In Search of the Centaur," 243–70.

7. My book was already at press when Laura Rascaroli's second monograph on the essay film, *How the Essay Film Thinks*, appeared. There, she extends her ambit beyond personal documentary through refreshing examples from global cinema, focusing on the essay film's disjunctive and dialectical inclination to explore various gaps and interstices—between genres, between fiction and documentary, between expressive components (whether visual or acoustic) in the film's fabric, between time frames, and so on. Rascaroli, *How the Essay Film Thinks* (New York: Oxford University Press, 2017), 1–21.

8. Corrigan, *The Essay Film*, 35.

9. Ibid.

10. Ibid., 35–36.

11. Robert Musil, *The Man without Qualities*, vol. 1, trans. Sophie Wilkins (New York: Knopf, 1995), 267–77.

12. Corrigan, *The Essay Film*, 147–53, 199–204.

13. Timothy Corrigan, "Essayism and Contemporary Film Narrative," in *The Essay Film: Dialogue, Utopia, Politics*, ed. Papazian and Eades, 15-27. Though Rascaroli limits her account of the essay film to documentary in *The Personal Camera*, her newer book includes fictional narrative. For a keen analysis of Aleksandr Sokurov's fictive *Elegy of a Voyage* (2001), see Rascaroli, *How the Essay Film Thinks*, 23–46.

14. Corrigan, *The Essay Film*, 16–17.

15. By "act" I mean to suggest a *performance*, relentlessly conscious of itself as such. On Montaigne's performative conception of the term *essai*, see Hugo Friedrich, *Montaigne*, ed. Philippe Desan (Berkeley: University of California Press, 1991), 1–30, 219–27; Richard Scholar, *Montaigne and the Art of Free-Thinking* (Oxfordshire, Eng.: Peter Lang, 2010), 67–90.

16. Jean Starobinski, "Can One Define the Essay?" trans. Lindsey Scott, in *Essayists on the Essay: Montaigne to Our Time*, ed. Carl H. Klaus and Ned Stuckey-French (Iowa City: University of Iowa Press, 2012), 112–13.

17. Michel de Montaigne, *The Complete Essays*, trans. M. A. Screech (New York: Penguin, 2003), 909. This edition is hereafter cited in text by book, chapter, and page number.

18. See Terrence Cave, "Locating the Early Modern," *Paragraph* 29 (2006): 12–26.

19. Eric Auerbach, "L'Humaine Condition," in *Mimesis: The Representation of Reality in Western Literature*, trans. Willard R. Trask (Princeton, N.J.: Princeton University Press, 2003), 303.

20. Antoine Compagnon, *La Seconde main, ou Le Travail de la citation* (Paris: Seuil, 1979), 279–312. See also Claire de Obaldia, *The Essayistic Spirit: Literature, Modern Criticism, and the Essay* (New York: Oxford University Press, 1995), 65–70, 85–87.

21. Hassan Melehy, *The Poetics of Literary Transfer in Early Modern France and England* (Surrey, Eng.: Ashgate, 2010), 139–60.

22. Montaigne also indulges in constant wordplay, exploiting the French language as a labyrinth of embedded, polysemous meaning. Puns and portmanteaux words (most of which are lost in translation) make his thought as wily as it is communicative. Godard's essayistic work is marked by similarly elaborate language games.

23. Mark Greengrass, "Montaigne and the Wars of Religion," in *The Oxford Handbook of Montaigne*, ed. Philippe Desan (New York: Oxford University Press, 2016), 138–57.

24. Auerbach, "L'Humaine Condition," 311.

25. See Deborah N. Losse, *Montaigne and Brief Narrative Form: Shaping the Essay* (London: Palgrave Macmillan, 2013).

26. Obaldia, *The Essayistic Spirit*, 214–15, 217, 236–37.

27. See Jean-Pierre Gorin's comments, included as a special feature on the Blu-ray edition of Marker's films *La Jetée* (1963) and *Sans soleil* (1983) released by The Criterion Collection. He mentions Godard's "dream to be Montaigne" in the section marked "Que sais-je?" of the supplementary features for *La Jetée*.

28. There are surprisingly few references to Montaigne in Godard's works and interviews. The most famous is the epigraph in *My Life to Live* (1962): "It is necessary to lend oneself to others and to give oneself to oneself." Lifted from Montaigne's "On Restraining Your Will" (III.10: 1134), this is not an unaltered quotation. Godard strikes "in my opinion" and seems to lend the sentence the feel of a motto instead of an instigative hypothesis. Yet Godard's film opens out and explores the implications of this statement through several types of social transactions, including prostitution and filmmaking, while Montaigne himself does not settle into a one-note argument, but weaves through examples to negotiate

Notes to Pages 11–20

an equilibrium between public and individual life, in a continual interplay of self and other.

29. Michael Witt, while referencing remarks by Jean-Louis Leutrat, writes of Godard's "protoplasmic oeuvre," arguing that "the disparate manifestations of his varied output and interventions are best thought of as the interconnected components of a vast installation under continual development on multiple fronts." Witt, *Jean-Luc Godard, Cinema Historian* (Bloomington: Indiana University Press, 2013), 7. Daniel Morgan comparably shows that Godard organizes multiple projects in his oeuvre as "series" that explore shared concerns. Morgan, *Late Godard and the Possibilities of Cinema* (Berkeley: University of California Press, 2013), 19–21.

30. For Friedrich Schlegel, "the essay is a mutual galvanism of author and reader" that ought to "combat intellectual arthritis and promote nimbleness." Quoted in John A. McCarthy, *Crossing Boundaries: A Theory and History of Essay Writing in German, 1680–1815* (Philadelphia: University of Pennsylvania Press, 1989), 189.

31. Essayistic cinema has begun to have its moment in film scholarship in part because of propitious changes in the viewing situation afforded by home video. Laura Mulvey, borrowing from Raymond Bellour and Victor Burgin, demonstrates how the home video spectator enters into "pensive" and "possessive" modes with regard to the spectacle. Mulvey, *Death 24x a Second: Stillness and the Moving Image* (London: Reaktion, 2006), 161–96. To be sure, the kind of spectatorial labor that cinematic essayism elicits is greatly assisted by such modes of viewing. A further sign of the essay's currency can be found in the recourse of scholars to the *production* of video essays on the web. Christian Keathley, Catherine Grant, and others have done much to establish the legitimacy of videographic scholarship, while connecting it to the history of the essay film. See Keathley and Grant's online journal for video essays, *[in]Transition*: http://mediacommons.futureofthebook.org/intransition/.

32. Adam Lowenstein, "The Master, the Maniac, and *Frenzy*: Hitchcock's Legacy of Horror," in *Hitchcock Past and Future*, ed. Richard Allen and Sam Ishii-Gonzáles (New York: Routledge, 2004), 184.

33. Jean-Luc Godard, "Interview with Jean-Luc Godard" (1962), in *Godard on Godard*, trans. and ed. Tom Milne (New York: Da Capo, 1972), 181. Hereafter cited in text and notes as GG.

34. T. S. Eliot, "Pensées of Pascal," in *Selected Essays* (New York: Harcourt Brace, 1950), 362.

Chapter 1

1. Carl H. Klaus, "Essayists on the Essay," in *Literary Nonfiction: Theory, Criticism, Pedagogy*, ed. Chris Anderson (Carbondale: Southern Illinois University Press, 1989), 155–74.

2. Timothy Corrigan argues that Godard self-consciously engages and furthers a Montaignean heritage. Corrigan, *The Essay Film*, 69–70. See also Alain Ménil, "Entre utopie et hérésie: Quelques remarques à propos de la notion d'essai," in *L'Essai et le cinéma*, ed. Suzanne Liandrat-Guigues and Murielle Gagnebin (Seyssel: Champ Vallon, 2004), 87–126.

226   Notes to Pages 20–24

3. András Bálint Kovács, *Screening Modernism: European Art Cinema, 1950–1980* (Chicago: University of Chicago Press, 2007), 117.

4. Rascaroli, *The Personal Camera*, 4–6.

5. Lopate, "In Search of the Centaur," 255.

6. Ibid. For Godard's work, Lopate instead prefers a term that is actually a cognate for "essay" in the director's own vocabulary: "research."

7. David Bordwell, *Narration in the Fiction Film* (Madison: University of Wisconsin Press, 1985), 312–13.

8. Ibid.

9. Ibid., 332–34.

10. Corrigan, *The Essay Film*, 51–55.

11. Godard, *GG*, 171.

12. Godard's attitude is compatible with Daniel Eisenberg's suggestion that there is no "essay film" genre as such; there is only the essayistic experiment out of which traits contingently emerge. See the interview with Eisenberg in the booklet accompanying the DVD box set of his films, *Postwar*, released through Video Data Bank, 2012.

13. Raymond Bellour argues for such terminological flexibility, which allows one to explore "not exactly the notion of the essay film, but of the essay as cinema." Bellour, "The Cinema and the Essay as a Way of Thinking," in *Der Essayfilm: Ästhetik und Aktualität*, ed. Sven Kramer and Thomas Tode (Konstanz: Verlagsgesellschaft, 2011), 53.

14. Thomas Harrison, *Essayism: Conrad, Musil, & Pirandello* (Baltimore: Johns Hopkins University Press, 1992); Obaldia, *The Essayistic Spirit*, 193–246; Randi Soloman, *Virginia Woolf's Essayism* (New York: Oxford University Press, 2012); and Stefano Ercolino, *The Novel-Essay, 1884–1947* (London: Palgrave Macmillan, 2014).

15. Rascaroli's *The Personal Camera* and Corrigan's *The Essay Film* take part in an international effort of canonization that includes Christa Blümlinger and Constantin Wulff, eds., *Schreiben Bilder Sprechen: Texte zum essayistischen Film* (Vienna: Sonderzahl, 1992); Alter, "The Political Im/perceptible in the Essay Film," 165–92; Sylvie Astric, ed., *Le Film-Essai: Identification d'un genre* (Paris: Centre Pompidou, 2000); Christina Scherer, *Ivens, Marker, Godard, Jarman: Erinnerung im Essayfilm* (Munich: Fink, 2001); Catherine Lupton, *Chris Marker: Memories of the Future* (London: Reaktion, 2005); Nora M. Alter, *Chris Marker* (Urbana: University of Illinois Press, 2006); Volker Pantenburg, *Film als Theorie: Bildforschung bei Harun Farocki und Jean-Luc Godard* (Bielefeld: Transcript Verlag, 2006); Dudley Andrew, "A Film Aesthetic to Discover," *CiNéMAS* 17, no. 2–3 (2007): 47–71; Sven Kramer and Thomas Tode, eds., *Der Essayfilm* (Konstanz: Verlagsgesellschaft, 2011); and Antonio Weinrichter, ed., *La forma que piensa: Tentativas en torno al cine-ensayo* (Pamplona: Gobierno de Navarra, 2007).

16. Hans Richter, "Der Filmessay: Eine neue Form des Dokumentarfilm," in *Schreiben Bilder Sprechen: Texte zum essayistischen Film*, ed. Blümlinger and Wulff, 197 (my translation is indebted to Richard Langston). For a recently available English translation, see Richter, "The Film Essay: A New Type of Documentary Film," trans. Maria P. Alter, in *Essays on the Essay Film*, ed. Alter and Corrigan, 89–92.

Notes to Pages 25–27

17. Richter, "Der Filmessay," 196–97, my italics. As a recent essayistic video that fulfills Richter's anticipations, Alexander Kluge's *News from Ideological Antiquity: Marx—Eisenstein—Das Kapital* (2008) explores the difficulties that economic processes pose to creative expression. See in particular the segment (23 minutes into the theatrical cut) where Kluge interviews Hans Magnus Enzensberger.

18. On the essay film's link to the avant-garde compilation film, see Paul Arthur, "Essay Questions," *Film Comment* 39, no. 1 (2003): 58–62; and Paul Arthur, "The Resurgence of History and the Avant-Garde Essay Film," in *A Line of Sight: American Avant-Garde Film since 1965* (Minneapolis: University of Minnesota Press, 2005), 61–73. Nicole Brenez has also mined this terrain through many of her curatorial projects and through her critical category of the "visual study." See her pieces "Recycling, Visual Study, Expanded Theory—Ken Jacobs, Theorist, or the Long Song of the Sons," trans. Adrian Martin, in *Optic Antics: The Cinema of Ken Jacobs* (Oxford: Oxford University Press, 2011), 158–74; and "Montage intertextuel et formes contemporaines du remploi dans le cinéma experimental," *CiNéMAS* 13, no. 1–2 (2002): 49–67. See also Christa Blümlinger, *Cinéma de seconde main: Esthétique du remploi dans l'art du film et des nouveaux médias* (Paris: Klincksieck, 2013).

19. Richter, "Der Essayfilm," 197.

20. Astruc would soon make films of his own, but his audiovisual work, with the exception of his scripted commentary for Jean-Daniel Pollet's *Bassae* (1964), does not meet the profile of the essay film as it has been so often defined on the basis of the *caméra-stylo*. His films are more inherently novelistic, which is not to discount their innovative uses of voiceover, mobile camera, and the long take. See Richard Neupert, *A History of the French New Wave*, 2nd ed. (Madison: University of Wisconsin Press, 2007), 46–56.

21. Astruc, "The Birth of a New Avant-Garde," in *The New Wave: Critical Landmarks*, ed. Peter Graham (Garden City, NJ: Doubleday, 1968), 18.

22. Jean-Paul Sartre, "What Is Literature?" trans. Bernard Frechtman, in *"What Is Literature?" and Other Essays* (Cambridge, Mass.: Harvard University Press, 1988), 216–17.

23. Astruc, "The Birth of a New Avant-Garde," 18–19.

24. Ibid., 21–23.

25. Ibid., 20.

26. Nora M. Alter has identified two alternative paths along which the audiovisual essay evolves: one stemming from Richter that tries, from within the art world, to merge the documentary with the experimental avant-garde film; and a second path stemming from Astruc that attempts to combine the documentary with the feature-length fiction film. For Alter, these legacies have intersected in the context of gallery installations. Alter, "Translating the Essay into Film and Installation," *Journal of Visual Culture* 6, no. 1 (2007): 52–57.

27. Astruc, "The Birth of a New Avant-Garde," 20–21.

28. Ibid., 19.

29. Timothy Corrigan, "The Essay Film as a Cinema of Ideas," in *Global Art Cinema: New Theories and Histories*, ed. Rosalind Galt and Karl Schoonover (New York: Oxford University Press, 2010), 218–37.

30. Corrigan, *The Essay Film*, 55–73.

31. Ibid. See also Corrigan, "The Essay Film as a Cinema of Ideas," 227.

32. Kate Ince, *Georges Franju* (New York: Manchester University Press, 2005), 11–45; Lupton, *Chris Marker*, 46–49.

33. If the Left Bank directors are the main exponents in this history, the Situationist essay films of Guy Debord, along with earlier Lettrist films like *Venom and Eternity* (Isidore Isou, 1951), make up an important underground strand. None of these films appear in Rascaroli's or Corrigan's accounts, but they are relevant to the definitional emphasis on the public sphere, audience interaction, and textual disruption.

34. Noël Burch, *Theory of Film Practice*, trans. Helen R. Lane (Princeton: Princeton University Press, 1981), 159.

35. Dai Vaughan, *For Documentary* (Berkeley: University of California Press, 1999), 29–41.

36. Lopate, "In Search of the Centaur," 248.

37. Virginia Bonner, "The New Executioners: The Specter of Algeria in Alain Resnais's *Night and Fog*," *Scope* 13 (2009), http://www.scope.nottingham.ac.uk/article.php?issue=13&id=1094.

38. William Rothman, *Documentary Film Classics* (Cambridge: Cambridge University Press, 1997), 44.

39. By "apostrophe," I refer to the rhetorical conceit—familiar to literature and to lyric poetry in particular—of addressing, invoking, and recruiting the absent receiver as a participant. I will have more to say about the relevance of this term to the essay form later in this study. For now, let me suggest that its desiring *but uncertain* play of absence and presence, distance and intimacy, makes it better suited conceptually to describe the relationship between audiovisual essayist and viewer than "direct address" and "interpellation."

40. Of this moment Lopate writes: "That 'but you have to know' . . . thrilled me like an unexpected, aggressive pinch: its direct address broke the neutral contract of spectatorship and forced me to acknowledge a conversation, along with its responsibilities.'" Lopate, "In Search of the Centaur," 248.

41. For a rich analysis of the film and the mode of spectatorship it enjoins, see Sandy Flitterman-Lewis, "Documenting the Ineffable: Terror and Memory in Alain Resnais's *Night and Fog*," in *Documenting the Documentary: Close Readings of Documentary Film and Video*, ed. Barry Keith Grant and Jeannette Sloniowski (Detroit, Mich.: Wayne State University Press, 1998), 204–22. See also Libby Saxton, "*Night and Fog* and the Concentrationary Gaze," in *Concentrationary Cinema: Aesthetics as Political Resistance in Alain Resnais'* Night and Fog (London: Berghahn, 2011), 140–51.

42. References to *Night and Fog* abound in essayistic cinema, as if to affirm its status as a prototype. Farocki, Godard, and others have worked with some of the same archival footage. The Eisler score resurfaces in Kluge's *The Patriot* (1979); a passage directed by Marker in *Far from Vietnam* (1967); and also Marker's more recent *The Case of the Grinning Cat* (2004). Vivid, pastoral landscapes in Godard's *Keep Your Right Up* (1987), marked by a barbed wire fence that the camera explores up close, evoke Resnais's film, and Godard cites the film in *A Married Woman* (1964), where it plays in a theater at the Orly airport. Shots from *Night and Fog* also appear in Godard's *Histoire(s) du cinéma* (1988–98) and the "Hell" montage in *Notre musique* (2004).

43. Corrigan, *The Essay Film*, 36–49.

44. André Bazin, "Bazin on Marker," trans. Dave Kehr, *Film Comment* 39, no. 4 (2003): 44.

45. Steven Ungar, "Radical Ambitions in Postwar French Documentary," in *Opening Bazin*, ed. Dudley Andrew and Hervé Joubert-Laurencin (Oxford: Oxford University Press, 2011), 254–61.

46. Bazin, "Bazin on Marker," 44, trans. modified. The term that Bazin coins has been translated as "horizontal" or "lateral," and some prefer "editing" to "montage." I prefer "lateral" because "horizontal" might be confused with the very kind of syntagmatic ("horizontal") succession from which Bazin means to distinguish his sense of the term. And Dudley Andrew has suggested that "montage" is the better term when Bazin defines new forms of organizing shots in documentary. Andrew, *What Cinema Is!* (Malden, Mass.: Wiley-Blackwell, 2010), 32–33, 62n8.

47. Raymond Durgnat argues that Marker's films, including *Letter from Siberia*, are tactically "pseudo-personal." Durgnat, "Resnais & Co.: Back to the Avant-Garde," *Monthly Film Bulletin* 54, no. 640 (1987): 135. See also Jonathan Rosenbaum, "Personal Effects: The Guarded Intimacy of *Sans Soleil*," The Criterion Collection, http://www.criterion.com/current/posts/484-personal-effects-the -guarded-intimacy-of-sans-soleil.

48. Jonathan Rosenbaum, "Orson Welles's Essay Films and Documentary Fictions," in *Discovering Orson Welles* (Berkeley: University of California Press, 2007), 129–45.

49. Rascaroli, "The Essay Film," 29.

50. This is how Solanas classifies *Hour of the Furnaces* in his 1969 interview with Godard. "Godard on Solanas/Solanas on Godard," in *Reviewing Histories*, ed. Coco Fusco (Buffalo, N.Y.: Hallwalls Contemporary Arts Center, 1987), 83. On the politicized *cine ensayo*, see Michael Chanan, "Documentary Film: Latin America," in *Encyclopedia of the Documentary Film*, ed. Ian Aitken (New York: Routledge, 2006).

51. Hamid Naficy, *An Accented Cinema: Exilic and Diasporic Filmmaking* (Princeton, N.J.: Princeton University Press, 2001). See also Paul Willemen, "Bangkok–Bahrain–Berlin–Jerusalem: Amos Gitae's Editing," in *Looks and Frictions: Essays in Cultural Studies and Film Theory* (Bloomington: Indiana University Press, 1994), 162–74.

52. Edgar Morin, quoted in Rascaroli, *The Personal Camera*, 39.

53. David Oscar Harvey rightly objects to definitions of the cinematic essay that outfit Astruc's *caméra-stylo* with a strict generic dependency on voiceover narration. He contends that "a non-vococentric essayistic subjectivity or manner of thinking has yet to be adequately theorized." Harvey, "The Limits of Vococentrism: Chris Marker, Hans Richter and the Essay Film," *SubStance* 41, no. 2 (2012): 7–9.

54. Jacques Rivette, "Letter on Rosselini," in *Cahiers du Cinéma: The 1950s: Neo-Realism, Hollywood, New Wave*, ed. Jim Hillier (Cambridge, Mass.: Harvard University Press, 1985), 202. While Rossellini's film has been released under the English-language titles *Voyage to Italy* and *Journey to Italy*, I refer to it as *Voyage in Italy* to preserve the more accurate "in" of its Italian title, *Viaggio in italia*.

230 Notes to Pages 36–44

55. Sandro Bernardi, "Rossellini's Landscapes: Nature, Myth, History," in *Roberto Rossellini: Magician of the Real*, ed. David Forgacs, Sarah Lutton, and Geoffrey-Nowell Smith (London: British Film Institute, 2000), 50–63.

56. Alain Bergala, *Voyage en Italie de Roberto Rossellini* (Crisnée, Belg.: Editions Yellow Now, 1990).

57. Corrigan, *The Essay Film*, 48. References to Deleuze's *Cinema 2* recur throughout Corrigan's argument.

58. Gilles Deleuze, *Cinema 1: The Movement-Image*, trans. Hugh Tomlinson and Barbara Habberjam (Minneapolis: University of Minnesota Press, 1986), x, xiv; Gilles Deleuze, *Cinema 2: The Time-Image*, trans. Hugh Tomlinson and Robert Galeta (Minneapolis: University of Minnesota Press, 1989), 280.

59. Durgnat, "Resnais & Co.," 133.

60. Denis Lévy, "Art et essai," in *L'Essai et le cinéma*, ed. Liandrat-Guigues and Gagnebin, 141–42.

61. Dorrit Cohn, *The Distinction of Fiction* (Baltimore, Md.: Johns Hopkins University Press, 1999), 7.

62. Jean-Pierre Gorin, in describing his own essayistic filmmaking, sympathetically defines "fiction" as a film's exertion of a shaping intellect. See Gorin, interview with Lynne Tillman, "Jean-Pierre Gorin," *BOMB Magazine* 23 (1988), http://bombmagazine.org/article/1056/jean-pierre-gorin.

63. Corrigan, "Essayism and Contemporary Film Narrative," 17, 25–26.

64. Ibid., 15–26.

65. *I'm Not There* invokes Godard's *A Married Woman* (1964), *Alphaville* (1965), *Masculine Feminine* (1966), *2 or 3 Things I Know About Her* (1967), and *La Chinoise* (1967) in revisionary ways that characterize Claire (Charlotte Gainsbourg) as a politically conscious modern woman and artist, over and against the sexism of her actor husband.

66. Gilles Deleuze, "Letter to Serge Daney: Optimism, Pessimism, and Travel," in *Negotiations, 1972–1990*, trans. Martin Joughin (New York: Columbia University Press, 1995), 70–72. Deleuze adapts the notion of audiovisual pedagogy from Daney.

67. Rossellini's *Voyage in Italy* already gives embryonic expression to this pedagogical bent, looking forward to his later work. Its allusions to Goethe's diaristic and epistolary *Italian Journey* (1816), from which it derives its title, imply an educational project that takes leave of preconception and begins from scratch.

68. Granted, fiction and narrative have their place in Marker's practice, too. Narrative essayism is at play in both of Marker's fiction films, *La Jetée* (1962) and *Level Five* (1997). And some of his more documentary-like films make use of fictionalization as a reflective strategy (e.g., invented characters, dramatic scenarios, and authorial personae in *Sans soleil*).

69. Brian Henderson, "*Godard on Godard*: Notes for a Reading," in *A Critique of Film Theory* (New York: E.P. Dutton, 1980), 82–105.

70. Ibid., 102.

71. Italo Calvino, "Cinema and the Novel: Problems of Narrative" (1966), in *The Uses of Literature*, trans. Patrick Creagh (San Diego, Calif.: Harcourt Brace Jovanovich, 1986), 79; Burch, *Theory of Film Practice*, 162.

Notes to Pages 44–50   *231*

72. Jonathan Rosenbaum, "Theory and Practice: The Criticism of Jean-Luc Godard," in *Placing Movies: The Practice of Film Criticism* (Berkeley: University of California Press, 1995), 21.

73. Colin MacCabe, "On the Eloquence of the Vulgar," in *The Eloquence of the Vulgar* (London: British Film Institute, 1999), 152–54.

74. Jacques Aumont, "The Fall of the Gods: Jean-Luc Godard's *Le Mépris* (1963)," in *French Film: Texts and Contexts*, ed. Susan Hayward and Ginette Vincendeau (London: Routledge, 2000), 174–75.

75. On *Contempt*'s relation to classicism, see Marc Cerisuelo, *Le Mépris* (Chatou: Transparence, 2006); Joe McElhaney, *The Death of Classical Cinema: Hitchcock, Lang, Minnelli* (Albany: SUNY Press, 2006), 1–3.

76. Godard, quoted in Bordwell, *Narration in the Fiction Film*, 315.

77. Gilberto Perez, *The Material Ghost: Films and Their Medium* (Baltimore, Md.: Johns Hopkins University Press, 1998), 87–91, 367–416.

78. Godard invokes the Hollywood melodrama through multiple references to Minnelli's *Some Came Running* (1958), a film that not coincidentally uses a large lampshade, positioned in the pictorial space between Dave (Frank Sinatra) and Gwen (Martha Hyer), to punctuate their emotional rift.

79. For an illuminating discussion of spatial "intervals" in cinema, including those that take effect between dramatis personae, see Alain Bergala, "L'Intervalle," in *La Mise en scène*, ed. Jacques Aumont (Brussels: De Boeck, 2000), 25–35. One also thinks of the Élie Faure recitation at the start of *Pierrot le fou* (1965) concerning Velázquez's interest in painting interspaces.

80. Although Godard stopped writing about Hitchcock in *Cahiers* as he drew closer to directing his own features, his top-ten lists and comments in interviews attest that Hitchcock's work remained a reference point for his own developing conception of modern cinema. In 1963 he ranked *Vertigo* as the third greatest American sound film (*GG*, 204), and in the 1965 interview "Let's Talk about *Pierrot*," he says, "Any great modern film which is successful is so because of a misunderstanding. Audiences like *Psycho* because they think Hitchcock is telling them a story. *Vertigo* baffles them for the same reason" (*GG*, 223).

81. P. Adams Sitney, *Modernist Montage: The Obscurity of Vision in Cinema and Literature* (New York: Columbia University Press, 1990), 19.

82. Aumont, "The Fall of the Gods," 177.

83. Alain Bergala, *Nul mieux que Godard* (Paris: Cahiers du Cinéma, 1999), 18–19, my translation.

84. Robert Musil, *The Man without Qualities*, vol. 1, trans. Sophie Wilkins (New York: Knopf, 1995), 10–13.

85. Godard, "Mots qui se croisent + rébus = cinéma donc:" [1967], in *Jean-Luc Godard par Jean-Luc Godard*, vol. 1: *1950–1984*, ed. Alain Bergala (Paris: Cahiers du Cinéma, 1998), 284, my translation.

86. Corrigan, *The Essay Film*, 51–55.

87. My argument is informed by Roland-François Lack's discussion of Godard's evolving forms of vocal self-inscription. Lack, "Sa Voix," in *For Ever Godard*, ed. Michael Temple, James S. Williams, and Michael Witt (London: Black Dog, 2005), 319.

88. See Thomas Y. Levin, "Dismantling the Spectacle: The Cinema of Guy Debord," in *Guy Debord and the Situationist International: Texts and Documents,* ed. Tom McDonough (Cambridge, Mass.: MIT Press, 2002), 425–28.

89. Douglas Morrey, *Jean-Luc Godard* (Manchester: Manchester University Press, 2005), 61–71.

90. See Georges Perec, *L'Infra-ordinaire* (Paris: Seuil, 1989), 11. In *Masculine Feminine,* when the characters visit a theater and watch a tedious Swedish art film, the voice of Jean-Pierre Léaud communicates his character's dissatisfaction by quoting from Perec's *Les Choses: Une histoire des années soixante* (1965).

91. Morrey, *Jean-Luc Godard,* 64.

92. In his audio commentary for The Criterion Collection DVD edition of the film, Adrian Martin observes that Godard's interest in finding poetry in a "broken," modern world carries over from his earlier work and reemerges in his later films starting in the 1980s.

93. The actress playing Juliette, Marina Vlady, contributes much of her performance while responding extemporaneously to remarks from Godard conveyed to her through a small earpiece. See Alain Bergala, *Godard au travail: Les années 60* (Paris: Cahiers du Cinéma, 2006), 323–42; and John Hulsey, "Godard's Remote Control," in *A Companion to Jean-Luc Godard,* ed. Tom Conley and T. Jefferson Kline (Malden, Mass.: Wiley-Blackwell, 2014), 263–81.

94. The constructive uncertainty of *2 or 3 Things* arguably has a precedent in a legendary work that is sometimes referenced as heralding the essay film: Jean Renoir's *The Rules of the Game* (*La Règle du jeu,* 1939). Such a perspective would find support in V. F. Perkins's account of Renoir's struggle to negotiate "the agonies of choice." As Perkins words it, "In a medium that insists on choice frame by frame, the style of *La Règle du jeu* collides the attempt to keep everything in view against the impossibility of doing so." Perkins, *La Règle du jeu* (London: British Film Institute, 2012), 94. Thomas Tode lists *The Rules of the Game* in his essay film catalog included in *Der Essayfilm,* ed. Kramer and Tode, 325.

Chapter 2

1. Of his closing voiceover remarks in *JLG/JLG: Self-Portrait in December* (1995), Godard claims: "I think it's a quote, but now to me quotes and myself are almost the same. I don't know who they are from; sometimes I'm using it without knowing." Godard, interview with Gavin Smith, "Jean-Luc Godard," in *Jean-Luc Godard: Interviews,* ed. David Sterritt (Jackson: University Press of Mississippi, 1998), 184. He has similarly described *Nouvelle vague* (1990), taking pride in the fact that almost all of its spoken dialogue is appropriated.

2. Godard's presentation of production credits deserves closer attention than I can give it here. This is part of his essayism in that the credits tend to disrupt the pretense of the work being "finished," and at times they graphically suggest conceptual relationships. For instance, at the end of *The Origins of the 21st Century* (2000), credits appear in all-caps without spacing between words. We barely discern the surnames "VANVOGT," "VACQUIN," "BERGSON," and "BATAILLE." Superimposed onto this text is "JLG" in red, as if to define Godard as a figure constituted by the other voices.

Notes to Pages 66–72 233

3. Jacques Rivette, spoken in Jean Narboni, Sylvie Pierre, and Rivette, "Montage," in Rivette: Texts and Interviews, ed. Jonathan Rosenbaum (London: British Film Institute, 1977), 74–75.

4. Jean-Pierre Gorin, quoted in Colin MacCabe, Godard: A Portrait of the Artist at Seventy (New York: Farrar, Straus and Giroux, 2003), 123.

5. By adding a TV monitor to the mix in his reenactment, Marker hints that in the age of newer media, the "Gorgon" has extended its domain through an endless flow of entertainment and information that invades the domestic sphere, inducing mindless acquiescence.

6. Consider the imbricated male-female pairings in the sequence: the male and female narrators, Vernant and Weil, Perseus and Medusa, and, of course, the man and woman in Hiroshima mon amour, Resnais's collaboration with Marguerite Duras.

7. Nicole Brenez, "For It Is the Critical Faculty That Invents Fresh Forms," trans. Michael Temple, in The French Cinema Book, ed. Michael Temple and Michael Witt (British Film Institute, 2004), 235.

8. Alessia Ricciardi, "Godard's Histoire(s)," in The Ends of Mourning: Psychoanalysis, Literature, Film (Stanford, Calif.: Stanford University Press, 2003), 167–205. Though Ricciardi's chapter overlooks certain critical aspects of Godard's early work, she provides a brilliant analysis of the citational poetics of shock in Godard's Histoire(s) du cinéma.

9. Godard's provocations in the mid-1960s bespeak a desire for what Raymond Bellour, writing a decade later, calls "material intimacy" with cinema: a circumstance allowing the film critic access to the same "matters of expression" as the film itself. Raymond Bellour, "The Unattainable Text," in The Analysis of Film, ed. Constance Penley (Bloomington: Indiana University Press, 2000), 21–27, 22. In a later piece, Bellour refers to Godard's provocations as a signal moment in the quest for a "between-the-two" of film criticism and filmmaking. Bellour, "A Bit of History," in The Analysis of Film, 5, 19.

10. Godard, GG, 213–15. Godard obliquely borrows here from Jean Epstein: "There are no stories. There have never been stories. There are only situations without order, without beginning, middle or end; with no right and no wrong side." Epstein, Bonjour cinéma (Paris: Éditions de la Sirène, 1921), 31–32, my translation. In episode 4B of Histoire(s) du cinéma, Godard revisits his own piece "Pierrot my friend" and has Sabine Azéma recite an altered version it, still riffing on this Epstein passage.

11. Linked with the French nouveau roman, Michel Butor had been trying since the mid-1950s to reshape the novel into a "stereophonic" form, drawing on nonliterary idioms and working to fashion a "volume" wherein all elements are simultaneous to each other at any given structural point. Michel Butor, "The Shape of the Novel," in Inventory, ed. Richard Howard, trans. Gerald Fabian (New York: Simon and Schuster, 1968), 37. See also David Bordwell, Narration in the Fiction Film (Madison: University of Wisconsin Press, 1985), 276–77, 317–18.

12. Jean-Luc Godard and Pauline Kael, "The Economics of Film Criticism: A Debate," in Jean-Luc Godard: Interviews, ed. David Sterritt (Jackson: University Press of Mississippi, 1998), 119–21.

234 Notes to Pages 72–81

13. Ibid.

14. *Histoire(s)* has been a constant reference point in discussions about the scholarly video essay and its presentational strategies. See Christian Keathley, "*La caméra-stylo*: Notes on Video Criticism and Cinephilia," in *The Language and Style of Film Criticism*, ed. Alex Clayton and Andrew Klevan (New York: Routledge, 2011), 179–81.

15. Adrian Martin points out that the pitch of the "cowboy film" soundtrack indicates that Godard has made a bootleg recording of Boetticher's film playing in a theater. Martin, "Recital: Three Lyrical Interludes in Godard," in *For Ever Godard*, ed. Michael Temple, James S. Williams, and Michael Witt (London: Black Dog, 2004), 255–62, 258.

16. Tom Conley, "Louis Aragon, 'Elsa je t'aime,' " in *Twentieth-Century French Poetry: A Critical Anthology*, ed. Hugues Azérad and Peter Collier (Cambridge: Cambridge University Press, 2010), 111–14.

17. Marie-Claire Ropars, "The Graphic in Filmic Writing: *À bout de souffle* or The Erratic Alphabet," *Enclitic* 5–6 (1982): 149.

18. Jorge Luis Borges, "Partial Magic in the *Quixote*," trans. James E. Irby, in *Labyrinths: Selected Stories & Other Writings* (New York: New Directions, 1964), 196.

19. Seeing that the intertitles begin to appear onscreen as subtitles, it is likely that Godard uses the notorious cut of Dreyer's film released by Joseph-Marie Lo Duca in France in the 1950s.

20. Maureen Turim makes the case that *My Life to Live* is not as thoroughly Brechtian as readings have tended to argue. "Without a doubt, Godard's distanciation effects were stronger for the original audience than those which remain today, but I would suggest that the instances usually put forward as the most Brechtian may also function as invitation to empathy." Turim, "Three-Way Mirroring in *Vivre sa vie*," in *A Companion to Jean-Luc Godard*, ed. Tom Conley and T. Jefferson Kline (Malden, Mass.: Wiley-Blackwell, 2014), 94–96.

21. Antoine de Baecque, "The Theory of Sparks: A History in Images, According to Jean-Luc Godard," in *Camera Historica: The Century in Cinema*, trans. Ninon Vinsonneau and Jonathan Magidoff (New York: Columbia University Press, 2012), 207–34; Antonie de Baecque, "Godard in the Museum," in *For Ever Godard*, ed. Temple, Williams, and Witt, 118–25; and Peter Wollen, "JLG," in *Paris Hollywood: Writings on Film* (London: Verso, 2002), 74–92.

22. Guy Debord and Gil J. Wolman, "A User's Guide to Détournement" (1956), in *Situationist International: Anthology*, revised and expanded, ed. and trans. Ken Knabb (Berkeley, Calif.: Bureau of Public Secrets, 1995), 14–21.

23. "The Role of Godard," in *Situationist International: Anthology*, ed. Knabb, 228–30; "Cinema and Revolution," in *Situationist International: Anthology*, ed. Knabb, 378–79.

24. Brian Price examines how Debord and the Situationists paradoxically advocate plagiarism *and* disparage Godard for just that. Price, "Plagiarizing the Plagiarist: Godard Meets the Situationists," *Film Comment* 33, no. 6 (1997): 66–69. For a comparison between Debord's cinema and Godard's that strongly prefers the former, see Thomas Y. Levin, "Dismantling the Spectacle: The Cinema of Guy Debord," in *Guy Debord and the Situationist International: Texts and Documents*, ed. Tom McDonough (Cambridge, Mass.: MIT Press, 2004),

Notes to Pages 82–88

425–28. For a more balanced account of both directors' contributions, see Nicole Brenez, "For It Is the Critical Faculty That Invents Fresh Forms," 230–46.

25. Serge Daney, "The T(h)errorized (Godardian Pedagogy)," trans. Bill Krohn and Charles Cameron Ball, available at http://home.earthlink.net/~steevee/Daney _Godard.html. For an alternate translation that is less faithful to Daney's writing style, but that includes important endnotes by Daney, see "Theorize/Terrorize (Godardian Pedagogy)," trans. Annwyl Williams, in *Cahiers du Cinéma, 1973–1978: History, Ideology, Cultural Struggle*, ed. David Wilson (London: Routledge, 2000), 116–23.

26. Wollen, "JLG," 78.

27. Daney, "The T(h)errorized," trans. Krohn and Ball.

28. In making this distinction between Debord and Godard, I don't mean to discount or make light of the fact that Debord's work responded to a need for precise activist direction in French leftist counterculture at the time, his essay films demonstrating what Olivier Assayas has called "strategic intelligence." Assayas, *A Post-May Adolescence: Letter to Alice Debord and Two Essays on Guy Debord*, trans. Adrian Martin and Rachel Zerner (Wien: Austrian Film Museum and SYNEMA, 2012), 49.

29. Martin Jay, "From the Empire of the Gaze to the Society of the Spectacle: Foucault and Debord," in *Downcast Eyes: The Denigration of Vision in Twentieth-Century Thought* (Berkeley: University of California Press, 1994), 416–34.

30. Guy Debord, *The Society of the Spectacle* (1967), trans. Donald Nicholson-Smith (New York: Zone Books, 1994), paragraph 35.

31. Morgan, *Late Godard and the Possibilities of Cinema*, 120–54.

32. According to Colin MacCabe, Godard said of his Dziga Vertov Group projects that they were "not movies" but had "some interesting moves in them." MacCabe, *Godard: A Portrait of the Artist at Seventy*, 216. In Godard's later work with Miéville, they use some of the same stylistic "moves" while modifying their general political approach and purpose. See McCabe's video essay, included on The Criterion Collection's Blu-ray edition of Godard's Every Man for Himself (1980).

33. James Roy MacBean, *Film and Revolution* (Bloomington: Indiana University Press, 1975), 67. What MacBean calls the "inky darkness" of the soundstage in the film can be seen as prototypical of *Histoire(s) du cinéma*; it prefigures the black screens against which fragmentary images form and fade, like fireworks in the night sky.

34. Kaja Silverman and Harun Farocki, *Speaking about Godard* (New York: New York University Press, 1998), 116.

35. Vincenz Hediger, "A Cinema of Memory in the Future Tense: Godard, Trailers, and Godard Trailers," in *For Ever Godard*, ed. Temple, Williams, and Witt, 153; Lack, "Sa Voix," in *For Ever Godard*, 14; Witt, *Jean-Luc Godard, Cinema Historian*, 55, 173.

36. MacBean, *Film and Revolution*, 142

37. We can view Godard's increased visibility and self-portraiture in his later work as a rectification of his insufficient bodily presence in his militant films, which had regressed from Godard's open interrogation of himself in the omnibus film *Far from Vietnam* (1967). The return of his onscreen figure has its most

extreme, self-castigating example in *To Alter the Image* (1982), where a shirtless Godard is bound to a chair and made to undergo violent physical abuse as he is asked to account for his failure, in the early 1970s, to help the newly formed Marxist government of Mozambique launch a radical type of television.

38. Video first appears in a crude form in the Dziga Vertov Group film *Vladimir and Rosa* (1971), but what Godard-Miéville achieve in *Ici et ailleurs* is vastly more sophisticated. On the place of video in Godard's work, see Philippe Dubois, "Video Thinks What Cinema Creates," trans. Lynn Kirby, in *Jean-Luc Godard: Son + Image, 1974–1991*, ed. Raymond Bellour with Mary Lea Bandy (New York: Museum of Modern Art, 1992), 169–85; and Michael Witt, "Shapeshifter: Godard as Multimedia Installation Artist," *New Left Review* 29 (2004): 73–89.

39. Witt, *Jean-Luc Godard, Cinema Historian*, 52–53.

40. Deleuze, *Cinema 2: The Time-Image*, 179–81.

41. Richard Brody, *Everything Is Cinema: The Working Life of Jean-Luc Godard* (New York: Metropolitan, 2008), 376–77.

42. Yosefa Loshitzky, *The Radical Faces of Godard and Bertolucci* (Detroit, Mich.: Wayne State University Press, 1995), 50.

43. For a reading that does justice to the segment's complexity of thought, see Morrey, *Jean-Luc Godard*, 107–14.

44. Godard-Miéville do not minimize or omit the Holocaust. Later in the film, the viewer is shown footage of the death camps and Miéville offers a brief meditation, following Primo Levi, on the use of the term *Muselmann* (Muslim) to describe any camp prisoners who had deteriorated to such a degree that purportedly other prisoners ignored them. This anticipates Godard's lecture in *Notre musique* (2004). See chapter 4.

45. Thomas Elsaesser, "The Future of 'Art' and 'Work' in the Age of Vision Machines," in *After the Avant-Garde: Contemporary German and Austrian Experimental Film*, ed. Randall Halle and Reinhild Steingröver (Rochester, N.Y.: Camden House, 2008), 31–49.

46. As his wordplay throughout the series demonstrates, Godard's title exploits the double sense of *histoire* in French, which translates either as "story" or "history."

47. Witt provides an indispensable evolutionary account of Godard's "comparative visual criticism," which culminates with *Histoire(s) du cinéma*. Witt, *Jean-Luc Godard, Cinema Historian*, 21–44.

48. Sam Rohdie, *Film Modernism* (Manchester: Manchester University Press, 2015), 171–72.

49. Jean Starobinski ascribes a comparable dynamic to Montaigne's use of citations. Starobinski, *Montaigne in Motion*, trans. Arthur Goldhammer (Chicago: University of Chicago Press, 1985), 106–20.

50. Even Godard's selection of cited films beyond his own oeuvre is an element of self-portraiture insofar as it attests to his personal history as a critic and viewer. The European and American concentration of the citations reflects Godard's formative cinephilia as a critic. Most of the films cited in the series antedate Godard's debut with *Breathless* (1960), thus privileging the history of cinema that made him want to make films. My thanks to Dan Morgan for assisting with this point.

Notes to Pages 95–105

51. It is likely that Godard misattributes this quotation to Bazin and that the passage comes from a 1959 Michel Mourlet article in *Cahiers du cinéma*. Jonathan Rosenbaum, "Trailer for Godard's *Histoire(s) du Cinéma* (1997), https://www.jonathanrosenbaum.net/1997/04/trailer-for-godard's-histoires-du-cinema/.

52. Morgan, *Late Godard and the Possibilities of Cinema*, 215–18.

53. Godard's series offers "the memory of a future, in which the heretofore unactualized powers of cinema return in another form." Scott Durham, "'An Accurate Description of What Has Never Occurred': History, Virtuality, and Fiction in Godard," in *A Companion to Jean-Luc Godard*, ed. Conley and Kline, 441–443.

54. Pierre Reverdy, "L'Image," in *Oeuvres complètes* (Paris: Flammarion, 1975), 73–75, my translation.

55. Michael Witt, "Montage, My Beautiful Care, or Histories of the Cinematograph," in *The Cinema Alone: Essays on the Work of Jean-Luc Godard, 1985–2000*, ed. Michael Temple and James S. Williams (Amsterdam: Amsterdam University Press, 2000), 33–50.

56. Nicole Brenez, "The Ultimate Journey: Remarks on Contemporary Theory," trans. William D. Routt, in *Screening the Past* 2 (1997), http://www.latrobe.edu.au/screeningthepast/reruns/brenez.html.

57. Godard's exclamation is a reworked passage from George Bernanos's novel *Diary of a Country Priest*: "What a marvel to be able to give what we don't possess! Miracle of our empty hands." See Morrey, *Jean-Luc Godard*, 225. The interrelation of sight and touch is already part of the sequence in *Histoire(s)*, in that Giotto's fresco portrays a biblical scene of the resurrected Christ instructing Mary Magdalene not to touch him.

58. Witt, *Jean-Luc Godard, Cinema Historian*, 132–33.

59. Samuel Beckett, "The Image," trans. Edith Fournier, in *Samuel Beckett: The Complete Short Prose, 1929–1989*, ed. S. E. Gontarski (New York: Grove, 1995), 165–68. In the Beckett sentence-story, which is a Proustian parody, this struggle is that of an aging man trying to recapture a memory of adolescent love.

60. Godard's use of superimpositions enacts a way of seeing and associating that he wishes to remain operative, *in our engagement with the work*, even where superimpositions are not literalized onscreen. As he says in a late interview, an "image" isn't an already-made picture but a relationship arising through the viewer's mentally combinatory contribution. "The image is the relation with me looking at it dreaming up a relation [to] someone else. An image is an association." Godard, interview with Gavin Smith, "Jean-Luc Godard," in *Jean-Luc Godard: Interviews*, ed. David Sterritt (Jackson: University Press of Mississippi, 1998), 190. The ending of Godard's *In Praise of Love* (2001) riffs on this sense of an image: over a contemplative video superimposition of a twilight seascape and the back of a character's head, the character comments that he can only think about something if he mentally compares it to something else.

61. Witt, *Jean-Luc Godard, Cinema Historian*, 18. See also James S. Williams, "*Histoire(s) du cinéma*," *Film Quarterly* 61, no. 3 (2008): 10–16, 12.

62. Morgan, *Late Godard and the Possibilities of Cinema*, 43–44.

63. Godard recognizes his incapacity to affirm the legitimacy of his montage in his earlier video essay *Scénario de "Sauve qui peut (la vie)"* (Scenario of "Every Man for Himself," 1979). As he tests out some of the same editing procedures

238 Notes to Pages 105–108

that shape *Histoire(s)*, he states: "What I'm trying to show you is how I see things, so that you can judge whether I am able to see, and what I have seen. I want to show you the relationships between images and then you would be as in a court of law where you are both the defendant and the prosecutor . . . and you can see if I see something. I show if there is something to see and how I see it. And you can say, 'No, he's wrong, there's nothing to see.' "

64. In French, *rapprochement* can refer to a reconciliation between enemies (at the level of nations) or between quarreling lovers. Elsewhere, Godard uses the term to evoke a juridical weighing: "There is a shot before and afterwards, and between the two, there is a support, which is the cinema. One sees a rich person, one sees a poor person, and there is *rapprochement*, and one says: it is not justice. Justice comes from *rapprochement*. The same idea [is at work] in montage. It is the scales of justice." Godard, "ABCD . . . JLG," in *Documents*, ed. Nicole Brenez et al. (Paris: Centre Pompidou, 2006), 330, my translation.

65. Lack, "Sa Voix," 326–27.

66. Sam Rohdie, "Deux ou trois choses . . . ," *Critical Quarterly* 51, no. 3 (2009): 85–99.

67. Jacques Rancière, "Godard, Cinema, (Hi)Stories," in *Film Fables*, trans. Emiliano Battista (London: Berg, 2006), 171–87; Rancière, "Godard, Hitchcock, and the Cinematographic Image," in *For Ever Godard*, ed. Michael Temple, James S. Williams, and Michael Witt (London: Black Dog, 2004), 214–31; Rancière, "Sentence, Image, History," in *The Future of the Image*, trans. Gregory Elliott (New York: Verso, 2007), 56–67.

68. Rancière, "Godard, Cinema, (Hi)Stories," 177, 184.

69. Rancière, "Godard, Hitchcock, and the Cinematographic Image," 230.

70. Rancière, "Sentence, Image, History," 62–63.

71. Jacques Aumont, *Amnésies: Fictions du cinéma d'après Jean-Luc Godard* (Lonrai: P.O.L., 1999), 120–21.

72. Hediger, "A Cinema of Memory," 157.

73. Rancière, "Godard, Cinema, (Hi)Stories," 179.

74. Friedrich Schlegel, "Dialogue on Poesy," in *Theory as Practice: A Critical Anthology of Early German Romantic Writings*, ed. and trans. Jochen Schulte-Sasse et al. (Minneapolis: University of Minnesota Press, 1997), 186.

75. Rancière illuminates several sequences in *Histoire(s)*, identifying links at once formal, political, and historical, only to then argue self-contradictorily that Godard's montage is spurious in the relations it weaves. He seems to base his critique on the supposition that an *average* viewer could not possibly make, or follow, these connections.

76. Morgan cogently argues that Godard's videographic montage follows the logic of Kant's notion of "subjective universality." That is, the combinations make a claim, as if in a universal key, while acknowledging that this claim may not work for some. Morgan, *Late Godard and the Possibilities of Cinema*, 228–29. For a similar interpretation of Godard's adherence to a "public aesthetics" in his late stage, see Richard Neer, "Godard Counts," *Critical Inquiry* 34, no. 1 (2007): 135–68.

77. No. 37 of the Athenaeum Fragments reads: "Many witty ideas are like the sudden meeting of two friendly thoughts after a long separation." Friedrich Schlegel, *Friedrich Schlegel's "Lucinde" and the Fragments*, trans. Peter Firchow

Notes to Pages 109–114

(Minneapolis: University of Minnesota Press, 1971), 166. Schlegel claims that *Witz* is most effective when "meant for a small audience" that "has the right" to exercise "freedom." Quoted in Michel Chaouli, *The Laboratory of Poetry: Chemistry and Poetics in the Work of Friedrich Schlegel* (Baltimore, Md.: Johns Hopkins University Press, 2002), 200–202.

78. An equally prolific cultivator of essayistic forms of twoness is Alexander Kluge, whether in the guise of his interviews or staged recitations where two people (sometimes Kluge himself, although usually from offscreen) read aloud a text.

79. Colin MacCabe, "Editorial," *Critical Quarterly* 51, no. 3 (2009): iii.

80. Godard, interview with Serge Daney, "Godard Makes (Hi)stories," trans. Georgia Gurrieri, in *Jean-Luc Godard: Son + Image, 1974–1991*, ed. Bellour with Bandy, 159.

81. In the stages of conceiving *Histoire(s)*, Godard spoke of citation as a gesture that simultaneously communicates "the impression of an expression" onto a human subject *and* "the expression of an impression" that reemerges from this subject. Jean-Luc Godard, *Introduction to a True History of Cinema and Television*, trans. Timothy Barnard (Montreal: Caboose, 2014), 42–44.

82. T. W. Adorno, "The Essay as Form," trans. Bob Hullot-Kentor and Frederic Will, *New German Critique* 32 (1984): 160–61.

83. Adorno recognizes that the essay dispenses with "creatio ex nihilo" and "catches fire . . . on what others have already done." Ibid., 152. Still, Godard's essayism displays a more deeply polyphonic style of thought and a more dispersive expression of the essayist's consciousness than Adorno entertains.

Chapter 3

1. Alter, *Chris Marker*, 96.

2. The couple is also a central theme in the essayistic corpus of Agnès Varda. In both *Jacquot de Nantes* (1991) and *The Beaches of Agnès* (2008), she pays loving tribute to her husband and fellow director Jacques Demy by spinning reflections around his life, films, declining health, and death.

3. Alain Bergala with Godard, "La vie vécue avant . . . ," in *Jean-Luc Godard par Jean-Luc Godard*, vol. 1: *1950–1984*, ed. Alain Bergala (Paris: Cahiers du Cinéma, 1998), 66–67, my translation. In certain ways, the Miéville years of Godard's career mount critiques of, and progress beyond, the chauvinistic attitudes and portrayals of women in some of Godard's early films, in particular those he made with Karina. For a reading of his "demiurgic" use of Karina as a "woman-child" figure, see Geneviève Sellier, *Masculine Singular: French New Wave Cinema*, trans. Kristin Ross (Durham: Duke University Press, 2008), 153ff.

4. Godard, quoted in Catherine Grant, "Home-Movies: The Curious Cinematic Collaboration of Anne-Marie Miéville and Jean-Luc Godard," in *For Ever Godard*, ed. Michael Temple, James S. Williams, and Michael Witt (London: Black Dog, 2004), 100.

5. MacCabe, *Godard: A Portrait of the Artist at Seventy*; Colin MacCabe, "The Commerce of Cinema," in *For Ever Godard*, ed. Michael Temple, James S. Williams, and Michael Witt (London: Black Dog, 2004), 94–99; Grant, "Home-Movies," 100–117; Jerry White, *Two Bicycles: The Work of Jean-Luc Godard* (Waterloo, Ont.: Wilfrid Laurier, 2013).

6. Chris Darke, *Alphaville* (Champaign: University of Illinois Press, 2005), 51.

7. The ending of *Alphaville* is decidedly chaste. Natacha is at last able to say and mean "I love you" to Caution as they drive out of the city, but there is no triumphant kiss, and no hint of libidinal energy between them.

8. Michael Witt, "Going Through the Motions: Unconscious Optics and Corporal Resistance in Miéville and Godard's *France/tour/détour/deux/enfants*," in *For Ever Godard*, ed. Michael Temple, James S. Williams, and Michael Witt (London: Black Dog, 2004), 200–213.

9. Michael Witt, "Going Through the Motions," 209.

10. Ibid., 207; Constance Penley, "Pornography, Eroticism (On *Every Man for Himself*)," in *The Future of an Allusion: Film, Feminism, and Psychoanalysis* (Minneapolis: University of Minnesota Press, 1989), 83.

11. Brody, *Everything Is Cinema*, 397–415.

12. White, *Two Bicycles*, 89, 107.

13. Godard, quoted in *Jean-Luc Godard par Jean-Luc Godard*, vol. 1, 461–62. I first encountered this quotation in Witt's "Going Through the Motions" (201) and have drawn on his translation, with slight changes.

14. Vilém Flusser, "The Gesture of Searching," in *Gestures*, trans. Nancy Ann Roth (Minneapolis: Minnesota University Press, 2014), 147–59.

15. Several scholars have turned to Giorgio Agamben's theorization of gesture as a way to examine Godard's late films. See Libby Saxton, "*Passion*, Agamben and the Gestures of Work," in *Cinema and Agamben: Ethics, Biopolitics and the Moving Image*, ed. Henrik Gustafsson and Asbjorn Gronstad (New York: Bloomsbury, 2015), 55–70; and James S. Williams, "Silence, Gesture, Revelation: The Ethics and Aesthetics of Montage in Godard and Agamben," in *Encounters with Godard: Ethics, Aesthetics, Politics* (New York: SUNY Press, 2016), 105–25.

16. Flusser, "The Gesture of Searching," 157.

17. Godard quotes this Rimbaud line in a handwritten notebook fragment in *Pierrot le fou* (1965).

18. Robert Stam, "Jean-Luc Godard's *Sauve qui peut (la vie)*," *Millennium Film Journal* 10/11 (1981): 197.

19. One of Godard-Miéville's discoveries is that the gesturing female body appears, on average, more resistant to forces of control than that of the opposite sex. In *France/tour/détour*, they observe that Camille's motions appear freer and less predictably uniform than those of her male counterpart. In *Every Man for Himself*, Denise's step-printed movements have a lyrical quality that Paul's, in their burlesque clumsiness, lack. The shots of her riding her bicycle in syncopated pauses and restarts resonate with a line she elsewhere writes in a reverie: "Something in the mind and body arches its back against routine and the void."

20. Flusser, "The Gesture of Loving," in *Gestures*, trans. Roth, 50–51.

21. White, *Two Bicycles*, 117–21.

22. Ellen Draper, "An Alternative to Godard's Metaphysics: Cinematic Presence in Miéville's *Le livre de Marie*," in *Jean-Luc Godard's* Hail Mary: *Women and the Sacred in Film*, ed. Maryel Locke and Charles Warren (Carbondale: Southern Illinois University Press, 1993), 73–74.

23. White, *Two Bicycles*, 124–25.

24. My reading is informed by Daniel Morgan, *Late Godard and the Possibilities of Cinema*, 114–15.

Notes to Pages 125–136

25. For a scrupulous study of *Hail Mary* and Godard's musical samplings throughout his late work, see James S. Williams, "Music, Love, and the Cinematic Event," in *Encounters with Godard*, 127–50.

26. The collaborative male-female situation echoes an earlier scene in *Hail Mary* that takes place in a classroom, where Eve covers the eyes of a spiky-haired male classmate named Pascal and provides vocal directions as he twists a Rubik's Cube. Prefiguring how Marie later guides Joseph, she says, "No . . . no . . . no . . . *Oui!*" Godard reuses this interpersonal setup in his 1987 television commercials for Marithé + François Girbaud jeans.

27. Morgan, *Late Godard*, 22–23, 43–44, 95–96, 109–10.

28. Susan Sontag, "Spiritual Style in the Films of Robert Bresson," in *Robert Bresson*, ed. James Quandt (Toronto: Toronto International Film Festival Group, 1998), 66.

29. Tennis references inflect Godard's treatment of interpersonal dialogue, coupling, and/or self-other interaction more generally in *Pierrot le fou* (1965), *Vladimir and Rosa* (1971), *Keep Your Right Up* (1987), *Nouvelle vague* (1990), *JLG/JLG: Self-Portrait in December, Histoire(s) du cinéma, The Old Place, Vrai faux passeport* (2006), and *Une catastrophe* (2008). See Rick Warner, "Tennis with Godard, or, Configuring the Elemental Between." *La Furia Umana* 33 (2018), http://www.lafuriaumana.it/index.php/66-lfu-33/742-rick-warner-tennis -with-godard-or-configuring-the-elemental-between.

30. Many of Godard's video dialogues resemble in their staging *one side of* a shot/countershot setup. In *Soft and Hard*, he self-consciously offers a variation on what Michel Chion calls the idiom of the suspended countershot. Chion, *Film, a Sound Art*, trans. Claudia Gorbman (New York: Columbia University Press, 2009), 471.

31. I am thinking of Godard's self-positioning in episode 2B, entitled "Jean-Luc." In 3B, Godard and Miéville use a different interview format as they question Marcel Raymond, a factory worker who also makes 8-mm nature films. As if a stand-in for Godard (or inspiration for Godard's later work), Raymond appears with his back to the camera, editing film strips while his nature scenes project onto the wall and his shadow superimposes with them. Miéville and Godard stay hidden and speak from offscreen, though Godard's gesturing hand occasionally enters the frame.

32. The tone of interaction varies across these videos. Godard is respectful of Serge Daney, whereas he belittles Woody Allen's filmmaking somewhat even as he praises *Hannah and Her Sisters* (1986). He all but ambushes Michel Piccoli with a pungent critique of the French celebration of cinema's centenary over which Piccoli was presiding.

33. At another point in their dialogue, Godard gesturally recalls the "V" and "Λ" hand signs from *The Book of Mary*, but puts an alternative spin on them by discussing them as vectors of projection and introjection that emanate from and impress upon the individual subject.

34. Godard elsewhere emphasizes Miéville's expressive cogency in vocal terms. In his preparatory materials for *Six fois deux*, he includes a photo of Miéville with a caption declaring that she is able to express "things no man could dream up." Godard, *Jean-Luc Godard par Jean-Luc Godard*, vol. 1, 395, my translation. *Histoire(s) du cinéma*, chapter 4A, begins with photos of women authors,

Miéville among them, and a recitation, in a female voice, of Paul Valéry's poem "Psalm on a Voice" ("In a soft and faint voice saying great things").

35. MacCabe, *Godard: A Portrait of the Artist at Seventy*, 241.

36. Montaigne's views on gender dramatically change over time. All four personal dedications in the *Essais* are to female readers, and his "Apology for Raymond Sebond" addresses itself to a female reader. Cathleen M. Bauschatz, "Leur plus universelle qualité, c'est la diversité: Women as Ideal Readers in Montaigne's *Essais*," *Journal of Medieval and Renaissance Studies* 19 (1989): 83–101.

37. In this sense, Godard's thematics of coupling compares to Alain Badiou's philosophical notion of the "Two Scene," whereby two lovers daringly experience the world from the perspective of difference instead of individual identity. See Badiou with Nicolas Truong, *In Praise of Love*, trans. Peter Bush (New York: New Press, 2012), 28, 38, 49, 51.

38. The artist-muse relation receives Godard's self-critical attention in *My Life to Live* (1962), in the scene where his voice, grafted onto the body of a male character looking at Nana (Anna Karina), recites Poe's "The Oval Portrait" (1842). The suggestion is that Godard's depiction of his own wife is possibly exploitative and hazardous. His work with Miéville differs from his earlier relationships in that Miéville—unlike Karina (whom Godard had first seen as a model in an advertisement) and Wiazemsky (whom Godard had first seen as a "model" in Bresson's *Au hasard Balthazar* [1966])—was a woman he did not initially encounter as a *product of* image-making. MacCabe, *Godard: Portrait of the Artist at Seventy*, 185–86.

39. Godard no doubt had Miéville in mind when he appeared on *The Dick Cavett Show* in 1980 to promote *Every Man for Himself* and said that women "have better ideas" than men. This remark signals a corrective shift away from the misogyny that mars, for instance, Godard and Jean-Pierre Gorin's *Letter to Jane: Investigation about a Still* (1972).

40. Empedocles, *Physics*, in *Early Greek Philosophy*, trans. Jonathan Barnes (New York: Penguin, 2001), 121–22.

41. Gregory Flaxman, *Gilles Deleuze and the Fabulation of Philosophy: Powers of the False, Volume I* (Minneapolis: University of Minnesota Press, 2011), 26–42.

42. Paul Willemen, "Through a Glass Darkly: Cinephilia Reconsidered," in *Looks and Frictions: Essays in Cultural Studies and Film Theory* (Bloomington: Indiana University Press, 1994), 223–57; Antoine de Baecque, *La Cinéphile: Invention d'un regard, histoire d'une culture 1944–1968* (Paris: Fayard, 2003).

43. Godard, "The Carrots Are Cooked," interview by Gideon Bachman, in *Jean-Luc Godard: Interviews*, ed. David Sterritt (Jackson: University Press of Mississippi, 1998), 132.

44. Godard, quoted in Grant, "Home Movies," 102.

45. On the temporal demands of friendship, see Alexander Nehamas, *On Friendship* (New York: Basic Books, 2016), 81–83.

46. Friendship is a distinct theme in a number of Marker's works. Here I will merely name *The Last Bolshevik* (1992), his made-for-television portrait of his friend and mentor, Alexander Medvedkin. The show presents itself as a continuation of friendly dialogue with the Russian director despite his death. As for Varda, many of her late endeavors are odes to the friends she has collected through and around her creative work over the years, for example, *The Beaches of Agnès* (2009) and *Agnès from Here to There Varda* (television, 2011).

Notes to Pages 138–144

47. Harun Farocki, "Written Trailers," trans. Antje Ehmann and Michael Turnbull, in *Against What? Against Whom?* ed. Antje Ehmann and Kodwo Eshun (London: Koenig, 2009), 225.

48. Godard, quoted in MacCabe, *Godard: Portrait of the Artist at Seventy*, 333.

49. MacCabe, "The Commerce of Cinema," 97–99.

50. White, *Two Bicycles*, 152–54.

51. John A. McCarthy, *Crossing Boundaries: A Theory and History of Essay Writing in German, 1680–1815* (Philadelphia: University of Pennsylvania Press, 1989), 29–31.

52. White, *Two Bicycles*, 153.

53. "A Prisoner of Love" carries two references. It is the title of Jean Genet's final, essayistic book of meditations, which was published posthumously in France in 1986. The book chronicles Genet's interactions with Palestinian fighters in the early 1970s, his visit being roughly contemporaneous with Godard and Jean-Pierre Gorin's trip to Jordan to shoot *Until Victory* (the film that Godard-Miéville critically dismantle in *Ici et ailleurs*). A second reference is to Godard-Miéville's *Six fois deux/Sur et sous la communication* (1976), the episode where Godard, in the role of a prison inmate, writes a love letter to Miéville.

54. Since *For Ever Mozart* (1996), Godard has treated the siege of Sarajevo as a culminating disaster of the twentieth century. Given the evocation of the fist of leftist solidarity, one thinks also of the battlefield death at the close of *British Sounds* (1969), the shot of a bloody fist (Godard's) reaching for a red banner.

55. On Weil's importance for Godard's late work, see Morrey, *Jean-Luc Godard*, 142–44, 152; and Nicole Brenez, "Jean-Luc Godard, *Witz* et invention formelle (notes préparatoires sur les rapports entre critique et pouvoir symbolique)," CiNéMAS 15, no. 2–3 (2005): 39–40.

56. "Logic of Images" referentially juxtaposes Benjamin's constellation concept with Jean Epstein's film theory. The phrase is the title of the first chapter of Epstein's *Esprit de cinéma* (1955), where he argues that cinematic images defy the verbal-centered logics and grammars that popular narrative cinema imposes on them. Epstein, "The Logic of Images," trans. Thao Nguyen, in *Jean Epstein: Critical Essays and New Translations*, ed. Sarah Keller and Jason N. Paul (Amsterdam: Amsterdam University Press, 2012), 330–33.

57. Walter Benjamin, *The Arcades Project*, trans. Howard Eiland and Kevin McLaughlin (Cambridge, Mass.: Belknap Press of Harvard University Press, 1999), 462–463 (convolute N3, 1).

58. On Godard's engagement with Benjamin, see Kaja Silverman, "The Dream of the Nineteenth Century," *Camera Obscura* 17, no. 3 (2002): 1–29; Monica Dall'Asta, "The (Im)possible History," in *For Ever Godard*, ed. Temple, Williams, and Witt, 350–63.

59. Walter Benjamin, "On the Concept of History" (1940), in *Walter Benjamin: Selected Writings,* vol. 4, *1938–1940*, ed. Howard Eiland and Michael W. Jennings (Cambridge, Mass.: Belknap Press of Harvard University Press, 2003), 389–400.

60. Witt, *Jean-Luc Godard, Cinema Historian*, 183.

61. Of course, this big bang in Ray's Cold War-era film already evokes thermonuclear disaster.

62. Alexander Kluge, "On Film and the Public Sphere," in *Alexander Kluge: Raw Materials for the Imagination*, ed. Tara Forrest (Amsterdam: Amsterdam University Press, 2012), 47–48.

63. Godard's encomium to Hitchcock as the cinema's "greatest creator of forms" in episode 4A of *Histoire(s)* has received much attention. As I have argued elsewhere, Godard confronts the master's work in order to distinguish, *through critical contrasts*, his own videographic montage. See Warner, "Difficult Work in a Popular Medium: Godard on 'Hitchcock's Method,' " *Critical Quarterly* 51, no. 3 (2009): 63–84.

64. In Godard's vocabulary, "thinking with one's hands" connects ethically with the trope of "dirty hands," which Godard explores in episode 2B of *Histoire(s)*, in a scene where he studies his own hands while seated at a typewriter. "Dirty hands" refers to Sarte's controversial 1948 play of the same name, which concerns the quandary of politically engaged individuals when unjust actions seem unavoidable on the path to achieving the greater collective good. See Morgan, *Late Godard and the Possibilities of Cinema*, 86–95.

65. Harun Farocki's *The Expression of Hands* (1997) considers this same horror through sampling *The Beast with Five Fingers* (1946), a remake of *The Hands of Orlac*. Farocki's work rivals Godard's in its attention to the gesturing body, and not unlike Godard, Farocki critically weighs his own gestures of montage. Farocki in fact once defined montage as "gestic thinking." Farocki, "What an Editing Room Is" (1980), in *Imprint: Writings*, ed. Susanne Gaensheimer and Nicolaus Schafhausen, trans. Laurent Faasch-Ibrahim (New York: Lukas and Sternberg, 2001), 78–85.

66. Another self-inscription of Godard and Miéville in *The Old Place* occurs when they sample a shot from Miéville's *We're All Still Here* (1997)—the ending in which the main couple (the male played by Godard) takes an evening stroll after an argument. Godard restages a similar shot of two side-by-side shadowy figures in *Goodbye to Language* (2014).

67. Margaret C. Flinn, "*The Old Place*, Space of Legends," in *A Companion to Jean-Luc Godard* (Malden, Mass.: Wiley-Blackwell, 2014), 511–12.

68. We might view this ternary inclusion of the spectator as a response to a problem Godard once formulated in his 1978 Montreal lectures, a problem of needing to be more than oneself. "I've found a woman, a friend [Miéville], so we say, 'We are one and a half,' one and a half because we are only half of three. . . . I have never succeeded in being three." Godard, *Introduction to a True History of Cinema and Television*, 119.

Chapter 4

1. Jacques Aumont elucidates Godard's mediumistic use of his own body in his late work and his "sorcerer-scientist" persona who is intent on relating his experimental method. Aumont, "The Medium," trans. Rachel Bowlby, in *Jean-Luc Godard: Son + Image, 1974–1991*, ed. Raymond Bellour with Mary Lea Bandy (New York: MoMA, 1992), 206–8.

2. Granted, Welles is an essayistic filmmaker, too, whose *F for Fake* (1975) and other films Godard references throughout episode 1A of *Histoire(s) du cinéma*. On the citational significance of *F for Fake* within *Histoire(s)*, see Witt, *Jean-Luc Godard, Cinema Historian*, 107–8.

Notes to Pages 154–162

3. See Timothy Corrigan's analyses of McElwee's and Moore's respective approaches in *The Essay Film: From Montaigne, After Marker*, 23–30, 172–73.

4. Rascaroli, *The Personal Camera*, 34.

5. Alexander Kluge's essayism also makes "communication" exceptionally difficult for the sake of enlivening the viewer's associative faculties. Christopher Pavsek compares Kluge and Godard in *The Utopia of Film: Cinema and Its Futures in Godard, Kluge, and Tahimik* (New York: Columbia University Press, 2013), 16, 37–38, 194, 225, 241.

6. Godard, interview with Serge Daney, "Godard Makes [Hi]Stories," trans. Georgia Gurrieri, in *Jean-Luc Godard: Son + Image, 1974–1991*, ed. Bellour with Bandy, 160.

7. See Philippe Dubois, "Video Thinks What Cinema Creates: Notes on Jean-Luc Godard's Work in Video and Television," trans. Lynne Kirby, in *Jean-Luc Godard: Son + Image, 1974–1991*, ed. Bellour with Bandy, 169–85.

8. Nicole Brenez nicely characterizes Godard's scenario-sketches: "the film to be made is confused in turn with the film that has already been made, and with the film that is impossible to make. The image becomes simultaneously optative, conditional, imperative, indicative." Brenez, "The Forms of the Question," in *For Ever Godard*, ed. Michael Temple, James S. Williams, and Michael Witt (London: Black Dog, 2004), 174–75.

9. For a compelling discussion of Godard's Montaignean use of video technology in *Scénario du film "Passion,"* see Michael Renov, "The Electronic Essay," in *The Subject of Documentary* (Minneapolis: University of Minnesota Press, 2004), 182–90.

10. Michael Fried, *The Moment of Caravaggio* (Princeton, N.J.: Princeton University Press, 2010), 9–37, 48–50.

11. See Michael Fried, "Orientation in Painting: Caspar David Friedrich," in *Another Light: Jacques-Louis David to Thomas Demand* (New Haven, Conn.: Yale University Press, 2014), 111–49.

12. Fredric Jameson, "High-Tech Collectives in Late Godard," in *The Geopolitical Aesthetic: Cinema and Space in the World System* (Bloomington: Indiana University Press, 1995), 163.

13. Godard, interview with Gavin Smith, "Jean-Luc Godard," in *Jean-Luc Godard: Interviews*, ed. Sterritt, 183.

14. Godard, quoted in Kaja Silverman, "The Author as Receiver," *October* no. 96 (Spring 2001): 24–25.

15. Godard, quoted ibid. See also Godard, *Jean-Luc Godard par Jean-Luc Godard*, vol. 2: *1984–1988*, ed. Alain Bergala (Paris: Cahiers du Cinéma, 1998), 306.

16. This line reworks a passage from Joseph Conrad's *Heart of Darkness*, where Marlow sizes up the man with whom he is doubled thematically, the deranged Kurtz: "Everything belonged to him—but that was a trifle. The thing was to know what he belonged to, how many powers of darkness claimed him for their own." Conrad, *Heart of Darkness* (1899), Norton Critical Edition, ed. Paul B. Armstrong (New York: W.W. Norton, 2017), 48–49.

17. Loud offscreen noise, from crow squawks to a ringing telephone that JLG appears loath to answer, recurrently express the film's concern with an outside encroaching on the inside. On the film's aural tactics, see Nora M. Alter,

"Mourning, Sound, and Vision: Jean-Luc Godard's *JLG/JLG*," *Camera Obscura* 15, no. 2 (2000): 75–103.

18. Karla Oeler, "The Housemaids of JLG," *Critical Quarterly* 51, no. 3 (October 2009): 25–40.

19. One chiaroscuro shot in *JLG/JLG* craftily condenses Godard's approach to filming himself. As he lights his cigar with a match, his face appears as an image within the image (reported back in the viewfinder of a video camera he is holding, its monitor indicating "insufficient light"). Meanwhile, the film's extra-diegetic camera frames his upper body over the shoulder. The staging thus resembles a shot/countershot alternation, as if JLG and JLG are squaring off in a dialogue.

20. Silverman, "The Author as Receiver," 20, my italics.

21. Ibid., 24–30, 32.

22. Ibid., 34.

23. Kevin J. Hayes, "*JLG/JLG—Autoportrait de Décembre*: Reinscribing the Book," *Quarterly Review of Film and Television* 19, no. 2 (2002): 155–64.

24. As I noted in chapter 3, the tennis match is one of Godard's favorite conceptual figures for reflecting on interpersonal relations.

25. Even when alone in the film, JLG sometimes has others in mind. One of his citations works as a nod to Anne-Marie Miéville. Smoking at his desk, he recites a poem by Paul-Jean Toulet while the soundtrack includes a fragment from Robert Bresson's *Diary of a Country Priest* (1951), the priest declaring how wonderful it is to give what one does not possess, a line Godard incorporates in *Histoire(s)* and other late projects. Toulet's poem reads: "While the orchestra plays its outdated repertoire, amid the crowd, I see you from afar. And you, divine, in silence, your chin poised on one finger, your eyes half-shut, you *think*. I want you to be thinking of me." After Godard looks up from the book, another French-language sound clip from a film plays offscreen—a woman's voice saying, "I am Anne-Marie."

26. Technically this comes from Diderot's addition to the original text. Denis Diderot, "Addition to the Preceding Letter," in *Diderot's Early Philosophical Works*, trans. and ed. Margaret Jourdain (Chicago: Open Court, 1916), 150, 152.

27. Diderot, *Letter on the Blind for the Use of Those Who See* (1749), in *Diderot's Early Philosophical Works*, 72–74, 87–88.

28. Brody, *Everything Is Cinema*, 557–60.

29. Ibid., 5–6.

30. This intertitle, while it refers to the film industry as well as JLG's collaboration with the blind editor, evokes Balzac's novel of political mystery, *Une ténébreuse affaire* (*A Murky Business*, 1841).

31. Denis Diderot, "Addition to the Preceding Letter," in *Diderot's Early Philosophical Works*, 153. Given our focus on male-female dyads in chapter 3, we should not ignore how Godard's interaction in this scene complies with this trope. When the female editor enters his studio, a poster for Miéville's first feature film, *My Favorite Story* (1988), looms in the background.

32. See Pavsek, *The Utopia of Film*, 39–41.

33. Maurice Merleau-Ponty, *The Visible and the Invisible*, ed. Claude Lefort, trans. Alphonso Lingis (Evanston, Ill.: Northwestern University Press, 1968), 140–41, trans. modified. As Silverman notes, the full spoken passage in *JLG/JLG*

Notes to Pages 170–177

is an "edited amalgamation" of several passages from Merleau-Ponty's original text. Silverman, "The Author as Receiver," 28.

34. Another important reference that informs Godard's project of auteurial suicide is E. M. Cioran's essay "The Temptation to Exist" (1956). Particularly relevant is Cioran's desire to dissolve himself into a field of transversal forces. Cioran, *The Temptation to Exist*, trans. Richard Howard (Chicago: University of Chicago Press, 1968), 216.

35. Morrey, *Jean-Luc Godard*, 209.

36. Pavsek, *The Utopia of Film*, 28.

37. Jean-Paul Sartre, *The Words*, trans. Bernard Frechtman (New York: George Braziller, 1964), 255.

38. Jean-Jacques Rossueau, *The Confessions*, trans. J. M. Cohen (New York: Penguin, 1953), 17.

39. See Jacques Morice, "4 x Godard," *Cahiers du cinéma* 483 (September 1994): 17.

40. Sam Rohdie, *Film Modernism* (Manchester: Manchester University Press, 2015), 170–72.

41. The quotation in Latin is from Virgil's *Aeneid* (6.125–29), where the Sibyl explains to Aeneas the task of resurfacing from the underworld. Poets from Ovid to Dante have reappropriated this line, shifting its context to the poetical process itself, and the difficulty it involves.

42. In Godard-Miéville's *Soft and Hard* (1985), a still of Hitchcock's Jeffries spying through his lens is combined associatively with a shot of Miéville studying images at an editing station.

43. Robert Bresson, *Notes on the Cinematographer*, trans. Jonathan Griffin (London: Quartet, 1986), 94 (French original modified by Godard). "Let every eye negotiate for itself" is from Shakespeare's *Much Ado About Nothing* (II.i.178).

44. Such an impulse to stress the work conducted at the editing station, and to give the spectator, as much as possible, a cutting-room experience without quite catering to technical interactivity, is a feature of many bravura examples of the audiovisual essay. Other examples include Dziga Vertov's *Man with a Movie Camera* (1929), Godard's *Scénario du film "Passion,"* and Pedro Costa's *Where Does Your Hidden Smile Lie?* (2001).

45. Jean Starobinski, *Montaigne in Motion*, trans. Arthur Goldhammer (Chicago: University of Chicago Press, 1985), 27–33. See also Terrence Cave, "Problems of Reading in Montaigne's *Essais*," in *Retrospectives: Essays in Literature, Poetics, and Cultural History*, ed. Neil Kenny and Wes Williams (Oxford, UK: Legenda, 2009), 20–37.

46. Daniel Morgan formulates Godard's role in comparable terms. See Morgan, *Late Godard and the Possibilities of Cinema*, 227.

47. Rascaroli, *The Personal Camera*, 56–57.

48. Jean-Luc Godard with Youssef Ishaghpour, *Cinema: The Archaeology of Film and the Memory of a Century*, trans. John Howe (New York: Berg, 2005), 34. Godard's line is subtler in French: "Pas tout le temps, mais en laissant penser, en montrant qu'elle est là" (*Archéologie du cinéma et mémoire du siècle: Dialogue* [Tours: Farrago, 2000], 27). "To remind" doesn't quite capture the sense, at once passive and constructive, of bringing an image to thought, letting it become mindful.

248 Notes to Pages 177–188

49. Corrigan, *The Essay Film*, 182.

50. James S. Williams, "European Culture and Artistic Resistance in *Histoire(s) du cinéma* chapter 3A, La Monnaie de l'absolu," in *The Cinema Alone: Essays on the Work of Jean-Luc Godard*, ed. Michael Temple and James S. Williams (Amsterdam: Amsterdam University Press, 2000), 129.

51. Rohdie, *Film Modernism*, 171.

52. Episode 4B teems with clips from within Godard's corpus: *Pierrot le fou* (1965), *Ici et ailleurs* (1976), *Scénario du film "Passion," Hail Mary* (1985), *King Lear* (1987), *Nouvelle vague* (1990), *Germany Year 90 Nine Zero* (1991), *Oh, Woe Is Me, JLG/JLG*, and *For Ever Mozart* (1996). Also, a woman's voice recites a modified section from Godard's "Pierrot my friend" article, which was published in *Cahiers du cinéma* in 1965.

53. Lack, "Sa Voix," in *For Ever Godard*, 329.

54. Benjamin, *The Arcades Project*, 458 (convolute N1, 8). This is a quote from Rudolf Borchardt's monograph on Dante, through which Benjamin defines the "pedagogic side" of his own "undertaking."

55. On the reenactment format within essayistic filmmaking in general, see Corrigan, *The Essay Film*, 196–98.

56. Laura Rascaroli insightfully interprets *Notre musique* as "an essay film that creates the conditions of its own communicative negotiation, and takes it as its subject matter as well as textual strategy." Rascaroli, *The Personal Camera*, 99. However, she plays down the film's fictional narrative as "not imping[ing] on the communication of an essayistic argument" (95). I would argue that the fiction is inextricably part of Godard's essayistic thinking in the film.

57. These shots are technically production stills, but Godard's critique still applies to Hawks's shot/countershot practice.

58. If this juxtaposition associates Israel with "fiction," and Palestine with "documentary," the point isn't to cast Israel's statehood as fictitious but, continuing from the interview scene with Darwish, to comment on why public sympathy in the West sides overwhelmingly with Israel against its Palestinian foes. "Fiction" suggests that Israel has a compelling, well-known *historical narrative* in the West, whereas Palestine doesn't.

59. In the film's larger structure, this line—less an explanation than a question that needs probing—connects with reflections on Emmanuel Levinas's philosophy of the face-to-face encounter (in one scene, the Israeli journalist reads Levinas's *Entre Nous: Thinking of the Other*, its cover plainly visible). The legacy of Montaigne is relevant here, too, in that his turn to essayistic writing was motivated partly by his desire to short-circuit the adversarial dogmatisms fueling the religious wars around him.

60. These attendees are not to be confused with those who hold the stills from *His Girl Friday*. Then again, Godard's opaquely varying treatment of the scene courts such disorientation. Without a clear *découpage*, it's hard to say which photograph these two audience members are looking at respectively. This ambiguity reflects the *Muselmann* term itself, which the lecture shortly invokes.

61. Primo Levi, *Survival in Auschwitz* (1958), trans. Stuart Woolf (New York: Touchstone, 1996), 88, 125, 128.

62. Burlin Barr points out that this scene integrates otherness in the form of characters who look on as observers, as key witnesses without whom no cogent

Notes to Pages 188–193

perception can emerge. Barr, "Shot and Counter-shot: Presence, Obscurity, and the Breakdown of Discourse in Godard's *Notre musique*," *Journal of French and Francophone Philosophy* 18, no. 2 (2010): 65–85.

63. The shot strongly echoes the swinging lamp in *Alphaville* (1965), which describes the spatial interval between Caution (Eddie Constantine) and Dickson (Akim Tamiroff) in the stairwell of the latter's hotel.

64. The one attendee who seems to "get" Godard's lecture is Olga (Nade Dieu), the young woman portrayed with her eyes closed, a Jewish-French student of Russian descent. Later in the film, we learn that she has sacrificed her own life in a Tel Aviv movie theater, in an act of protest for peace. While Olga is shown in "Paradise" at the end of *Notre musique*, her suicide is *not* what Godard wanted his lecture to inspire, as his response upon hearing of her death indicates; her deed is yet another index of his failed communication.

65. Rascaroli, *The Personal Camera*, 102.

66. Ibid.

67. Godard's method here is closer to both the absorptive tradition of self-portraiture in Western painting and the tenuousness of lyric address in poetry when the reader is positioned to *overhear* the speaker's verse. In the words of Northrop Frye, "lyric is the genre in which the poet, like the ironic writer, turns his back on his audience." Frye, *Anatomy of Criticism: Four Essays* (Princeton, N.J.: Princeton University Press, 1957), 249–50, 271.

68. Harun Farocki, "Cross Influence/Soft Montage," in *Harun Farocki: Against What? Against Whom?* ed. Antje Ehmann and Kodwo Eshun (London: Koenig, 2009), 73.

69. Farocki associates his own montage process with what Gilles Deleuze calls Godard's "method of AND." Farocki, "Diary," in *Harun Farocki: Soft Montages*, ed. Yilmaz Dziewior (Bregenz: Kunsthaus, 2010), 207.

70. Farocki, "Cross Influence/Soft Montage," 72.

71. Farocki: "Whether it is Bresson, Godard or the Straubs, watching their films or writing about them is like learning to read. In order to read a philosophical text, you have to have a certain amount of training; the text requires a different mode of reading than a newspaper or a novel. The same goes for these films." Harun Farocki, interview with Thomas Elsaesser, "Making the World Superfluous: An Interview with Harun Farocki," in *Harun Farocki: Working on the Sightlines*, ed. Thomas Elsaesser (Amsterdam: Amsterdam University Press, 2004), 179.

72. Alexander Kluge, quoted in Christian Schulte, "Television and Obstinacy," in *Alexander Kluge: Raw Materials for the Imagination*, ed. Tara Forrest (Amsterdam: Amsterdam University Press, 2012), 319.

73. Christa Blümlinger, "Memory and Montage: On the Installation *Counter-Music*," trans. Michael Turnbull, in *Harun Farocki: Against What? Against Whom?* ed. Antje Ehmann and Kodwo Eshun (London: Koenig, 2009), 101–9.

74. Farocki, "Diary," 65.

75. Serge Daney, quoted in Farocki, "Diary," 65.

76. For an alternate translation of the full article that Farocki cites, see Serge Daney, "Montage Obligatory: The War, the Gulf, and the Small Screen," trans. Laurent Kretzschmar, *Rouge* 8 (2006), http://www.rouge.com.au/8/montage .html. Daney theorizes "obligatory" montage as the (television) viewer's mental and combative supplement to material form.

250   Notes to Pages 193–203

77. Godard's absence from his work sometimes abrogates what I have called his inviting spectator address. Consider his absence from *Film Socialism* (2010), a film that does quite the opposite of invitingly engage its audience: the intertitles "access denied" and "no comment" seem to signal a blocked channel of understanding and dialogue between the film and the spectator. Yet Godard alludes to his role as director when in the same film he samples a shot of an elderly Michelangelo Antonioni silently inspecting a statue in *The Gaze of Michelangelo* (2004). By invoking Antonioni's self-portrait as an artist defined through his studious gaze, Godard characterizes his own approach in such terms, as if it necessarily mutes his authorial voice ("no comment").

Coda

1. *Cave of Forgotten Dreams* continues many investigative features from Herzog's earlier "excursive" essay films, as Timothy Corrigan calls them in *The Essay Film*, 121–26.

2. "Hyper-haptic" is a term I take from Miriam Ross, *3D Cinema: Optical Illusions and Tactile Experiences* (London: Palgrave Macmillan, 2015), 21–35.

3. See Barbara Klinger, "*Cave of Forgotten Dreams*: Meditations on 3D," *Film Quarterly* 65, no. 3 (2012): 38–43.

4. Ross, *3D Cinema*, 104.

5. Ibid., 105–6.

6. Godard, "In Conversation with Jean-Luc Godard," interview by Cécile Mella. Canon Professional Network, http://cpn.canon-europe.com/content/Jean -Luc_Godard.do.

7. Witt, *Jean-Luc Godard, Cinema Historian*, 6.

8. This shot of three dice is reused from Godard-Miéville's *France/tour/détour/ deux/enfants* (1977).

9. The video integrates a famous photo of a young Guy Debord on damaged stock. This situates Debord as a prophet of disaster while suggesting that an even worse society of the spectacle is upon us than he imagined.

10. Deren's *Meshes of the Afternoon* (co-directed with her husband, Alexander Hammid, 1943), is an important reference for Godard's *Goodbye to Language*. Godard loosely borrows from its repetitive, fragmentary dream structure and elliptical eruptions of violence. Godard, like Deren, uses his own residence as the main location. A young woman in *Goodbye* is filmed slowly descending the stairs, with just her bare feet in the frame, in a stark homage to the close-ups of Deren's ambulatory feet in *Meshes*.

11. My study of Godard's references in *Goodbye* is informed by Ted Fendt's comprehensive list. See Fendt, "*Adieu au langage/Goodbye to Language*: A Works Cited," MUBI (2014), https://mubi.com/notebook/posts/adieu-au-langage -goodbye-to-language-a-works-cited.

12. Godard, "A Long Story," interview by Jacques Rancière and Charles Tesson, in *The Future(s) of Film: Three Interviews 2000/01*, trans. John O'Toole (Bern: Gachnang and Springer, 2002), 21.

13. Roland Barthes, "Longtemps, je me suis couché de bonne heure . . ." (1978), in *The Rustle of Language*, trans. Richard Howard (Berkeley: University of California Press, 1989), 278–80, 284.

Notes to Pages 203–212

14. Ibid., 281–83. Barthes's description of Proust's method bears affinities with how Corrigan defines the "*digressive or dissipative*" function of essayism in Terrence Malick's *The Tree of Life* (2011). See Corrigan, "Essayism and Contemporary Film Narrative," 15–27.

15. Nico Baumbach, "Starting Over," *Film Comment* 50, no. 6 (2014): 34–41; David Bordwell, "*Adieu au langage*: 2+2 x 3D," *Observations on Film Art* (2014), http://www.davidbordwell.net/blog/2014/09/07/adieu-au-langage-2-2-x-3d/; James Quandt, "Last Harrumph," *Artforum* 53, no. 1 (2014): 127–28; Blake Williams, "Cannes 2014: *Adieu au langage* (Jean-Luc Godard, France)," *Cinema Scope* 59 (2014), http://cinema-scope.com/spotlight/adieu-au-langage -jean-luc-godard-france/; James S. Williams, "Coda: Cinema after Language," in *Encounters with Godard: Ethics, Aesthetics, Politics* (New York: SUNY Press, 2016), 247–54.

16. Godard, "In Conversation with Jean-Luc Godard," http://cpn.canon -europe.com/content/Jean-Luc_Godard.do.

17. Bordwell, "*Adieu au langage*: 2+2 x 3D," http://www.davidbordwell.net /blog/2014/09/07/adieu-au-langage-2-2-x-3d/.

18. Jacques Ellul, "Victoire d'Hitler?" *Réforme* 14 (1945): 1, 3.

19. Jacques Ellul, *The Technological Society*, trans. Tom Wilkinson (New York: Vintage, 1964), 319–35.

20. Godard has called Levinas's fixation on the face-to-face encounter a "bad," overly reductive use of the shot/countershot principle. Godard, "The Future(s) of Film," interview by Emmanuel Burdeau and Charles Tesson, in *The Future(s) of Film: Three Interviews 2000/01*, trans. John O'Toole (Bern: Gachnang and Springer, 2002), 64.

21. In the first prologue, the addition of Levinas to the bookstall table also serves to offset the anti-Semitism linked with other authors who appear: Ezra Pound, Aleksandr Solzhenitsyn, and Fyodor Dostoevsky (who was nevertheless a major influence on Levinas).

22. Emmanuel Levinas, *Time and the Other*, trans. Richard A. Cohen (Pittsburgh: Duquesne University Press, 1987), 74–94.

23. Emmanuel Levinas. *Totality and Infinity*, trans. Alphonso Lingis (Pittsburgh: Duquesne University Press, 1969), 42–48.

24. Emmanuel Levinas and Richard Kearney, "Dialogue with Levinas," in *Face to Face with Levinas*, ed. Richard A. Cohen (Albany: SUNY Press, 1986), 16–17.

25. Ibid., 17.

26. Targeting Heidegger and Sartre, Levinas contends that existential ontology founds itself on an egoism allied with the logic of State tyranny. Levinas, *Totality and Infinity*, 46–47. In the opening titles of *Goodbye*, Godard refers to Heidegger's controversial ties with the Nazi Party by posing the question: what if "non-thought" contaminates thought?

27. Baumbach, "Starting Over," 37.

28. Godard, "Jean-Luc Godard: 'Le Cinéma, c'est un oubli de la réalité,'" interview by Philippe Dagen and Frank Nouchi. *Le Monde*, June 10, 2014, http:// www.lemonde.fr/culture/article/2014/06/10/jean-luc-godard-le-cinema-c-est-un -oubli-de-la-realite_4435673_3246.html.

29. Vadim Rizov, "Goodbye to 3-D Rules," *Filmmaker Magazine*, October 20, 2014, http://filmmakermagazine.com/87878-goodbye-to-3-d-rules/#.V7ndW 16Jlg3. Rizov reports that according to Fabrice Aragno, the cinematographer on *Goodbye*, Godard shot the promenades with Roxy by himself, during walking sessions with the dog, using amateur-grade video cameras by Fuji and Sony.

30. Emmanuel Levinas, "The Name of a Dog, or Natural Rights," in *Difficult Freedom: Essays on Judaism*, trans. Seán Hand (Baltimore, Md.: Johns Hopkins University Press, 1997), 151–53.

31. *Goodbye*'s forest trope (which the film's narrator traces to an Apache definition of "world" as "forest") further interconnects with the theme of couplehood through the repeated clip from *People on Sunday* (Robert Siodmak and Edgar G. Ulmer, 1930). This grainy scene shows a young man chasing a young woman into a forest. It marks a prelapsarian moment before the catastrophe that Godard conveys through references to Ellul, traumatic history, and dystopian science fiction.

32. In *Stalker*, a German shepherd materializes in the Zone and returns to the Stalker's ramshackle home. The dog is *a link between these spaces* and a testament to the Zone's actuality. In *Goodbye*, the oscillation between Roxy's promenades and scenes of downtime in the couple's house effectively refashions *Stalker*'s interplay between an exterior landscape of mystical potentiality and a domestic space of beaten-down hope.

33. In the coda, there are also references to films directed by Miéville. A fleeting glimpse of two side-by-side shadow figures evokes a shot from the ending of *We're All Still Here* (1997), a shot sampled in *The Old Place* as well.

34. At the time of the film's premiere at Cannes, murmurs of the couple having become estranged surfaced in the French press. I do not know the latest status of their personal relationship, but it seems clear that *Goodbye* memorializes the mode of twoness they have embodied together.

35. This is a gesture of viewer apostrophe that Godard has used before. Consider the two beach chairs positioned side by side in his installation exhibit at the Pompidou Centre. Agnès Varda similarly uses empty chairs as an overture to the spectator in the second episode of her TV series *Agnès from Here to There Varda* (2014).

36. Godard, "In Conversation with Jean-Luc Godard," http://cpn.canon -europe.com/content/Jean-Luc_Godard.do. While Roxy's role in this sense is far from obvious, the film invites us to consider Roxy's aptitudes within a circuit of associations that includes past revolutionary causes. Early in *Goodbye* we see a close-up of a young woman singing with a crowd from Jean Renoir's *La Marseillaise* (1938); the clip is recycled from Godard's own *Histoire(s)* with its added graphic title "something," one of the bywords of Emmanuel-Joseph Sieyès's 1789 pamphlet *What Is the Third Estate?*

37. Godard, "Jean-Luc Godard: 'Le Cinéma, c'est un oubli de la réalité,' " http://www.lemonde.fr/culture/article/2014/06/10/jean-luc-godard-le-cinema -c-est-un-oubli-de-la-realite_4435673_3246.html. In interviews, Godard has mentioned Brunschvicg's text *Descartes et Pascal: Lecteurs de Montaigne* (1944) as the source of this quotation. Godard, "Jean-Luc Godard—Elias Sanbar," *Politis*, January 16, 2005, http://www.france-palestine.org/article3140.html.

Notes to Page 221

38. See Timothy Barnard's entry on Léon Brunschvicg in *Reading with Jean-Luc Godard*, ed. Kevin J. Hayes and Timothy Barnard (Montreal: Caboose, forthcoming 2018).

39. Blaise Pascal, *Pensées* (1669), ed. and trans. Roger Ariew (Indianapolis, Ind.: Hackett, 2005), 106 (S405/L373).

40. Godard, "Jean-Luc Godard: 'Le Cinéma, c'est un oubli de la réalité,'" http://www.lemonde.fr/culture/article/2014/06/10/jean-luc-godard-le-cinema-c-est-un-oubli-de-la-realite_4435673_3246.html. See also Godard, "Jean-Luc Godard—Elias Sanbar," *Politis*, January 16, 2005, http://www.france-palestine.org/article3140.html.

INDEX

Abdeli, Kamel, 205
"accented cinema," 33
Addison, Joseph, 6
Adorno, Theodor, "The Essay as Form" (1958), 110
aesthetics: intertwined with history, 12; of obscurity, 194; of third cinema, 33; 3D aesthetics, 204, 215
Agnès from Here to There Varda (Varda, 2011), 155, 242n46, 252n35
Akerman, Chantal, 33
Alexander Nevsky (Eisenstein, 1938), 95, 96
Algerian war, 29
Allen, Woody, 131; *Hannah and Her Sisters* (1986), 241n32
allusions, 26, 47, 65. *See also* intertextuality
Alphaville (Godard, 1965), 85, 230n65, 240n7, 249n63; gesture of love in, 115–16, 126, 135; Vogt's science fiction and, 206
Alter, Nora M., 3, 227n26
Althusser, Louis, 50; "Ideology and Ideological State Apparatuses" (1970), 84
anamorphic widescreen format, 44
Anderson, Thom, 93
Andrew, Dudley, 229n46
anti-Semitism, 89, 165, 166
Antonioni, Michelangelo, 45, 66, 112, 126; *Eclipse* (1962), 38, 111; *The Gaze of Michelangelo* (2004), 250n77
Apocalypse Now (Coppola, 1979), 200
Apollinaire, Guillaume, 74
apostrophe, 30, 62, 66, 136, 161, 228n39, 252n35
appropriations, 9, 12, 58, 65
Aragon, Louis, 74

Arcades Project, The (Benjamin), 143
archival footage, 25, 31
Arendt, Hannah, *The Origins of Totalitarianism* (1951), 114
Aristotle, 136, 137
Artaud, Antonin, 76, 77, 78
art cinema, European, 21
art et essai theaters, 27
art film, 73
Arthur, Paul, 3
Artist on the Road to Tarascon, The (Van Gogh, 1888), 181
Artists Under the Big Top: Perplexed (Kluge, 1968), 38
Assayas, Olivier, 235n28
Astaire, Fred, 95, 196
Astruc, Alexandre, 32, 37, 40, 227n20, 227n26, 229n53; "The Birth of a New Avant-Garde: La Caméra-stylo" (1948), 24, 25–27; on cinema of thought, 34
As You Can See (Farocki, 1986), 138
audiovisual essay, 5, 22, 67; *Letter from Siberia* as locus classicus in debates over, 30; "pedagogy of perception" and, 40; reflective task of, 51; retraining of viewer by, 17. *See also* essay film
Auer, Mischa, 179
Auerbach, Erich, 8
Au hasard Balthazar (Bresson, 1966), 242n38
Aumont, Jacques, 44, 107, 244n1
Auschwitz death camp, 29
auteurism, 16, 66
authorship, Romantic ideas of, 66
avant-garde, 26
Avant-scène du cinéma, L' (journal), 51
Avatar (Cameron, 2009), 195, 199

255

256   Index

Bacchus and Ariadne (Tintoretto, 1576), 159, 161
Bacon, Francis, *Study for a Portrait of Van Gogh II* (1957), 180
Bad and the Beautiful, The (Minnelli, 1952), 43
Badiou, Alain, 242n37
Baecque, Antoine de, 80
Baldwin, James, 6
"Ballad of Hanged Men" (Villon), 159–60
Band of Outsiders (Godard, 1964), 50, 113
Band Wagon, The (Minnelli, 1953), 95, 96
Bardot, Brigitte, 45
Barefoot Contessa, The (Mankiewicz, 1954), 200, *201*
Barthes, Roland, 203
Bassae (Pollet, 1964), 227n20
Bataille, Georges, 177
Battleship Potemkin (Eisenstein, 1925), 183
Baudelaire, Charles, 19, 66, 123; *The Flowers of Evil* (1857), 61–62
Baumbach, Nico, 204, 211
Baye, Nathalie, 120
Bazin, André, 31, 42, 237n51; "evolution" of film style, 26; on "lateral montage," 30, 52, 229n46
Beaches of Agnès, The (Varda, 2008), 154, 155, 239n2, 242n46
Beast with Five Fingers, The (Florey, 1946), 244n65
Beckett, Samuel, "The Image" (1959), 101, 102
Being and Nothingness (Sartre, 1943), 210
Belkhodja, Catherine, 112
Bellour, Raymond, 225n31, 226n13, 233n9
Belmondo, Jean-Paul, 73, 77, 79
Benjamin, Walter, 117, 243n56; *The Arcades Project*, 143
Bergala, Alain, 48, 66, 113
Bergman, Ingmar: *Prison* (1949), 104, *104*, 105–6, 149, 200; *Summer with Monika* (1953), 75
Bergman, Ingrid, 35, *36*, 112
Berr, Betty, 116

Berto, Juliet, 84, *85*
"Birth of a New Avant-Garde, The: La Caméra-stylo" (Astruc, 1948), 24, 25–27
Bitomsky, Hartmut, 25
Bjørnstad, Ketil, 181
black screen: in Debord's *Howls for Sade*, 83; in Farocki's video installations, 191; in Godard-Miéville Marian diptych, 122–23; in *Goodbye to Language*, 205, 220; in *Histoire(s) du cinéma*, 93, 95, 100; in *Ici et ailleurs*, 87; in *JLG/JLG*, 169, 171; in *Nouvelle vague*, 203; in *Notre musique*, 185
Blaise Pascal (Rossellini, 1972), 40
Blum, Léon, 89
Blümlinger, Christa, 3
Boetticher, Bud, *Westbound* (1959), 74, 234n15
Boltanski, Christian, 140
Book of Imaginary Beings, The (Borges and Guerrero, 1976), 150
Book of Mary, The (Miéville, 1985), 114, 122–24, 131, *133*, 241n33
Bordwell, David, 21, 204, 205
Borges, Jorge Luis, 6, 23, 76, 210, 221; *The Book of Imaginary Beings* (with Guerrero, 1976), 150; "The Dream of Coleridge" (1952), 180
borrowings, 3, 65, 66. *See also* citation
Bosnian War, 183
Breathless (*À bout de souffle*, Godard, 1960), 41, 73–75, 79, 153, 236n50
Brecht, Bertolt, 25, 66
Brenez, Nicole, 68, 99, 227n18, 245n8
Bresson, Robert, 34, 174; *Au hasard Balthazar* (1966), 242n38; *Diary of a Country Priest* (1951), 246n25; *Notes on the Cinematographer*, 102, 174; *Pickpocket* (1959), 126, 128
Brezhnev, Leonid, 89
British Sounds (Godard/Dziga Vertov Group, 1970), 84, 87, 243n54
Broch, Hermann, 23; *The Death of Virgil* (1945), 129
Brody, Richard, 89, 114, 165
Broken Blossoms (Griffith, 1919), 95
Bruneau, Zoé, 205

Index 257

Brunschvicg, Léon, *Descartes et Pascal* (1994), 221, 252n37
Brutality in Stone (Kluge/Schamoni, 1961), 30
Buñuel, Luis: *Un chien andalou* (co-dir. Dalí, 1929), 179; *Land without Bread* (1933), 23
Burch, Noël, 19, 21, 28, 40, 44
Burgin, Victor, 225n31
Butor, Michel, 72, 233n11

Cahiers du cinéma, 22, 23, 34, 237n51; Godard interview (1962), 17, 41–42; Godard's writings for, 41, 71–72, 231n80
Calvino, Italo, 44
Camera-Eye (Godard/Dziga Vertov Group, 1967), 153
Cameraperson (Johnson, 2016), 33
caméra-stylo (camera pen), 25–27, 32, 227n20; authorial personality and, 43; fiction filmmaking and, 34; overlap of "second" and "third cinema" cultures and, 33; voiceover narration and, 229n53
Cameron, James, *Avatar* (2009), 195, 199
Camus, Albert, 26
capitalism, 54, 60, 90, 117, 121
Captain Blood (Curtiz, 1935), 200
Carabiniers, Les (Godard, 1963), 73
Caravaggio, 159, 193
Carracci, Annibale, 159
Case of the Grinning Cat, The (Marker, 2004), 228n42
Cassavetes, John, 96, 154
Catastrophe, Une (Godard, 2008), 241n29
Cave of Forgotten Dreams (Herzog, 2010), 196, 197, *197*, 199
Cayrol, Jean, 29
Chaplin, Charlie, 154; *Modern Times* (1936), 94
Charisse, Cyd, 95
Chevallier, Richard, 205
Chien andalou, Un (Buñuel/Dalí, 1929), 179
Child, Abigail, 25
Chinoise, La (Godard/Dziga Vertov Group, 1967), 86, 163, 230n65

ciné-clubs, 27
cinema: film noir, 183; French impressionist films (1920s), 176; Godard's quasi-spiritual faith in, 100; history of, 14; iconoclastic, 83–86; of ideas, 25; of thought, 34. *See also* Hollywood, classical
Cinema 2: The Time-Image (Deleuze), 37–38, 39–40
CinemaScope, 45, 48
cinéma vérité, 44
Cioran, E. M., "The Temptation to Exist" (1956), 247n34
citation, 9–10, 13, 65–70, 104; citation as historical montage, 92–110, *98*, *103*, *104*; copyright and, 66–67; within an essayistic filmmaker's own corpus, 71, 79, 173; diachronic function of, 69; film criticism and, 70–73; film within a film, 73–77, *78*, 79; Godard's collage versus Debord's *détournement*, 79–86, 235n28; material and textural effects and, 69; post-militant adoption of video and, 86–92, *91*, *92*; self-portraiture and, 156
Citizen Kane (Welles, 1941), 150
City (Simak, 1952), 202
"city symphony" genre, 50
Clift, Montgomery, 100
Close-Up (Kiarostami, 1990), 5–6
Cocteau, Jean, 103, 154; *Le Testament d'Orphée* (1960), 72; *Orpheus* (1950), 102, 103, *103*
Cohen, Jem, *Museum Hours* (2012), 39
Cohn, Dorrit, 39
Cold War, 31, 75, 90, 184
Coleridge, Samuel Taylor, 6, 180
Colette, Anne, 41
colonialism, 29
Communism, Soviet, 200, 201
Communist Manifesto (Marx and Engels, 1848), 84
Comolli, Jean-Louis, 71
Confessions (Rousseau, 1782), 171
Conley, Tom, 74, 75
Conrad, Joseph, 23; *Heart of Darkness* (1899), 245n16
Constantine, Eddie, 115, 249n63
consumerism/consumer society, 55, 56, 79

Contempt (*Le Mépris,* Godard, 1963), 12, 44–49, 47, 95, 212; citation in, 65–66, 69; cited in *Histoire(s) du cinéma,* 103, 173; cited in *Soft and Hard,* 134; cited in *The Book of Mary,* 123; couple in, 44–46, 49, 111, 121; Godard's cameo in, 153; lampshade as spatial interval between couple, 45, *45,* 46, 49, 61, 131; musical score, 123

Coppola, Francis Ford, *Apocalypse Now* (1979), 200

copyright, 66, 67

Cornell, Joseph, 25

Corrigan, Timothy, 3, 5–6, 23, 37, 225n2; *The Essay Film,* 5, 226n15; on essayistic cinema as performance, 27; on essayistic strategies in film, 39

Costa, Pedro, *Where Does Your Hidden Smile Lie?* (2001), 113–14

coupling, as thematic concern, 13, 15, 74–76, 111–15, 133; in *Alphaville,* 126; in *Contempt,* 44, 45, 46, 49, 111; demands of love and work, 120–22, 128, 137; in *Every Man for Himself,* 120–22; in *Goodbye to Language,* 204, 211–12, 215; in *Le Gai Savoir,* 84–85; in *The Old Place,* 141; in *Soft and Hard,* 128–31, *132,* 133–38, *133*; spectatorship and, 104, *104,* 105; tennis references and, 128, 130, 241n29. *See also* "twoness," dialogical

Courbet, Gustave, 159

Coutard, Raoul, 49, 134

Cozarinsky, Edgardo, 25

Crucified Lovers, The (Mizoguchi, 1954), 95

cultural capital, 70

Curtains (Raven, 2014), 196

Curtiz, Michael, *Captain Blood* (1935), 200

Dalí, Salvador, *Un chien andalou* (co-dir. Buñuel, 1929), 179

Daney, Serge, 131, 156, 173, 241n32; on Godard's "pedagogy," 82–83, 84; on "the image" and "the visual," 192–93

Dans le noir du temps [*In the Darkness of Time*] (Godard-Miéville, 2002), 199

Darke, Chris, 115

Darling, David, 170

Darwish, Mahmoud, 87, 184, 187, 248n58

Dean, James, 144

Death of Virgil, The (Broch, 1945), 129

Debord, Guy, 13, 25, 32, 84, 235n28, 250n9; *détournement* practice of, 67, 80, 81, 82; essay films of, 228n33; Godard harshly critiqued by, 80–82; as influence on Godard, 50. *See also* Situationists

Debord, Guy, works of: *Howls for Sade* (1952), 83; *In girum imus nocte et consumimur igni* (1978), 81, 183; *The Society of the Spectacle* (1967; film version, 1973), 81, 82, 195

découpage, 35, 248n60

De Gaulle, Charles, 75

Delahaye, Michel, 71

Deleuze, Gilles, 37–40, 52, 88, 116, 137, 230n66

Demy, Jacques, 239n2

De Palma, Brian, *The Fury* (1978), 96–97, 98, 99, 107

Deren, Maya, *Meshes of the Afternoon* (1943), 202, 250n10

Descartes, René, 26, 27

Descartes et Pascal: Lecteurs de Montaigne (Brunschvicg, 1994), 221, 252n37

Détective (1985), 133

détournement, 67, 80, 81, 82

Deutsch, Gustav, 25

dialogue, 10–11, 32, 122, 130, 151, 184; beyond language, 212; failure of, 189; "lover's dialogue," 115; reduction of, 202

Diary of a Country Priest (Bernanos novel), 237n57

Diary of a Country Priest (Bresson, 1951), 246n25

Dickinson, Angie, 102

Diderot, Denis, *Letter on the Blind for the Use of Those Who See* (1749), 164–65, 166, 168

Dieu, Nade, 249n64

direct address, 4, 176, 189, 228n39

Disprezzo, Il (Moravia, 1954), 44

Index 259

documentary, 17, 21, 85, 93; archival footage in, 25; pseudo-documentary, 32. *See also* fiction/documentary division
Dostoevsky, Fyodor, 23
Draper, Ellen, 124
Dray, Albert, 116
"Dream of Coleridge, The" (Borges, 1952), 180
Dreyer, Carl Theodor, *The Passion of Joan of Arc* (1928), 76–77, 78
Duchamp, Marcel, 140
Du côté de la côte (Varda, 1958), 28
Duel in the Sun (Vidor, 1946), 105
Duras, Marguerite, 32, 233n6
Dürer, Albrecht, 8
Durgnat, Raymond, 229n47
Dutronc, Jacques, 120
Dziga Vertov Group, 32, 82, 108, 218, 220, 235n32; collectivist ethos of, 83, 163; Godard-Miéville partnership as critique of, 86–87; Godard's development as essayist and, 84

Eclipse (Antonioni, 1962), 38, 111, 112
Ecran français, L' (journal), 25
editing, 22, 31, 46, 174, 229n46, 247n44. *See also* montage
Eisenberg, Daniel, 25, 226n12
Eisenhower, Dwight D., 75
Eisenstein, Sergei, 25; *Alexander Nevsky* (1938), 95, 96; *Battleship Potemkin* (1925), 183
Eisler, Hanns, 29, 228n42
Eisner, Lotte, 44
Elephant (Alan Clarke, 1989), 5
Eliot, T. S., 18
Ellul, Jacques: "Hitler's Victory?" (1945), 206, 209, 215; *The Technological Society* (1954), 206–7
Elsaesser, Thomas, 92
Éluard, Paul, 115
Empedocles, 137
Empire Strikes Back, The (Kershner, 1980), 143
Engels, Friedrich, 84
Entre Nous: Thinking of the Other (Levinas, 1991), 207, 248n59
Enzensberger, Hans Magnus, 227n17

Epstein, Jean, 117, 233n10; *Esprit de cinéma* (1955), 243n56; *The Intelligence of a Machine* (1946), 179
Esprit de cinéma (Epstein, 1955), 243n56
Essais (Montaigne, 1580, 1582, 1588), 7–11, 12, 20, 242n36; "consubstantial" relation to Montaigne, 154; Greco-Roman debates over *philia* and, 137; readers' awareness of physical setting of study, 174
"Essay as Form, The" (Adorno, 1958), 110
essay film, 3, 6, 20; canonical history of, 24, 226n15; distinctive attributes of, 3–4; essayistic mode beyond, 33–41; Godard's early work and, 23; literary essay transposed to, 110; Marker as key figure, 32; post-militant turn of, 13; as quasi-genre, 12, 111, 226n12; "utopian" mission of, 4. *See also* audiovisual essay
Essay Film, The: From Montaigne, After Marker (Corrigan), 5, 226n15
essayism, 5, 6, 37, 70; collaborative thinking of, 18; gesture and, 119; Godard-Miéville partnership and, 114; long-term filmmaker–spectator relationship, 16; narrative film and, 12, 38–39, 122; non-dogmatic character of, 84; origins of Godard's essayism, 41, 43; pedagogy of perception and, 40; of Rossellini, 35
Every Man for Himself (Godard, 1980), 114, 118, 120–22, 126, 240n19
experimental avant-garde, 25, 227n26
Expression of Hands, The (Farocki, 1997), 174, 244n65

Faces Places (Varda/JR, 2017), 33
Falconetti, Renée, 76, 77, 78
Far from Vietnam (omnibus, 1967), 228n42, 235n37
Farocki, Harun, 5, 8, 25, 31, 67, 86, 249n71; *caméra-stylo* definition and, 32; as critic-turned-director, 71; as innovator, 20; leftist engagement of, 191; self-portraiture of, 14; "soft montage" of, 191, 192

260   Index

Farocki, Harun, works of: *As You Can See* (1986), 138; *The Expression of Hands* (1997), 174, 244n65; *Images of the World and the Inscription of War* (1988), 30, 176, 183; *Inextinguishable Fire* (1969), 191; *Interface* (1997), 191

Faulkner, William, 26

Faure, Élie, 209, 231n79; *History of Art: Modern Art* (1937), 77

Faust (Murnau, 1926), 95, 96, 99

F for Fake (Welles, 1975), 18, *18*, 32, 35, 172, 174, 244n2

fiction/documentary division, 6, 32, 50; hybrid combination, 3–4, 32, 205; refusal of, 67; rethinking of, 23; stereo format and, 195

fiction films, 3, 13, 21, 33, 62, 93, 230n62. *See also* narrative film

Fieschi, Jean-André, 71

film criticism, 70–73, 93

"Film Essay, The: A New Form of Documentary Film" (Richter, 1940), 24–25

Filming Othello (Welles, 1978), 32

Film Socialism (Godard, 2010), 150, 200, 250n77

Final Destination 5 (2011), 199

"first-person" perspective, 4

Flaxman, Gregory, 137

Fleming, Victor, *Gone with the Wind* (1939), 102, 129, 130

Flowers of Evil, The (Baudelaire, 1857), 61–62

Flusser, Vilém, 119, 122

Ford, John, *Rio Grande* (1950), 82

For Ever Mozart (Godard, 1996), 243n54

Foucault, Michel, 116

found footage, 4, 87, 227n18. *See also* citation

France/tour/détour/deux/enfants (Godard/Miéville, 1977), 114, 116–19, *117*, 121, 131, 200, 240n19

Franju, Georges, 30, 36, 43; *Hôtel des Invalides* (1952), 28–29, 111; Left Bank group and, 3, 23; short film and, 28, 41

Frankenstein (Shelley, 1818), 218

French Revolution (1789), 87, 88, 211

Fried, Michael, 159

Fright Night (2011), 199, 200, 202

Frye, Northrop, 249n67

Fury, The (De Palma, 1978), 96–97, *98*, 99, 107

Gainsbourg, Charlotte, 230n65

Gai Savoir, Le (*The Joy of Learning*, Godard, 1969), 13, 79, 81, 84–86, *85*, 200

Gaze of Michelangelo, The (Antonioni, 2004), 250n77

Germany Year 90 Nine Zero (Godard, 1991), 140, 179

Gesamtkunstwerk ("total work of art"), 107

gesture, 17, 114–15, 122, 197; of apostrophe, 30, 228n39; of citation, 70; couple as theme and, 115–19; Godard-Miéville's altered motion exercises and, 116–22; of loving, 122, 124–25, *127*, 131, 135, 143; montage and, 13; as pictorial basis of montage associations; of searching, 119. *See also Old Place, The*: "think with one's hands" motif

Getino, Octavio, *Hour of the Furnaces* (co-dir. Solanas, 1968), 33

Gish, Lillian, 95, 102–3, 146

Gleaners and I, The (Varda, 2000), 155

Godard, Jean-Luc: as actor/performer, 14, 15, 131; address to spectator, 13; as auteur, 14, 16, 156; on being a self-critical essayist, 19; *Cahiers du cinéma* interview (1962), 17, 41–42; on cinema as thinking form, 177; as cinematic essayist, 11–15; "collage" method, 80–81, 85, 107; course–discourse pairing in metacinema, 43, 44, 49, 50, 71, 72; as critic-turned-director, 218; as "director of the couple," 112–13; Dziga Vertov Group and, 32, 82, 163, 235n32; as essayist, 22, 41, 69; exemplary status of, *5*; hybrid role as critic and filmmaker, 70–73; lyric address of, 249n67; Maoist (Marxist-Leninist) phase, 79, 81, 83, 84–86, 141–42, 148, 218, 219; New Wave films of, 44, 50, 70, 73, 84, 113, 218; pairing of "novel"

Index 261

and "essay," 22, 34, 41, 43; on self-portrayal, 153; self-retrospective tendency of, 113, 173, 181, 198, 219; visit to Jordan and Lebanon, 86, 243n53; on writing as filmmaking, 42; writings in *Cahiers du cinéma*, 41, 71–72, 231n80

Godard, Montaignean lineage and, 6, 11, 50, 66, 174, 225n2; multiple works linked over time, 11, 69, 93, 151, 195; "piling up" of citations, 95; synthesis of authorial and spectatorial roles, 175

Godard, post-militant phase of, 13, 93, 109, 183, 190, 191; adoption of video technology and, 87, 92; partnership with Miéville and, 90; tempered political consciousness, 109

WORKS: *Alphaville* (1965), 85, 115–16, 126, 135, 206, 230n65, 240n7, 249n63; *To Alter the Image* (1982), 236n37; *Band of Outsiders* (1964), 50, 113; *Breathless* (*À bout de souffle*, 1960), 41, 79, 153, 236n50; *British Sounds* (1970), 84, 87, 243n54; *Camera-Eye* (1967), 153; *Contempt* (*Le Mépris*, 1963), 12; *Dans le noir du temps* (*In the Darkness of Time*, 2002), 199; *Détective* (1985), 133; *Every Man for Himself* (1980), 118, 120–22, 126, 240n19; *Film Socialism* (2010), 150, 200, 250n77; *For Ever Mozart* (1996), 243n54; *Germany Year 90 Nine Zero* (1991), 140, 179; *The Great Swindler* (1964), 79; *Hail Mary* (1985), 114, 122–26, 127, 128, 131, 212, 241n26; *In Praise of Love* (2001), 216, 237n60; *Je vous salue, Sarajevo* (1993), 141; *JLG/JLG: Self-Portrait in December* (1995), 14, 89, 142–43, 153, 155, 241n29; *Keep Your Right Up* (1987), 103, 122, 153, 228n42, 241n29; *King Lear* (1987), 153; *La Chinoise* (1967), 86, 163, 230n65; *Le Gai Savoir* (*The Joy of Learning*, 1969), 13, 79, 81, 84–86, 85, 200; *Les Carabiniers* (1963),

73; *Letter to Jane: Investigations about a Still* (co-dir. Gorin, 1972), 21, 242n39; *Made in USA* (1966), 50; *A Married Woman* (1964), 44, 51, 77, 115, 228n42; *Masculine Feminine* (1966), 44, 46, 53, 230n65, 232n90; *Meetin' WA* (1986), 131; *Message of Greetings: Swiss Prize / My Thanks / Dead or Alive* (2015), 153; *Nouvelle vague* (1990), 122, 203, 212, 232n1, 241n29; *Oh, Woe Is Me* (1993), 168; *Opération "beton"* (1955), 41; *The Origins of the 21st Century* (2000), 140–41, 232n2; *Passion* (1982), 122; *Pierrot le fou* (1965), 51, 71–72, 77, 209, 231n79, 241n29; *Pravda* (1970), 87, 218; *Prénom Carmen* (1983), 113, 122, 153, 218; *Scénario de "Sauve qui peut (la vie)"* (1979), 237n63; *Small Notes Regarding the Film "Hail Mary"* (1983), 124; *Struggle in Italy* (*Lotte in Italia*, 1971), 84, 220; *The Three Disasters* (*Les trois désastres*, 2013), 14, 197–202, 200–201, 201, 212, 219; *2 or 3 Things I Know about Her* (*2 ou 3 choses je sais que d'elle*, 1967), 12, 20, 22, 23, 162; *2 x 50 Years of French Cinema* (1995), 131; *Une catastrophe* (2008), 241n29; *Until Victory* (with Gorin, unfinished), 86, 87; *Vladimir and Rosa* (1971), 236n38, 241n29; *Voyage(s) in Utopia, JLG, 1946–2006: In Search of a Lost Theorem* (2006), 198; *Vrai faux passeport* (2006), 67, 241n29; *Week-end* (1967), 21, 103; *Wind from the East* (co-dir. Gorin, 1970), 84, 102, 108–9, 113. See also *Contempt*; *Goodbye to Language*; *Histoire(s) du cinéma*; *My Life to Live*; *Notre musique*; *Scénario du film "Passion"*; *2 or 3 Things I Know about Her*

Godard-Miéville partnership, 15, 86–92, 106, 200; cinephilia and, 137–38, 151; coda of *Goodbye to Language* and, 218–19, 221, 252n33; couple

262 Index

Godard-Miéville partnership, *continued*
as theme and, 113, 239n3; essayism
and, 114; friendship as crux of
essaying, 136; gestures in films of,
116–19; Marian diptych, 122–26,
127, 128; Miéville aligned with verbal
expression, 120; post-militant and
post-filmic mode, 90; as song of two
humans, 128–31, *132*, 133–38, *133*;
Straub-Huillet partnership compared
with, 113–14
WORKS: *France/tour/détour/deux/
enfants* (1977), 114, 116–19, *117*,
121, 131, 200, 240n19; *Numéro
deux* (1975), 153, 191; *Six fois
deux/Sur et sous la communication*
(1976), 119, 153, 241n31, 241n34;
Soft and Hard (1985), 13, 114,
128–31, *132*, 133–38, *133*,
241n30. See also *Ici et ailleurs*;
Old Place, The
Goddard, Paulette, 94
Godet, Héloïse, 205
Goethe, Wolfgang von, 230n67
Gone with the Wind (Fleming, 1939),
102, 129, 130
Goodbye to Language (*Adieu au
langage,* Godard, 2014), 14, 15,
197–98, 200, *208, 209*, 244n66; as
cinematic "third form" (Barthes),
203; as essayistic love story, 202–10;
forest trope, 216, 252n31; *Meshes of
the Afternoon* as key reference for,
202, 250n10; remembrance in coda
of, 219–22, *220*; Roxy the dog as
intercessor, 211–16, *213, 214*, 217,
218, 252n29
Gorin, Jean-Pierre, 11, 21, 32, 224n27,
230n62; *caméra-stylo* definition and,
32; Dziga Vertov Group and, 82;
on Godard's assault on intellectual
property, 66; visit to Jordan and
Lebanon with Godard, 86, 243n53
Gorin, Jean-Pierre works of: *Letter to
Jane Investigations about a Still* (co-
dir. Godard, 1972), 21, 242n39; *Tout
va bien* (co-dir. Godard), 120; *Until
Victory* (co-dir. Godard, unfinished),
86, 87, 88; *Wind from the East* (co-
dir. Godard, 1970), 84, 102, 108–9

Gospel According to St. Matthew, The
(Pasolini, 1964), 148
Grant, Cary, 144, 185, 186, *186*
Grant, Catherine, 114, 225n31
Great Swindler, The (Godard, 1964), 79
Greenaway, Peter, 8, 32; *Just in Time*
(2013), 196
Grégori, Christian, 205
Griffith, D. W., 43; *Broken Blossoms*
(1919), 95
Grin without a Cat, A (Marker, 1977),
16, 31, 141
Guattari, Félix, 116
Guégan, Gérard, 71
Guerrero, Margarita, 150
Gutiérrez Alea, Tomás, *Memories of
Underdevelopment* (1968), 38
Guzmán, Patricio, *Nostalgia for the
Light* (2011), 33

Habermas, Jürgen, 206
Hail Mary (Godard, 1985), 114, 122–
26, *127, 128*, 131, 212, 241n26
Hampton, Rebecca, 123
Hands of Orlac, The (Wiene, 1924),
147, 244n65
Hannah and Her Sisters (Allen, 1986),
241n32
Harvey, David Oscar, 229n53
Hawks, Howard, 45, 186–87, 248n57;
His Girl Friday (1940), 185, 186, *186*,
248n60; *Rio Bravo* (1958), 102
Haynes, Todd, *I'm Not There* (2007),
39, 230n65
Heart of Darkness (Conrad, 1899),
162–64, 245n16
Hediger, Vinzenz, 86, 107
Heidegger, Martin, 66, 206, 208, 210,
251n26
Henderson, Brian, 42, 43
Herzog, Werner, 5, 32; *Cave of
Forgotten Dreams* (2010), 196, 197,
197, 199
Hiroshima mon amour (Resnais, 1959),
38, 68, 111, 233n6
His Girl Friday (Hawks, 1940), 185,
186, *186*, 248n60
Histoire(s) du cinéma (1988–98), 13,
14, 18, 30, 131, 144; audience of
friends, 138; on auteurism, 156;

Index

episodes as "chapters," 93; citation as historical montage, 92–110, *98*, *103*, *104*, 146, 147; citation in, 70, 72–73, 233n8, 233n10; "dirty hands" trope, 244n64; expanded into stereoscopic form, 198–202; "form that thinks" in, 177–78; Godard as "first viewer" in/ of, 174–76; Godard's self-portraiture in, *155*, 160, 172–82, *180*; Godard's subjunctive approach to cinema history in, 173; Hindemith sonata reprised in *JLG/JLG*, 169; image as "ensemble being" in, 99; *Le Gai Savoir* as prototype of, 86, 235n33; as perceptual revelation, 97, 100, 105, 173, 182; superimposed images in, 93–94, 99–100, 101, *104*, 160, *175*, 176–77; tennis references in, 241n29; titles and voiceover narration, 17; "twoness" in, 114; video as "becoming medium," 179–82

History of Art: Modern Art (Faure, 1937), 77

Hitchcock, Alfred, 35, 42, 45, 66, 147, 154, 194

Hitchcock, Alfred, works of: *I Confess* (1953), 47; *North by Northwest* (1959), 111; *Psycho* (1960), 231n80; *Rear Window* (1954), 173–74, 178, 247n41; *Spellbound* (1945), 77; *To Catch a Thief* (1955), 144; *Vertigo* (1958), 47–48, 112, 231n80; *The Wrong Man* (1956), 47

Hitler, Adolf, 89, 206, 219

Hölderlin, Friedrich, 66

Hollywood, classical, 44, 46, 93, 130, 183

Holocaust, 29–30, 97, 100, 101, 140, 177, 236n44. *See also* Nazism

Hôtel des Invalides (Franju, 1952), 28–29, 111

Hour of the Furnaces (Solanas/Getino, 1968), 33

Howls for Sade (Debord, 1952), 83

How the Essay Film Thinks (Rascaroli), 223n7

Huillet, Danièle, 13, 32, 113; *Not Reconciled* (co-dir. Straub, 1965), 38

Huppert, Isabelle, 122, 160, 161

Hyer, Martha, 231n78

Hypothesis of a Stolen Painting, The (Ruiz, 1979), 32

I Am Not Your Negro (Peck, 2017), 33

Ici et ailleurs (*Here and Elsewhere*, Godard and Miéville, 1976), 13, 21, 82, *91*, 114, 199, 236n44; accusation of anti-Semitism against Godard, 89, 165; gesture in, 116; Godard-Miéville partnership and, 86–92, 113; post-militant essayism and, 183; *Soft and Hard* compared with, 133; superimposition of images in, 88, 89, 92

I Confess (Hitchcock, 1953), 47

"Ideology and Ideological State Apparatuses" (Althusser, 1970), 84

Illumination (Zanussi, 1972), 38

"Image, The" (Beckett, 1959), 101, 102

"Image, The" (Reverdy, 1918), 99

Images of the World and the Inscription of War (Farocki, 1988), 30, 176, 183

I'm Not There (Haynes, 2007), 39, 230n65

implicit address, 73, 186

improvisation, 7, 28, 35, 43, 119

India: Matri Bhumi (Rossellini, 1959), 33

indirect address, 14, 178, 194

Inextinguishable Fire (Farocki, 1969), 191

Inflation (Richter, 1928), 25

In girum imus nocte et consumimur igni (Debord, 1978), 81, 183

In Praise of Love (Godard, 2001), 216, 237n60

In Search of Lost Time (Proust, 1913), 102, 203

intellectual property, 66

Intelligence of a Machine, The (Epstein, 1946), 179

Interface (Farocki, 1997), 191

interpellation, 228n39

intertextuality, 48, 66, 68, 69, 206

intertitles, 18, 50, 66, 76, 84, 163

Isou, Isidore, 228n33

Israel, 89, 165, 187–88, 248n58

Ivens, Joris, 32; *A Story of Wind* (1988), 33, 102

"I-You" communication structure, 4, 14, 155, 176

264 Index

Jacobs, Ken, *Seeking the Monkey King* (2011), 196
Jacquot de Nantes (Varda, 1991), 239n2
James, Henry, "The Middle Years" (1893), 141–42
Jay, Martin, 83
Jean-Luc Godard par Jean-Luc Godard (1985), 113
Jennings, Humphrey, 32
Jetée, La (Marker, 1963), 112, 224n27, 230n68
Je vous salue, Sarajevo (Godard, 1993), 141
JLG/JLG: Self-Portrait in December (Godard, 1995), 14, 89, 142–43, 153, 155, *167*, 232n1, 241n29; authorial death in, 163, 170–72, *171*; blindness motif, 164–65, 168–70, 174, 179, 246n30; Godard's public image and, 161–62; interaction with others in, 161, 164; "legend of stereo" lesson, 165, 177, 184; Vogt's science fiction and, 166, 168, 206, 218–19
Johnson, Kirsten, *Cameraperson* (2016), 33
Jones, Jennifer, 105
Just in Time (Greenaway, 2013), 196

Kael, Pauline, 72, 93
Kant, Immanuel, 238n76
Karina, Anna, 76, 77, 85, 113, 115; artist-muse relationship with Godard, 137, 242n38; Godard's New Wave phase and, 113
Keathley, Christian, 225n31
Keaton, Buster, 154
Keep Your Right Up (Godard, 1987), 103, 122, 153, 228n42, 241n29
Keiller, Patrick, 32
Kelly, Grace, 144, 178
Keuken, Johan van der, 32, 40
Khittl, Ferdinand, *The Parallel Street* (1961), 75
Kiarostami, Abbas, *Shirin* (2008), 76
King Lear (Godard, 1987), 153
Kluge, Alexander, 119, 146, 245n5; *caméra-stylo* definition and, 32; as innovator, 20; on montage as activity of reading constellations,

146; on "muscles" of perception, 192; "twoness" in works of, 239n78; utopic form of citation, 67
Kluge, Alexander, works of, 8, 25, 32, 67; *Artists Under the Big Top: Perplexed* (1968), 38; *Brutality in Stone* (co-dir. Schamoni, 1961), 30; *News from Ideological Antiquity* (2008), 227n17; *The Patriot* (1979), 228n42; *Yesterday Girl* (1966), 38
Koestler, Arthur, *Darkness at Noon* (1940), 200
Korzybski, Alfred, 166; *Science and Sanity* (1933), 168
Kracauer, Siegfried, 44
Kramer, Robert, 32

La Boétie, Étienne de, 10, 136
Lacan, Jacques, 50
Lack, Roland-François, 86
Land without Bread (Buñuel, 1933), 23
Lang, Fritz, 42, 66; in *Contempt*, 173; *Rancho Notorious* (1952), 95
Langlois, Henri, 80
Last Bolshevik, The (Marker, 1993), 31, 154, 242n46
Last Year at Marienbad (Resnais, 1961), 95, 97
La Tour, Georges de, 193
Léaud, Jean-Pierre, 84, *85*, 232n90
Left Bank group, 3, 23, 27–28, 29, 228n33. *See also* New Wave
Leigh, Vivien, 102
Leiris, Michel, 94
Lenin, Vladimir, 89
Leopard, The (Visconti, 1963), 95, 96
Letter from Siberia (Marker, 1957), 30–31, 229n47
"Letter on Rossellini" (Rivette, 1955), 34–35, 37
Letter on the Blind for the Use of Those Who See (Diderot, 1749), 164–65, 168
Letter to Jane: Investigations about a Still (Godard/Gorin/Dziga Vertov Group, 1972), 21, 242n39
Lettrist films, 228n33
Level Five (Marker, 1997), 112, 154, 230n68
Levi, Primo, 236n44

Index

Levinas, Emmanuel, 251n20; *Entre Nous: Thinking of the Other* (1991), 236n46, 248n59; *Time and the Other* (1947), 207–8, 211, 215; *Totality and Infinity* (1961), 209, 211, 251n26
Lévy, Denis, 38
Life Is a Dream (Ruiz, 1986), 76
Lightning over Water (Wenders, 1980), 32
literature, 9, 19, 27, 30, 71, 139; apostrophe in, 228n39; essay as genre, 20; essayistic narrative fiction 5, 23; film and video combined with, 12; Godard's written articles and, 65; Montaignean essay, 25
Lopate, Phillip, 3, 20–21, 63, 226n6
Los Angeles Plays Itself (Anderson, 2003), 93
Lowenstein, Adam, 16
Ludwig, Daniel, 205
Lukács, Georg, 139
Lumière, Auguste and Louis, 17
Lyotard, Jean-François, 116

MacBean, James Roy, 84–85, 235n33
MacCabe, Colin, 109–10, 114, 235n32; on Godard and Montaigne, 135–36; on *The Old Place*, 138–39
Made in USA (Godard, 1966), 50
Majewski, Lech, *The Mill and the Cross* (2011), 39
Makavejev, Dušan, 32
Malevich, Kazimir, 140
Malick, Terrence, *The Tree of Life* (2011), 6, 39
Malone, Dorothy, 103
Malraux, André, 26, 80
Manet, Édouard, *A Bar at the Folies-Bergère* (1881–82), 177
Mankiewicz, Joseph L., *The Barefoot Contessa* (1954), 201, *201*
Mann, Anthony, *Man of the West* (1958), 43
Man of the West (Mann, 1958), 43
Man Who Left His Will on Film, The (Oshima, 1970), 38
Man with a Movie Camera (Vertov, 1929), 23, 201, *201*, 247n44
Man Without Qualities, The (Musil), 5, 49

Maoism, 84, 141
Marcuse, Herbert, 206
Marker, Chris, 5, 12, 25, 33, 50; *caméra-stylo* definition and, 32; citation used by, 67–68; Debord's spectator address contrasted to, 81; documentary format and, 40; essayistic ethos of repeated scrutiny of images, 16, 31; friendship as theme, 138, 242n46; as innovator, 20; Left Bank group and, 3, 23; leftist engagement of, 191; notion of "the Zone," 16; self-portraiture of, 154; short film and, 28, 30–31
Marker, Chris, works of: *The Case of the Grinning Cat* (2004), 228n42; *A Grin without a Cat* (1977), 16, 31, 141; *La Jetée* (1963), 112, 224n27, 230n68; *The Last Bolshevik* (1993), 31, 154, 242n46; *Letter from Siberia* (1957), 30–31, 229n47; *Level Five* (1997), 112, 154, 230n68; *Night and Fog* (Resnais, 1955), 29–30, 38, 77, 166, 183, 228n42; *One Day in the Life of Andrei Arsenevich* (1999), 16; *The Owl's Legacy* (1989), 67, 111, 233nn5–6; *Sans soleil* (1983), 16, 31, 35, 224n27, 230n68; *Statues Also Die* (co-dir. Resnais, 1953), 29; *Toute la mémoire du monde* (co-dir. Resnais, 1956), 29. See also *Sans soleil*
Married Woman, A (Godard, 1964), 44, 51, 77, 115, 228n42
Marsaillaise, La (Renoir, 1938), 252n36
Martin, Adrian, 232n92, 234n15
Martin, Arnaud, 116
Marx, Karl, 84
Marxism-Leninism, 79, 81, 83
Masculine Feminine (Godard, 1966), 44, 46, 230n65, 232n90; film within the film, 73; Perec cited in, 53, 232n90
Matheson, Richard, 164
Matisse, Henri, 159
May 1968 revolts in Paris, 82, 141, 207, 216
McElwee, Ross, 5, 154
Medvedkin, Alexander, 242n46
Meetin' WA (Godard, 1986), 131
Meir, Golda, 89
Mekas, Jonas, 32, 33
Melehy, Hassan, 10

Index

Méliès, Georges, 17, 154
melodrama, 34, 44, 46, 131, 212, 231n78
Memories of Underdevelopment (Gutiérrez Alea, 1968), 38
memory, 32, 66, 101, 174; of the future, 237n53; videographic layered montage and, 180
Merleau-Ponty, Maurice, 170; *The Visible and the Invisible* (1968), 169
Meshes of the Afternoon (Deren and Hammid, 1943), 202, 250n10
Message of Greetings: Swiss Prize / My Thanks / Dead or Alive (Godard, 2015), 153
Messiah, The (Rossellini, 1975), 40
meta-film, 43. *See also* reflexivity
"Middle Years, The" (James, 1893), 141–42
Miéville, Anne-Marie, 13, 111, 235n32, 236n44, 246n25. *See also* Godard-Miéville partnership
Miéville, Anne-Marie, works of: *The Book of Mary* (1985), 114, 122–24, 131, *133*, 241n33; *My Favorite Story* (1988), 246n31; *We're All Still Here* (1997), 114, 140, 244n66, 252n33
Mill and the Cross, The (Majewski, 2011), 39
Minnelli, Vincente, 43, 45, 48, 66, 231n78; *The Band Wagon* (1953), 95, 96
miracle/miraculous, 35, 100, 108, 124, 125–26, 169, 237n57
mise en scène, 22, 45, 46; in *Goodbye to Language*, 207, 208–9; in *Scénario du film "Passion,"* 160; in *2 or 3 Things I Know about Her*, 53
Mizoguchi, Kenji, *The Crucified Lovers* (1954), 95
modern art, 140
Modern Times (Chaplin, 1936), 94
Monet, Claude, 216
montage, 3, 4, 13, 32, 112, 120; avant-garde of 1920s and, 26; commentated, 29; as constellation, 144, *145*, 146; gesture and, 244n65; in *Goodbye to Language*, 219; in *Histoire(s) du cinéma*, 70, 94, 97, 99, 100–103, 139, 173; historical investigation and, 156;

in *Ici et ailleurs*, 116; "lateral," 30, 52, 82, 229n46; in *Notre musique*, 183, 187; in *The Old Place*, 140, 147–48, 150–51; physical gesture and, 13; rapprochement of "distant" elements, 99–100, 101, 144, 176, 238n64; "soft montage," 191, 192; in *2 or 3 Things I Know about Her*, 54; viewer as montagist, 101
Montaigne, Michel de, 6, 7–11, 16, 50, 93, 224n22; on citation (borrowing), 65; Debord's style contrasted to, 81; as diachronic essayist across multiple writings, 7; dialogue with La Boétie, 136; evasive manner of, 18; as "first reader" of the *Essais*, 175; on learning how to die, 163; library of, 10, 135; on observation of animals, 215; references to, in Godard films, 224n28; on relation of author and work, 152; Rossellini and tradition of, 34; tennis reference of, 130. *See also Essais*; Godard, Montaignean lineage and
Moore, Michael, 154
Moravia, Alberto, 44
Moretti, Nanni, 5
Morgan, Daniel, 96, 105
Morin, Edgar, 34
Morrey, Douglas, 55
Mourlet, Michel, 237n51
Mr. Arkadin (Welles, 1955), 82, 179
Mulvey, Laura, 225n31
Murnau, F. W., *Faust* (1926), 95, 96, 99
Museum Hours (Cohen, 2012), 39
musical scores, 12, 74; in *The Book of Mary*, 123, 124; in *Contempt*, 123; in *Goodbye to Language*, 213, 220; in *Hail Mary*, 125; in *Histoire(s) du cinéma*, 95, 169, 181; in *JLG/JLG*, 163, 169; in *The Old Place*, 142, 148; in *2 or 3 Things I Know about Her*, 56, 57, 61
Musil, Robert, 6, 23; *The Man Without Qualities*, 5, 49
My Favorite Story (Miéville, 1988), 246n31
My Life to Live (*Vivre sa vie*, Godard, 1962), 22, 46, 170, 224n28; artist-muse relation in, 242n38; Brechtian

reflexivity in, 77, 234n20; Dreyer film within, 76–77, 78; as part of trilogy, 51

Nadeau, Maurice, 26
Naficy, Hamid, 33
narrative film, 11, 15, 38, 83; in citations, 93, 107; conventional shot structures of, 26; coupling theme and, 112, 204, 205, 215, 218, 219; course–discourse pairing and, 49; disjointed stratification of, 38; essayist as narrator, 11; essayistic gestures in, 12–14, 34, 38–39, 111, 122, 202–3; ideological constraints of, 85; point-of-view structures of, 30; shot/countershot principle in, 185, 187; syntax of, 187; teleologies of, 5, 39, 87, 203; 3D cinematography in, 195, 197; videographic effects in, 118. See also fiction films
Nazism (National Socialism), 89, 146, 147, 208, 215; death camps, 29, 90, 169, 177, 187; Heidegger and, 251n26; invasion of Russia, 96; pro-Vichy attitudes in Godard's family, 166; White Rose resisters against, 179. See also Holocaust
Nelson, Ricky, 102
New Left, 16, 141
News from Ideological Antiquity: Marx—Eisenstein—Das Kapital (Kluge, 2008), 227n17
New Wave, 16, 27, 41, 44, 70, 84. See also Left Bank group
Nietzsche, Friedrich, 137
Night and Fog (Resnais, 1955), 29–30, 38, 77, 166, 183, 228n42
Nixon, Richard, 89
North by Northwest (Hichcock), 111
Nostalgia for the Light (Guzmán, 2011), 33
Notebook on Cities and Clothes (Wenders, 1989), 32
Notes on the Cinematographer (Bresson), 102, 174
Notes Toward an African Orestes (Pasolini, 1970), 32
Not Reconciled (Straub/Huillet, 1965), 38

Notre musique (Our Music, Godard, 2004), 14, 153, 155, 200, 228n42, 236n44; Godard's self-portraiture in, 182–94, *190;* Levinas's philosophy and, 207, 248n59; "Paradise" section, 249n64; "Purgatory" section, 184; shot/countershot principle and, *186*
nouveau roman ("new novel"), 80, 233n11
Nouvelle vague (Godard, 1990), 122, 203, 212, 232n1, 241n29
Novak, Kim, 47, 48
Numéro deux (Godard and Miéville, 1975), 153, 191

object, as relational link between subjects: in *Contempt,* 45–46, *45;* in *2 or 3 Things I Know about Her,* 57, 58, *59*
objectivity, chimera of, 31
Odyssey, The (Homer), 179
Of Great Events and Ordinary People (Ruiz, 1979), 32
Oh, Woe Is Me (Godard, 1993), 168
Old Place, The (Godard/Miéville, 1999), 13, 111, 114, 138–39, 199, 241n29; charitable attention motif, 140–43; coda of *Goodbye to Language* compared to, 219, 252n33; as exercises in artistic thinking, 139–40; image as constellation motif, 143–44, *145,* 146; as intellectual poem, 139, 148; "Logic of Images" exercise, 143, *145,* 146, 243n56; "Prisoner of Love" exercise, 141, 243n53; "think with one's hands" motif, 146–51, 244n64; "three persons" aphorism in, 111, 142, 151, 178
On Certainty (Wittgenstein, 1969), 164, 168
One Day in the Life of Andrei Arsenevich (Marker, 1999), 16
Opération "beton" (Godard, 1955), 41
Origins of the 21st Century, The (Godard, 2000), 140–41, 232n2
Origins of Totalitarianism, The (Arendt, 1951), 114
Orpheus (Cocteau, 1950), 102, 103, *103*
Ô Saisons, ô châteaux (Varda, 1957), 28, 111

Oshima Nagisa, *The Man Who Left His Will on Film* (1970), 38
otherness, 188, 193, 210, 248n62
Otte, Hans, 183
Overney, Pierre, 141
Owl's Legacy, The (Marker, 1989), 67, 111, 233nn5–6
Ozu Yasujiro, 40

Païni, Dominique, 149
Painlevé, Jean, 30
painting, 34, 65, 72, 93, 118, 139, 140, 142, 158, 160, 162, 177, 180, 193, 196–7, 199, 218, 231n79, 249n67
Palestine/Palestinians, 86, 165, 187–88, 248n58
Parain, Brice, 170
parallax effects (in 3D cinema), 14, 196, 207, 209, *209*, 213
Parallel Street, The (Khittl, 1961), 75
parody, 65, 249n59
Pascal, Blaise, 199; *Pensées* (1669), 221
Pasolini, Pier Paolo, 178; *The Gospel According to St. Matthew* (1964), 148; *La Rabbia* (1963), 32; *Notes Toward an African Orestes* (1970), 32
Passion (Godard, 1982), 122
Passion of Joan of Arc, The (Dreyer, 1928), 76–77, 78
passive viewing, annihilation of, 17; partial maintenance of, 222
Patriot, The (Kluge, 1979), 228n42
Pavsek, Christopher, 170
Peck, Gregory, 105
Peck, Raoul, *I Am Not Your Negro* (2017), 33
Penley, Constance, 118
Pensées (Pascal, 1669), 221
People on Sunday (Siodmak and Ulmer, 1930), 95, 252n31
perception, pedagogy of, 40, 119, 192
Perec, Georges, 53
Périer, François, 103
Perkins, V. F., 232n94
Perlov, David, 32
persona, as textual fiction, 9
Personal Camera, The: Subjective Cinema and the Essay Film (Rascaroli), 4–5, 155, 176, 189, 223n13, 226n15

Personal Journey with Martin Scorsese through American Movies (Scorsese, 1995), 93
Picabia, Francis, 140
Piccoli, Michel, 45, 131, 241n32
Pickpocket (Bresson, 1959), 126, 128
Piero della Francesca, *The Legend of the True Cross*, 178
Pierrot le fou (1965), 51, 71–72, 77, 209, 231n79, 241n29
Piranha 3D (2010), 199
Place in the Sun, A (Stevens, 1951), 100, 169
Plato, 10, 11, 67, 68, 111
Poe, Edgar Allan, "The Oval Portrait" (1842), 242n38
poetry, 10, 106, 228n39, 232n92; literary essay as "intellectual poem," 139; "progressive universal poetry," 106–7
point of view, 39, 60, 76, 104, 126, 149; citational process and, 80; "psychological mimesis" and, 48
Pollet, Jean-Daniel, 38, 227n20
postmodernism, 70
post-structuralism, 116
Postwar (DVD box set, Eisenberg, 2012), 226n12
Pound, Ezra, *Cantos*, 179, 181
Pravda (Godard/Dziga Vertov Group, 1970), 87, 218
Preminger, Otto, *Whirlpool* (1949), 74
Prénom Carmen (Godard, 1983), 113, 122, 153, 218
Price, Brian, 234n24
Prison (Bergman, 1949), 104, *104*, 105–6, 149, 200
production credits, 66, 232n2
Proust, Marcel, 23, 216; *In Search of Lost Time* (1913), 102, 203
Public Enemy, The (Wellman, 1931), 95, 96

Quandt, James, 204

Rabbia, La (Pasolini, 1963), 32
Radziwilowicz, Jerzy, 160
Rancho Notorious (Lang, 1952), 95
Rancière, Jacques, 106–8, 238n75

Index

Rascaroli, Laura, 3, 4–5, 23, 176, 223n7, 233n13; on *caméra-stylo* formulation, 33; on *Notre musique*, 189, 248n56; *The Personal Camera*, 4, 223n13, 226n15

Raven, Lucy, *Curtains* (2014), 196

Ray, Nicholas, 43; *Rebel without a Cause* (1955), 144

Raymond, Marcel, 241n31

Rear Window (Hitchcock, 1954), 173–74, 178, 247n41

Rebel without a Cause (Ray, 1955), 144

reception, 16, 27, 30, 99, 119, 148, 149, 160, 173, 189

reflexivity, 33, 43, 68, 71, 84, 92; in *Breathless*, 75; Maoist *autocritique* protocol and, 84; in *My Life to Live*, 77; in *2 or 3 Things I Know about Her*, 62

Rembrandt van Rijn, 8, 39, 193

Renoir, Jean, 34, 35, 154; *La Marseillaise* (1938), 252n36; *The Rules of the Game* (1939), 94, 95, 96, 232n94

Renov, Michael, 3

Republic (Plato), 67

research, 61, 63, 70, 83, 120, 226n6; *caméra-stylo* definition and, 33; gestures and, 115, 161; grammar of popular cinema and, 62; interpersonal dialogue/exchange and, 112–13; necessitated by past failures, 88; paired with spectacle, 17, 40, 43, 176; "pure research," 51; self-portraiture and, 153; television and, 119

Resnais, Alain, 12, 30; Debord's spectator address contrasted to, 81; Left Bank group and, 3, 23; short film and, 27–28, 41

Resnais, Alain, works of: *Hiroshima mon amour* (screenplay: Duras, 1959), 38, 68, 111, 233n6; *Last Year at Marienbad* (1961), 95, 97; *Night and Fog* (1955), 29–30, 38, 77, 166, 183, 228n42; *Statues Also Die* (co-dir. Marker, 1953), 29; *Toute la mémoire du monde* (co-dir. Marker, 1956), 29

Reverdy, Pierre, 101, 105, 144, 176; "The Image" (1918), 99

revolution: failure or impossibility of, 15, 60, 184; ghost of, 219–20

Ricciardi, Alessia, 233n8

Richter, Hans, 32, 34, 40, 227n17, 227n26; "The Film Essay: A New Form of Documentary Film" (1940), 24–25; on reflective task of audiovisual essay, 50–51

Rilke, Rainer Maria, *Duino Elegies*, 215

Rimbaud, Arthur, 110; *A Season in Hell* (1873), 120

Rio Bravo (Hawks, 1958), 102

Rio Grande (Ford, 1950), 82

Rivette, Jacques, 48, 66, 68; on Godard's use of citation, 65; "Letter on Rossellini" (1955), 34–35, 37

Rocha, Glauber, 102, 108

Rodin, Auguste, 149; *The Thinker* (1904), 142, 211

Rohdie, Sam, 94

Romanticism, German, 106–7. *See also* Schlegel, Friedrich

Rome Open City (Rosselllini, 1945), 34

Ropars, Marie-Claire, 75

Rosenbaum, Jonathan, 44, 229nn47–48, 237n51

Ross, Miriam, 196

Rossellini, Roberto, 12, 41, 42, 112

Rossellini, Roberto, works of: *Blaise Pascal* (1972), 40; *India: Matri Bhumi* (1959), 33; *The Messiah* (1972), 40; *Rome Open City* (1945), 34; *The Taking of Power by Louis XIV* (1966), 40; *Voyage in Italy* (1954), 34–37, *36*, 48, 111, 229n54, 230n67

Rothman, William, 29

Rouch, Jean, 30, 43

Rougemont, Denis de, 146, 147

Rousseau, Jean-Jacques, *Confessions* (1782), 171

Roussel, Myriem, 113, 124

Ruchat, Marie, 205

Ruiz, Raúl, works of, 3; *The Hypothesis of a Stolen Painting* (1979), 32; *Life Is a Dream* (1986), 76; *Of Great Events and Ordinary People* (1979), 32

Rules of the Game, The (*La Règle du jeu*, Renoir, 1939), 94, 95, 96, 232n94

Russell, Rosalind, 185, 186, *186*

salutes, 65

Sanders, George, 35

Sans soleil (Marker, 1983), 16, 31, 35, 224n27; as canonical work, 73; couple in, 111–12; fictionalization as reflective strategy in, 230n68; gestural insertions in, 92; *Goodbye to Language* compared with, 216, 217; tranquil female narrator in, 183

Sartre, Jean-Paul, 19, 66, 251n26; *Being and Nothingness* (1943), 210; *Dirty Hands* (1948), 244n64; "Situation of the Writer in 1947," 26; *The Words* (1964), 171, 172

Scénario du film "Passion" (Godard, 1982), 155, 157–61, 172, 174; Godard's self-inscription in, 14, *158*; "seeing first" method in, 158, 161, 182, 189

Schamoni, Peter, *Brutality in Stone* (co-dir. Kluge, 1961), 30

Schlegel, Friedrich, 15, 106, 139, 225n30

Scholl, Sophie, 179, 200

Science and Sanity (Kozybski, 1933), 168

Season in Hell, A (Rimbaud, 1873), 120

Seberg, Jean, 74, 79

"second cinema," 33

Seeking the Monkey King (Jacobs, 2011), 196

self-portraiture, 14, 153–56, 235n37; citations and, 156; Godard-Miéville double self-portrait in *The Old Place*, 149, *149*; in *Histoire(s) du cinéma*, 94–97, *98*, 155, 172–78, 236n50; Montaigne's manner of, 8–9; in *Notre musique*, 182–94, *190*; in painting, 159; in *The Three Disasters*, 201. See also *JLG/JLG: Self-Portrait in December*

Shelley, Mary, *Frankenstein* (1818), 218

Shelley, Percy Bysshe, 218

Shirin (Kiarostami, 2008), 76

short film, 27–28, 41

shot/countershot principle, 130, 186, 192, 248n57; in *Contempt*, 46–47, *47*, 48, 49; face-to-face and encounter and, 251n20; in *Goodbye to Language*, 211; in *My Life to Live*,

76–77, *78*; in *Notre musique*, 184–91, *186*

Shub, Esfir, 25

Silverman, Kaja, 163

Simak, Clifford D., 215; *City* (1952), 202

Sinatra, Frank, 231n78

Siodmak, Robert, *People on Sunday* (co-dir. Ulmer, 1930), 95, 252n31

Sirk, Douglas, *Written on the Wind* (1956), 103

Sitney, P. Adams, 48

Situationists: *détournement* practice of, 67, 80, 81, 82; Godard harshly critiqued by, 80–82. See also Debord, Guy

"Situation of the Writer in 1947" (Sartre), 26

Six fois deux/Sur et sous la communication (Godard/Miéville, 1976), 119, 131, 153, 241n34

Sjöström, Victor, *The Wind* (1928), 103, 146

"sketch," improvised, 28

Small Notes Regarding the Film "Hail Mary" (Godard, 1983), 124

Snow White and the Seven Dwarfs (Disney, 1937), 102

Society of the Spectacle, The (Debord, 1967; film version, 1973), 81, 82, 195

Soft and Hard (Godard/Miéville, 1985), 13, 114, 128–31, *132*, 133–38, *133*, 241n30; living room scene, 140; *The Old Place* compared with, 138, 140, 142, 151; *Rear Window* cited in, 247n41

Sokurov, Aleksander, 32–33

Solanas, Fernando, *Hour of the Furnaces* (co-dir. Getino, 1968), 33

Some Came Running (Minnelli, 1958), 231n78

Sonimage, 114

Sontag, Susan, 126

Soulages, Pierre, 140

spectacle, 17, 21, 40

spectators, 91, 194; address to, 250n77; direct address and, 4; gestures of address to, 13; as montage-based thinkers, 192; reading of the image, 40; (re)training of, 17, 40, 63, 192, 249n71

Index

spectatorship, 37, 52, 150; address to, 155–56; authorship entangled with, 161; character interiority and, 75; as coupling, *220*; essayistic, 15–18; implicit address and, 73; repeat viewings, 15–16; superimposition of images and, 176–77

Spellbound (Hitchcock, 1945), 77

Stalin, Joseph, 200

Stalker (Tarkovsky, 1979), 16, 216, *217*, 252n32

Stam, Robert, 120

Starobinski, Jean, 175, 236n49

Starry Night, The (Van Gogh, 1889), 143

Statues Also Die (Resnais/Marker, 1953), 29

stereo cinema, 14, 195–98, 199–202. *See also* 3D cinematography

Stevens, George, *A Place in the Sun* (1951), 100, 169

Stewart, James, 47, 173–74

Stock Market, The (Richter, 1939), 25

Stone, Sharon, 146

Story of Wind, A (Ivens, 1988), 33, 102

Straub, Jean-Marie, 13, 32, 67; creative relationship with Huillet, 113; *Not Reconciled* (co-dir. Huillet, 1965), 38

Struggle in Italy (*Lotte in Italia,* Godard/Dziga Vertov Group, 1971), 84, 220

subjectivity, 13, 39, 176, 210, 221; authorial, 6, 12, 21, 67, 155; citation and, 66, 67; documentary and, 17; of essayist, 4, 5; loss of, 222; from singularity to twoness, 109; spectatorial, 21; unified and centered, 63; "unsettled subjectivity," 27, 29

Summer with Monika (Bergman, 1953), 75

Sunset Boulevard (Wilder, 1950), 43

superimposition, of images: in *Histoire(s) du cinéma*, 93–94, 99–100, 101, *104*, 160, *175*, 176–77; in *Ici et ailleurs*, 88, 89, 92; in *Scénario du film "Passion,"* 160; viewers' engagement with film and, 237n60

Svilova, Elizaveta, 201

Swing Time (Stevens, 1936), 196

syntax, 38, 43, 58, 203; of narrative cinema, 187; shot/countershot, 49, *78*, 191; violations of classical syntax, 40

tactile perception, 126, 164–65, 169, 197, 237n57, 250n2

Taking of Power by Louis XIV, The (Rossellini, 1966), 40

Tamiroff, Akim, 249n63

Tarkovsky, Andrei, *Stalker* (1979), 16, 216, *217*

Tati, Jacques, 154

Taylor, Elizabeth, 99–100, 101

Technological Society, The (Ellul, 1954), 206–7

television, 12, 27, 42, 67, 158; Godard-Miéville collaboration and, 116–17, *117*; Godard-Miéville critique of, 128, 131, *132*, 134; invention of, 206

"Temptation to Exist" (Cioran, 1956), 247n34

Testament d'Orphée, Le (Cocteau, 1960), 72

Thinker, The (Rodin, 1904), 142, 211

"third cinema," 33

3D cinematography, 14–15, 197–202; in *Cave of Forgotten Dreams*, 196–97; in *Goodbye to Language*, 204, 206, 208, 209, 212, 213, *214*, 215–16; resurgence of, 195

Three Disasters, The (*Les trois désastres,* Godard, 2013), 14, 197–202, *201*, 212, 218, 219

Time and the Other (Levinas, 1947), 207–8, 211, 215

"time-image" (Deleuze), 37

Tintoretto, *Bacchus and Ariadne* (1576), 159, 161

Titanic (Cameron, 2012), 199

To Alter the Image (1982), 236n37

To Catch a Thief (Hitchcock, 1955), 144

Tokyo-Ga (Wenders, 1985), 32

Totality and Infinity (Levinas, 1961), 209, 211, 251n26

Toulet, Paul-Jean, 246n25

Toute la mémoire du monde (Resnais/Marker, 1956), 29

Tout va bien (Godard/Gorin/Dziga Vertov Group, 1972), 120

Tree of Life, The (Malick, 2011), 6, 39

272 Index

Trinh T. Minh-ha, 32, 33
Truffaut, François, 17
Turim, Maureen, 234n20
"twoness," dialogical, 13–14, 105, 109, 173, 239n78, 252n34; as history (expired), 219; "oneness" of the state versus, 200, 201; as similar to Badiou's "Two Scene," 242n37; unbalanced, 137. *See also* coupling, as thematic concern
2 or 3 Things I Know about Her (2 ou 3 choses je sais que d'elle, Godard, 1967), 12, 20, 23, 49, 162; allusions in, 65–66; café scene, 56–58, *59–60,* 60–61, 63, 66; DVD edition, 232n92; as essayistic reflection, 62–63; features of essay film in, 50–51; as Godard's initial foray into essay film, 22; Godard's voiceover narration, 52–56, 57–58, 81; as part of trilogy, 51; prostitution as topic, 51, 52, 54, 56; sociological goal of, 51–52; time as measured quantity versus lyrical time, 54–56, *55*
2 x 50 Years of French Cinema (Godard, 1995), 131

Ulmer, Edgar G., *People on Sunday* (co-dir. Siodmak, 1930), 95, 252n31
Until Victory (Godard/Gorin/Dziga Vertov Group, unfinished), 86, 87, 88

Valéry, Paul, 142, 143, 210
Van Gogh, Vincent: *The Artist on the Road to Tarascon* (1888), 181; *The Starry Night* (1889), 143
van Vogt, A. E., 207, 215; *The World of Null-A* (1948), 166, 168, 206, 218–19
Varda, Agnès, 5, 8, 12, 30, 32, 33, 36; *caméra-stylo* definition and, 32; couple as thematic concern, 239n2; Debord's spectator address contrasted to, 81; friendship as theme, 138, 242n46; as innovator, 20; Left Bank group and, 3, 23; self-portraiture of, 14, 154–55; short film and, 27–28, 41
Varda, Agnès, works of: *Agnès from Here to There Varda* (2011), 155, 242n46, 252n35; *The Beaches of Agnès* (2008), 154, 155, 239n2,

242n46; *Du côté de la côte* (1958), 28; *Faces Places* (co-dir. JR, 2017), 33; *The Gleaners and I* (2000), 155; *Jacquot de Nantes* (1991), 239n2; *Ô Saisons, ô châteaux* (1957), 28, 111
Védrès, Nicole, 25, 30
Veidt, Conrad, 147
Venom and Eternity (Isou, 1951), 228n33
verbocentrism, 158, 214
Vernant, Jean-Pierre, 67–68
Vertigo (Hitchcock, 1958), 47–48, 112, 231n80
Vertov, Dziga, 117; *Man with a Movie Camera* (1929), 23, 200, *201,* 247n44
video, 12, 14, 173; Godard-Miéville collaboration and, 134–35; Godard's adoption of, 87, 92, 236n38; multilayered cited material, 91, *91, 92;* ready-made images and sounds in, 72
Vidor, King, *Duel in the Sun* (1946), 105
Vietnam War, 51, 79
Vigo, Jean, 30
Villon, François, "Ballad of Hanged Men," 159–60
Virolleaud, Camille, 116
Visconti, Luchino, *The Leopard* (1963), 95, 96
Visible and the Invisible, The (Merleau-Ponty, 1968), 169
Vitti, Monica, 112
Vladimir and Rosa (Godard/Dziga Vertov Group, 1971), 236n38, 241n29
Vlady, Marina, 232n93
voiceover, 4, 17, 22, 29; *caméra-stylo* formulation and, 229n53; Debord's use of, 81; in *Histoire(s) du cinéma,* 95, 97; in *JLG/JLG,* 162; versus non-vococentric essay film, 229n53; in *Notre musique,* 188; in *The Old Place,* 139, 142
Voices of Silence, The (Malraux, 1951), 80
Voyage in Italy (Rossellini, 1954), 34–37, *36,* 48, 111, 112, 229n54, 230n67
Voyage(s) in Utopia, JLG, 1946–2006: In Search of a Lost Theorem (Godard, 2006), 198

Index

Vrai faux passeport (Godard, 2006), 67, 241n29

Warhol, Andy, 140
Week-end (Godard, 1967), 21, 103
Weil, Simone, 67, 68, 143
Welles, Orson, 3, 14, 34, 154
Welles, Orson, works of: *Citizen Kane* (1941), 150; *F for Fake* (1975), 18, *18*, 32, 35, 172, 174, 244n2; *Filming Othello* (1978), 32; *Mr. Arkadin* (1955), 82, 179
Wellman, William, *The Public Enemy* (1931), 95, 96
Wenders, Wim, 7; *Lightning over Water* (1980), 32; *Notebook on Cities and Clothes* (1989), 32; *Tokyo-Ga* (1985), 32
We're All Still Here (Miéville, 1997), 114, 140, 244n66, 252n33
Westbound (Boetticher, 1959), 74, 234n15
Western ("cowboy film") genre, 74, 75, 234n15
Where Does Your Hidden Smile Lie? (Costa, 2001), 113–14
Whirlpool (Preminger, 1949), 74
White, Jerry, 114, 118, 123, 139, 141
Wiazemsky, Anne, 113, 137, 242n38
Wiene, Robert, *The Hands of Orlac* (1924), 147, 244n65

Williams, Blake, 204
Williams, James S., 204, 241n25
Wind, The (Sjöström, 1928), 103, 146
Wind from the East (Godard/Gorin/ Dziga Vertov Group, 1970), 84, 102, 108–9, 113
Witt, Michael, 86, 88, 100, 198, 225n29; on Godard-Miéville partnership, 114, 116; on "saccadic" motion, 117–18; on videographic montage, 110
Wittgenstein, Ludwig, 66, 165, 166; *On Certainty* (1969), 164, 168
Wollen, Peter, 80
Wood, Natalie, 144
Woolf, Virginia, 6, 23
wordplay, 53, 104, 194, 207, 224n22, 236n46
Words, The (Sartre, 1964), 171, 172
World of Null-A, The (van Vogt, 1948), 166, 168, 206, 218–19
Written on the Wind (Sirk, 1956), 103
Wrong Man, The (Hitchcock, 1956), 47
Wyborny, Klaus, 25

Yesterday Girl (Kluge, 1966), 38

Zampatti, Jeremy, 205
Zanussi, Krzysztof, *Illumination* (1972), 38
Zworykin, Vladimir, 206